*"Why should not the New Englander
be in search of new adventures?"*
THOREAU: *Walden*

THE BERKSHIRE TRAVELLER PRESS
Stockbridge, Massachusetts 01262

Country Inns and Back Roads

VOLUME XII

BY THE BERKSHIRE TRAVELLER
Norman T. Simpson

THE BERKSHIRE TRAVELLER TRAVEL SHELF
Country Inns and Back Roads 1978, North America
Country Inns and Back Roads, Europe (Revised June 1978)
Country Vacations, USA
New Brunswick Inside Out
Canada's Capital Inside Out
Montreal Inside Out
Great Montreal Walks
The Inn Way . . . Switzerland
The Inn Way . . . Caribbean

Library of Congress #78-51116
ISBN 0-912944-47-1
Copyright 1978 Berkshire Traveller Press
Printed in U.S.A.

COVER PAINTING, BOOK DESIGN, AND DRAWINGS: Janice Lindstrom

Printed in Dalton, Massachusetts by The Studley Press

The American country inn, along with the church and the New England town meeting, ranks as one of the oldest continuing institutions in our country. Town records from the mid-17th century indicate that many communities were required by law to provide some type of accommodations and provender for travelers by whatever name they might be called—inn, ordinary, hostelry, or what-have-you.

The American Colonial inn was kept by an innkeeper and his family and was the center of village activity. Those early inns also temporarily served as churches, gaols, blockhouses, courtrooms, and hospitals. Their *alter egos* include lecture halls, theatres, mortuaries, bordellos, runaway slave stations, grist mills, ferry stops, mountain shelters, smugglers' hideaways, and political campaign headquarters.

Inns were established in villages in the 17th and 18th centuries when travel was by foot or horseback; however, many later inns had their beginnings as stagecoach and freight wagon stops. Inns were also built on the great toll roads like the "National Pike." During the developmental years of our country, innkeeping moved west along with the settlers, and the tradition of finding refuge and food in ranches and cabins on the prairies and in the mountains later turned many a farm and ranch into an inn.

Although its real development was to come many years later, the precedent for the American resort was established in Colonial days when a royal governor grew weary of the heat and humidity in Boston, and began a summer colony high in the New Hampshire mountains. The American resort-inn was born. As early as Washington's youth some people started to follow the European custom of journeying to the numerous mineral springs.

In the early part of the 19th century, railroads replaced the stagecoach, and the American inn at stagestops began to disappear. As the century moved forward, small towns grew up along the railroads and travelers stayed at what became known as commercial hotels. By the last quarter of the century the railroads encouraged the vacation concept. Riding the "steam cars" on twin tracks that were frequently engineering marvels, families from the city would travel to the mountains, seashore, and mineral springs resorts to spend many weeks during the summer. Tremendous hotels requiring large staffs were built and for 75 years these were a significant part of the American vacation scene. These in turn were augmented by local farms in the vicinity who took in boarders.

In the early 1920s the railroads were displaced by the automobile, which made Americans more mobile and gradually changed vacation and holiday styles from summer-long stays to a few days or a weekend. One by one the large resort hotels disappeared, although the smaller, summer boarding houses and farms adapted themselves more readily to the shorter stays. In the 1950s these would emerge in importance, particularly with the development of the ski vacation.

The automobile awakened an insatiable desire to travel in Americans. All over the country, the signs "Guests" and "Tourist Home" could be seen in the windows of private homes. The American version of European "bed and breakfast" was keeping the spirit of personal innkeeping alive. It became quite a popular pastime for families to load up the car and see where the road would take them. Travel was fun and although at first the tires were rim changers, repair shops infrequent, and the road frequently muddy, the great American love affair with the automobile was well under way.

Salesmen and business people, who had previously made great use of the railroads, now bought a Ford or a Dodge and started making business trips by automobile. Now a new accommodation concept developed—the motel, or motor hotel. The railroad, like the stagecoach, began to disappear, and with it the small commercial hotel.

The new travel fad, the motel, displaced the tourist home and the chain motel came into being wherein prefabricated buildings could be erected in a relatively short time and the mass-produced accommodations had many advantages: quick reservation systems, readily accessible rooms, a casual informality in dress, TV, and telephones, and a certain standardization of design and decoration. The European visitor to America could travel all over the country, stay in motels, but perhaps wonder in the morning whether he was in Wichita or Chattanooga.

Meanwhile, the American country inns that had survived 150 years of changing travel styles, now almost faded from sight. True, here and there, there were some inns located on main highways that made adjustments and added a few features that might make them competitive with nearby motels. They even constructed motel units as a concession to the motoring-conscious public. However, most of them had been converted to other uses or torn down to make way for gasoline stations, supermarkets, or even motels. In the 1950s there was a mere handful of country inns in existence.

Looking back, I believe it was about the middle of the 1960s when the renaissance of the American country inn began. A small but growing segment of the American traveling and vacationing public began searching for an alternative to the efficient, but impersonal style of motel traveling. They began to "discover" the antithesis of the large motel—the country inn, where personalized innkeeping, individually furnished rooms, home-cooked food, quiet countryside surroundings, and an atmosphere that included living rooms and parlors with bookshelves and fireplaces, encouraged conversation with new friends. These inns were not found on the interstates, but on the meandering lesser roads. In many respects the country inn became a tangible symbol of the American search for some of the desirable virtues of the past.

It was a slow process at first, but many wonderful things began to happen. For example, some of the inns of the 18th and 19th centuries that had been converted to other uses came back into their own. False ceilings were ripped away to find beautiful, heavy beams. Walls were removed to disclose handsome fireplaces. Layers of wallpaper were carefully peeled away to reveal beautiful 18th century stenciling. Many buildings were saved from being torn down literally in the knick of time. Furthermore, as country inns grew in popularity we were all amazed at how well they adapted to their original use!

Perhaps best of all, many American communities without village inns or small hotels since the late Victorian days, now found new vigor and pride in their own restored inns.

In the 1960s and '70s a new genre of innkeepers came into being. These were men and women who had been successful in other occupations and were attracted to the idea of moving to the country with their families in order to find a new way of life. Usually they had been guests in several country inns and found that the idea of owning one was something that appealed to their sense of adventure. They are dedicated, intelligent, eager to learn, adaptable, friendly, and most of all, they really like people. Many participate in active outdoor sports like tennis and skiing. They enjoy the idea of operating an inn as they would their own home, and many have furnished their inns with their own private antiques. Some have had practical experience in the hospitality field and a few have even attended hotel schools. On the other hand, many began as enthusiastic amateurs.

They all agree that they have not found it a bed of roses. Innkeeping is a very hard master. Long hours, economic conditions, the weather, the energy crisis, and government regulations all contribute to make the going very rough at times.

True American innkeeping (which flickered, but was never really extinguished) now burns brighter than ever. I have discovered inns in villages where the great attraction is beautiful homes and gardens, tree-lined streets, antique shops, and museums. Still other inns have evolved as a result of being located in the mountains or next to the seashore. In many cases the country boarding house became an inn. Many inns have grown up near centers of active sports such as tennis, golf, horseback riding, and skiing. Several inns include many different combinations, as Americans prove how varied and subtle are their recreational tastes and preferences.

PREFACE TO 12TH EDITION

In its twelve years of publication, this book was never intended to be a complete guide to country inns in North America. It contains my continuing experiences in visiting a carefully selected group of inns in each region. The purpose is to encourage travelers to visit country inns, whether included in this book or not, and to experience this unique type of personal hospitality.

Because there are always improvements taking place in country inns — some inns going out of business, or changing hands, as well as discovering new inns to be included — a new edition is necessary every twelve months.

From the very beginning, I looked for inns that I felt would continue to operate for many years to come. Consequently, there are a number of inns that have been included in the book each year since the late 1960s. The innkeepers' young families have grown up and some are carrying on in their parents' tradition.

When an inn changes ownership it is my general practice to omit it from subsequent editions until the new innkeeper has had the opportunity to become firmly established. A steady stream of letters has assured me that this sense of continuity is most important.

Incidentally, I receive many letters each year. Through them I am richer for some deep and lasting friendships. Many of them recommend inns that I have not visited; some contain praise for inn-going adventures; and a few have criticisms. In the latter case, the information is passed on to the individual inn. I am in continual contact with each inn and try to re-visit as many inns as possible each year.

If the reader finds as much about people as he does about crewel bedspreads, Yankee pot roast, and curly maple tables, it is because I believe the real heart and soul of an inn is the innkeeper and his guests. The setting, food, accommodations, service, furnishings, diversions, and surroundings are of prime importance, but the cementing factor that makes a country inn so unique and enjoyable is the personal involvement. It was true in colonial days and is even more so now.

In 1966, the *first* year that *Country Inns and Back Roads* was written, I invited a group of innkeepers and their wives for dinner and discovered that they were delighted to have the opportunity to exchange ideas and to help solve the problems unique to country inns. We had such a good time that first evening that we decided to meet again the following year and thereafter. From those early meetings has evolved something that I can see now was inevitable: the formation of an informal, independent innkeepers' association that would provide a forum for innkeepers continually to exchange ideas and supply each other with practical and moral support. These meetings continue and the association is thriving. Membership invitations are extended to inns selected for *Country Inns and B ck Roads.*

I do not include lodging rates in my descriptions for the very nature of an inn means that there are lodgings of various sizes, with and without baths, in and out of season, and with plain and fancy decoration. Travelers should call ahead and inquire about the availability and rates of the many different types of rooms.

Rates are comparable to those at hotels, motels, and resorts in the same geographic area. To me, this represents a travel bargain for there is so much more offered at a country inn. The italicized paragraphs following the account of my visit to each inn provide factual information and travel directions. In a few instances, I have included some outstanding country restaurants that do not have lodgings. This is carefully noted in the information paragraphs.

European plan means that rates for rooms and meals are separate. American plan means that meals are included in the cost of the room. Modified American plan means that breakfast and dinner are included in the cost of the room. Some inns include a Continental breakfast with the lodging.

For new readers, welcome to the wide, wonderful world of country inns as an interesting, alternate style of travel. The warm, generous, friendly spirit of innkeeping continueth. Visiting country inns is one of the best ways really to get to know America and Americans.

Norman T. Simpson
Stockbridge, Massachusetts
February 27, 1978

Contents

Preface

Arizona
    LODGE ON THE DESERT, Tucson 300
    RANCHO DE LOS CABALLEROS, Wickenburg 302
    TANQUE VERDE, Tucson 303

California
    BENBOW INN, Garberville 305
    HARBOR HOUSE, Elk 307
    HERITAGE HOUSE, Little River 309
    NORMANDY INN, Carmel 311
    OJAI VALLEY INN, Ojai 313
    SUTTER CREEK INN, Sutter Creek 314
    THE INN, Rancho Santa Fe 316
    VAGABOND HOUSE INN, Carmel 318
    WINE COUNTRY INN, St. Helena 320

Canada
Quebec
    CUTTLE'S TREMBLANT CLUB, Mont Tremblant 351
    HOVEY MANOR, North Hatley 353
    WILLOW PLACE INN, Como 355

New Brunswick
    ELM LODGE, St. Stephen 345
    MARATHON HOTEL, Grand Manan Island 347
    MARSHLANDS INN, Sackville 349

Nova Scotia
    INVERARY INN, Baddeck 338
    KILMUIR PLACE, Northeast Margaree 339
    MILFORD HOUSE, South Milford 341

Ontario
GRANDVIEW FARM, Huntsville 357
OBAN INN, Niagara-on-the-Lake 359

Prince Edward Island
SHAW'S HOTEL, Brackley Beach 343

Connecticut
BOULDERS INN, New Preston 20
CURTIS HOUSE, Woodbury 22
GRISWOLD INN, Essex 24
MOUNTAIN VIEW INN, Norfolk 26
SILVERMINE TAVERN, Norwalk 28
TOWN FARMS INN, Middletown 30
WHITE HART INN, Salisbury 32

Florida
BAY SHORE YACHT CLUB, Ft. Lauderdale 252
BRAZILIAN COURT HOTEL, Palm Beach 254
CHALET SUZANNE, Lake Wales 256
LAKESIDE INN, Mount Dora 257

Indiana
DURBIN HOTEL, Rushville 273
NEW HARMONY INN, New Harmony 269
PATCHWORK QUILT, Middlebury 275
RED GERANIUM AND SHADBLOW RESTAURANTS, New Harmony 271

Kentucky
BOONE TAVERN HOTEL, Berea 208
DOE RUN INN, Brandenburg 210
ELMWOOD INN, Perryville 212
INN AT PLEASANT HILL, Shakertown 214

Louisiana
LAMOTHE HOUSE, New Orleans 260

Maine
ASTICOU INN, Northeast Harbor 74
BLACK POINT INN, Prouts Neck 76

CAPTAIN LORD MANSION, Kennebunkport 78
CLAREMONT, Southwest Harbor 80
DOCKSIDE GUEST QUARTERS, York 82
GREY ROCK INN, Northeast Harbor 84
HOMEWOOD INN, Yarmouth 85
ISLAND HOUSE, Ogunquit 88
OLD FORT CLUB, Kennebunkport 89
SQUIRE TARBOX HOUSE, Westport Island 91
WHISTLING OYSTER, Ogunquit 94
WHITEHALL INN, Camden 95

Maryland
MARYLAND INN, Annapolis 216
ROBERT MORRIS INN, Oxford 219

Massachusetts
BRADFORD GARDENS INN, Provincetown, Cape Cod 33
BRAMBLE INN, Brewster, Cape Cod 35
INN AT HUNTINGTON, Huntington 39
INN AT PRINCETON, Princeton 42
INN FOR ALL SEASONS, Scituate Harbor 37
JARED COFFIN HOUSE, Nantucket Island 44
LONGFELLOW'S WAYSIDE INN, South Sudbury 46
NAUSET HOUSE INN, East Orleans, Cape Cod 47
RALPH WALDO EMERSON, Rockport 49
RED INN, Provincetown, Cape Cod 51
RED LION INN, Stockbridge 53
STAGECOACH HILL INN, Sheffield 55
VICTORIAN, Whitinsville 56
VILLAGE INN, Lenox 59
YANKEE CLIPPER, Rockport 61
YANKEE PEDLAR INN, Holyoke 62

Michigan
BOTSFORD INN, Farmington Hills 277
NATIONAL HOUSE, Marshall 280
STAFFORD'S BAY VIEW INN, Petoskey 282

Minnesota
LOWELL INN, Stillwater 284

Missouri
    CHESHIRE INN, St. Louis   286
    ST. GEMME BEAUVAIS INN, Ste. Genevieve   288
    WILDERNESS LODGE, Lesterville   290

New Hampshire
    COLBY HILL INN, Henniker   98
    DANA PLACE, Jackson   100
    DEXTER'S INN, Sunapee   102
    JOHN HANCOCK INN, Hancock   104
    LOVETT'S, Franconia   106
    LYME INN, Lyme   107
    NEW LONDON INN, New London   109
    PHILBROOK FARM, Shelburne   112
    ROCKHOUSE MOUNTAIN FARM, Eaton Center   114
    SPALDING INN CLUB, Whitefield   116
    STAFFORD'S-IN-THE-FIELD, Chocorua   118
    WOODBOUND INN, Jaffrey   121

New Jersey
    MAINSTAY INN, Cape May   148

New York
    ALGONQUIN HOTEL, New York   150
    ALMSHOUSE INN, Ghent   152
    ASA RANSOM HOUSE, Clarence   154
    BEEKMAN ARMS, Rhinebeck   156
    BIRD & BOTTLE INN, Garrison   158
    BULL'S HEAD INN, Cobleskill   160
    CLARKSON HOUSE, Lewiston   162
    GLEN IRIS INN, Castile   164
    GREENVILLE ARMS, Greenville   165
    HOLLOWAY HOUSE, East Bloomfield   168
    LINCKLAEN HOUSE, Cazenovia   170
    OLD DROVERS INN, Dover Plains   172
    OLIVER HOUSE, Ancram   174
    REDCOAT'S RETURN, Tannersville   176
    SPRINGSIDE INN, Auburn   178
    SWISS HUTTE, Hillsdale   180
    THREE VILLAGE INN, Stony Brook   182

North Carolina
    HEMLOCK INN, Bryson City   221
    HOUND EARS LODGE, Blowing Rock   223
    NU-WRAY INN, Burnsville   225
    PINE CREST INN, Tryon   226
    SNOWBIRD MOUNTAIN LODGE, Robbinsville   228

Ohio
    BUXTON INN, Granville   293
    GOLDEN LAMB, Lebanon   295
    WELSHFIELD INN, Burton   297

Pennsylvania
    CENTURY INN, Scenery Hill   184
    FAIRFIELD INN, Fairfield   187
    HICKORY BRIDGE FARM, Orrtanna   189
    INN AT STARLIGHT LAKE, Starlight   191
    MOSELEM SPRINGS INN, Moselem Springs   193
    OVERLOOK INN, Canadensis   195
    PINE BARN INN, Danville   197
    PUMP HOUSE INN, Canadensis   198
    1740 HOUSE, Lumberville   200
    STERLING INN, South Sterling   202
    THE TAVERN, New Wilmington   204

Rhode Island
    INN AT CASTLE HILL, Newport   64
    LARCHWOOD INN, Wakefield   67
    1661 INN, Block Island   69

South Carolina
    SWORDGATE INN, Charleston   261

Vermont
    BARROWS HOUSE, Dorset   123
    BLUEBERRY HILL, Goshen   125
    CHESTER INN, Chester   126
    EDSON HILL MANOR, Stowe   128
    GREEN MOUNTAIN INN, Stowe   131
    INN AT SAWMILL FARM, West Dover   132

INN ON THE COMMON, Craftsbury Common   134
KEDRON VALLEY INN, South Woodstock   136
NORTH HERO HOUSE, North Hero   138
RABBIT HILL INN, Lower Waterford   141
VILLAGE INN, Landgrove   143

Virginia
    ALEXANDER-WITHROW HOUSE, Lexington   238
    GRAVES MOUNTAIN LODGE, Syria   236
    GRISTMILL SQUARE, Warm Springs   240
    HOLLYMEAD INN, Charlottesville   232
    OLD CLUB RESTAURANT, Alexandria   234
    WAYSIDE INN, Middletown   230

Virgin Islands
St. Croix
    KING CHRISTIAN HOTEL, Christiansted   334

Washington
    CAPTAIN WIDBEY INN, Coupeville   322
    FARMHOUSE, Port Townsend   324
    JAMES HOUSE, Port Townsend   326
    LAKE QUINAULT LODGE, Quinault   328
    PARTRIDGE INN, Underwood   330

West Virginia
    COUNTRY INN, Berkeley Springs   242
    GENERAL LEWIS INN, Lewisburg   244
    RIVERSIDE INN, Pence Springs   246
    WELLS INN, Sistersville   248

Index

Country Inns
and Back Roads

Southern New England

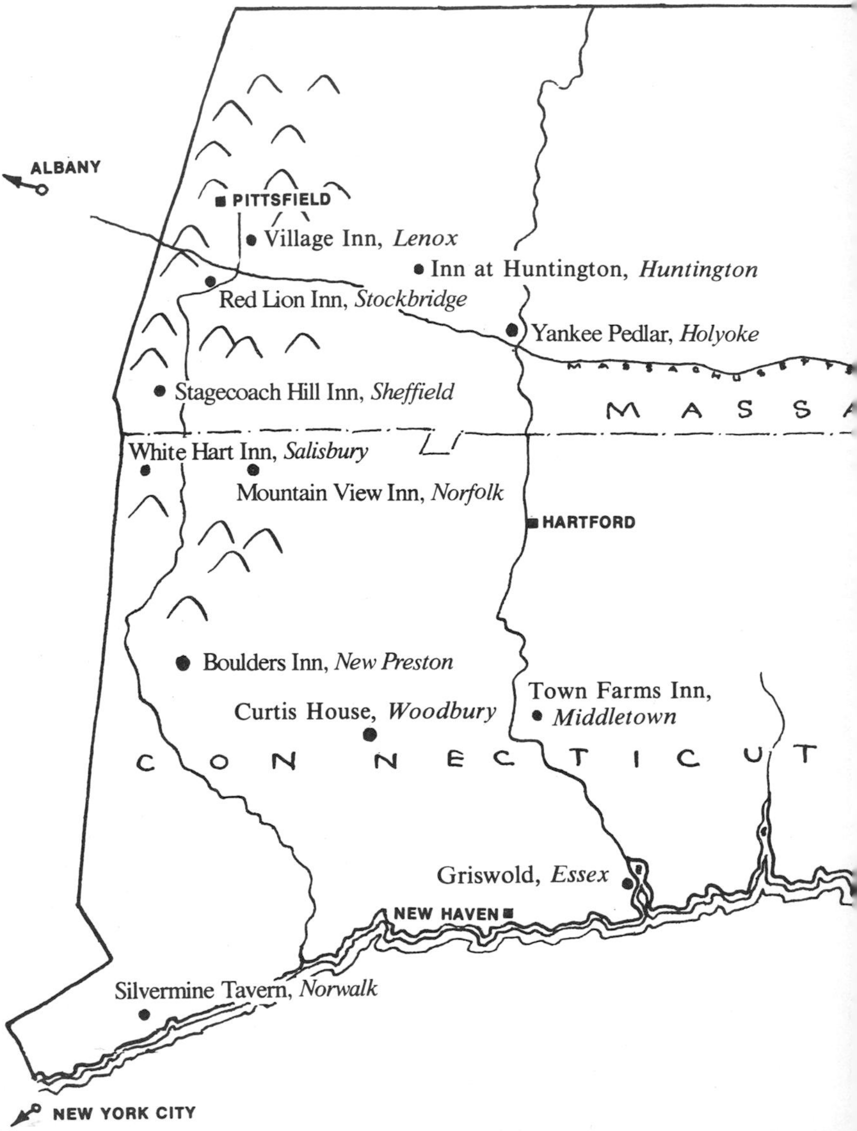

ALBANY
PITTSFIELD
Village Inn, *Lenox*
Inn at Huntington, *Huntington*
Red Lion Inn, *Stockbridge*
Yankee Pedlar, *Holyoke*
MASSACHUSETTS
Stagecoach Hill Inn, *Sheffield*
MASSA
White Hart Inn, *Salisbury*
Mountain View Inn, *Norfolk*
HARTFORD
Boulders Inn, *New Preston*
Town Farms Inn,
Middletown
Curtis House, *Woodbury*
CONNECTICUT
Griswold, *Essex*
NEW HAVEN
Silvermine Tavern, *Norwalk*
NEW YORK CITY

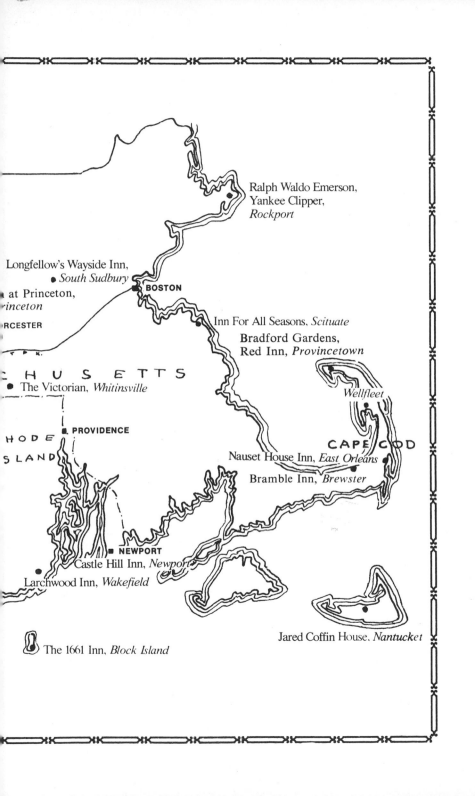

Ralph Waldo Emerson,
Yankee Clipper,
Rockport

Longfellow's Wayside Inn,
● *South Sudbury*

at Princeton,
rinceton

BOSTON

RCESTER

Inn For All Seasons, *Scituate*

**Bradford Gardens,
Red Inn,** *Provincetown*

─ H U S E T T S

● The Victorian, *Whitinsville*

Wellfleet

H O D E
S L A N D

■ **PROVIDENCE**

CAPE COD

Nauset House Inn, *East Orleans*

Bramble Inn, *Brewster*

■ **NEWPORT**

Castle Hill Inn, *Newport*

Larchwood Inn, *Wakefield*

The 1661 Inn, *Block Island*

Jared Coffin House, *Nantucket*

Connecticut

BOULDERS INN
Lake Waramaug, Connecticut

The letter was postmarked New York City and read in part as follows: "My wife and I want to tell you what a wonderful Memorial Day weekend we spent at the Boulders Inn. Dick and Jane Lowe really made us feel at home and we very much appreciated their sincere hospitality.

"We stayed in Brook Cottage which is only a few feet from an honest-to-goodness babbling brook and we highly recommend it to you the next time you are passing through. We cannot imagine a more picturesque setting in which to get away from the hustle of Manhattan. It was our type of vacation: good food, lots of sleep, tennis, reading in the evening, and most of all the manners and courtesy of this slower pace of life. And we are not so old that the slower pace is all we can keep up with; in fact, we are only thirty. Unfortunately, my new job will take me to Austin, Texas and I notice that your book, *Country Inns and Back Roads,* has no listing for the entire state. I guess we will just have to fly back to the Boulders from time to time."

I spoke to Jane Lowe about that letter and she said, "Oh yes, I do remember them. That was a really sensational weekend. It sort of gets the season under way and we had quite a few families with us as well. That is when we begin our full daily meal service which continues until mid-October. We have bed and breakfast the remainder of the year except for some special weekends."

I was enjoying my annual visit to the Boulders, this time once again with Fran and Roger Wunderlich. Roger is our representative to all the bookstores on the East Coast between Boston and Washington, and has visited many of the inns in this book. It was a comfortably-busy mid-summer night, and quite a few of us gathered in the living room to watch a spectacular thunderstorm come up over Lake Waramaug.

Oddly enough, the talk turned to cross-country skiing, and Dick Lowe was telling me how many people try it for the first time here at the Boulders during the winter. "We have a very good ski touring center nearby," he said. "And, everybody in the family can be outfitted. It is a good place to start cross-country skiing, because the beginners can ski on our snow-covered lake. As people get more

proficient they can use our trails which, by the way, become walking trails during the summer."

Jane Lowe, looking very pretty in a green-and-white print dress, chimed in, "Well, dedicated downhill skiers can ski at the Woodbury Ski Area which is just down the road a piece."

Chef Wayne Wellmaker came out of the kitchen, complete with his big white hat, and I had a chance to meet this young man who, among other things, originated the BI Pumpkin Nut Bread. We had a brief talk about the new menu which he had in mind for 1978, which would stress New England country foods. We were joined by another member of the inn's fourth generation, Pete Franklin, who is now really managing the inn, giving Dick and Jane a little more time to concentrate on some expansion plans.

"This has always been a place for young people," said Jane. "My grandfather's idea of a perfect summer was to come up from Greenwich by horse and carriage and spend the season entertaining his friends until Labor Day. He started all this. Then Dick and I began in the big house the year after we were married. I worked for my family every teen summer as a waitress and so forth, and both Wes and Tuck, our sons, have also grown up here working at the inn."

The Boulders Inn sits back and above the shores of Lake Waramaug, which is one of the prettiest lakes in northwest Connecticut. It offers a great many attractions that appeal to people of all ages. The lake has sailing, boating, canoeing, swimming, fishing, and water sports, and the 250 acres have miles of woodland delights as well. There is tennis on the inn's own courts, and golf, and horseback-riding nearby.

Accommodations vary to provide for both families and couples. Some rooms are in the main buildings, others are scattered in small lodgings on the hillside and in the valley.

BOULDERS INN, Lake Waramaug, New Preston, Conn. 06777; 203-868-7918. A 30-room year-round resort-inn, 1½ mi. north of New Preston, 20 mi. from Danbury. All plans available. Breakfast, lunch, and dinner served daily to travelers from late May to mid-October and some weekends through the year. European plan and breakfast available rest of year. Monday dinner served to house-guests only. Rooms and breakfast only on Thanksgiving. Closed Christmas. Tennis, swimming, boating, sailing, fishing, hiking, bicycles, xc skiing, tobogganing. Golf and riding nearby. Dick and Jane Lowe, Innkeepers.

Directions: From I-84, take Exit 7 and follow Rte. 7 north to Rte. 202 (formerly 25) through New Milford. Proceed 8 mi. to New Preston then 1½ mi. to inn on Rte. 45.

CURTIS HOUSE
Woodbury, Connecticut

The Curtis House opened in 1754 and is, according to my information, the oldest inn in the state of Connecticut. It was first opened by Anthony Stoddard and was known as the Orenaug Inn.

Four of the subsequent owners have been named Curtis although all were unrelated. The Hardisty Family has been operating the inn since early 1950.

I visited it on a chilly Saturday afternoon in January after a pleasant snowfall the night before. Everything combined to make it idyllically New England. The countryside was at its best in its white mantle and the towns and villages of northwest Connecticut with their 18th-century homes and churches gleamed in the bright sunshine.

I walked through the front door, down a corridor, past the stairway to the lodging rooms on the two floors above, and entered the low-ceilinged, heavily-beamed parlor with its wide floor boards and cheery fireplace. There were many antiques, including drop leaf tables, Windsor chairs and settees.

Waitresses were bustling about the dining room carrying trays laden with plates of beef pot pie, Yankee pot roast, roast beef hash, scallops, and blueberry pancakes. There were quite a few families dining with sons and daughters who were students at local prep schools.

My luncheon included a delicious fresh fruit and sherbet cup and a beef pie. From the desserts I chose an apple crisp which was served with vanilla ice cream. What could be more New England?

Luncheon and dinner are served daily except Christmas Day and reservations are not accepted with the exception of New Year's

Day, Mother's Day, Easter, and Thanksgiving.

There are 18 lodging rooms in this old inn, many of them with canopied twin or double beds. Twelve of the rooms have private baths. There are four additional modern rooms in the nearby Carriage House.

The large sign in front of the inn is the work of Wallace Nutting who included many of the Woodbury buildings in his book, *Connecticut The Beautiful.* Woodbury is one of the antiquing centers of New England and there are many antique shops on Routes 6 and 47. The Glebe House which was the birthplace of the American Episcopal Church is only a ten-minute walk from the inn.

Woodbury and Southbury are ideal towns for browsing. Visitors in late June can enjoy an outdoor auction of antiques and treasures sponsored by a local church, followed by a strawberry festival. I understand that on that one day every year it almost never rains.

I left Woodbury and the Curtis House as the setting sun created great red and orange streaks over the snowy hills and the lights of the inn were already casting their warm, beckoning glow. This is the way it has been for well over 200 years.

CURTIS HOUSE, Route 6 (Main St.), Woodbury, Conn., 06798; 203-263-2101. An 18-room village inn, 12 mi. from Waterbury. Open year-round. European Plan. Lunch and dinner served daily except Christmas. No pets. Antiquing, skiing, tennis, platform tennis, horseback riding nearby. The Hardisty Family, Innkeepers.

Directions: From N.Y. take Sawmill River Pkwy. to I-84. Take Exit 15 from I-84 in Southbury. Follow Rte. 6 north to Woodbury. From Hartford take I-84 to Exit 17, follow Rte. 64 to Woodbury.

GRISWOLD INN
Essex, Connecticut

The Griswold Inn is proof positive of the old saw: "Nothing succeds like success." When I mentioned this to innkeeper Bill Winterer, he laughed modestly and said, "I'm not so sure we're successful, but I know we're working very hard at what we're doing and we love it."

Bill is one of the most enthusiastic people I have ever met. He visited Essex and saw the inn when he was an officer candidate at nearby New London Coast Guard Academy, and after a few years in the world of high finance, he and his wife Vicky decided to start life anew here as innkeepers.

"Can you imagine," he said, "only five families have owned this building since 1776. It was the first three-story structure in Connecticut and except for a couple of small changes, it remains the same. The Tap Room was built in 1738 and was the first schoolhouse in Essex. It was rolled on logs down the main street to its present location by a team of oxen.

"We call the original parlor of the inn 'The Library' and we've lined it with books. Some of the firearms in the Gun Room date back to the 15th century. Our Covered Bridge Room is a dining room constructed from an abandoned New Hampshire covered bridge and moved to Essex." This room has a very impressive collection of Currier and Ives steamboat prints and temperance banners.

As if all this weren't enough for Bill (who is a very enthusiastic sailor and has his own yawl, the *Axia*), there is also the Steamboat Room whose decor and furnishings simulate the dining salon of a riverboat of 100 years ago. On one wall of the room is a mural depicting an offshore perspective of the Essex shoreline as it appeared at the turn of the century. The amazing thing is that the entire mural rocks slowly up and down creating the impression for people in the dining room of actually being on a moving ship! "Vicky and I just couldn't resist the whole idea," he said. "It has been great fun."

"Great fun," perhaps is the dominating theme of the Griswold. I think the epitome of this fun is found in a red popcorn wagon which provides snowy snacks for the Griswold guests. The feeling of fun is further projected by the old-fashioned pot-bellied stove, and many humorous posters and prints among the really impressive collection of memorabilia and antiques, including marine oils, ships' bells, clocks, ships' models, and running, and mast lights.

There are 18 guest rooms at the "Gris," most of which have private baths and all are furnished in early Essex.

The food at the "Gris" is basically American. Local and salt water fish, beef, and lamb dishes have been popular. A Hunt Breakfast is served every Sunday, which includes long tables of fried chicken, herring, lamb kidneys, eggs, grits, creamed chipped beef, and special sausage. This sausage is made from a 200-year-old recipe.

Essex, besides being a waterfront town where there are many yachts, sailboats, cruisers, and shipyards, also has many, many very attractive shops. Some of these are located in Griswold Square which is an interesting group of late Colonial, early Federalist, buildings and a restored barn just across the street from the inn. Much of this was Vicky Winterer's particular area of interest.

Bill and Vicky have just completed the restoration of the Town Farms Inn in Middletown, Connecticut, the latest inn to be included in this edition.

Every time I visit the "Gris," I find something hanging on the walls, or in one of the corners, that I had missed on a previous visit. There are many interesting and odd examples of memorabilia. This time I found a small plaque which was really a birthday ditty dated the seventh day of the seventh month of 1776. It reads:

"To my dear son Fred:
  I send you this my little gun, do not handle it in fun
  But with it make the British run
  Join ye ranks of Washington
  When our independence is won we will take a drink of good old rum."

John Francis Putnam

25

GRISWOLD INN, Main St., Essex, Conn. 06426; 203-767-0991. A 16-room inn in a waterside town, steps away from the Connecticut River, and located near the Eugene O'Neill Theatre, Goodspeed Opera House, Ivoryton Playhouse, Gillette Castle, Mystic Village, Valley Railroad and Hammonasset State Beach. Some rooms with private baths. European plan. Complimentary Continental breakfast served daily to inn guests. Lunch and dinner served daily to travelers. Hunt breakfast served Sundays. Closed Christmas Eve and Christmas Day. Day sailing on inn's 44-foot ketch by appointment. Bicycles, tennis and boating nearby. Victoria and William G. Winterer, Innkeepers.

Directions: From I-95 take Exit 69 and travel north on Rte. 9 to Exit 3, Essex. Turn right at stop light and follow West Ave. to center of town. Turn right onto Main St. and proceed down to water and inn.

MOUNTAIN VIEW INN
Norfork, Connecticut

I was sitting in the lobby of the Mountain View Inn chatting with Joan Jokinen and admiring the exceptional collection of clocks. They were large and small, ornate and plain, foreign and domestic. However, there was one clock with something a little odd about it. I couldn't quite figure it out.

Karl Jokinen came in from the kitchen resplendent in his immaculate chef's outfit. "How about having the duck tonight?" he asked. I can hardly resist Karl's duck l'orange. "You'd be surprised how many people have ordered it after reading about it in *Country Inns and Back Roads*," he said.

While it's true that duck is one of my favorites, I have also enjoyed the Steak Tartare, Chicken Papillote, bay scallops, and veal curry, at this inn in northwest Connecticut. Karl also waxes creative with a cold Gaspé Bay salmon in an aspic mold garnished with vegetables and egg whites. "We change our menu frequently," he said. "We adjust it to what our guests tell us they enjoy the most, and at the same time I like to keep adding new things."

There are also some unlisted surprises on the menu including apples stuffed with mincemeat, fresh squash with a remarkable seasoning, romaine lettuce and avocado salad with orange dressing.

"We've always done some canning, but this year we're quite heavy on it," said Karl. "The only thing we will have to buy is flour, sugar, salt and things that you really cannot make. We stay as far away as possible from processed foods and stick pretty much to the natural things."

"Where is your star helper?" I asked.

"Oh, our son Larry, who really learned his trade here in the kitchen since before he started high school, has taken a temporary leave of absence. He is on his own in school in New Haven. He comes back now and then and gives me a hand," said Karl.

"Jennifer, our daughter, is even more of a help than ever. It is hard to realize she is almost twelve."

Rooms at this inn are a little larger than one might expect because it was originally a private home. They are all comfortably furnished with typical country inn furniture.

Norfolk is one of the sequestered towns in northwest Connecticut. For many summers, I have enjoyed the Yale Summer School of Music concerts offered on weekends. However, in fall and winter, these hills and valleys have exceptional back roading and woodland walks.

I finally could not contain my curiousity any longer. I took Karl by the arm, and we both walked across the room where I pointed to one of the clocks. "Karl," I said, "there is something different about that clock. Am I right?"

"You certainly are," he answered. "It's running backwards."

MOUNTAIN VIEW INN, Norfolk, Conn. 06058; 203-542-5595. A 7-room village inn, 40 mi. west of Hartford in the picturesque Litchfield Hills. European plan. Breakfast, lunch and dinner served daily to travelers except Mondays and Christmas Day. Open year-round. Golf, tennis, hiking, swimming, mountain climbing, bicycles, ice fishing, Alpine and xc skiing nearby. Karl and Joan Jokinen, Innkeepers.

Directions: Norfolk is on U.S. 44 which runs east-west. North-south roads which intersect 44 include U.S. 7, I-91, and U.S. 22. Inn is located off Rte. 44, ¼ mi. on 272 South.

SILVERMINE TAVERN
Norwalk, Connecticut

"Meet Miss Abigail," said Frank Whitman. "She's the only woman permitted by Connecticut law to stand within three feet of a bar."

I spoke courteously, but Miss Abigail just stood there in her crinoline and lace, looking inscrutable. The walls behind her and, in fact, in all of the dining rooms were covered with old farm implements and tools, as well as American primitive paintings.

Frank and I continued our tour of the Silvermine Tavern. "The Tavern was named for the town," he asserted. "That name, in turn, came from an old as-yet-unfounded rumor about a silver mine discovered by an early settler. The old post office was here at the four corners.

We passed through two low-ceilinged sitting rooms, both brimming with antiques. There were fireplaces in each and one had an old clock with wooden works. Frank pointed out the beams from the original inn as well as the old-fashioned colonial hinges on the doorway. Some of the oil paintings of the colonial ladies and gentlemen looked rather forbidding.

I followed him up a winding staircase and found typical country inn bedrooms without television or telephones.

"You can imagine that we're quite popular with honeymooners," he said. "They like to wander the country roads and to feed the ducks and swans on the Mill Pond." There is a Country

Store just across the street from the Tavern where the old counters and display tables have some very interesting adaptations of colonial skills and crafts. In the back room of the store, a museum has antique tools and gadgets and a fine collection of Currier and Ives prints.

The Tavern at various times, has served as a country inn, a gentleman's country seat, and a town meeting place. It has a very large outdoor dining area overlooking the Silvermine River and the Mill Pond with ducks and swans. Summer terrace dining among the oaks, maples, pines and poplar trees is very popular with playgoers at the Westport Playhouse and the Stratford Shakespeare Theatre nearby. I like the Silvermine in the winter also, when the many fireplaces are crackling.

Some of the New England dishes on the menu include Indian pudding, bread pudding, honeybuns, native scrod, lobster, scallops, and oysters. On Thursday night there is a buffet that includes roast beef, corned beef and fried chicken. On Wednesday and Friday night during the summer there is a barbecue, and there is a Sunday brunch buffet which has as many as 25 different offerings on the big tables.

When my tour of the Tavern and all the buildings at the Crossroads was over, I went back to ask Miss Abigail if she'd care to join me for dinner. I suggested the chicken pie. No reply. I pointed out that all the breads and desserts were homemade —even the ice cream. Still she remained inscrutable.

But I didn't feel too badly when Frank assured me that she hasn't spoken to anyone in years.

SILVERMINE TAVERN, Perry Ave., Norwalk, Ct. 06850; 203-847-4558. A 10-room country inn in the residential section of Norwalk. Long Island Sound and beaches 6 mi. away. European plan includes Continental breakfast. Lunch and dinner served to travelers daily. Open year-round. Closed Christmas Day and Tuesdays during winter. Golf, tennis and fishing nearby. Francis C. Whitman, Innkeeper.

Directions: From New York or New Haven via I-95, take Exit 15. Pick up the new Rte. 7 going north. At the end of Rte. 7 (approx. 1 mi.) turn right, go to first stoplight, turn right. At next stoplight by firehouse turn right onto Silvermine Ave. Proceed down Silvermine Ave. about 2 mi. to Tavern. From I-84 and Danbury take old Rte. 7 south to Norwalk. Watch for Kelly Greens ½ mi. south of Merritt Pkwy. on the left, turn right on Perry Ave. opposite Kelly Greens. Follow Perry Ave. 2 mi. to Tavern. From Merritt Pkwy. take Exit 39 south on old Rte. 7 and follow directions above.

TOWN FARMS INN
Middletown, Connecticut

The winter's afternoon was brilliant. Following Bill Winterer's unfailing directions, I turned off Route 9 at Silver Street in Middletown, turned left and followed the road through the Connecticut Valley Hospital complex. I crested a hill and, looking down into a valley next to the Connecticut River, I saw a mellowed-red-brick building that I was certain would be the Town Farms Inn. A few minutes later, I walked through the front door and all around me was the hustle and bustle of carpenters, bricklayers, cabinetmakers, and electricians at work. I stood there for about thirty seconds and was joined by Bill and Vicky Winterer, their faces aglow with enthusiasm. "You're right on time, come on, let's take a quick tour and I'll explain what its all about."

We walked into the parlor, and through wide doors into a room which had a low ceiling with red beams and red paneling. Two fireplaces at one end, each with an Indian portrait over the mantle. "This is the American Indian Room," said Bill. "It is a dining room and lounge area." We were joined by another man whom he introduced as J.P. Chadwick Floyd, the architect for the renovation. "Incidentally, our application is in the works for being listed in the National Historic Register," said Vicky.

The tour continued into a striking, two-storied dining room with several French doors, all providing a most generous view of the river. "Originally this part of the building had two floors," said Mr. Floyd, "however, we saw the possibility of removing the ceiling, and making it a very light, airy room with lots of windows that were originally on the second floor. It is a perfect example of a Palladian room and we have installed a Palladian window at one end which has three parts and a curve over the center section. This will be the main dining room." Vicky pointed out the balcony at the opposite end, where they were planning to have concerts by string quartets and other small groups. By this time, I was thoroughly caught up in their enthusiasm — I began to see the entire unfoldment of the Town Farms Inn, which was scheduled for a grand opening in just three weeks.

The setting is ideal ... just a few steps from the banks of the Connecticut River in a valley surrounded by low, verdant hills. To top it off, a spur of the old Connecticut Valley Railroad runs alongside the inn and a train comes through once a day, just about lunchtime.

"These buildings were the county poor farm for many years," said Vicky. "Most recently it was an inn. Bill came to lunch here about

four years ago and saw its possibilities. We learned last summer that it was for sale, so we both came over to take a closer look and fell in love with the place. It has been great fun fixing it up."

The Winterers both have a great deal of experience "fixing things up" because they are also the proprietors of the Griswold Inn in Essex, Connecticut, which is down the river just a few miles.

The Town Farms Inn has a second floor with several rooms that will be ideal for lodgings, but these will not be available until 1979.

My tour took the better part of the afternoon, and Bill took me outside to show me where the dining terrace would be located next to the railroad tracks and river.

"Vicky has already started on her cutting garden with zinnias and marigolds. She is planting flowering shrubs around the building."

We talked about the menu: "There will be a lot of New England dishes: oysters, Boston scord, bluefish, lemon sole, Cape Cod scallops, and things like that," he said. "But we will also have roast Canadian quail, hare cooked in wine and fresh mushrooms, chicken Cordon Bleu, and beef Stroganoff. We will also have a children's menu."

Unfortunately, I wasn't able to be present at the official opening of the inn which took place on February 3rd, and featured as guests of honor Governor Ella Grasso and her husband, Dr. Thomas Grasso of Connecticut. However, I was looking forward to a midsummer visit at this rural inn, the most recent addition to *Country Inns and Back Roads.*

TOWN FARMS INN, Silver St., Middletown, Conn. 06457; 203-347-7438. A riverside restaurant just a few minutes from the center of

*Middletown. Lodging rooms available in 1979. Lunch and dinner
served daily except Christmas Eve and Christmas Day. Wesleyan
Univ. nearby. Long Island Sound about 40 min. away. Bill and Vicky
Winterer, Innkeepers.*

*Directions: From I-91 follow Rte. 9 south to Middletown and take
Exit 12 to Silver St. Then proceed ½ mi. eastward, following signs to
Connecticut Valley Hospital whose grounds resemble a college
campus. The inn is on the left side of the road at the bottom of the
hill, a red brick building with a black mansard roof.*

WHITE HART INN
Salisbury, Connecticut

"Northwestern Connecticut has names like Litchfield, Kent,
Cornwall Bridge, Sharon and Salisbury. There are winding roads,
picket fences, old Colonials, horses, high hedges, and an appreciation for fine leathers and imported tweeds. The village of
Salisbury sums it all up very nicely, and plump in the middle of it, is
the White Hart Inn, and the adjoining Country Store.

"There was a memorable day about six months ago when I held a
five-minute conversation with the wooden Indian at the entrance of
this Country Store, thinking it was Innkeeper, John Harney. (There
is a resemblance.)

"John says of the White Hart Inn: 'We're as New England as
Mom's apple pie.' He ought to know. Unlike Ethan Allen, the hero
of fort Ticonderoga, who went from Salisbury to Vermont. John
went the other way, from Vermont to Salisbury.

"The White Hart is a rambling old place with many fireplaces and
chimney corners. The guest rooms are big and comfortable, and the
food is plentiful. Sunday night buffets bring out many of the
interesting people, who have migrated to both the Litchfield Hills
and the Berkshires, from the metropolitan area. A lot of them have
their first taste of real New England, as a result of staying at the
White Hart on an earlier weekend visit.

"The Country Store is a replica of a similar emporium of 75 years
ago, and sells all of the gimcracks, candles, soaps, spices, penny
candy, etc., that we have come to associate with the late 1890s.
However, I noted that there are quite a few new gadgets that may well
be considered gimcracks in another hundred years. I have always
found it very difficult just to browse and not to buy."

The above paragraphs are what I wrote in 1968 on one of my
very first visits to the White Hart Inn. Everything I wrote then is true
today, the only difference being that the White Hart has since

celebrated its 100th birthday, and John Harney insists that he has been there at least 110 years!

Over the past few years I have described John beating me at checkers (I'm sure he's honest but why does he win every time?), John beating me at darts (I know he practices on the side), and John giving me history lessons about the lost community called Dudleytown. I have described the gingerbread village which is on display at the inn during every Christmas season, and also John's successes and failures in the world of politics.

Just as John Harney and the White Hart are a tradition in northwest Connecticut, I guess one might say they are also a tradition in *Country Inns and Back Roads*, since they were both in the first edition in 1966!

WHITE HART INN, Salisbury, Conn. 06068; 203-435-2511. A 25-room village inn, 55 mi. west of Hartford. European plan. Breakfast, lunch, dinner served to travelers daily. Alpine and xc skiing, ski-jumping, golf, swimming nearby. John Harney, Innkeeper.

Directions: Exit the Taconic Pkwy. at Millbrook, N.Y. Proceed east on U.S. 44 to Salisbury. Inn is located at Jct. of U.S. 44 and 41.

Massachusetts

BRADFORD GARDENS INN
Provincetown, Cape Cod, Massachusetts

"Provincetown," said Jim Logan, "can be many different things. To the artist, it may be the combination of old houses that frame the

harbor, the rare quality of light, the boats, the narrow streets. To the writer, the eternal tides, the distant hills of Plymouth riding the horizon across the bay, or just a skirt of gulls convoying the dawn.

"To the vacationer it may be the little lanes, the field of finely washed sand as the sun beats down, or just the fun of walking down Commercial Street."

I have been visiting the Bradford Gardens Inn since 1973, and it has been great fun to watch its growth during the years. Letters from readers praise the breakfast, the comfortable rooms, many with fireplaces, the growing art collection, and the feeling that there is somebody around who actually cares.

Each of the lodging rooms has its own character and descriptive name such as the Honeymoon Suite, which has a bedroom and sitting room with a garden view and a Franklin stove; the Jenny Lind Salon which has a beautiful spool bed; the Yesteryear Room with its astonishing brass bed; the Cherry Tree Room which is particularly lovely the last two weeks in June when the famous tree shows off; and the Sun Gallery Room which has its own private entrance, a fireplace, a garden view and an excellent harbor view. Behind the inn, there is the Loft Lodge, which accommodates six people in two loft bedrooms. It has a deck, patio, fireplace, and includes a full kitchen with a washer and dryer. The inn also has a modern apartment building and motel overlooking the Provincetown Harbor.

Breakfast is the only meal served, and Jim does this himself—he might cook shirred eggs Mornay, the unusual and good Quebec pork pie or corn pancakes from an old, secret family recipe, depending upon his whim. During the hot summer months, a lighter, European-type breakfast is served in the rose garden.

I have visited Provincetown in almost every month of the year, and personally prefer the comparative solitude of fall and winter. I like to bundle up well and walk the full length of Commercial Street looking in the windows of the small shops, many of which are open, and perhaps do a bit of Christmas shopping. One of the Portuguese bakeries supplies me with a small warm roll. It is a quiet scene, with other weekend visitors strolling about greeting each other and having the opportunity to enjoy the old buildings and streets of the town more fully. Bicycling and walking are a pleasure, and I share the dunes and beaches with the permanent residents, the sea birds.

I can wind up the day with dinner at the Red Inn, which fortunately is open year-round, and then make my way back to the Bradford Gardens where Jim, the thoughtful innkeeper, has laid a fire in my bedroom. It is a good place for a winter break.

BRADFORD GARDENS INN, 178 Bradford St., Provincetown, Mass. 02657; 617-487-1616. A small 8-room village inn with working fireplaces overlooking Provincetown Bay. European plan includes complimentary breakfast. No other meals served. Open year-round. Within walking distance of Provincetown harbor and shops. Bicycles, swimming, riding, tennis, golf and dune buggies nearby. Jim Logan, Innkeeper.

Directions: Follow Rte. 6 to Provincetown.

THE BRAMBLE INN
Brewster, Cape Cod, Massachusetts

Revisiting the Bramble Inn, which is located in Brewster on the north shore of Cape Cod, Massachusetts, was great fun. I found Karen Etsell and Elaine Brennan ecstatic about their progress during the previous twelve months.

"It has been a wonderful season and we feel very proud of the things that have been happening here," said Karen. "The art work from our gallery sold very well, and the addition to our menu of the quiche and the crepes was extremely well received."

"Yes, and we are going to make lots more improvements in the upcoming year," said Elaine. "We are planning to do more remodeling and landscaping. We've met some wonderful people this year, and some of the most memorable have come to us through *Country Inns and Back Roads.* We were especially taken by the two girls you directed to us when you met them at the Larchwood Inn in the middle of the summer. They went out to the Jared Coffin House on Nantucket and had lunch, as I recall. We also met a wonderful

couple from Louisville, Kentucky, who sent us some Kentucky cheese. They knew we were great cheese lovers."

The Bramble Inn is a dandy. It is a marvelous example of what I delight in finding in country inns. For one thing, it expresses the innkeepers' individual interests and personalities. In this case, these two attractive women decided they would like to try their hand at innkeeping, and brought to the business a background of professional social work. Elaine is also a photographer, and many of her works are on the walls, along with those of local artists.

The tone of the inn is set by this collection of watercolors, oil paintings, lithographs, pastels, and wood lathe art, which is a combination of wood lathe blocks and barn siding creatively arranged in a rough frame. The walls and woodwork are sparkling white and the floorboards of differing widths have been refinished in a contrasting warm brown. Plants hang from the ceiling and there is much ivy (which had grown considerably since my last visit).

Brunch and lunch seemed to go on indefinitely here, and the menu includes Cape Cod clam chowder, home-baked bread, cheese plates — including one called breakfast cheese plate (a delightful repast which I grew accustomed to while traveling in Europe), consisting of a light cheese for morning meal. Most of these are accompanied by fruits. The luncheon plate consists of fruits served with a choice of Brie, Camembert, and Vermont cheddar cheese, and more of that wonderful baked bread. A delicious quiche and two crepe dishes round out the menu. Dessert is something special and original, called Bramble a la Mode, which is an old-fashioned Cape Cod delicacy with raisins and cranberries wrapped in a tender pastry and topped with vanilla ice cream.

There are two lodging rooms at the top of the stairs, one with a double bed and one with a single bed. Both have flowered wallpaper and country furniture. Elaine and Karen told me that my mentioning there were but two, caused people, in some cases, to feel the rooms would not be available, when in fact, they were. "Please tell your readers to call ahead, because on many nights last year we did have a room available."

THE BRAMBLE INN GALLERY AND CAFE, Route 6A, Main St., Brewster, Cape Cod, Ma. 02631; 617-896-7611. A village inn and art gallery in the heart of one of cape Cod's northshore villages. Lodgings include Continental breakfast. Lunch and dinner served daily except Mondays. Open May through mid-October. Small, intimate inn does not meet the needs of most children. No pets. Swimming, sailing, water sports, golf, recreational and natural attractions within a short drive. Adjacent to tennis club. Elaine Brennan and Karen Etsell, Innkeepers.

Directions: Take Exit 10 from Rte. 6. Follow to the intersection of Rte. 6A (4 mi.). Turn right, one-tenth mile to inn.

INN FOR ALL SEASONS
Scituate Harbor, Massachusetts

The fire was crackling and aromatic, and afforded a welcome respite from the chilly air of Scituate Harbor in December. I settled back in the rocking chair and contemplated the mixture of turn-of-the-century and Art Nouveau decor of the parlor of the Inn For All Seasons.

The wallpaper was in black and gold stripes with flocking, the corner cabinets had little china pieces and there was a chest of drawers with a marble top. On top of the piano was a ceramic of a zebra. There were elegant beaded curtains at the window. Looking into the formal dining room I was gazing right into the eyes of a two-and-a-half foot leopard seated on the edge of the sideboard. He wasn't real, but he could have been.

The outer door swung open and two houseguests to whom I had been introduced by Dorothy Wondolowski earlier, came immediately to the fire, hands outstretched. "Oh boy, this feels good. I love Scituate in December, it seems so natural." The woman's cheeks were glowing and she took off a Scottish tam-o-shanter and shook her hair loose. "I love to see those seabirds in the harbor and watch the fishing boats. The water is so blue today."

I discovered that they were from Detroit and that the man had to make occasional trips to Boston. "I discovered last year that it is

really quite easy to pick up my rental car at Logan Airport and come directly here and use this as a base of operation," he said. "It is only about an hour from the airport. Laura can go up to Boston with me while I take care of my business, or she can stay here and walk the beaches and visit the town." Elaine and Dorothy Wondolowski, two of the four innkeepers at the inn, joined us with a large silver tea tray and our new friends from the Midwest seemed to have dozens of questions about the inn.

"Well, the four of us, and that includes Elaine's husband, Ed, and my husband, Stan, decided to turn this lovely building into an inn in 1972.

"We really wanted to have an exceptional inn and we decided that we wouldn't make any sacrifices or short cuts. For instance, we take two days to prepare our stock for the soups and sauces, we insist that vegetables must be handled precisely to provide full flavor and freshness, and we take enough time to prepare each individual dish for each guest.

"We change both the menu and decor four times each year and try to have the colors and mood of the season reflected in the atmosphere and food. We serve heartier meals in the fall and winter, and lighter and more delicate food in the summer and spring. For example, our fall menu has Wellington of chicken, crab Crown Pompadour, veal Oscar, and beef Wellington. But our spring and summer menus would have things like our own fresh water fish which is served during all seasons also.

Dorothy suggested that since it was mid-afternoon and a great many of the expected houseguests had not checked in as yet, we might like to see some of the guest rooms above stairs. There were seven of them, most furnished in a Victorian style with antique beds, wicker furniture, patchwork quilts, country furniture. Each was entirely different. I was happy to see many books and magazines and a basket of apples on the upstairs landing.

When we returned to the first floor, I happened to pick up a brochure that spoke about seminars for the distinctive diner. Elaine explained that there are dining seminars scheduled at various times during the year which enable a guest to talk directly with the chef who explains the upcoming dinner and discusses the preparation and presentation. "We have no set schedule on these, but the next one is in about two weeks and our chef, Paul McGee, has already scheduled clam stew, cheese Helene, lemon sole amandine, winter salad, and poached pears Helene. Our guests telephone us frequently to learn the schedule."

An imaginative menu, attractive homelike bedrooms, the beckoning sea, historic sites, and plenty of activities —this is the Inn For All Seasons. It is all provided in an atmosphere of elegance and great attention to detail.

INN FOR ALL SEASONS, 32 Barker Rd. Scituate Harbor, Mass. 02060; 617-545-6699. An 8-room inn in a picturesque south shore sea town, 32 mi. from Boston. Shared baths. European plan. Continental breakfast, lunch, and dinner served to travelers daily except Mondays. Reservations for all meals advised. Open year-round. Children over 12 years old and attended pets allowed. Bicycles, fishing, golf, swimming, tennis, antiquing, and deep-sea fishing nearby. The Wondolowskis, Ed, Elaine, Stan, and Dorothy, Innkeepers.

Directions: From Boston, take Southeast Expressway south to Rte. 3. Continue south on Rte. 3 to Exit 31. Turn left at bottom of ramp and take right on Rte. 123 at traffic light. Go approximately 8 mi. to traffic lights intersecting Rte. 3A. Come across Rte. 3A, and follow signs for Scituate Harbor. At end of town take a right turn at set of traffic lights on to Jericho Rd. Take second left after Pier 44 on to Barker Rd. The inn is two blocks up on the right.

THE INN AT HUNTINGTON
Huntington, Massachusetts

As I stepped into the rather austere elegance of the Inn at Huntington, the sense of "something special" grew from the moment I was greeted by the strains of baroque instrumental music, to the moment I had taken my last delightful mouthful of creme caramel.

In the setting of this vintage 1760 inn, Murray and Barbara Schuman have hewn to a standard of simplicity and beauty in the hand-fashioned cherry tables, Windsor chairs, sparkling table settings with flowers, candles in hurricane lamps, and the walls hung with interesting prints.

Although Murray's ideas upon graduating from the Ecole Hoteliere in Lausanne, Switzerland were on a grand scale in terms of having a formal and elaborate restaurant with Limoges china and sterling silver, and men in tuxedos, he finally discovered he really wanted a country inn that was more American and functional.

Coming originally from Detroit and Philadelphia, respectively, Barbara and Murray met in 1972 at the Culinary Institute in Hyde Park, where he was Dean of Instruction and she came to develop the 200-book library which now, thanks to her efforts, houses about 15,000 volumes. Out of their mutual dream of a certain kind of "special" country inn has grown their concept of total integration of decor, service, and menu with each part complementing the other. "Barbara and I also have a strong feeling that the inn should be a part of the community. Everyone who works here, except myself and the sous chef, comes from the local area. We have taken people who have never waited on tables before and trained them."

Food is paramount, of course, with Murray. He thinks of his kitchen as being more of a cooking studio where "I learn to deal with food, to discover basic flavors and combinations of flavors, to combine and complement them with herbs and sauces, and simple garnishes, and to present different aromas, textures, and colors that are aesthetically pleasing to the American palate."

The menu of the Inn at Huntington changes frequently, reflecting not only available fresh fruits and vegetables, but Murray's ideas and inspirations. "For specials of the evening I usually choose dishes I have never tried before. Perhaps I've heard about something that interests me, so I try it and then I may decide to keep it on the menu for a week or so. That's what happened with one of our most popular dishes, duckling with raspberries (aux framboises). I had never seen it done elsewhere, but after I got the idea, I couldn't resist the temptation to give it a whirl.

"Lobster Pocket is another such dish—it's chunks of fresh lobster in a lobster bisque which forms a sort of croquette mixture and is wrapped in phyllo dough—the paper thin leaves that are used in making baklava—with a langoustino sauce around it—very crispy with a creamy sauce—just delicious.

"All of our baking is done here, except for the rolls which are made to our specifications by a marvelous baker. I think we have some desserts that are really special, too. This month we are featuring something called Poire William—ice cream topped with pear marmalade made with pears from our own tree and a pear brandy from Switzerland. Our torte de la maison always has three to four layers of sponge cake with pastry cream, fruit or nuts, and a cream topping; and our creme caramel is elegant.

"Along with our junior innkeepers, Hans and Aaron Schuman, we are having a lovely time here."

The Inn at Huntington reminds me of other chef-owned country inns featured in this book: Murray and Barbara, along with those other innkeepers, bring a true love of food and a dedication that seems very much in place in the mountains and the hills. It has been an interesting journey for them starting in Philadelphia and Detroit, and arriving in Huntington by way of Switzerland and Hyde Park.

There are no lodging rooms available at the moment, but the Schumans are happy to recommend places nearby.

THE INN AT HUNTINGTON, Worthington Rd., Huntington, Ma. 01050; 413-667-8868. A restaurant featuring European countryside cuisine on Rte. 112 (Worthington Rd.) 1 mi. from downtown Huntington. No lodgings. Dinner served nightly except Monday. Reservations strongly suggested. Open February 1st to December 31st. Closed Thanksgiving, Christmas Eve, Christmas Day. Murray and Barbara Schuman, Innkeepers.

Directions: Huntington is on Rte. 112, off U.S. Rte. 20, halfway between the Westfield and Lee exits of the Mass. Tpke. From Northampton use Rte. 66 to Rte. 112 to Huntington.

INN AT PRINCETON
Princeton, Massachusetts

It was a gentle evening in mid-September. We were all out on the terrace of this quiet, rather sequestered inn, when Suzanne Reed said, "I think it has grown dark enough now to see the lights of Boston."

"Really? But Boston is at least fifty miles away," I exclaimed.

"Well, come and see for yourself," she said, and we walked to the end of the terrace which is the highest point on the inn property. Sure enough, there, twinkling in the distance, I could see some of the lights of the Boston skyline.

"Yes, and when it gets pitch dark a little later on they look like little diamonds in the blackness," said Liz Sjogren, who with Suzanne is joint-owner of the inn.

The Inn at Princeton is really a jewel. It was once a mansion, with a lower story of beautiful fieldstone and an upper story of traditional weathered New England shingles. It is set slightly apart from the town in its own spacious gardens and lawns. Like so many other country inns, it represents a wish fulfillment — in this case, for two attractive women who discovered a few years ago that they each wanted to leave the teaching profession and open a country inn.

"It has been tons of fun and tons of work," said Suzanne, "but the moment we saw the house, we knew it had to be ours — it was exactly what we wanted. Although the outside of the building was beautiful, it did require quite a few repairs; but the interior needed to be almost completely done over. We worked after school, on weekends and vacations for months; cleaning, scraping, painting and wallpapering. We scoured the antique shops; begged and borrowed from our families and friends. We both had always been interested in art, and the art work seemed to fall into place. The miniature dollhouse with its tiny furnishings on display on the stairway landing represents part of our individual collections of miniatures."

"Meanwhile," said Liz, "we interviewed many chefs and cooks, and realized that this was going to be a real problem. Then we became acquainted with Walter Hawley, who is a graduate of the Culinary Institute, and he is our chef now. He has been wonderful, and our guests rave about his dishes. He is happy here, because he is able to do the things he likes best — to create his own dishes and experiment with ideas. As a result of his inspiration. We now have a special section on the menu called 'Menu du Chef'."

From the Sun Room, one of the two dining rooms on the first floor, there is a lovely view of lawn, trees, and a country road through the ten handsome bay windows. The other dining room overlooks the great sweeping valley with rolling fields, and in the evening, the lights of Boston in the distance.

Guests entering through the front door are greeted by a fireplace on the right, and by an expansive living room on the left with a collection of very colorful and cleverly-lit oil paintings and watercolors. An old trunk holds firewood for the living room fireplace. There is an air of style and grace about these rooms with their highly polished parquet floors.

Decorated in attractive period furnishings and bright cheery wallpaper, the bedrooms have many special touches, such as the cradle I found in one, and cleverly framed old photographs.

For dinner that night I had sweetbreads which were served on a bed of spinach with a most unusual sauce. I was especially fond of the squash which was wonderfully spiced. I also had the opportunity to meet Walter who came out of the kitchen wearing his jaunty chef's hat. Among the other items of continental cuisine are paupiettes du veau, lamb chops en croute, and scallops Provencale. Dessert was a fresh fruit trifle — delicious.

After dinner, I decided to take another short constitutional on the terrace, and sure enough, now that the night was inky black, the distant lights of Boston seemed ever so much closer.

INN AT PRINCETON, Mountain Rd., Princeton, Ma. 01541; 617-464-2030. A 5-room village inn 60 mi. from Boston and 14 mi. from Worcester near Mt. Wachusett State Reservation. European plan. Dinner served to travelers except Sunday and Monday. Open year-round. Closed Christmas. No pets. Not oriented for younger children. Tennis, swimming, skiing, hiking nearby. Suzanne W.

Reed and Elizabeth A. Sjogren, Innkeepers.

Directions: From Boston: Rte. 2 west to Intersections of Rte. 2 and 31. From Conn. and Mass.: Mass. Tpke. to Rte. 122A to Holden Center, right at Rte. 31. From Vt.: I-91 to Rte. 2 to Rte. 31.

JARED COFFIN HOUSE
Nantucket Island, Massachusetts

I receive letters almost every day from the people who visit the country inns written about in *Country Inns and Back Roads.* I remember this one letter in particular. I received it about eight years ago:

"A few years ago my husband and I ran across a copy of one of your books which shows a gentleman skater on the cover. (That would be about 1968!) On page 17 there was a map of Nantucket Island and a description of your visit there in February, and how you stopped at the Jared Coffin House. Later we got an edition with a green cover showing what I presume was the same gentleman fishing with his dog, (that was 1969), and again you were quite enthusiastic about visiting the Jared Coffin House and Nantucket Island. We read all about the Chippendales, the Sheratons, the Crewel Room where you had accommodations and the Quahaug chowder, the Bay scallops, the roses, the moors, and the beaches.

"The 1975 edition was the last straw. You mentioned spending part of the Christmas holiday there and talked about the winding cobblestone streets, bicycling out to the other end of the island, visiting the bird sanctuary and again, the excellent food and accommodations at the Jared Coffin House.

"We could stand it no longer. I must say that planning a trip to an island thirty miles at sea is not something that one does lightly. I'm glad you suggested that it wouldn't be necessary to take our automobile, so we left it at the Woods Hole parking lot. The trip was just long enough to give us a feeling of being at sea and we were delighted with Nantucket.

"Mr. Read was a marvelous host and he even went out of his way to show us some of the back roads on the moors. He even told us about the time you and he got lost on one of them.

"Of course, the inn is just like living in a museum and I am happy to say that we also were able to reserve the Crewel Room, and that four-poster bed with the crewel-embroidered spread and canopy was a beauty. The sun came in the windows in the morning and there was the aroma of breakfast just as you promised."

In mentally reviewing things that have happened at the Jared

Nantucket waterfront

Coffin House in the last ten years, probably the most significant is that Peggy and Phil Read are now the sole proprietors of this classic country inn, as well as being the innkeepers. The most recent news is that a beautiful 1821 Federal house on Center Street, across the street from the inn on the dining room side, has been purchased and is being converted into six lovely rooms decorated and furnished in keeping with the Federal style.

Innkeepers from inns in this book have had an annual meeting at the Jared Coffin House twice in the past and we all have enjoyed it so much that we are making plans to meet there again in November of 1978.

JARED COFFIN HOUSE, Nantucket Island, Mass. 02554; 617-228-2400. A 41-room village inn 30 mi. at sea. European plan. Breakfast, lunch, dinner served daily. Strongly advise verifying accommodations before planning a trip to Nantucket in any season. Swimming, fishing, boating, golf, tennis, riding, and bicycles nearby. Philip and Margaret Read, Innkeepers.

Directions: Accessible by air from Boston and Hyannis, or by ferry from Woods Hole, Mass. Automobile reservations are usually needed in advance. Seasonal air service from New York and ferry service from Hyannis are available May thru October. (617-426-1855.) Inn is located 300 yards from ferry dock.

LONGFELLOW'S WAYSIDE INN
South Sudbury, Massachusetts

There have been two paintings of Longfellow's Wayside Inn especially created for the covers of *Country Inns and Back Roads.* The first was in 1970, and the second, a few years later. As a result, we have been receiving an increasing number of letters from our readers who have had occasion to visit the famous inn, said to be the oldest, continuously-operating inn in America. One of the most interesting letters came as a result of a visit on Thanksgiving Day a few years ago. In substance it read as follows:

"We had planned to bring our children to New England during the late fall of the year because we felt it would best create a sort of 'Puritanical' atmosphere. We also felt that it would be less crowded and I am happy to say you were right, because our visit to Cape Cod at that time of the year was most delightful. The climax would be our reservation and Thanksgiving dinner at Longfellow's Wayside Inn.

"We arrived the day before, and the first thing we did was take a guided tour which enabled us to put everything into its proper perspective. We soon realized that the Wayside was actually not a museum but a kind of living treasure — a bridge between the early 18th century and the late 19th century. It developed that the early inn was a simple two-room structure with a tap room below and a chamber above, in which as many as five travelers slept at one time. Both of my sons, who were studying American history, were fascinated with the idea that the Sudbury Militia actually gathered in the tap room and went off to the Battle of Concord. Incidentally, we found that this entire trip was very valuable for them to get a good picture of their American heritage.

"We were all certainly very excited going to bed that night and we were able to reserve the room of which you have spoken in the old part of the inn. The wind whistled around the corners and the boys said that they really heard the rattle of drums.

"Thanksgiving Day dawned clear and frosty and we could already smell the turkeys cooking in the kitchen. We all took a walk up to the Grist Mill and looked in on the Chapel and the Little Red School House to work up an appetite before dinner.

"We were fascinated to learn that the Wayside Inn changed its name to Longfellow's Wayside Inn as a result of the publication of his book *Tales From A Wayside Inn*. I never realized that he actually visited here and that there was so much Longfellow memorabilia connected with the inn. Just before dinner we had a chance to meet Mr. Koppeis, the innkeeper, and he was kind enough to show us to our table in the dining room.

"It was exactly what we had hoped for, a fabulous turkey and all kinds of vegetables and hot breads and pastries, warm pies and even spiced whipped cream. Of course, we all had some Indian pudding to celebrate the occasion. It was a Thanksgiving Day that I'm sure none of my family will ever forget!"

LONGFELLOW'S WAYSIDE INN, Wayside Inn Rd., off Rte. 20, South Sudbury, Mass. 01776; 617-443-8846. A 10-room historic landmark inn, midway between Boston and Worcester. Within a short distance of Concord, Lexington, and other famous Revolutionary War landmarks. European plan. Lunch and dinner served daily except Christmas. Breakfast served to overnight guests. Francis Koppeis, Innkeeper.

Directions: From the west, take Exit 11A from I-95 to Rte. 495 N. Proceed north on 495 to Rte. 20. Follow Rte. 20 east to inn. From the east, take Exit 49 from Rte. 128. Follow Rte. 20 west to inn.

NAUSET HOUSE INN
East Orleans, Cap Cod, Massachusetts

I was looking at my Christmas card from Jack and Lucille Schwarz at the Nauset House Inn. It showed one end of the inn dining room with its red brick floors, pristine white walls, the long, family-style table and the ladder-back rocker in front of a blazing hearth.

With the exception of a large holly wreath, it was exactly as I remembered it from my trip in late September. On that particular morning the warm, late-summer sun had drawn many guests outside to the terrace to enjoy a second cup of coffee and the wine-like aroma

of the apple orchard. The roses and beach plums were still in bloom and there was an occasional goldfinch or cardinal darting among the trees.

I had just come down for breakfast and Jack introduced me to people at the table from Montreal and Philadelphia.

"Have some cranberry muffins, I'll be right back with more sausage to go with the scrambled eggs," he said over his shoulder.

I found out that the people from Montreal had been at the inn for three days. They told me about their favorite beach walks and bike trails. "You'll probably want to go for a dip around 2:00 p.m.," they said. "It's very warm. This is the best time of year to be here."

The Nauset House Inn is about three-fourths of the way out to the end of Cape Cod within sight of Nauset Beach, which has some of the best surf in New England. The inn is small enough for everyone to become quite friendly. Breakfast is the only meal served, and all sorts of New England and Cape Cod things are offered, including real maple syrup from the Schwarz's farm in Vermont. For lunch and dinner, they are happy to recommend restaurants from Chatham to Provincetown.

Jack and Lucille are knowledgeable collectors of antiques and this is reflected throughout the entire inn. All the beds, chests, secretaries, tables, clocks, highboys and such are handsome Early American pieces, and available for purchase. They also have a tiny antique shop in the orchard just behind the inn with still more choice selections.

The Cape is a particularly happy experience from late May through early June and after Labor Day. There's much more of an opportunity then to enjoy all of the beauty and history. It's also fun walking on Nauset Beach and finding it almost deserted.

In the meantime, our breakfast circle widened and we were

joined by guests from England, Winnipeg, Canada, San Francisco, New Orleans, Atlanta and Dallas. It was almost like an international breakfast meeting at the U.N.

Jack returned with the sausage and set the plate down with a flourish. "This morning," he said, "we'll call it Sausage Samuel, after Samuel Champlain, who landed in Nauset Harbor and named it after the Indian tribe who paddled out to the ship to greet him."

Now, that was some Christmas card, wasn't it?

NAUSET HOUSE INN, P.O. Box 446, Nauset Beach Rd., East Orleans, Cape Cod, Mass. 02643; 617-255-2195. A 12-room country inn 90 mi. from Boston, 27 mi. from Hyannis. Breakfast served to inn guests only. No other meals served. Some rooms with shared bath. Open daily from April 1 to Nov. 15. No children under 10 yrs. No pets. Within walking distance of Nauset Beach. Riding and bicycles nearby. Jack and Lucy Schwarz, Innkeepers.

Directions: From the Mid-Cape Hwy. (Rte. 6), take Exit 12. Bear right to first traffic light. Follow signs for Nauset Beach. Inn is located 1/4 mi. before beach on Nauset Beach Rd.

RALPH WALDO EMERSON
Rockport, Massachusetts

The telephone call came from Ohio and the man on the other end had this to say: "I've lived out here in the mid-West all of my life, and one of the things I've always wanted to do was to travel to New England and spend some time by the ocean. Where would I go to find lots of ocean and rocks to climb, where it's real 'New England'?"

I thought instantly of the Ralph Waldo Emerson. Its broad veranda has an unobstructed view of the ocean and it has some of the best climbing rocks that can be found anywhere.

The "Emerson," as it's called in Pigeon Cove, is made for people who are fascinated by the sea. It is possible to walk from that broad front porch across the lawn, through the natural rock garden, across a little dirt road to the rocks on the shores. And what rocks they are! A marvelous collection of boulders and great slabs of granite which are relics of the ice age. Among them are hundreds of small tidal pools. The sea gulls dive and zoom continually. Offshore there are dozens of little buoys which indicate where the lobster traps are in the waters below.

I tried to explain all of this as lucidly as possible. He asked me if they served typical New England food. "Well," I replied, "How do lobster, clams, fresh saltwater fish and homemade pies sound to you?" He agreed.

I told him about Pigeon Cove and strolling along the tree-shaded streets with the rambler of roses and the New England houses. I explained about the lanes that led down to the sea to provide access to the rockbound coast, and how much they reminded me of lanes in Sussex and Surrey which for centuries have provided a path between the fields and into the woods.

To his inquiry about whether children would like it, I explained that when I was there last, there seemed to be a fair number in evidence. "They enjoy the pool at the ocean," I pointed out.

Before he rang off, he asked whether Ralph Waldo Emerson, the famous New England essayist, had ever stayed at the inn. "They say he did," I answered. "In his diary he made this entry: 'Returned from Pigeon Cove where we made the acquaintance of the sea for seven days. 'Tis a noble, friendly power and seemed to say to me: "Why so late and slow to come to me? Am I not here always thy proper summer home"?'"

"Well," he replied, "if it is good enough for Ralph Waldo Emerson, I think it certainly will be good enough for me. I am going to make my reservations for July right now."

RALPH WALDO EMERSON, 1 Cathedral Ave., Rockport, Mass. 01966; 617-546-6321. A 36-room oceanside inn, 40 mi. from Boston. Modified American and European plans. Breakfast and dinner served to travelers daily. Snack bar luncheon in season. Season: July 1 through Labor Day. Open Memorial Day through Nov. 1. No pets. Pool, sauna and whirlpool bath on grounds. Tennis, golf nearby. Courtesy car. Gary Wemyss, Innkeeper.

Directions: Take I-95 to Rte. 128 to 127 (Gloucester). Proceed 6 mi. on Rte. 127 to Rockport and continue to Pigeon Cove.

THE RED INN
Provincetown, Cape Cod, Massachusetts

"We have the off-season," said Ted Barker, helping himself to another portion of striped bass, "and we have the off-off-season here in Provincetown."

We were having an early dinner in the new, three-level, terraced Greenhouse dining room, which has been reserved for non-smokers. Overhead the skylights gave full range to the Cape Cod sky, and I was taking a mental note of the profusion of greenery, some in large oak barrels, others in clay pots hanging from the ceiling, and in the brick planters separating the three levels. I realized that no matter where one might sit in this room there was a splendid view of the harbor at Provincetown with its myriad boats, seabirds, and the Long Point lighthouse in the distance.

"It seems to me," I said, "that there has been some major restoration and construction going on here at the Red Inn for the last couple of years."

"Yes, that's true," he replied, "but I think we are completely caught up. The first step was the new kitchen where Marcie is so happy, and then we had the new lounge and the new outside landscaping."

Marcie and Ted Barker and various members of their family have made the Red Inn a genuine Cape Cod institution even before my first visit in 1972. In a tourist-oriented locale where new restaurants open with the arrival of the birds in the spring each year and then close their doors forever, the Red Inn has thrived with each passing year. I believe that this can be attributed to the fact that it is a family-run restaurant, and therefore projects a sense of continuity. This feeling of permanency is one of the features I look for in deciding which of the many fine inns and restaurants that I visit each year will be included in the book.

Naturally, being a restaurant, the continuing success of the Red Inn is based on the menu, which includes a great variety of seafood dishes, and various cuts of western beef. There are different shrimp dishes, scallops, and lobsters (which seem harder to get with each passing year). Desserts include Strawberries Romanoff, Orange Delight, Indian pudding, and baked apples.

"What's this about the off-off-season?" I asked.

"We find that from December through March Provincetown is a sort of special place for people to recharge. They like to come here," he said, " and enjoy the walks on the beaches and the quiet streets. Thanksgiving, Christmas and New Year's weekends are also very popular. We have advance reservations each year."

The Red Inn now serves lunch throughout the year, and the daytime view from the dining room windows is spectacular in any weather. The fireplaces add an inner and outer warmth during that aforementioned off-off-season.

The Red Inn still continues to be family-operated. Alan, the Barkers' oldest son, and his wife Debbie now have a new member, Katie, making it three grandchildren for Ted and Marcie. Their son Paul finished college in the West, and is usually on hand during the summer season. Brad and Kathy are finishing school, and will also

continue to join in the family endeavors. Ted's sister's oldest boy, Eric, has been with the inn during the summer, and has decided that he likes the inn business and is on deck fulltime. The Barkers' other sons, Rick and Jim, are by this time old standbys and continue their careful and concerned contributions.

As Ted says, "We are blessed."

THE RED INN, 15 Commercial St., Provincetown, Mass. 02657; 617-487-0050. A waterside country restaurant with a striking view of Provincetown Harbor. No lodgings. Open for lunch and dinner every day of the year. Within walking distance of all Provincetown lodging accommodations and recreational activities and attractions. Ted and Marcie Barker, Innkeepers.

Directions: Follow Rte. 6 to end of Cape Cod.

RED LION INN
Stockbridge, Massachusetts

The Red Lion Inn is over 200 years old. At least there has been an inn on this site for over 200 years. There have been some changes in the various buildings, just as the methods of reaching Stockbridge have changed. First, it was only by horseback. Then the Springfield-Albany Stage came through. Railroads used to run dozens of trains to Stockbridge and the Red Lion buggies met guests at the Stanford White-designed railroad station. Now it is about two and a half hours from New York and Boston by auto.

I was having dinner outdoors in the flower-laden courtyard at the Red Lion with innkeepers Jack and Jane Fitzpatrick. (He is also a State Senator.) It was a soft, fine evening and the lanterns on the trees swayed in the gentle breeze.

We were talking about how Stockbridge has changed through the years from an 18th-century Indian village discovered by missionaries, to a secluded retreat for prominent artists, musicians, writers in the 19th century, and how, today, Tanglewood, the Berkshire Playhouse, and Jacob's Pillow attract people from everywhere.

"Don't forget we have the Corner House with Norman Rockwell's original paintings, Chesterwood, the Mission House, and Naumkeag as well," said Jane.

Speaking of Norman Rockwell, almost every guest room in the inn has a print of a Norman Rockwell painting. There is a generous sprinkling of Rockwell's Huckleberry Finn lithographs in the hallways.

Like many other country inns, the Red Lion is also a family affair, with the Fitzpatricks' daughter, Nancy, very much involved with the hospitality of the inn. Their other daughter, Ann, has gained well-deserved praise for her candy sculpture which can be seen at Gumdrop Square, a small shop located in the former village fire station.

As often as I have walked through the lobby and parlors of this community-minded village inn, I am always impressed by the beautiful collection of antiques which include tables, cabinets, highboys, clocks, paintings, and prints that seem to be very much at home in the low-ceilinged setting. A collection of teapots was actually started in the middle of the 19th century by a Mrs. Plumb, who owned the inn at that time.

One of the continuing blessings at this inn are the unusual flower arrangements made by Ann Bramen. Her love of gardening is reflected by the imaginative flower arrangements, which can be seen every day at the inn.

Stockbridge has five seasons. Summer, autumn, winter, spring, and fall foliage. I see many visitors who are guests at the Red Lion as they pass the window of my office on Pine Street, enjoying a quiet New England town with fresh air, lots of trees, and friendly people, many of whom migrated here from the city themselves.

The three of us ended up, as most people do, in rocking chairs on the broad front porch, and the conversation turned quite naturally to the Berkshire Playhouse in which all of three of us had a more than casual interest. We waved and called out to our Stockbridge

neighbors who were passing in front of the broad porch on an early September evening promenade.

"It's hard to realize," said Jane, "that we will have snow here in a few months. I am already planning my Christmas decorations for the inn."

RED LION INN, Stockbridge, Mass. 01262; 413-298-5545. A 95-room historic village inn dating back to 1773 in the Berkshire Mountains. Adjacent to Tanglewood, Norman Rockwell's Old Corner House Museum, The Berkshire Playhouse, Jacob's Pillow, Chesterwood Gallery, Mission House, and major ski areas. European plan. Breakfast, lunch, and dinner. Open year-round. Outdoor heated pool. Tennis, golf, boating, fishing, hiking, mountain climbing, and xc skiing nearby. Jack and Jane Fitzpatrick, Owners.

Directions: From the Taconic State Pkwy, take Exit 23 (N.Y. Rte. 23) to Mass. Rte. 7. Proceed north to Stockbridge. From the Mass. Tpke. exit #2 Lee, follow Rte. 102 to Stockbridge.

STAGECOACH HILL
Sheffield, Massachusetts

One evening last winter when the roads were all glazed and the snow was pelting against my windshield, I stopped off at the Stagecoach, returning from a trip to Connecticut. It was the perfect evening to visit this English inn in the Berkshires.

I opened the huge front doors and I walked up the steps to the lounge where there were 18 to 20 people seated in the romantic semi-darkness which was lighted by the glow from two fireplaces and the candles hidden in red hurricane lamps. There was soft piano music coming from one corner of the room.

Scottie Burns came in with an armload of firewood and said, "Welcome. 'Tis not a fit night to be out!"

Scottie's accent is as thick as the crust on the steak and kidney pie which is one of the favorites at the Stagecoach. The old, red brick building, part of which used to be the town poor house a hundred years ago, looks very much as if it had been picked up from Sussex or Surrey and dropped at the base of a mountain here in Sheffield. We call it an English inn with a Scottish favor.

Stagecoach Hill, as has already been suggested, is a wee bit on the intimate side. The local folks find its atmosphere most congenial, and the guests who come up from the city almost every weekend · appreciate the fact that it is somewhat small and really quite cozy. For winter fun, it is near several South Berkshire ski areas and, in the summer, it is within an easy drive to Tanglewood, theatres, and other seasonal attractions.

Good food is another reason why Stagecoach has so many devoted followers. Wilbur Wheeler, Scottie's partner, is the chef and he has such creations as the Aldermen's Carpetbag, which is a sirloin steak lined with oysters, as well as several different kinds of veal dishes and steaks.

Other dishes in his repertoire include Chicken Livers Rumaki which consist of delicious baked chicken livers wrapped in bacon and served on a bed of brown rice with a generous helping of pecan sauce.

It's always difficult to choose among desserts here. There are homemade chocolate eclairs, Bavarian cream pies, and the ever popular English Trifle. I also enjoy the Stilton cheese which is rather rare in these parts. I found it a perfect way to top off the dinner.

There are lodgings at the Stagecoach, however they are rather austere. "We are fixing them up one by one," said Scottie, "but even so, we very seldom have a vacancy on the weekend."

As I was leaving, a young couple from the city were just making their way into the dining room. I heard her say, "Oh, it's just like it says in the book. I recognized it from the front cover of the 1977 edition. I know we're going to like it here."

STAGECOACH HILL INN, Undermountain Road, Sheffield, Mass. 01257; 413-229-8585. A British inn with Scottish overtones on Rte. 41 midway between Salisbury, Conn. and Great Barrington, Mass. Motel accommodations available. European plan. Dinner served nightly and all day Sunday. Closed in March. Closed Christmas Eve, Christmas Day and Wednesdays. Near South Berkshire ski areas, Tanglewood, Jacob's Pillow and all summertime attractions. Scottie Burns and Wilbur Wheeler, Innkeepers.

Directions: From Mass. Tpke., take Exit 2 and follow Rte. 102 west to Stockbridge. Take Rte. 7 south to Great Barrington, then follow Rte. 41 south to inn.

THE VICTORIAN
Whitinsville, Massachusetts

Walking into an imposing mansion that sits regally above the street on a grassy slope, a visitor would expect to find rich wood paneling everywhere, spacious rooms and halls, high ceilings, a stately staircase, tall doors, and windows, and many large fireplaces. The Victorian has all of that, but who would also expect to find hand-tooled leather wainscoting in a charming third-floor room with lovely arched windows, or intricately tiled floors in the bathrooms, or a dressing-room in one bedroom with full-length mirrors mounted on the mahogany, walk-in closet doors? Marty and Orin Flint are still marveling at their good fortune in finding this fine example of Victorian architecture which was kept in excellent repair by the Whitin family—for whom the town of Whitinsville was named.

Looking in on the six bedrooms, I was impressed with the sense of graciousness and comfort inherent in all of them with their roomy, tiled bathrooms. The third-floor rooms have a shared bathroom.

Being a bit early, I still had my choice of their three dining rooms—the formal, stately blue and gold room with its blue moire-covered walls, ceiling-high windows draped with gold swags, gilt-edged mirrors, and a beautiful chandelier; or the book-lined, softly-lit dining room with its huge fireplace and two bay window dining nooks. The third room was engaged for a private party.

I'm particularly partial to book-lined rooms, and so we sat down near some shelves that featured a set of "Tom Swift and His Adventures." Seeing a book by Edward Everett Hale, I thought I'd stump them with a question on what famous story he had written. Quick as a flash, Phil, the waiter, replied, "Man Without a Country." Orin explained Phil actually taught French and was pinch-hitting that evening for one of their waitresses. The sense of camraderie and cooperation between the staff and the innkeepers is a pleasure to see, and I'm sure contributes to the enjoyment of their guests.

Although Marty is no longer doing the cooking, they are very pleased with their new chef, who is continuing to uphold the high standards she has set. Making a choice from their French menu proved to be a difficult job. Marty said, "Our most popular dishes are filet of beef with Madeira sauce and shrimp Scampi—but I think my favorite is lamb chops Souvarov, which is done like a beef Wellington with a pastry jacket."

"Fricassee de Lapin" caught my eye—rabbit braised with wine and vegetables. Or I could have had prime rib, frogs' legs Provencale, oysters Florentine, filet of sole stuffed with salmon mousse, boneless breast of chicken with cream and seasoning, blanquettes de veau—chunks of veal with onions and mushrooms in a cream sauce—or boiled lobster. Salad is served in the Continental manner after the main course.

To choose between the desserts, as might be expected, is pure torture. I got to sample several, since we all chose a different dish—the crepe with glazed fruit and a generous dollop of ice cream was superb; the apricot sherbet (which really isn't sherbet) is like nothing I've ever tasted: absolutely marvelous; the strawberry Chantilly looked like a huge piece of feathery-soft, pink and white cake—and tasted like some heavenly ambrosia.

A gracious conclusion to dinner at the Victorian is a tiny goblet of mulled wine served to every diner, compliments of the host and hostess.

As I drove down the curving driveway, I thought it is true that the house looks very grand and imposing, but the spirit of warm and friendly hospitality makes everyone feel delightfully "at home" in the Victorian.

THE VICTORIAN, 583 Linwood Ave., Whitinsville, Mass. 01588; 617-234-2500. A Victorian mansion with six lodging rooms available in a quiet town 15 mi. from Worcester, Ma. and 40 mi. from Narragansett Bay in R.I. European plan. Dinner served to travelers daily except Mondays. Lunch served to travelers daily except Mondays and Saturdays. Overnight guests receive Continental breakfast. Very small pets only. Lawn games, ice skating, fishing on grounds. Golf and tennis nearby. Orin and Martha Flint, Innkeepers.

Directions: From Providence, follow Rte. 146 north and take the Uxbridge exit. From the traffic light in Uxbridge, proceed north on Rte. 122 approximately 1½ mi. to Linwood Ave. (there will be a sign on the corner saying "Whitinsville — Left"). Bear left here. The inn is a few hundred yards around the corner. From Worcester, follow Rte. 146 south to the Whitinsville-Purgatory Chasm exit. Proceed into Whitinsville and keep right at the set of traffic lights onto Linwood Ave. The inn is on the left at the other end of Linwood Ave. — about 1½ mi.

THE VILLAGE INN
Lenox, Massachusetts

Although they share a common location in western Massachusetts, Berkshire towns and villages each have their own individuality. For example, Lenox is only about a twelve-minute drive from Stockbridge but it is impossible to mistake one for the other.

A group of us, mostly from Stockbridge, were having breakfast at the Village Inn and discussing this very subject when innkeeper Dick Judd came through the Yankee dining room and became involved. "I think Lenox and Stockbridge were pretty much the same during colonial times," he said, "but the discovery of the area north of Lake Mahkeenac by the New York millionaires in the late 1800s, and the establishment of so many estates has definitely left an impression on the village."

Meanwhile the attractive waitress had taken our orders for breakfast which ranged from New England flapjacks and syrup with bacon or sausage to waffles, eggs, and French toast.

Peggy Rogers said, "We just love to come up here for breakfast as well as lunch, but tell me how has the response been to your not serving dinner?"

Dick Judd smiled and replied, "It has worked out beautifully. You know, we are open every day of the year and we have 'all morning' breakfasts which are served from 8 a.m. to 11:30. Lunch goes from noon to 2:30. Marie and I always like to be able to chat for a few moments with everybody who comes into the inn, and either or both of us are here all the time. When we were serving three meals that meant a 14 to 16 hour day. We decided to put all our efforts into two meals and then suggest that guests enjoy dinner in some of the other restaurants in Lenox that we think are quite excellent. We have been able to put more time into putting in the new carpeting in the dining room and redesigning and redecorating a great deal of the inn."

"We think that the inn looks lovely," said Mary Harrison, "and it was so beautifully decorated at Christmas."

"We have to give Marie credit for that," said Dick.

"Did I hear my name being mentioned?" This was Marie Judd, who joined us all at the table. "If you are talking about food, let me say a word or two about our luncheons. We've added all kinds of quiches such as mushroom and quiche Lorraine and also a wide variety of crepes. Almost everything is made from scratch including zucchini soup with Italian sausage and cabbage borscht."

A good word for the Village Inn is snug. The early 19th century building has low ceilings, flowered wallpaper and many old Victorian prints and photographs. Guests frequently enjoy impromptu concerts by Dick on the electric organ in the front parlor. The building is a two-and-a-half story yellow clapboard with a basic Federal design that blends well with others in the vicinity. Plantings of iris, daffodils, tulips, peonias, roses, and petunias brighten the picture.

In warm weather breakfasts and lunches are served on the porch overlooking a small pool with a fountain. Maples provide the shade and an American flag adds an appropriate bright touch. Speaking of flags, the dining room was decorated with many different varieties of American flags as well as an explanation for each.

Lodging rooms are furnished with comfortable, homelike furniture kept spotlessly clean.

The inn is located in the center of Lenox within an easy walking distance of an outstanding library as well as many churches and shops. It is also a pleasant twenty-minute walk to the front gate of Tanglewood where the Boston Symphony presents summer concerts.

The Berkshire Playhouse, Jacob's Pillow Dance Theatre, and many other cultural and natural attractions of the Berkshires, both summer and winter, are at the doorstep.

THE VILLAGE INN, Church St., Lenox, Mass. 01240; 413-637-0020. A 25-room inn in a bustling Berkshire town 4 mi. from Stockbridge, 8 mi. from Pittsfield, and 1 mi. from Tanglewood. Lenox is located in the heart of the Berkshires with many historical, cultural, and recreational features.

Breakfast and luncheon served daily to travelers. Open every day of the year. No pets. Swimming pool privileges across the street from inn. All seasonal sports available nearby. Richard and Marie Judd, Innkeepers.

Directions: After approaching Lenox on Rte. 7, one of the principal north-south routes in New England, exit onto Rte. 7A to reach the Village Center and Church Street. When approaching from the Mass. Tpke. (Exit 2) use Rte. 20N about 4 mi. and turn left onto Rte. 183 to center of town.

YANKEE CLIPPER
Rockport, Massachusetts

Fred Wemyss and I were sitting on Flagpole Point, a rocky promontory overlooking the sea a few steps from the inn. We were talking about Rockport.

"Rockport has been an artist colony for over forty years," he explained. "Once it was a sleepy fishing village, but then it was 'discovered' by artists during the depression of the Thirties. Some of the most important people in painting have either visited or lived in Rockport. Now it attracts all kinds of creative people, including photographers, writers and craftsmen, as well as artists.

"The Rockport Art Association's annual exhibitions are always a big event. Rockport has been referred to as one of America's most highly paintable locations. We have open ocean, snug harbors, picturesque fishing boats and those great, gorgeous rocks."

I observed that the town itself was filled with fetching little houses with beguiling roof lines, inviting gardens and winding elm-shaded streets. Furthermore, I am sure there must be at least one hundred different, fascinating shops in this little seaside community.

The Wemysses came to Rockport in 1946 for a vacation, when the idea of turning three adjacent homes into an inn occurred to them. The three buildings include the main inn itself, where the dining area is located and where there are many large rooms with a sea view. A few paces away, there is the Quarterdeck which has an unobstructed view of the ocean and gardens. The third is called the Bullfinch House, and is noted particularly for its beauty. It is of colonial Greek design, created and named for its designer, who also created the Boston Statehouse. I believe that it's the same Bullfinch who, in the early 19th century, designed several stately houses in Orford, New Hampshire, overlooking the Connecticut River, north of Hanover.

"We've had a great time here," exclaimed Fred. "The family grew up here and my son Gary is the innkeeper at the Ralph Waldo Emerson. We've met hundreds of guests who have become good friends. We try to do everything we can to make them feel really at home. Besides wandering through Rockport, climbing the rocks, and doing the beaches, there's swimming right here in our own pool and golf, tennis and fishing nearby. Lots of people prefer just to relax up here on the rocks."

Fred looked at his watch and said: "Oh, oh, I think we'd better go back, it's almost time for dinner. We're having lobster tonight."

"Come on," I said, "I'll race you."

YANKEE CLIPPER, Rockport, Mass. 01966; 617-546-3407. An intimate 26-room inn on the sea, 40 mi. from Boston. European plan available year-round; Modified American plan from May 15 to July July 1 and Sept. 5 to Nov. 1. Breakfast and dinner served daily. Lunch served during July and August. Meals served to travelers by reservation only. No pets. Ocean view, shoreline walks, many antique shops and other stores nearby. Fred and Lydia Wemyss, Innkeepers.

Directions: Take 1-95 to Rte. 128 to 127 (Gloucester). Proceed 6 mi. on Rte. 127 to Rockport and continue to Pigeon Cove.

YANKEE PEDLAR
Holyoke, Massachusetts

It was Thursday—Italian Night at the Yankee Pedlar. New owners, Frank and Clair Banks and I were going over the menu: "We love Italian food," said Frank, "and we think that almost everybody else does, so we've set aside one night a week when everybody can be Italian.

"The first course could be roasted peppers with anchovies,

Calamari Bianco or real proscuitto ham and salami served with melon. This is followed by minestrone soup and then by the pasta course which might be green noodles with proscuitto and cheese, spaghetti Bolognese, our own homemade noodles Alfredo, linguine with clam sauce, or ravioli with butter and cheese. The entree could be chicken Cannelloni in a Mornay sauce, grilled Italian sausage and peppers, veal Scallopini, Saltimbocca Romana, or a mixed grill Tuscany, to name a few.

"We finish off with fromagi, dolci, frutta, or gelati."

For me this was like being back in Italy once again. I hadn't seen such a well-balanced Italian menu since my visit there the previous fall. Incidentally, the regular menu features traditional New England fare.

Visiting the Yankee Pedlar is like looking through a kaleidoscope at the 18th and 19th centuries. For example, one of the many dining rooms has the paneling, heavy beams, old utensils and tools which date back to Colonial America. Another has the look of elegance and ornamentation of the 19th century with many varieties of framed prints from Mrs. Godey's book. There are engravings of gentlemen in high silk hats and peg-bottom trousers, and drawings and paintings of some of the principal events of the last century. Among the prints are General Grant looking better than I've ever seen him, and George Washington looking rather portly.

A Victorian theme is found in the Gilded Cage and Oyster Bar which is reminiscent of the rollicking days at the turn of the century. Whenever I walk in, I expect to see men wearing derbies and ladies with leg-o'-mutton sleeves. The relishes and salads which are served with the hearty sandwiches look like the long forgotten "free lunch."

The Opera House, which is a special dining room set aside for

weddings, banquets, business meetings, and theatre, completes the Victorian theme. The ornate furnishings and decorations would provide a fitting background for some of the great entertainers of that time such as Anna Held, Fritzi Scheff, and Eleanora Duse.

In talking with Clair and Frank about their future plans, they explained that ten more rooms were being added in the Williamsburg House, which is among the houses of the town adjacent to the inn. These would be decorated with Williamsburg furniture and canopied beds. Clair will do the designing and decorating.

Frank and Clair met when they were both students at the Culinary Institute and have been in the hotel business in various ways ever since. Three of their four daughters are also working at the inn.

As our waitress, looking as if she had stepped out of the cast of "Upstairs, Downstairs" and with a faint touch of an Irish brogue, wheeled in the five-decker dessert cart, I asked Frank a question in all seriousness.

"Frank, I know that you have been the manager of both the Waldorf-Astoria and the St. Regis Hotels in New York, certainly two of the most distinguished large hotels in the world. Tell me, what did it feel like, after everything was settled, and you walked in here the first day as the new owner of a traditional country inn in a small city in western Massachusetts?"

A big smile spread across his face, and he reached over and patted Clair's hand. "It's what we always wanted," he said, "even from the very beginning. We felt like we had died and gone to heaven."

YANKEE PEDLAR, Holyoke, Mass. 01040; 413-532-9494. A 37-room village inn with antiques, 8 mi. north of Springfield, 3.5 mi. north of Mass. Pike. Breakfast, lunch, and dinner served to travelers daily except Christmas. Oyster Bar open until 12:30 a.m., Gilded Cage Lounge with live entertainment open to 1:00 a.m. Historic 19th-century mill town with anique canal system. Mt. Tom ski area, golf, tennis nearby. Bess Stathis, Innkeeper.

Directions: From I-91 take Exit 16. The Inn is located at junction of Rtes. 202 and 5.

Rhode Island

THE INN AT CASTLE HILL
Newport, Rhode Island

There is a definite European flavor at this inn. In many ways it reminds me of several different places I visited in Sweden, Holland,

Germany, France, and Italy. The marvelous Victorian exterior would be quite in place on the banks of the Rhine or the Rhone. The rich paneling and intricate woodwork of the interior could grace several of the French chateaux and Italian villas I have seen.

The menu is definitely Continental, and the service with the headwaiter and assistant waiters all moving about very smartly is reminiscent of several fine European restaurants.

I reflected on these things as I was driving through the city of Newport, finding my way down Thames Street, watching for the sign that said "Ocean Drive." I passed Fort Adams State Park and several of the famous Newport mansions and once again, in the distance, could see the sign for the Inn at Castle Hill.

The road from Ocean Drive winds through a small section of woods that immediately reminded me of the forest of Barbizon, about two hours south of Paris, which inspired a school of French painters, lead by Millet.

As soon as I emerged from the woods and came to the front entrance I realized that it was this, above all things that makes this inn most unique. There could be no mistaking the sweeping waters of Narragansett Bay and the Atlantic Ocean for any other place. For many travelers, this must be the *sine qua non* of waterside inns.

Alexander Agassiz, the famous naturalist, built Castle Hill 100 years ago as a summer residence. It has remained unchanged in character, and many of the original furnishings, including Oriental rugs and the handcrafted oak and mahogany paneling, are still in tact.

Accommodations at the inn vary from the mansion-like rooms with a view of the water—some with enormous bathrooms, to housekeeping cottages which are rented by the week during the summer and fall.

For many years, the innkeeper, Paul McEnroe, was the proprietor of DeLaVergne Farms in Amenia, New York, which was completely destroyed by fire in 1974. "Some people must use copies of *Country Inns and Back Roads* for quite awhile," he observed. "Because I am still getting mail requests for reservations at the Amenia inn. Of course, we are delighted to have them visit us here in Newport."

Although I have stayed in the room used by Thornton Wilder, which he describes in his book *Theophilus North,* on this particular visit I was in a corner room with a halfmoon window overlooking the entrance to the bay on one side, and on the other side there were large windows with an impressive view of the Newport Bridge. Like most of the inn rooms it had been redecorated in 1977. The patterned green of the wallpaper was echoed in the print of the quilt and the cushions of the white wicker furniture. There were also two wicker loveseats and two wicker chests of drawers. I had a chance to see all of the other rooms in the main house which were equally handsome and elegant.

When I remarked to Paul on the resemblance to inns I had visited in Europe, Paul responded enthusiastically, "That is exactly what we are trying to achieve," he said. "After all, this inn was built as a mansion and we are trying to re-create the elegance of Newport's past by having a menu, service and furnishings that best suit our ideals. Our menu is basically European with a generous number of New England specialties. That is undoubtedly the way it was 75 years ago."

INN AT CASTLE HILL, Ocean Drive, Newport, R.I. 02840; 401-849-3800. A 20-room mansion-inn on the edge of Narragansett Bay. Near the Newport mansions, Touro Synagogue, the Newport Casino and National Lawn Tennis Hall of Fame, the Old Stone Mill, the Newport Historical Society House. European plan. Continental breakfast served to house guests only. Lunch and dinner served daily to travelers. Possibly closed from January to end of April. No pets. Swimming, sailing, scuba diving, walking on grounds. Bicycles and guided tours of Newport nearby. Jens Thillemann, Manager. Paul McEnroe, Innkeeper.

Directions: After leaving Newport Bridge follow Bellevue Ave. which becomes Ocean Dr. Look for inn sign on left.

LARCHWOOD INN
Wakefield, Rhode Island

On my recent trip to the Larchwood Inn in August of 1977, I had a delightful time, particularly enhanced by making the acquaintance of two very attractive young ladies, Susan Solomon from Torrance, California, and Mary Jane Morris from South Pasadena, California. We started a conversation in the living room, and I discovered that they were visiting several different inns in *Country Inns and Back Roads* on their holiday. "We are going to the Bramble Inn on Cape Cod tomorrow," said Susan, "and then on to the Island House in Ogunquit, and to Grey Rock in Northeast Harbor, Maine." They were having a wonderful time, and were very enthusiastic about being in the East for the first time.

Our conversation became so animated that I suggested the three of us have dinner together, and so the hostess arranged for us to sit in the Crest Room, which has shields and tartans of Scottish clans intertwined with thistles. Other dining rooms include the South County Room, which depicts Rhode Island's regional history with murals depicting the Gilbert Stewart House, which is a short drive

67

trom Wakefield; St. Paul's Church; the Wright Homestead (which is now the Larchwood Inn); and scenes of nearby fishing villages. I noted the repetition of the old-fashioned pineapple theme, a pleasing symbol of hospitality throughout the inn.

Our dinner began with a delicious cup of fresh fruit and sherbet and was followed with a choice of salads — these are brought in on a tray and the guest may choose the most tempting. My dinner that night was flounder stuffed with seafood and bread crumbs, and drenched with a delicious cream sauce. The baked potato and carrots were also extremely tasty.

Susan and Mary Jane were particularly impressed with the grounds at the Larchwood Inn because it is a former mansion which is in a park-like setting, considerably back from the main street of the village. There are a great many beech and ginkgo trees, blue spruces, and pines. Rhododendron bushes, tuberous begonias, roses, and forsythia round out the very impressive landscaping.

Visitors at the Larchwood Inn are not likely to meet Frank Browning, the innkeeper, as he is chef and spends almost all of his time in the kitchen making certain that everything is as close to perfection as possible. The guests are taken care of by cordial young ladies at the inn office. The inn has gained considerable reputation as a restaurant during the many years of its existence, being carefully nurtured by both Frank and the previous owners, Mr. and Mrs. Cameron, who established the basic Scottish theme. Since my last visit, a telephone call has confirmed the fact that the lodging rooms are now almost completely redecorated and refurnished.

My evening with Susan and Mary Jane was drawing to a close, but I did suggest that they would enjoy a trip to Nantucket on the ferry and hoped that they would give my best wishes to Innkeeper Phil Read at the Jared Coffin House. I heard later that they enjoyed themselves tremendously at the other inns as well. I was so glad that we had met at the Larchwood.

LARCHWOOD INN, 176 Main St., Wakefield, R.I. 02879; 401-783-5454. An 11-room village inn just 3 mi. from the famous southern R.I. beaches. Some rooms with shared bath. European plan. Breakfast, lunch, dinner served every day of the year. Swimming, boating, surfing, fishing, xc skiing and bicycles nearby. Francis Browning, Innkeeper.

Directions: From Rte. 1, take Pond St. Exit and proceed ½ mi. directly to inn.

1661 INN
Block Island, Rhode Island

The letter was dated July 22nd, 1977 and was postmarked New York City. It read in part:

"Let me simply say that we agree wholeheartedly with your strong recommendation of the 1661 Inn. We found that it has comfortable beds, clean rooms, and prompt service all at very reasonable prices. There is a friendly, cheerful atmosphere with courteous service in every respect. From our room we had a spectacular view of the Old Harbor and we could watch the boats go by and the swans swimming in the fresh water pond just beyond the back yard.

"The food was superb. The cuisine in itself attracts people and we counted ourselves fortunate to be able to eat there each day as weekly residents. Other features such as a daily wine and cheese hour, badminton and croquet games, and the inn's own vegetable garden for its dining table, all contributed to the special style that we found so impressive.

"We plan to go back there again and again, and we've already started telling everyone we know to arrange for a visit. Your judgment in highlighting the 1661 Inn in your book was amply affirmed by our experience there. We give it the highest possible praise."

Thank you very much, and I am sure that all of the Abrams — Justin, Joan, Rita, Ricky, and Mark join me in saying that we appreciate letters like this and at the same time it makes us all work harder.

Block Island may be reached by ferry from Providence,

Point Judith, and Newport, Rhode Island, and New London, Connecticut. I flew over from New London in July of 1977 on one of the most glorious days of the summer. Rita met me at the airport and gave me a running account of Block Island lore that included the fact that there were 365 fresh water ponds on this 3½ x 7-mile island which is 22 miles around. The road from the airport to the inn was bordered by stone walls which are typical of Block Island roads which, incidentally, are marvelous for bicycling. The inn has excellent Schwinn three-speed bikes. We had to stop briefly at a sign that said "Slow, Duck Crossing," and we drove out to the Mohegan Cliffs which are the highest point on the island, looking down over the great waves coming in from the Atlantic. The green water, blue sky, and lighthouse, with the traditional, red brick Victorian design, made it a world apart.

The inn, as usual, was bustling. This time I had a chance to meet the chef, Peter Cooper, who, during the wintertime is assistant director of Career Planning at the Culinary Division of the Johnson and Wales College in Providence. He is a very enthusiastic, talented man who is quite creative in the kitchen. For example, he makes a flounder, banana, and walnut dish which is sauteed with a dash of curry. The dinner menu, as he explained, is Continental, including frogs legs Provencale, and shrimp scampi served with sauteed mushrooms, tomato, and garlic. These are backed up with fresh seafood which is caught in the waters of Block Island.

I should say a word or two about the desserts, including the homemade eclairs and a concoction called Joan's Delight which is a sour cream pie with blueberries, pineapple, and whipped cream.

The dining room is very attractive at all times. It faces the sea, and flowers from the garden, are on the table and the waitresses are dressed in patchwork uniforms.

The inn is an old, white house, partially hidden from the road by thick hedges. The guest rooms are decorated with attractive wallpaper and braided rugs.

At the wine and cheese party that evening I overheard one lady say, "I spend the first day I come here doing absolutely nothing but lying in the sun; on the second day, I rent a bike and go riding in the morning and go to the beach in the afternoon. From there on in I'm in the swing of everything—tennis, snorkeling, fishing, picnicking, birdwatching, and loafing."

THE 1661 INN, Box 367, Block Island, R.I. 02807; 401-466-2421 or 2063. A 21-room island inn off the coast of R.I. and Conn. in Block Island Sound. Modified American and European plans. Most rooms with shared baths. Open from Memorial Day through Oct. 4. Breakfast and dinner served to travelers daily. Lawn games on grounds. Tennis, bicycling, ocean swimming, sailing, snorkeling, diving, salt and fresh water fishing nearby. Block Island is known as one of the best bird observation areas on the Atlantic fly-way during migrations. The Abrams Family, Innkeepers.

Directions: By ferry from Providence, Pt. Judith and Newport, R.I. and New London, Ct. By air from Newport, Westerly and Providence, R.I., New London and Waterford, Ct., or by chartered plane. Contact inn for schedules.

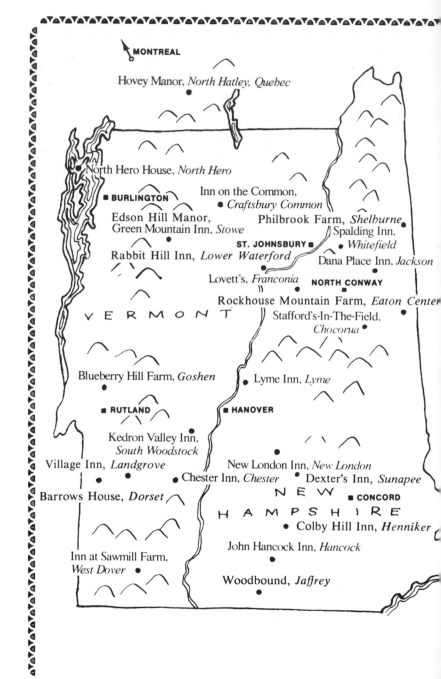

MONTREAL

Hovey Manor, *North Hatley, Quebec*

North Hero House, *North Hero*

■ BURLINGTON

Inn on the Common,
● *Craftsbury Common*

Edson Hill Manor,
Green Mountain Inn, *Stowe*

Philbrook Farm, *Shelburne*

Spalding Inn,

ST. JOHNSBURY ■ ● *Whitefield*

Rabbit Hill Inn, *Lower Waterford*

Dana Place Inn, *Jackson*

Lovett's, *Franconia*

NORTH CONWAY

Rockhouse Mountain Farm, *Eaton Center*

V E R M O N T

Stafford's-In-The-Field,
Chocorua ●

Blueberry Hill Farm, *Goshen*

Lyme Inn, *Lyme*

■ RUTLAND

■ HANOVER

Kedron Valley Inn,
South Woodstock

Village Inn, *Landgrove*

New London Inn, *New London*

Chester Inn, *Chester* ● Dexter's Inn, *Sunapee*

Barrows House, *Dorset*

N E W ■ CONCORD

H A M P S H I R E

Colby Hill Inn, *Henniker*

John Hancock Inn, *Hancock*

Inn at Sawmill Farm,
West Dover ●

Woodbound, *Jaffrey*

Northern New England

MAINE

CALAIS ■

■ BANGOR

Asticou Inn,
Grey Rock Inn,
Northeast Harbor

Whitehall Inn, *Camden*

Squire Tarbox,
Westport Island

Claremont Inn,
Southwest Harbor

Homewood Inn,
Yarmouth

PORTLAND ■

Black Point Inn, *Prouts Neck*

Captain Lord, Old Fort Club, *Kennebunkport*

Island House,
Whistling Oyster,
Ogunquit

Dockside Guest Quarters, *York*

Maine

ASTICOU INN
Northeast Harbor, Maine

It was Thursday night at the Asticou Inn in Northeast Harbor, Maine and Thursday nights are particularly special to people who are summering or visiting in the Bar Harbor area, because that is the night that the buffet is served.

George and Esther Stiles, the innkeepers, had invited fellow-innkeeper Janet Millet from nearby Grey Rock Inn and me to be their guests for dinner, and it was a gala evening in every respect. the big, long table was laden with culinary delights, each more impressive than the other. Among the most popular features, which unfortunately are inedible, are the ice carvings which are different each week.

George introduced me to the ice-carver, head chef Allen Weigman. He has been here for a number of years and has made the acquaintance of many of the guests.

Our table was by the window which overlooks the harbor, and we could easily see the deck lights of the sailboats and cruisers bobbing in the soft evening breeze.

I'm not really sure how long the Asticou has been in Northeast Harbor, but a rough guess would be at least fifty years. In the early days, guests would spend a great deal of the summer here, arriving by train or boat and staying until the end of the season when they would return to the city. Now there are a very few of these medium-size resort inns that have the many little touches that give them such a special appeal. The Asticou still has beautiful table linen, fresh flowers, and turn-down service.

1977 was the first full year for the Asticou swimming pool, and George Stiles was most enthusiastic about it. "We've had the same people coming back here for many years, and now their children and grandchildren are returning," he said. "The Asticou is growing with the times. For example, in former days guests used to go swimming in the cold waters of the harbor, but today's guests enjoy our swimming pool because it is just a few steps away from the deck of the inn. I can also tell you that we have tennis courts in our plans.

"Today's guests at the Asticou are much more active. We have so many things here on Mt. Desert that attract outdoor-minded people who are concerned about ecology and nature. Our guests stay here on the Modified American plan which omits lunch and allows everyone to enjoy the one hundred different activities on Mt. Desert Island."

Although the Asticou was for many years a "carriage trade" accommodation, there is a most informal feeling here, with the head waiter, the chef, and the front desk personnel all very helpful and friendly. I was particularly impressed with Charlotte Justice, who seemed to have patient answers to all of the guests' questions.

After dinner, the four of us went outside on the deck where the lights from the dining and living rooms reflected on the yellow umbrellas that are so very welcome at midday. It was a pleasant picture, seeing gentlemen dressed in colorful summer jackets and ladies in their pastel dresses, obviously enjoying themselves and their surroundings.

"Every time I come here," said Janet Millet, "it makes my little Grey Rock Inn seem so small, because this is such a grand place."

"That's the fascinating thing about inns," replied George. "No two of them are alike, and I think the guests at Grey Rock enjoy your particular type of quiet intimacy, just as the people who keep returning here prefer our more lively resort atmosphere."

ASTICOU INN, Northeast Harbor, Me. 04662; 207-276-3344. A 60-room elegant resort-inn on the northern coast of Maine. Near Acadia National Park, Cadillac Mountain, Abbey Rockefeller Gardens, Thuya Lodge and Gardens, and Jackson Laboratory. Modified American plan omits lunch. Breakfast, lunch and dinner served daily to travelers from late June to mid-September. Swimming pool and extensive gardens on the grounds. Bicycles, golf, tennis, sandy beaches nearby. George M. Stiles, Innkeeper.

Directions: Exit Maine Tpke. (Rte. 95) at Bangor. Follow Alt. Rte. 1 to Mt. Desert Island.

BLACK POINT INN
Prouts Neck, Maine

Ever since the summer of 1971, I have kept on the windowsill of my Berkshire office a small egg-shaped granite rock. I refer to it as my "Prouts Neck talisman." It is a memento of one of the first visits I made to Innkeepers Hank and Mary Petteys at the Black Point Inn. I picked it up on my walk around Prouts Neck next to the sea. No doubt the continuous action of the water had bounced it around, grinding it against the bowl of rocks in which I had found it, making it smooth and satisfying to the touch.

Even now, I can remember that morning. Under a brilliant Maine August sun, I set out after breakfast to walk the Prouts Neck path. The usual course is to follow the path directly from the front of the inn. However, this time I decided to walk counter-clockwise and wound my way up through the beautiful trees and cottages that make up the private residential area of the community. Most of these are built of brown, weathered shingles with white trim, the same design as the inn. Some of the same families have been summering here for generations.

Following Hank's directions, I cut through to the ocean at a point where I could see the Winslow Homer Studio, and then started walking in the marshlands and thickets beside the sea. Eventually, the path came out on the rocks and led to the sandy beach favored by inn guests who like chilly salt water.

The path came out on a ledge above the sea, and I stretched out on the warm rock and began to muse about the conversation I had had at dinner last night when Hank had mentioned the fact that

Prouts Neck was first settled about 1630, and in 1690, the trouble with the French and Indians caused the colonists to leave it for 12 years. In 1702, they started a new trading post. However, in 1713, 19 men were ambushed and killed by Indians at the southern end of Massacre Pond, which is just across the road from the Prouts Neck golf course.

"It became popular as a summer resort in the middle of the 19th century," he pointed out. "In 1886 there were a half-dozen summer cottages. One of them was occupied by Charles Savage Homer whose son, Winslow, became one of America's most well-known artists. He must have gotten his inspiration for some of those great paintings of the Maine coast from just walking on the rocks and the beaches here."

It was now about twelve noon and I could hear the tuning-up of the small orchestra which plays both for the poolside buffet at noon, and for dancing after dinner at the inn. I continued on up to the pool area where Mary and Hank were sitting underneath one of the gay umbrellas, waving for me to join them.

The Black Point Inn is one of the few remaining American plan hotels that flourished in New England for about 100 years. It has quiet dignity, personal service, attention to details, ocean bathing, excellent tennis courts, a golf course, exceptional food, and an unpretentious elegance. Men wear coats for dinner and many of the ladies enjoy wearing their gay, summer dresses. Dressing up is part of the fun. That is the way it has been ever since I have been visiting this inn which, like the Asticou at Northeast Harbor, and the Spalding Inn in Whitefield, New Hampshire, provides one of the last few remaining intimate resort-inn experiences. There is one thing that I have noticed about all three of these places, however, and that is that young people are discovering them in greater numbers every year. Along with the Rolls Royces, Cadillacs and Lincolns, there is a sprinkling of Porsches and Audis in the parking lot. The Black Point still remains a lovely lady.

BLACK POINT INN, Prouts Neck, Me. 04070; 207-883-4311. A 76-room luxury resort-inn on Rte. 207, 10 mi. south of Portland. American plan. Breakfast, lunch and dinner served to travelers. Open late-June to early-September. No children under age 12. No pets. Pool, bicycles, sailing, dancing, golf, tennis and ocean bathing all within a few steps. Henry Petteys, Innkeeper.

Directions: From Maine Tpke. take Exit 7. Turn right on Rte. 1. Proceed 2.7 mi. to Rte. 207. Turn left. This is the road to Prouts Neck.

CAPTAIN LORD MANSION
Kennebunkport, Maine

"We really ought to call this "The Berkshire Traveller Room," said Shirley Throumoulos as she ushered me through the door leading to the left front bedroom on the top floor of the Captain Lord Mansion. The fireplace was already laid, and extra wood was neatly stacked on one corner of the hearth. "I think you've stayed here on each one of your visits," she said.

I guess it's true that this is my favorite room, although they are all most attractive. However, I particularly like this one because there is a circular window in the bathroom.

The Captain Lord Mansion is a regal yellow building with a lookout cupola similar to the one at the Mainstay in Cape May. Like its New Jersey counterpart, it is a perfect place for getting above it all. The inn has larger-than-usual lodging rooms, and all but two of them now have their own bathrooms. Many have working fireplaces. It was built during the War of 1812, and additions and subtractions have been made over the years.

Now it is not only a quiet guest house, but a way of life for Shirley and Jim Throumoulos. They met in the spring of 1973 when Shirley came to Kennebunkport, where she met Jim who had seen the possibilities of making an inn out of this lovely old mansion in 1972. In due process they fell in love and were married. In fact, the wedding pictures in the front hall of the mansion show Jim and Shirley being married in the Congregational Church in Kennebunkport. The reception was held at the inn on a beautiful day in the spring of 1974. The event is recorded for posterity in needlepoint, which is hung on the walls of the cozy kitchen where guests gather for breakfast.

"I have so many things to tell you," Shirley said. "But the first thing I want to do is to show you my completed brick walk. It runs from the drive to the side door. I have wanted to do it for three years." Shirley, whose first love is flowers and plants (she has a degree in landscape architecture), has done a great deal of the exterior landscaping as well as filling the rooms with houseplants.

"I wish you could be here between Thanksgiving and Christmas," she said enthusiastically. "It's just beautiful. Almost every church in the village will have a fair, and two of the fairs are quite large because they invite artists and craftspeople to take booths. Our own Dock Square Shops, as well as L.L. Bean and the incredible shops in the Old Port Exchange in Portland, really provide marvelous shopping. Most of all, I like the real New England Christmas spirit without the plastic tinsel and the mob scene."

As we were passing through the Music Room she said, "Oh, here's something else I wanted to be sure and show you. Do you see these marks? These are the records of the heights of the original Captain Lord's children. They date way back to before 1850. It's so wonderful to know something about the people who lived here then.

"This Music Room is being used all the time. We have little impromptu concerts by our guests, and people really read my books, which makes me very happy. They also seem to enjoy the collection of *National Geographic, Yankee,* and *National Wildlife,* which my mother and father gave us. People say it is so nice to have them around, because this is a place where you can finally sit down next to the fire and catch up on what's happening and do some of the reading you always wanted to do. "We find that people love to sit around the kitchen, and I'm happy to say they like my zucchini bread and date muffins. You know, they are even more popular than the blueberry."

THE CAPTAIN LORD MANSION, Box 527, Kennebunkport, Me. 04046; 207-967-3141. An 8-room seacoast village inn, 3 tenths of a mi. from Dock Square in Kennebunkport, off Ocean Ave. Near Rachel Carson Wildlife Refuge. Shaker community and Alternative Energy Research Structures open to the public. Lodgings include breakfast. No other meals served. Some rooms with shared bath. Not oriented to children. No pets. Open year-round. Check-in time between 2 and 8 p.m. Bicycles, hiking, xc skiing, canoeing, deep sea fishing, golf, and indoor swimming and tennis nearby. Shirley and Jim Throumoulos, Innkeepers.

Directions: From Boston follow I-95 into Maine. Take Exit 3 and follow signs to Kennebunkport.

THE CLAREMONT INN
Southwest Harbor, Maine

It is a distinct honor for an inn or a hotel to be nominated for inclusion in the National Register of Historic Places. The nomination of the Claremont Inn was made in the fall of 1977 at a quarterly meeting of the Maine Historic Preservation Commission. It read in part:

"The oldest surviving summer hotel on Mt. Desert Island and one of the oldest in the state, the Claremont, according to the nomination, stands as one of the last reminders of Maine's early summer resort period of the 1870s and 1880s ... such establishments became a kind of community in themselves, a home away from home where guests pursued quiet pastimes.

"Overlooking Somes Sound in what is now Acadia National Park, the Claremont is significant of its own merits and is a reminder of a prosperous, relaxed, and seasonal way of life that no longer exists."

I am delighted to know the Claremont has been nominated, and I am also delighted to know that many significant changes have been made at the Claremont in the last two years which will continue to make it an enjoyable vacation experience.

In 1977, only the Claremont cottages were open, while the proprietors, the McCue Family and the present innkeeper, Matthew Landreau, carefully drew up plans which would involve some major refurbishing of the beautiful, old main building of the inn and updating it for use by today's vacationers.

The results are very dramatic. For one thing, the demolition of the annex has been completed and at the time this book went to press, the foundations for a new dining room had been poured and with the coming of spring, a completely new building, semi-attached to the main hotel on the shore side will begin. It will have a pyramid roof with the same pitch as the porches of the hotel. The exterior will be cedar shingles, the interior will be a smooth finish, beamed ceiling with matching central column and wainscoting. There will be ten picture windows with opening wings to take advantage of the fantastic view of Somes Sound and the mountains of Acadia.

Breakfast and dinner will be served, and box lunches will be provided by arrangement at the main desk. Rooms will be primarily on the Modified American plan but European plan will also be available. The cottages at the Claremont are European plan but Modified American plan is available for cottage guests if desired. The dining room will be open to the public on a limited basis.

The newly re-opened Claremont will have 22 rooms in the main building, which has elevator service. There are also additional rooms in the Philips House and the Clark House, and eight completely-equipped cottages that have fireplaces.

All of these changes are going to make the Claremont, which has always been a great vacation experience, even more attractive. However, I am happy to say there are a number of things that will not be changed: the hammock, which is strung between a birch and a pine on the broad lawn leading to the water's edge, the boathouse which is a great gathering place for guests at the end of the day, the spectacular views of both land and water, a very active tennis program, and all of the never-changing, but ever-differing, natural attractions of the Mt. Desert area which attracted people to this part of Maine in the 1870s, and will continue to do so for still hundreds of years to come.

I will be at the new-old Claremont in September of 1978. It is an ideal time for a Mt. Desert vacation.

CLAREMONT HOTEL AND COTTAGES, Southwest Harbor, Me. 04679; 207-244-5036. A 22-room rambling summer hotel on Somes Sound, Mt. Desert Island, 20 mi. east of Ellsworth. Modified American plan omits lunch. Some rooms with shared baths. Hotel open June 28 to Sept. 6. Adjacent housekeeping cottages. Cottages open Memorial Day weekend to Oct. 15. Breakfast and dinner served daily to travelers on a limited basis. Tennis, rowboats, croquet, badminton, dock, and deep water moorings on grounds. Fresh water swimming, golf, bicycles, riding, boating, and sailing rentals nearby. The McCue Family, Owners; C. Matthew Landreau, Innkeeper.

Directions: From Maine Tpke., exit at Augusta and proceed east on Rte. 3 to US #1. At Ellsworth, pick up Rte. 3 again and follow Rte. 102 on Mt. Desert Island to Southwest Harbor. Follow inn signs approaching and in Southwest Harbor.

DOCKSIDE GUEST QUARTERS
York, Maine

The day was sparkling. There was a brilliant blue, late-September sky as I crossed the bridge from York Harbor to Harris Island and threaded my way past the boatyards up to the entrance of the Dockside Guest Quarters. Once again the panorama of York Harbor spread out in front of me. There were sailboats, launches, working fishing boats and even a yacht or two.

In the parking lot, I noticed that there were a considerable number of cars from outside New England including Ohio, Illinois, Virginia, and even California. Late September and early October days in York can be spent walking the sandy beaches and swimming when the sun is highest at midday and early afternoon. Golf and tennis are available at the golf club nearby and many guests enjoy picking their own apples at local orchards.

The continental breakfast was still being served in the lobby; Harriette Lusty handed me a cup of tea and suggested that I take some of the fresh coffee cake, and sit with her out on the front porch.

"I have lots of news," she said. "We've had a perfectly wonderful year with many, many people traveling with *Country Inns and Back Roads*. Our sons, Paul, who will be graduating from Franklin Marshall College in 1978, and Eric, who is a midshipman at the Maine Maritime Academy, have been busy all summer giving guided boat trips and sailing lessons. Now we have several small outboards and bay sailers for our guests."

Almost on cue, Paul came walking around the outside of the inn and said, "Hi, would you like another sail on the harbor today?"

He dropped the bag of sails from his shoulder, frightening a semi-dozing kitten who had apparently hidden in the bushes. We all laughed as she scampered into the flowerbed.

Paul went off to sail, Harriette answered the telephone, and I wandered into the downstairs sitting room of the Main House where there were lots of games, a shell collection, many carved boats, and owl andirons in the fireplace, similar to those in the Sutter Creek Inn in California. The small, highly-polished brass cannon pointed its muzzle out of the doorway into the harbor. It is rolled out on the lawn and used on ceremonial occasions.

Harriette returned, and we walked down under the trees toward some of the additional lodgings. These are of a contemporary design, and each has its own porch and water view; some have a casual studio feeling. "Some of these have connecting doors; they make pleasant accommodations for small reunion groups or large family get-togethers."

A few years ago David and Harriette added the Dockside Dining Room, managed by Steve and Sue Roeder, which serves lunch and dinner and has a great many seafood specialities headed, of course, by lobster. One of the non-sea offerings, which is a favorite of mine, is roast duckling "a la Hickory Stick," which is crisp on the outside and moist on the inside.

I asked Steve whether or not anyone had seen the mysterious Scots piper recently whose wraith-like figure can sometimes be faintly seen in the evening when the fog rolls in.

"Oh, yes," he said, "someone sees and hears him almost every week."

DOCKSIDE GUEST QUARTERS, Harris Island Rd., York, Maine 03909; 207-363-2868. An 18-room waterside country inn 10 mi. from Portsmouth, N.H. Some larger quarters in newer multi-unit cottages. York village is a National Historic District. American plan available. Continental breakfast served to houseguests only. Dockside Dining Room serves lunch and dinner to travelers daily except Mondays. Open from Memorial Day weekend in May through Columbus Day. Fishing, sailing and boating from premises. Golf, tennis, hiking and swimming nearby. David and Harriette Lusty, Innkeepers.

Directions: From U.S. 1 or I-95, take Exit at York to Rte. 1A (the main street of York). Take Rte. 103 (a side street off Rte. 1A) and follow signs to Harris Island Rd.

GREY ROCK INN
Northeast Harbor, Maine

Janet Millet and I were seated on rocking chairs on the porch of Grey Rock. It was a sunny afternoon in late July and she was bringing me up to date on all the activities at the inn since my last visit.

"We've had simply wonderful guests," she said enthusiastically. "They come from all over the United States, Canada, and even other parts of the world. Sometimes it is very exciting to keep a country inn. Just look at the license plates on the cars out there now." We noted that there were people from North Carolina, New Mexico, California, Illinois, and British Columbia. While we were talking, another car pulled up and Janet said excitedly, "Oh, here are some people from Ohio."

While she showed them to their room and explained about the Continental breakfast which is served every morning, I wandered for a few moments in the dining and living rooms of the inn. There is a very elegant cabinet with quite an impressive collection of hand-painted china and fine glassware. Everywhere I saw attractive wicker furniture. There is a wicker desk that is positively one of a kind, and a few lamps with wicker bases.

This time I noticed four Oriental paintings which depict the costumes of four Chinese dynasties. Janet returned long enough to tell me that a visitor from China told her it was possible that these were painted at the time of Marco Polo. All around were many flower arrangements and other touches that express Janet's feeling for design and color.

We walked out to the front porch from which I could see some of the boats on Northeast Harbor. "Do you know that many of my guests get up early in the morning to drive to the top of Cadillac Mountain to watch the sun rise?" she said. "In fact, many of them try to stay an extra day or two, because there is really a number of things to experience here on Mt. Desert Island."

Grey Rock Inn was built as a private estate in the early 1900s. The bedrooms are quite large, many with handsome brass beds, which are turned down for the guests each night. Each room faces the harbor and has its own bath. They are cool and shady in the summertime and pleasantly decorated.

The inn has an alpine setting of evergreens and berry bushes and has quite a few woodland walks on the property.

My first visit was in the summer of 1974 when I discovered that Janet is British, having been brought up in England. Her father still lives in a small cottage in one of the Cotswolds' villages. Being British, of course, means that very frequently Janet invites her guests to join her in the living room for a cup of tea in the late afternoon. The scene reminds me very much of an English country house.

"Everyone is now checked in for the day," she said, "let's take a walk down into the village center. There is a new art gallery that I would like to see, and if I remember correctly, you like the shops down there."

GREY ROCK INN, Harborside Rd., Northeast Harbor, Me. 04662; 207-276-9360. A 10-room village inn in the town of Northeast Harbor, Me. adjacent to Acadia National Park and all of the attractions of this unusual region. European plan. Continental breakfast served to houseguests only. No other meals served. Season from early Spring to Nov. 1. Children 14 yrs. and older preferred. No pets. Janet Millet, Innkeeper.

Directions: Located on the right-hand side of Rte. 198 approaching the town of Northeast Harbor. Note sign for inn. Do not try to make a right-hand turn at this point but proceed about one block, turn around and approach the inn on the left up the steep hill.

HOMEWOOD INN
Yarmouth, Maine

July was showing off her best weather for me during my last visit to the Homewood Inn. It was clear and bright when I walked out of my lodging room into the brilliant sunshine of a freshly-washed Maine morning. Here were the picnic tables which are

ordinarily used for clambakes on Monday nights; however, last night a downpour put us all into the new dining room where the clambake continued uninterrupted. Fred Webster had kidded me as he handed me a freshly-cooked lobster. "We've had just wonderful weather on Mondays; I guess in honor of your coming, the skies opened up."

As I sauntered across the lawn, I came to the tennis court, already in use, and just a few steps beyond, the swimming pool overlooking Casco Bay. Sunlight sparkled on the wet grass and small garden where Maine summertime flowers were blooming in profusion.

At that moment Fred came around the corner, and we decided to walk the grounds together. He introduced me to Leon Martin, who has worked here as a caretaker since April, 1924. "He does a marvelous job," said Fred.

We stepped inside the dining room to be greeted by hostess Peg Smith. Colleen Webster joined us for breakfast.

"I'll show you after breakfast," said Colleen, "there have been a lot of changes. The Lodge now contains the dining room, and what was once the dining room has been made into lovely lodging suites with antiques, and some very nice water views. We've tried to do everything as carefully as possible and all of our guests seem very pleased."

"Very pleased" is the theme of many postcards and letters I receive every year from readers who have stayed at the Homewood Inn. One of them came from Ned Smith, who is the innkeeper of the Wine Country Inn in St. Helena, California. He said, in part, "We saved the last three days of our vacation to spend at the Homewood Inn. It was a choice we will never regret. The food was superior, the staff friendly and responsive to our needs, and the recreational facilities were all first-rate. I guess the' high point of our vacation was sailing on Casco Bay in a charter boat furnished through the inn. I hope we will be able to visit New England again soon, and if we do, a return to the Homewood will be high on our list."

I have been visiting the Homewood Inn since 1972, and each time I have met guests who have returned year after year. It is a very homey, family-type place. Once again, I met one of the Webster's daughters, Julie Webster, who waited on my table on previous visits. This year, she is involved in maintenance work at the inn. "She's going to be a real innkeeper — in fact, she is already," said Fred.

One of the enjoyable things about returning to the Homewood is the chance to see Fred's mother, Doris and her husband, Ted Gillette. They run the Maine Craft Shop, which features all kinds of Maine crafts. "Doris and I will travel everywhere in Maine, and we are having more fun looking up various people who do carved ducks, stone creations, ships' models, painting on slate, etc.," explained Ted.

Lodgings at the Homewood are in single and double cottages which make up most of the inn complex. Many of them have fireplaces and water views, and are set among the juniper, cedar, maple, and Norway pines. Guests are frequently delighted to find that they are sharing the waterside environment with dozens of varieties of land and shore birds. It is a great place for children of all ages.

And so things go forward at the inn on Casco Bay which has been here for so many years. On each visit I find new plans and new progress. Like so many other guests, "I am always very pleased."

HOMEWOOD INN, Drinkwater Point, Yarmouth, Me. 04096; 207-846-3351. A 46-room waterside inn on Casco Bay north of Portland. European plan. Breakfast and dinner served to travelers daily except Mondays when Continental breakfast and steak or lobster cookout at night available (by advance reservation). Open June 10 through Oct. 15. (Some rooms and cottages with kitchenettes available from May 1 and after Oct. 15.) Bicycles (incl. tandems), pool, tennis, croquet court, boating, hiking, salt water swimming on grounds. Golf, riding, fishing, state parks, theatre nearby. Fred and Colleen Webster, Ted and Doris Gillette, Innkeepers.

Directions: From the south, take Exit 9 from Maine Tpke. (I-95) to Rte. 1-N and follow signs to inn. From the north, take Exit 11 from I-95 at Gray and follow Rte. 115 to Yarmouth. Follow signs to inn.

THE ISLAND HOUSE
Ogunquit, Maine

Sometimes letters tell the story of an inn more succinctly than I can. Here is an excerpt from New York City:

"My wife and I have just returned from a little vacation in New England and I think we have you and your book to thank for a lot of our fun. We stayed at the Island House and dined at the Whistling Oyster in Ogunquit. We also stayed at the Colby Hill Inn in Henniker, New Hampshire.

"The Island House was perhaps the most spectacular for us because we arrived there directly from the city. A door at the rear of our room, which I assumed led to a closet, was tightly stuck. My wife said that she saw light through the crack so we both pulled on the knob and when the door sprang open, it revealed a small porch and the ocean itself crashing over enormous rocks. I had no idea that we would be that close to the sea.

"Paul Laurent was very nice. He seemed to be expecting us when we arrived and even remembered which street we lived on in New York. He had grown up in the same neighborhood. Anyway, the Island House, right down to the wildflowers, was everything you said it would be."

Of course, we always like to get letters like that. Incidentally, when we get complaints, which we do every once in awhile, we contact the innkeepers and also try to straighten things out with the disappointed guest.

Well, back to the Island House. It sits on the end of Perkins

Cove, out on the rocks, which have a cover of honeysuckle and sumac. There are snapdragons, blue thistles, marigolds, and many other flowers. Cormorants, gulls, mourning doves, ducks and humming birds abound in the area.

There are two points I must make about the Island House. First, children under twelve years of age simply would not be happy there. There are no facilities to entertain young people. Neither are there facilities for pets. The second is that during the height of the season, which in Ogunquit is July and August, it is almost always necessary to have reservations in advance.

This means that June and September are more plausible times if you like to travel casually without advance reserving.

The Island House serves a continental breakfast to its guests. Many of them take their coffee either on the porch overlooking the cove, or stroll out to the rocks at oceanside. No other meals are served. However, the Whistling Oyster which is within a short walking distance serves both lunch and dinner.

ISLAND HOUSE, Ogunquit, Me. 03907; 207-646-8811. A 6-room oceanside inn overlooking Perkins Cove, 15 mi. from Portsmouth, N.H. Lodgings include Continental breakfast, served daily except Sundays to house guests only. (Lunch and dinner available at the Whistling Oyster nearby.) No children under 12. No pets. Open from Memorial Day to Oct. 1. Advance reservations necessary. Golf, tennis, swimming, fishing, scenic walks, interesting shops and art galleries, all within walking distance. Paul and Marge Laurent, Innkeepers.

Directions: From Maine Tpke., exit at York or Wells. Follow U.S. #1 to Ogunquit. Go 1 mi. on Shore Rd. to Perkins Cove. Inn is last house in Perkins Cove.

OLD FORT CLUB
Kennebunkport, Maine

I just couldn't imagine who she might be. She certainly was an impressive lady, semi-recumbent on a Persian couch, with a Near Eastern headdress, sans most of her clothing. An alert lion sat at her feet staring me right in the eye. She might be Aida, Potiphar's wife or even Cleopatra; in any case she was a larger than life painting covering most of the wall in the Old Fort Club House.

"Antique collecting has been going on here in Kennebunkport for years," explained Marjorie Brass, as she noted my preoccupation. "The seafarers who lived in this section of Maine during the 19th

century, brought home a tremendous amount of furniture, orna-
ments, and knicknacks from ports all over the world. I am always
amazed at the things I find for our shop that probably had their
origins in the Spice Islands, India, or the Far East a hundred years
ago. It is one of the reasons why antique collecting is such great fun."

While we were talking some other guests, carrying on a conversation in voluble French, came through the Club House on their way
out to the swimming pool and tennis courts. They courteously
switched over to English to ask the Old Fort manager, Mrs.
Dickerson, about where to eat dinner that evening. Mrs. Dickerson
was good enough to introduce us and I learned that they, like many
other Old Fort Club mid-summer and fall guests, are from Canada.
"Since so many United States people go there, I consider Kennebunkport a kind of cultural exchange," explained Marjorie.

Quite a few noteworthy changes have taken place since my last
visit to this resort-inn on the Maine coast. A new apartment has
been added to the Club House, and the front entrance now sports a
very attractive lattice-work portico.

"I'm really into old books," explained Marjorie, as she pointed
out the many bookshelves that have been added in the antique shop,
which now also has two matching bay windows.

She was also pleased to have reacquired the original Old Fort
Inn sign. Made of ornate wrought-iron in about 1885, it is a
handsome piece and looks beautiful set in a circular rock foundation
in the front of the inn, with many flowers planted around it.

The lodging rooms are in what was once an impressive stone
carriage house for a hotel which flourished for a number of years,
but has since been torn down. There are 12 efficiency apartments

with daily maid service and an enclosed garage. The apartments are carefully designed with a real decorator touch. Harmonizing draperies and slip-covers provide a gay feeling. Their dimensions are large enough so that people can stay for several days without feeling cramped.

Although these apartments have fully equipped kitchen facilities and many of the guests prepare their own meals, Yale and Marjorie are very happy to provide their guests with a complete run-down on all of the area restaurants. "Of course we think very highly of the Whistling Oyster in Ogunquit; it's open year round," said Yale, who is an airline pilot on the days when he is not an innkeeper. "But during the warm months there are literally dozens of fascinating places and we try to keep up to date with all of them. I have to play a lot of tennis to offset our adventures in eating."

Speaking of tennis, it is a very popular activity at the Old Fort Club, and when I was there the tennis pro, Anne Burr, was very much involved in arranging games, reserving court times and providing instruction and encouragement. "I guess I am sort of a social director cum gardener," she said. "I love to work with the flowers here, they are such a joy."

"Yes," joined in Marjorie. "She keeps our club house and reception desk in fresh flowers all of the time."

As I was leaving this time, I turned once more to the lady in the painting. I'd like to meet her but I'd never get past that lion.

OLD FORT CLUB, Old Fort Ave., Kennebunkport, Me. 04046; 207-967-2709 or 3980. A 12- apartment resort- inn on Cape Arundel within walking distance of the ocean in an historic Maine town. No meals are served but a full kitchen is provided with each apartment. Daily maid service. Balconied club room. Open from Memorial Day to Oct. 1. No pets. Heated pool, tennis court, shuffleboard on grounds. Bicycles, golf, salt water swimming and boating nearby. Yale and Marjorie Brass, Innkeepers.

Directions: Use Exit #3 (Kennebunk) from Maine Tpke. Turn left on Rte. 35 to Kennebunkport and follow signs to inn.

SQUIRE TARBOX INN
Westport Island, Maine

I was driving north up the coast of Maine on U.S. Route 1. I passed through Bath and started looking for Route 144, which turns off the main road on the right and leads to Westport Island. I remembered that if I passed the Wiscasset Information Booth I had

gone too far. Sure enough, there was the sign, so I turned right and followed the blacktop road through the countryside and over the bridge. There were about six more twisty, turny miles, and then once again, I saw the familiar shape that is the Squire Tarbox Inn.

I found everything literally in apple-pie order, because on that particular day there were three apple pies fresh out of the oven, and Annie McInvale invited me to have a bite with a piece of delicious cheese.

I carried the apple pie along with a glass of cold milk out to the freshly painted deck with the new wooden tables and gay umbrellas which is in a sheltered nook between two of the buildings. Elsie White pointed with pride to a screened-in gazebo decorated with pots of geraniums. I asked Elsie who, with Anne McInvale, is an innkeeper of this tidy little inn, how she enjoyed her new vocation.

"Oh, I love it," she replied, "and we have had so much encouragement from our new Westport Island friends and guests." She handed me a copy of a very attractive brochure about the Squire Tarbox Inn. "You will remember that I told you that one of our guests who had an advertising agency in Wisconsin designed this for us at the end of last year."

The Squire Tarbox is a very quiet inn in a section of Maine that is sufficiently off the beaten track to be unspoiled and natural. The bedrooms are very cozy in a real "upcountry" manner, and there is plenty of opportunity to sit around in front of the fireplaces in the sitting and dining rooms, and enjoy conversation.

Guests can go blueberrying or raspberry picking, walk down the pine-needled path to Squam Creek and swim or fish in Montsweag Bay, nearby.

Perhaps the real feeling at the Squire Tarbox is expressed by a letter I received from a gentleman in Cincinnati who wrote me about his experiences there during the summer of 1977:

"Elsie White and Anne McInvale are operating this inn with one thought in mind—the comfort, relaxation and pleasure of their guests. Anne is one of those people who actually enjoys cooking! What she can do with squash, beets, zucchini and other vegetables! We have never in all our travels had such interesting and delicious meals, and getting up in the morning was a real treat because she greeted us with fresh, homebaked blueberry muffins and homemade toasted bread.

"Our room in the barn area was clean and comfortable, and the whole atmosphere of the place made it so easy to rest and relax. I could go on, but I did want you to have a brief outline of our pleasurable stay at the Squire Tarbox Inn. After this experience we look forward to staying at other inns in your book whenever the opportunity affords it." It is true that the rooms in the barn have that wonderful, delightful feeling that comes from years of aging and mellowing. Filled with books and photographs and reproductions of the work of Andrew Wyeth, the sitting room in the barn has a great old wood stove to take the chill off on nippy mornings. I should add that the bedrooms in the main house are, as might be expected, homey and comfortable.

Travelers passing through the Wiscasset area might be interested in having dinner at the Squire Tarbox, but let me advise a telephone call for reservations. The dining room is very small and reservations are almost always necessary.

SQUIRE TARBOX INN, Westport, Island, R.D. #2, Box 318, Wiscasset, Me. 04578; 207-882-7693. A restored Colonial home on Rte. 144 in Westport, 10 mi. from Wiscasset. European plan. 6 rooms with shared baths; two with private bath. All lodgings include Continental breakfast. Breakfast served to house guests only. Dinner served to travelers by reservation. Open from May 1 to Oct. 31. No pets. Golf, tennis, pool, sailing nearby. Anne McInvale and Elsie White, Innkeepers.

Directions: From Maine Tpke. take Exit 9 follow Rtes. 95 and 1 to Rte. 144, 8 mi. north of Bath. Follow Rte. 144 to Wiscasset-Westport Bridge. Inn is located 6 mi. south of bridge on Westport Island.

WHISTLING OYSTER
Ogunquit, Maine

I made two visits to the Whistling Oyster in 1977. The first was in February, on a brilliant sunshiny day with about six inches of new-fallen snow. The sparkling quality of the day portended well for the future. The reason for my being there was the fact that in the late summer of 1976, the original Whistling Oyster was completely destroyed by fire. This was a special trip to Ogunquit to tour the half-finished building with John Parella, and to learn about the new Whistling Oyster.

"We've designed a new building," he said to me at that time, "with some of the best concepts of the old." He pointed out the location of the dining rooms, the lounge area, the kitchen, and the gift shop. At that time the carpenters were busy at work sawing, hammering, and measuring; and the plumbers and the electricians were on the job as well. The building was a shell, but everyone, including Chef Bill Cardwell, was working hard to be ready by late spring.

The second trip came in July when I could see the glorious result of such dedicated activity. The Whistling Oyster has indeed been restored and what I could only imagine in February was now a reality.

The distinctive staircase, the coordinated decorations and furnishings, gleaming silverware, and yellow chrysanthemums were already the objects of admiration.

Everything at the inn was twice as exciting as before. There were many more dining and observation levels including an impressive top deck from which to view Perkins Cove. The round and square tables were set once again with brown placemats, gleaming silverware, and a profusion of flowers —this time yellow chrysanthemums. The waiters with their brown vests and white shirts were moving deftly among the guests serving fruit soups, lamb, veal, native fresh fish, and poached salmon. Everything about the inn reflected elegance and taste. Even the gardens had been completely restored and looked more impressive with a lattice-work fence.

The famous Whistling Oyster gift shop now occupies considerably more space than before. I was delighted once again to see the painted tiles and also the Lladro porcelains from Spain were very intricate and appealing. This shop is internationally famous.

Innkeeper John Parella, the long ordeal of reconstruction and redesigning behind him, was in high spirits. "Actually, the real story here is the people who worked so hard to make it all happen. Everyone working on the job caught the spirit. Many times when I came back at night or on Sundays I found the plasterers or the carpet layers or other people putting in extra time because we all wanted it to be finished as quickly as possible. It never could have been done without everybody feeling that it was a community effort. Those people were just lovely.

"Our chef, Bill Cardwell, has been terrific and he has completely redesigned the layout of the kitchen and the storerooms. He has added several new dishes to our menu and we are already starting to work on our special gourmet dinners for the fall and winter.

"I know that you weren't able to be with us on April 30th when we had our inaugural dinner for the new Oyster, but I have saved a menu for you. That was really a wonderful night and instead of celebrating our 70th birthday, we were actually commemorating its rebirth."

Let me add my congratulations and best wishes.

WHISTLING OYSTER, Perkins Cove, Ogunquit, Me. 03907; 207-646-9521. A waterfront restaurant in Perkins Cove at Ogunquit. No lodgings. Lunch and dinner served daily. Open throughout the year. Reservations advisable. (For accommodations: the Island House just a few steps away.) John Parella, Innkeeper.

Directions: From the south, take the York exit from I-95. Turn north on Rte. 1 to Ogunquit Square. Proceed south on Shore Rd. for about 1 mi. to Perkins Cove turnoff.

WHITEHALL INN
Camden, Maine

I thought that I was acquainted with every possible nook and cranny of the Whitehall Inn. During previous visits I had enjoyed rocking on the front porch which overlooks the lawn and the main

Camden Harbor

street and many of the beautiful houses of Camden. It also has a generous glimpse of Penobscot Bay and the islands. I had browsed in the Edna St. Vincent Millay Room looking at the portraits and photographs of the famous American poet who had been born in Camden. I had visited with Heidi Dewing in the kitchen and had a delicious slice of bread with homemade apple butter. I also found a very pleasant view from the living room of the annex, which is located across the street from the main inn building.

However, this time while roaming through the public rooms of the inn in search of innkeeper Ed Dewing, I found a brilliantly sunlit side terrace whose existence I had never suspected. It was here that I met Mrs. Shenstone. She was enjoying a late morning cup of tea with her daughter.

"The Dewings have been very kind," she said. "You know, at 92, I find the stairs very difficult so they have found ways to overcome that predicament. They quietly send breakfast to my room and do so many little things that make such a difference in my stay. I really feel like one of their family."

The Dewing family is a working, happy innkeeping team. I remember in 1972 when Ed Dewing gave up a thriving advertising career in Boston, and he and Jean moved to Camden and became keepers of this highly reputable village inn. Their children, Jonathan, Chip, and Heidi may have had some misgivings about leaving their city friends to move to a small seaside town in Maine, but they soon found that the family project was great fun and they have all been involved almost since the beginning.

Two of them, Heidi and Jonathan, have decided to make careers out of the hospitality business, and they are both very enthusiastic about country inns. Jonathan graduates from the University of Maine hotel program in 1978, and will be working with my good friend, Dick Knowlton, of the Gasparilla Inn in Boca Grande, Florida. His father says that he will be returning to the Whitehall as assistant manager during the summer.

Heidi's interest in food developed from working in the Whitehall kitchen, and in a recent letter to me, she writes that she has been employed as a pastry baker at the Ritz-Carlton Hotel in Boston — the first woman to be hired in the kitchen as a cook or a baker. It is a wonderful opportunity to learn the finer points of pastry baking . . . "I love country inns," she wrote, "but I am going to spend a few years learning to be the best baker I can."

Chip Dewing will graduate from Nason College in June and, like his brother and sister, has been a familiar figure among the guests of the inn.

Each time I have visited the Whitehall there has been something new and interesting. This time it was the fact that the Dewings' own personal island in Penobscot Bay, Little Green Island, is very popular with their guests. "It has a lobsterman's shack on it, and it is also a game preserve," said Ed. "There are 17 varieties of wild flowers. It is a wonderful place to spend a day in quiet and contemplation."

Quiet and contemplation are not the only things available to visitors to Camden. Here are some notes I took from the inn bulletin board: chamber concerts at the Rockport Opera House; the Maine Festival is held in late July; there is a continuing group of sailing festivals; Ed and Jean can direct guests to a lobsterman who will be happy to take inn guests out in his boat when he hauls in the traps. There is a very wide variety of Penobscot Bay cruises; an antique show; harp concerts at the inn every week, as well as theatre in the village. There are many drives in the area, including the one to the top of Mt. Battie.

WHITEHALL INN, Camden, Me. 04843; 207-236-3391. A 38-room village inn in a Maine seacoast town, 75 mi. from Portland. Modified American and European plans. Breakfast and dinner served daily to travelers. Open June through October. Tennis, bicycles, shuffleboard, day sailing, harbor cruises on grounds. Golf, hiking, swimming, fishing nearby. Jean and Ed Dewing, Innkeepers.

Directions: From Maine Tpke. take Exit 9 to coastal Rte. 95. Proceed on 95 to Rte. 1 at Brunswick. Follow Rte. 1 to Rte. 90 at Warren, to Rte. 1 in Camden. Inn is located on Rte 1, ¼ mi. north of Camden.

New Hampshire

COLBY HILL INN
Henniker, New Hampshire

The comfortable chair by the big fireplace was so inviting that I picked up the guests' register at the Colby Hill Inn and settled down to browse through some of the comments. Guest registers are fun. Most of the time there are happy, and sometimes witty and bright, comments from enthusiastic guests.

Don Glover, Sr., came down the stairs and through the living room, noticing what I was reading. "It's interesting how many people pick up the guest register, just the way you have. It makes fun reading, don't you think so?"

Don and his wife June were classmates of mine at Bucknell University, and a couple of years ago they, along with their son, Don, Jr., and his wife, Margaret, acquired this classic New Hampshire inn from Bettie Gilbert. Don, Jr., has been running the inn for more than a year, awaiting the final moment of the Senior Glover's departure from business in New Jersey and his taking up residence in Henniker.

The inn is on the outskirts of this small village which, among other things, is the home of New England College. The ceilings are low, the walls are hung with oil paintings and prints, and the furnishings are country antiques. A grandfather clock ticks away in one corner. There are birds during all seasons and a gorgeous flower garden during spring and summer. In earlier times, the living room fireplace where I was enjoying a cozy respite, was used for baking bread.

Lodging rooms at the inn are typical country New England.

Many have candlewick bedspreads, hooked rugs, old bowl-and-pitcher sets, which are reminiscent of the days when water was brought in from the outside. Some of them have shared bathrooms and all of them have that wonderful, old "home" feeling.

"June and I are going to have our first full winter at the inn," said Don. "This is great cross-country skiing terrain and we have an arrangement with the ski shop in town to provide our guests with any equipment they may need. There are forty miles of trails in this vicinity and a great many of our guests, including their children, come up for long weekends or even mid-week when it is possible."

At that moment I caught the aroma of freshly baked bread coming from the kitchen, so Don and I wandered back to where Don, Jr., and Regine, the second cook, were getting things ready for dinner. Don, Jr., and I had a short conversation about the expanding menu. "We've added beef kabob Teriyaki," he said. "And this, along with our fresh seafood, has been received very well. We have crab Imperial, shrimp Scampi and usually a fresh fish of the day. My mother has her own little baking corner here and she does the chocolate cakes, the cinnamon buns, the biscuits, and the apple-sauce. We have a lot of things on the menu that have grown in our garden, including juice from our own tomatoes. She also made some jelly from wild grapes that grow out behind the barn."

One of my favorite things at this inn is a delightful swimming pool sheltered by an L formed by the two huge barns adjacent to the inn. It is most welcome on hot days of the southern New Hampshire summer.

This inn is enjoyable in many seasons because this section of New Hampshire has many lakes, state parks, golf courses, summer theatres, and antique shops which add to the attraction for vacationers or weekenders.

COLBY HILL INN, Henniker, N.H. 03242; 603-428-3281. An 8-room inn on the outskirts of a New Hampshire college town. European plan. Some rooms with shared baths. Breakfast served to house guests only. Dinner served to travelers Tuesdays through Sundays. Open year-round. No children under 6. No pets. Swimming pool on grounds. Alpine and xc skiing, tennis, golf, canoeing, hiking and bicycling nearby. The Glover Family, Innkeepers.

Directions: From I-89, take Exit 5 and follow Rte. 202 to Henniker. From I-91, take Exit 3 and follow Rte. 9 through Keene and Hillsborough to Henniker, on W. Main St., one half mile west of the center of town.

THE DANA PLACE INN
Jackson, New Hampshire

Betty Jennings and I were standing in the middle of her garden and she was explaining that the entire output is used on the menu at the inn. "Well, there is the squash, the tomatoes, the parsley, lettuce, the carrots," she said, "and then we have a few herbs which are increasing in number every year."

We continued our walk through the grounds along the Ellis River, and she explained how the cross-country ski trails can also be used for walking during the summertime. The path led around the great boulders, through an orchard and came out at a pool formed by a natural basin in the river. "This is where we cross over in the winter," she said, "If it is too icy, there is a little trolley on a cable and you can pull yourself across the river to get to the other side. It is possible to ski from here right on down into Jackson, and a great many of our guests do it. Also, the people from Jackson come up for our lunches. It is just the right kind of a distance."

It was early September and I dipped my hand into the pool and found the water was still warm. I was tempted to dive off the rocks at the deep part. It looked so clear and inviting.

"Mal and I have had a wonderful time since we came here," she said. "Page, our daughter, was "relish girl" this summer and Chris, who will be ready for college shortly, was also a great help. It has made a very nice way of life for all of us, although you should tell your readers, many of whom ask us about going into the country inn business, that it is a great deal of work all the time."

The Dana Place is an historic inn. There has been an inn here since the late 1800s. At one time it was a farm, as is evidenced by the many apple trees. Like so many New England dwellings, it has been through additions, with buildings snuggled up against each other. Now its L-shape has many comfortable, homey bedrooms of different sizes and shapes.

The location within the White Mountain National Forest offers opportunities for mountain climbing, hiking, walking, and has some access to alpine trails above the timber line for the avid and experienced climber. The lower mountains invite those who prefer easier walking and enjoy the pleasure of beautiful woodland paths and x-country skiing. Guests can order picnic lunches for walks or drives through the countryside or into the mountains.

Betty and I continued our stroll and talked for a moment about the food. "We think of ourselves as sort of country gourmet," she said. "For example, this summer we had a cold peach soup on the menu which was very popular. Our veal and ham in a casserole, and veal sauteed with butter, fresh mushrooms, wine and artichokes was also very well received. We also serve chicken Gloria which is chicken sauteed in butter with brandy and apricots. I do all the desserts, including a cranberry torte pie which is just wonderful. I also do the cheesecake and French chocolate custard served with whipped cream."

By this time we had completed our big circle next to the river, through the woods and open fields and were walking toward the inn with its white clapboard buildings. The green mountains provided a contrasting background. It is the same view that is included in Jan Lindstrom's scratchboard drawing.

Betty sighed contentedly and said, "It is really beautiful here most of the year. I love the summers and fall, but to me there is nothing like seeing all this covered with snow and having lots of cross country skiers gathering together at night around the fireplace. I am so glad we are innkeepers."

DANA PLACE INN, Route 16, Pinkham Notch, P.O. Box 157-B, Jackson, N.H. 03846; 603-383-6822. A 14-room resort inn, 5 miles from Jackson, N.H. in the heart of the White Mountains. Rates include lodging and full breakfast. Lunches served on winter weekends only. Dinners served to travelers daily from late May to late October and from mid-December to late April. Closed Thanksgiving Day. Two tennis courts, natural pool, trout fishing, xc skiing on grounds. Hiking trails, indoor tennis, 5 golf courses, downhill skiing nearby. Malcolm and Betty Jennings, Innkeepers.

Directons: Follow Rte. 16, north of Jackson Village toward Pinkham Notch.

DEXTER'S INN AND TENNIS CLUB
Sunapee, New Hampshire

"Tennis is one of our middle names, and so is cross-country skiing in the winter." Shirley Simpson and I were enjoying a walking tour of Dexter's Inn, when she stopped for a moment to return an errant tennis ball that came rolling across the lawn after one of the guests had hit an overhead smash that bounded over the fence. "Our three tennis courts are all-weather so we can play as early in the spring as possible and even on warmish days in November and December.

"Last winter we had sensational cross-country skiing weather for our 9½ miles of trails. These are used for walking in the summer and fall. You should really come during the last week of September. The leaves are already turning and it is the best time to be in New Hampshire. It's not crowded at all."

We walked past the swimming pool and into the cool deep woods for a few yards and came out at a lovely little chapel. "This was built some years ago," she said. "Many of our guests enjoy this walk—it is so quiet and peaceful, and it is a good place for bird-watching, or for picking the wildflowers in the fields."

When I asked her how she and her husband Frank had discovered Dexter's Inn, which has such a beautiful view of Lake Sunapee and the valley, she replied that they had come here as guests from Cincinnati about nine years ago. "The visit changed our life completely. We decided that we not only wanted to own a country inn, but that this was the only place where we would be happy, so we all came, including our son Aaron. He is very much involved with what we are doing."

The lodging rooms at Dexter's Inn are fun. The accent is on very bright and gay colors, in wallpaper and curtains and bedspreads. The ten rooms in the main house are reached by using funny little hallways that zig-zag around the various wings.

The front parlor has a baby grand piano, a lovely old antique desk with copies of newspapers and magazines, a very inviting fireplace, and lots of books. There is also a little gift shop.

There are other bedrooms with a rustic flavor located in barns across the street. These barns also have a recreation room which is keyed for young people who need a place of their own. There is ping pong, bumper pool, a television set, and just about every indoor game that has ever been invented.

"The cooking is done by ladies who live nearby and for the most part it is mainly good American food. Among our specialties we have a French Market (baked onion) soup, scallops Francoise which are baked in a wine and cheese sauce, turkey Divan, Yorkshire fish which is deep-fried in a special beer batter, and also breast of chicken done with wine and mushrooms. The cooks also do apple crisps and blueberry buckles and speaking of baking, there is homemade bread, fresh everyday."

Dexter's is a resort-inn and there is something for almost everybody to enjoy. Many guests stay for quite a few days and even a couple of weeks at a time. During the summer and winter, the rates include the cost of breakfast and dinner. It is possible to visit in June and September on the European plan.

Later when Frank and Shirley and I were seated on the sunny terrace, I asked them, "What about people who come up here never having played tennis before or even been near cross-country skis?"

"We have instructors available for both sports," said Frank, "and all the equipment that our guests might need. Our tennis pro will arrange informal games among guests of similar abilities."

Yes, Dexter's Inn has many middle names — one of them is "friendly."

DEXTER'S INN AND TENNIS CLUB, Stagecoach Rd., Sunapee, N.H. 03782; 603-763-5571. A 15-room country inn in the central New Hampshire mountain and lake district. Mod. American and European plans available. Breakfast, lunch and dinner served to travelers. Lunches served only July, Aug.; Dec., Feb. Open from Memorial Day to mid-October; December 26th through mid-March. Closed Thanksgiving and Christmas Day. Pets allowed in Annex only.

Three tennis courts, pool, croquet, shuffleboard, 9½ mi. of xc skiing on grounds, downhill skiing and additional xc skiing nearby. Frank and Shirley Simpson, Innkeepers.

Directions: From east: use Exit 12, I-89. Continue west on Rte. 11, 8 mi. just past Sunapee. Sign at Winn Hill Rd. Turn left up hill and after 1 mi. bear right on Stagecoach Rd. From west: use Exit 8, I-91, follow Rte. 103 east into N.H. through Newport, ½ mi. past Junction with Rte. 11. Look for sign at "Young Hill Rd." and go 1½ mi. to Stagecoach Rd.

JOHN HANCOCK INN
Hancock, New Hampshire

Starting with the 1975 issue I have shared with our readers a yearly letter from Pat Wells that enables us all to be up to date with the happenings at the John Hancock Inn. Here are a few observations from her most recent letter (any italics are mine).

"We really seem to be happiest with a dozen projects underway. This year we've continued refurbishing the guest rooms, adding some lovely hooked rugs and antiques, as well as painting and papering. As you know, we have always tried to make any changes with respect for the past, restoring whenever we can, but attempting to provide the comfort all travelers are glad to find. We are especially excited when the work gives us a glimpse of the past—where renovations unearth early wallpapers, bark insulation, old newspapers and bottles, or sections of mural-covered plaster, the past seems right with us.

"Just last month another find came to light. We've always felt that *somewhere* there should have been stencils by Moses Eaton. He lived near Hancock and many of the houses decorated with Rufus Porter murals also had Eaton's stencils. In the process of relocating a doorway, some lovely examples of Eaton's work were uncovered. As you can imagine we were very excited."

There is a room on the second floor with murals at least 150 years old. It is nothing short of miraculous that they have been preserved this long.

"The holiday seasons are so busy, with reservations at capacity many weeks in advance. There is really quite a challenge to provide the personal touches that our guests and our family enjoy. The meals have earned scores of new friends, since many times, luncheon and dinner guests discover our lodgings and return to spend more time as houseguests. Our first-time visitors seem amazed to find the richness of the Monadnock region, both in the beauty of the land and in the talents and abilities of our people.

"Guests enjoy walking through the village where strangers become friends, or a hike or a ride through the hills to find a quiet spot—perhaps by a rushing stream or a lovely lake with a distant mountain beyond."

The John Hancock is New Hampshire's oldest operating inn. It was open in 1789, and I understand that Mr. Hancock himself never appeared on the scene, but because he owned all the land, they named the community and the inn after him. The inn is a traditional New England village inn located in the Mt. Monadnock region, where every season has its special appeal. It is interesting to know that every year on the 4th of July the Hancock church bells ring from 12 midnight to 1 a.m.

THE JOHN HANCOCK INN, Hancock, N.H. 03449; 603-525-3318. A 10-room village inn on Rtes. 123 and 137, 9 mi. north of Peterborough. In the middle of the Monadnock Region of southern N.H. European plan. Breakfast, lunch and dinner served daily to travelers. Closed Christmas Day and one week in spring and fall. Bicycles available on the grounds. Antiquing, swimming, hiking, Alpine and xc skiing nearby. Glynn and Pat Wells, Innkeepers.

Directions: From Keene, take either Rte. 101 east to Dublin and Rte. 137 north to Hancock or Rte. 9 north to Rte. 123 and east to Hancock. From Nashua, take 101A and 101 to Peterborough. Proceed north on Rtes. 202 and 123 to Hancock.

LOVETT'S BY LAFAYETTE BROOK
Franconia, New Hampshire

"Almost like a club" is one of the frequent comments I receive from the readers who have stayed at Lovett's. It is a sophisticated country inn with considerable emphasis on excellent food and service, and is well into its second generation of one-family ownership. Many of the guests have been returning for years; their fathers and mothers came before them. There is a very definite spirit that pulls everybody together.

Perhaps this is best illustrated by a letter: "My mother, a friend and I spent two days and nights at Lovett's in June. We had traveled over 3500 miles in the New England states and eastern Canada by the time we reached Franconia. Seldom had we experienced warmth and hospitality such as that offered at Lovett's, ranging from the young man who greeted us upon arrival to our waitress, Barbara. The meals were excellent, especially the omelet creations and the desserts. The ingredients are as tasty as the names are enticing. We are looking forward to another opportunity for a visit."

Summer in Franconia has many delights—antiquing, horse shows, summer theatre, flower shows, auctions and country fairs. Most of the ski areas run their lifts during the summer and autumn. Shopping seems to intrigue Lovett's guests, and there is a sprinkling of country stores and craft shops throughout the mountains.

On the campus-like grounds of the inn there are small chalets with mountain views and living rooms, many of them with fireplaces. There are also poolside chalets, as well as several bedrooms in the main house and in two nearby houses.

Of the two swimming pools, one has rather chilly mountain water that comes right off nearby Canon Mountain, and the other has a solar heater; one of the first in the area, I am sure.

With Lovett's impressive reputation for its food, it is difficult to make a choice from the tempting menu.

When I pressed Charlie Lovett to tell me which dish was most favored, he had this to say, "We're particularly proud of our cold bisque of native watercress, our eggplant caviar, and our pan-broiled chicken in brandy, herbs, and cream. People also tell us they enjoy our braised sirloin of beef Beaujolais, and lamb served with our own chutney."

Just for the fun of it, I am going to list a few of the desserts: strawberry shortcake, hot Indian pudding with ice cream, angel cake a la mode, macaroon crumble pie, grasshopper pie, meringue glace with strawberries, and butterscotch ice cream puff.

When I spoke to Charlie about the letter of commendation, he said, "Well that's simply marvelous. Of course, the whole idea is to run a comfortable inn and we have been trying to do it for over thirty years."

LOVETT'S BY LAFAYETTE BROOK, Profile Rd., Franconia, N.H. 03380; 603-823-7761. A 32-room country inn in New Hampshire's White Mountains. Modified American plan omits lunch, although box lunches are available. Breakfast and dinner served by reservation to travelers. Open daily between June 20 and Oct. 15 and Dec. 26 and April 1. No pets. Two swimming pools, xc skiing, badminton, lawn sports on grounds. Golf, tennis, alpine skiing, trout fishing, hiking nearby. Mr. and Mrs. Charles J. Lovett, Jr., Innkeepers.

Directions: 2½ mi. south of Franconia on N.H. 18 business loop, at junction of N.H. 141 and I-93 South Franconia exit. 2¾ mi. north of junction of U.S. 3 and 18.

LYME INN
Lyme, New Hampshire

I followed Fred and Judy Siemons into Room 11 on the third floor of the Lyme Inn. "This one has a hidden fireplace in the closet," said Judy, "and when we redecorate the room we are going to rearrange it so that the fireplace will be exposed."

"This whole third floor was once a ballroom," said Fred, "I guess the people who lived here in the mid-19th century liked a good time as much as we do."

107

Fred and Judy were having a good time as innkeepers. They had taken over the Lyme Inn on the first of July from my good friends, Ray and Connie Bergendoff, and were enjoying their new life in the country very much.

"Fred and I grew up across the street from one another in a little town called Ridgefield Park, New Jersey, where my parents had a delicatessen called 'Oscar's'. When Fred came out of the service he went to the Culinary Institute and has been in the food service business for a long time."

"We had some good friends who had a place in the Catskills where we worked summers while we were in college and we started to go up there when our children were small. As they got older, they worked in the same hotel in a variety of positions. Fred very often went up and ran the kitchen if there was need, and I ran the front office for them. This gave us some experience."

We continued our tour of the inn, and they were proudly showing me some of the redecorating that had been done previously. The bedrooms in the Lyme Inn have poster beds, hooked rugs, handstitched quilts, wide pine floorboards, a stencilled wallpaper, wingback chairs, and all kinds of beautiful antique furniture which guests frequently become very attached to and purchase. "In that case," said Judy, "we replace them."

We walked down the stairs to the second floor where the floorboards in the hallway are painted a Shaker red; on the third floor, they are painted green. On the fourth floor, which is reached by a funny little narrow stairway, the floors are blue, and there is blue and red striped wallpaper, and red and blue furniture.

We walked back down to the first floor and stopped in the dining room with its exposed beams, round and square tables, and beautiful glassware. When I picked up a copy of the menu, Fred said, "We really haven't changed very much in the inn or on the menu, because Connie and Ray had done such a marvelous job. We still serve beer batter shrimp, Nantucket Bay scallops, wiener schnitzel, hunter-style veal, and lapin a la creme which is rabbit lightly simmered in onions and sour cream."

Everyone sat down around one of the tables for some hot muffins, fresh from the oven. "We find that it takes about three days really to enjoy the area," said Fred. "Dartmouth College theatre, the backroads, local shops, fairs, auctions, and the great emphasis on handcrafts in the area, plus the skiing, both cross-country and downhill, encourage guests to extend their holidays."

"I think it is the quiet here, too, that makes the difference," said Judy. "We only have one TV in the side sitting room and there are loads and loads of books. We even encourage our guests to take home partially read copies and return them when finished."

LYME INN, on the Common, Lyme, N.H. 03768; 603-795-2222. A 15-room village inn, 10 mi. north of Hanover on N.H. Rte. 10. Convenient to all Dartmouth College activities including Hopkins Center and with music, dance, drama, painting, and sculpture. European plan year-round. Some rooms with shared baths. Breakfast and dinner served daily to travelers, except dinner on Tuesdays. Closed three weeks following Thanksgiving and three weeks in late spring. No children under 8. No pets. Alpine and xc skiing, fishing, hiking, canoeing, tennis, and golf nearby. Fred and Judy Siemons, Innkeepers.

Directions: From I-91, take Exit 14 and follow Rte. 113A east to Vermont Rte. 5. Proceed south 50 yards to a left turn, then travel 2 mi. to inn.

NEW LONDON INN
New London, New Hampshire

First a little bit of history and then a letter.

The New London Inn has seen many changes of owners and innkeepers since it was built by Ezekiel Sargent in 1792. Owners most recent are John and Sally Biewener who purchased the inn from its previous owners, Frank and Lois Conklin, late in the fall of 1976.

I am sure that Sally would not mind if I shared a letter she

wrote to me. It probably provides more insight to the nature of the inn than anything I could write:

"It's hard to believe that only one year ago, almost to the day, John and I saw the New London Inn and decided that we wanted to be innkeepers. It was a momentous decision and it changed our lives completely. We feel it was the right decision and have an interesting and successful year behind us and are looking forward enthusiastically to many, many more.

"We have made quite a few changes at the inn and have received enough compliments to feel that we are on the right track. The dining room has been redecorated with new wallpaper, tables, placemats, and napkins. It is more cozy and inviting and less formal. We are redoing the coffee shop to make more of a dining room out of it, although it will still be casual and informal and serve breakfast and luncheons.

"I find a great deal of satisfaction in redecorating the bedrooms. It has been fun finding old dressers, beds, and other furnishings to make the rooms more 'country innish'.

"Our three daughters have been invaluable (we should have ten children to help us run an inn); we found that we can really count on them in an emergency. Cathy, the daughter whom you met, who is interested in the theatre, stayed six months to help us get started. When she went back to New York, our college age daughter Carol came for the summer. We miss both of them, but fortunately our youngest daughter Judy is only 15 and will be here for a few years. She is an excellent waitress and we are really proud of her. Our dog Chris and cat Morris contribute their share to give the inn a homey atmosphere.

"In the coming year John and I need to relax and plan more time for ourselves. We find it too easy to put in 24-hour days, seven days a week. Hope to see you soon. Sincerely, Sally."

I am sure that everyone will agree that this is a most interesting and delightful picture of some of the aspects of running a country inn.

Let me add that New London Inn is located in a beautiful college town in south central New Hampshire, a few miles from Lake Sunapee, near some excellent cross-country and downhill skiing in the winter and many engaging summertime activities.

It is a three-story, white clapboard town landmark with a long, two-story porch on the side, facing the main street. The lobby and parlor, each with its own fireplace, provide homelike surroundings, and in warmer seasons the porch, lawn, and gardens are excellent places for relaxation.

Congratulations to John and Sally for what was, at the time of this writing in December, 1977, a full year of innkeeping. I know it is hard, rewarding work, but it sounds like you are also having a good time!

NEW LONDON INN, New London, N.H. 03257; 603-526-2791. A 24-room village inn in a college town, 35 mi. from Hanover and Concord N.H. Near Lake Sunapee and King Ridge and Mt. Sunapee ski areas. European plan. Breakfast, lunch and dinner served daily to travelers. Open year-round. Closed Christmas Day. Swimming, boating, climbing, hiking, bicycles, snowshoeing, Alpine and xc skiing nearby. John and Sally Biewener, Innkeepers.

Directions: From I-89, take either Exit 11 or 12 and follow signs for New London. Inn is in the center of town.

The morning was clear and bright. The sun on the turning leaves brought out the iridescent colors of red, yellow, russet and transformed late September in northeastern New Hampshire, into a paean to autumn.

I was enroute to Whitefield, New Hampshire, having just left Bethel, Maine, driving along Route 2 (that very picturesque and highly useful road which runs from Maine across to Vermont), when I saw the sign that said "Philbrook Farm Inn." As always for me, an inn sign on a country road is like a firebell for a Dalmatian. I turned off in the town of Shelburne and followed the road through meadowland for about a half-mile, and then across a long, single-lane bridge over the Androscoggin River. The bridge boards went "clippity-cloppity" under the wheels of the car, and I was immediately drawn back to the days when a Sunday drive in the country with my father and mother meant hearing this sound a half dozen times.

Arriving at a cross road, a charming sign with a painted pastoral scene directed me to turn down a shaded road through elms and maples and evergreens with a hill on one side and the meadows and the river on the other. Then I came in full sight of the buildings of Philbrook Farm Inn on the left, with their white clapboards, shutters and dormers. While on the right, a large herd of handsome Herefords grazed in the meadow across the road. A garden of hundreds, perhaps even thousands, of flowers was a spirit-lifter if ever I saw one.

PHILBROOK FARM INN
Shelburne, New Hampshire

I parked the car underneath an old apple tree and walked across the screened porch into the main entrance. My nostrils were assailed by the absolutely heavenly aroma of freshly-baked bread. I could hear someone in the inn playing the organ and I still recall that the melody was "Seeing Nellie Home." Later on, I saw several song-books with all the great old songs. I became aware of beautiful paneling; many, many paintings and photographs and maps, obviously of the farm and the surrounding area and of a small fire in the fireplace in the reception hall, which was rather welcome, as there was just a bit of a nip in the air.

As I stood looking out the window at the gorgeous view—the meadows with the contented cattle and the White Mountains beyond—a voice behind me said, "Good morning, I am Connie Leger, welcome to Philbrook Farm Inn." I introduced myself and explained that I had seen the sign on Route 2, and we started talking immediately about country inns and innkeeping. She invited me into the kitchen to meet her sister, Nancy Philbrook, who along with a lady from Shelburne and one of the inn guests was beginning to prepare for the noontime meal on an old woodburning range. When I remarked on the fact that a guest was actually helping in the kitchen, Nancy said that it happens all the time here. "Many of our people have been coming back for so many years they know the kitchen almost as well as we do, and they love to come down and peel the potatoes or cut the beans or shell the peas or just sit and visit. We have a lovely time."

"A lovely time" is one of the strongest feelings I had while touring the inn and seeing the great old farmhouse bedrooms with the flowered wallpaper and the furniture that has been collected over many, many years. One of the things I liked very much was the large selection of books on most every subject, well-worn and obviously loved.

We ended up sitting in rocking chairs on the front porch enjoying a morning cup of tea and I listened to some of the history of this fascinating place alternately recited by Nancy and Connie as each of them went back either to check the bread or to take care of the needs of some of the guests.

"The latch string has been out continuously for three generation," said Connie, "and we are the fourth. What we are doing is carrying on in the family tradition."

I asked about the food at the Inn: "Well, we have a typical New England menu. It is all homemade with no mixes. There is one main dish each night and the dinner usually consists of a homemade soup, some type of pot roast, pork roast, or roast lamb. The vegetables are all fresh and we try to stay away from fried foods. Most of the guests enjoy roasts because these days they are not served as much at home.

"All the desserts are homemade and there is pie, ice cream and pudding. For lunches we serve chowder, salads, hot rolls, hash, macaroni and cheese and things like that. We always serve a full breakfast with a choice of juice, hot or cold cereal, eggs, bacon, toast or muffins. On Sunday morning we have New England fish balls and corn bread. On Saturday night we have a New England baked bean supper. Almost always we have a roast chicken dinner on Sunday noon."

As we sat in the sunshine talking, I learned that there has always been music at the inn, especially in the winter when people sit around and play the piano and the organ, and there is a Sunday night sing-a-long.

Winter is a jolly time here, too, as there is cross-country skiing on the 900 acres of farmland, plus downhill skiing just a few miles away with all of the sensational ski lifts in the White Mountains between Shelburne and North Conway.

I'm sure that Harvey Philbrook who came here in 1834 would be very pleased to know that the latch string is still out at the Philbrook Farm Inn.

PHILBROOK FARM INN, North Rd., Shelburne, N.H. 03581; 603-466-3831. A 20-room country inn in the White Mountains of northeastern N.H., 6 mi. from Gorham and just west of the Maine/N.H. line. American, Mod. American & European plans available. 6 rooms with bath, 1 with ½ bath, 13 with shared bath. Breakfast, lunch and dinner served daily to travelers. Open May 1st to October 31st; December 26th to April 1st. Closed Thanksgiving, Christmas. Pets allowed only during summer season in cottages. Shuffleboard, horseshoes, badminton, ping pong, pool, hiking trails, xc skiing, snowshoeing trails on grounds. Swimming, golf, hiking, back roading, bird watching nearby. Nancy C. Philbrook & Constance P. Leger, Innkeepers.

Directions: The inn is just off U.S. Rte. 2 in Shelburne. Look for inn direction sign and turn at North Rd., cross r.r. tracks and river, turn right at crossroad, and the inn is at the end of road.

ROCKHOUSE MOUNTAIN FARM
Eaton Center, New Hampshire

It was about 6 p.m. on a late September afternoon. The maples, aspens and oak trees in this rugged part of New Hampshire were already beginning to turn into glorious colors. I was driving up the dirt road from Eaton Center and in the distance I could see what I thought were horses who seemed to be loping across the road near the front of Rockhouse Mountain Farm Inn. What a wonderful sight they were, running free down into the valley below.

Later, Johnny Edge explained to me that the horses are allowed to run like this in the summertime, "As long as the grass is green they won't wander away." I learned that when the grass is greener in other places, there are times when they have wandered down into the town and have to be rounded up.

The horses are just part of a completely self-contained farm vacation. They are used for trail rides which are conducted by Johnny. There are also cows, ducks, geese, chickens, pigs, piglets, ponies, and guinea hens, and believe it or not, they all have their own names. There is a great barn filled with hay in which the younger guests have made tunnels and played circus on rainy days.

All of this wonderful vacationing atmosphere has been maintained by the Edge family, John and Libby, with their now-grown son and daughter, Johnny and Betsi Ela, who is married to Bill. I think it is marvelous that Johnny and Betsi, who have grown up here, are continuing in the family tradition. Betsi is in charge of the kitchen and Johnny is in charge of all the activities outside, including conducting canoe trips every week.

Didn't we all have a great time that evening at dinner? Among the other guests there were two who have been returning for many years, plus another couple, who were first-timers at Rockhouse Mountain Farm. The latter said they had read about it in *Country Inns and Back Roads* and that they had decided to come for a week. At first, they had been concerned about running out of things to do, but now after five days, they realized that "you can never run out of things to do here. There is just so much to see and do, not only here on the farm, but in the nearby vicinity."

This happened to be lobster night, and I think for one of the few times in my life I actually had my fill of lobster. Libby had made three different kinds of pies in the afternoon, and I had a small piece of all three.

Of course, after a dinner like this accompanied by much joking and laughing, it was necessary to take a walk outside in the

September night, and John Edge joined me for just a few minutes. I asked him whether or not this would be a good place for family reunions. "The best." he replied enthusiastically. "You know we have raised our own family here, and I think we know what children and young people really enjoy the most. Many of our guests came here when they were newly married, and now their children are bringing *their* children with them to visit. Sometimes grandparents meet their children and their grandchildren here by prearrangement. The younger crowd can milk the cows, feed the calf, help with the haying, hike up to the Indian cave, go on canoe trips and cookouts, and use the canoes and sailboats at Crystal Lake, which has a beach.

"In the meantime, there is tennis, golf, hang gliding, soaring, bicycling, hiking, fishing, summer theatre, antiquing, and lots of things for their grandparents and parents to enjoy."

The next morning after a breakfast of hot cakes made from scratch with maple syrup, I wandered out to the corral where Johnny was whistling for the horses to come up and get their breakfast. We could see them grazing down in the valley, and soon they were on their way, manes flying and hoofs pounding, right through the gate to the troughs where the aromatic grain had been poured. There they were, close enough to touch. It is one of the many beautiful things about RMF.

ROCKHOUSE MOUNTAIN FARM INN, Eaton Center, N.H. 03832; 603-447-2880. A complete resort in the foothills of the White Mountains, (6 mi. south of Conway), combining a modern 18-room country inn with life on a 350-acre farm. Some rooms with private bath. Mod. American plan. Open from June 15th through October. Own saddle horses, milk cows, and other farm animals; haying, hiking, shuffleboard; private beach on Crystal Lake with swimming, rowboats, sailboats, and canoes — canoe trips planned; stream and lake fishing; tennis and golf nearby. The Edge Family, Innkeepers.

Directions: From I-93, take Exit 23 to Rte. 104 to Meredith. Take Rte. 25 to Rte. 16, and proceed north to Conway. Follow Rte. 153 six mi. south from Conway to Eaton Center.

SPALDING INN CLUB
Whitefield, New Hampshire

The Spalding Inn Club is an excellent example of the entertainment and hospitality that can be provided for a family with many different vacation preferences. For example, on the inn grounds there are tennis courts, a swimming pool, a nine-hole par-three

golf course, two championship lawn bowling greens and shuffle-board. Five 18-hole golf courses are within fifteen minutes and there is plenty of trout fishing, boating, canoeing and many enticing back roads for motoring. The entire White Mountain Range of northern New Hampshire is practically at the doorstep, and the Appalachian Trail system for mountain climbing is a short walk from the inn.

I personally prefer to have a balance of vigorous activity as well as some quiet times, so I was pleased to find the extensive library, a card room, and a fine collection of jigsaw puzzles. I also enjoyed some quiet walks in the nearby woods among the beautiful birch, maple and oak trees native to northern New Hampshire. The Spalding Inn has over 400 acres of lawns, gardens and orchards, and innkeeper Ted Spalding explained that it takes a staff of nine gardeners to keep everything up to par.

This lovely old place is one of what, I believe, are just four remaining New Hampshire American plan resort-inns that were originally built in the 19th century. It is the smallest of the four, and this well suits my taste. Many of the amenities of earlier times are still preserved, including gracious dining room service, where the menu changes daily and includes such offerings as broiled scrod, poached salmon, sweetbreads, Maine lobster, raspberry pie and Indian pudding. Incidentally, a gentleman wouldn't think of going in to dinner without a jacket and tie. It sort of goes with the finger bowls, and turn-down service in the spacious bedrooms.

In spite of all this elegance there are real country inn touches everywhere. The broad porch is ideal for rocking, and the main living room has a fireplace with a low ceiling, lots of books, a basket of apples, and a barometer for tomorrow's weather. There is even a jar of sourballs available for everyone.

The inn also maintains completely furnished and equipped cottages. They are available for rental periods of three days or longer from December to April. This makes winter activities, including downhill and excellent cross-country skiing as well as snowmobiling and snowshoeing, available during the beautiful New Hampshire winter.

There used to be fifty of these New Hampshire resorts, but the decline of the railroad and the coming of the automobile changed the vacation habits of many people. I am delighted to say that the Spalding Inn has maintained the old standards and adapted itself admirably to the traveling and vacation needs of today. Long may it thrive!

SPALDING INN CLUB, Mountain View Road, Whitefield, N.H. 03598; 603-837-2572. A 70-room resort-inn in the center of New Hampshire's White Mountains. American plan only from early June to mid-October when breakfast, lunch and dinner are served daily to travelers. Housekeeping cottages only from mid-December to April. Heated pool, tennis courts, 9-hole par 3 golf course, 18-hole putting green, two championship lawn bowling greens and bicycles on grounds. Also guest privileges at 5 nearby golf clubs. Trout fishing, boating, summer theater and backroading nearby. Ted and Topsy Spalding, Innkeepers.

Directions: From New York take Merritt Pkwy. to I-91; I-91 to Wells River, Vt. Woodsville, N.H. exit; then Rte. 302 to Littleton, then Rte. 116 thru Whitefield to Mtn. View Rd. intersection — 3 miles north of village. From Boston take I-91 north thru Franconia Notch to Littleton exit; then Rte. 116 thru Whitefield to Mtn. View Rd. intersection — 3 miles north of village. From Montreal take Auto Route 10 to Magog; then Auto Route 55 and I-91 to St. Johnsbury, Vt.; then Rte. 18 to Littleton, N.H. and Rte. 116 as above. The inn is situated 1 mi. west on Mountain View Rd.

STAFFORD'S IN-THE-FIELD
Chocorua, New Hampshire

As I believe I have indicated on several occasions, innkeepers in this book have ample opportunities to meet each other and very frequently visit each other's inns. Here is an excerpt I received from Bill Winterer, who keeps two inns featured in CIBR: The Griswold Inn is Essex, Connecticut and the Town Farms Inn in Middletown, Connecticut.

"Vicky and I had a very delightful experience that I would like to share with you. We took our three little boys up to Stafford's-in-the-Field for a five-day cross-country skiing holiday. I can honestly say I have never been treated better anywhere. Fred and Ramona are charming hosts and they made us feel completely at home.

"The only liability connected with the holiday was the food. It was so delicious and so beautifully served that Vicky and I each added about five pounds during that short period. It was really a joy each time we sat down in the dining room."

Stafford's-in-the-Field (hereinafter to be known as Stafford's) is the inn at the end of the road for which so many people seem to be searching. It has a wide porch running around three sides and overlooks broad meadows which disappear to a distant line of trees. Sitting on the edge of a New Hampshire forest, it has a long history of being an inn—and is, in fact, a farmhouse inn. For example, there is a huge classic New England barn which has been marvelously preserved and is today used for such rural diversions as barn dances, concerts, operettas, and the like, during the summer.

Lodging rooms are located in the main building, which has country bedrooms on three floors. In addition, there are cottages scattered about the park-like grounds, some of which have Franklin stoves and others, fireplaces. The inn is a very informal place with the type of relaxed atmosphere that encourages guests to do as they wish — read books, pick blueberries, go for walks, or enjoy outdoor sports in both winter and summer.

Besides spending the evenings in conversation by the fireplace, or listening to music, guests frequently gather around an old player piano which must be pumped furiously to perform. Small antique oil or kerosene lamps complete this nostalgia-laden scene.

Bill Winterer mentioned Ramona Stafford's country-gourmet cooking which includes lamb curry, ginger chicken, prime ribs, chiles rellenos con queso, and spareribs cooked in maple syrup. Ramona says that no matter how long a guest remains, the entrees are different each night.

All the desserts and breads are homemade, and this is where the Stafford's daughter, Momo, joins in. She creates cheesecakes, lemon cream cake, French silk pies, sauteed apples in puff pastry, and baked Alaska. Her popovers melt in the mouth. Small wonder that Bill and Vicky were so generous in their praise.

All three of the Stafford children have grown up since my first visit in 1971. As Fred Stafford said during a recent conversation, "They're like all other kids, they're in and out, they return to the nest intermittently. They all will be home at least part of the summer, because we will be doing our fourth Gilbert and Sullivan presentation, and they are the singing stars of the show. We hold it at the end of August every year. It's hard to realize that Momo is 24, Hansel is 20, and Fritz is 21."

STAFFORD'S-IN-THE-FIELD, Chocorua, N.H. 03817; 603-323-7766. An 8-room resort-inn with 5 cottages, 17 mi. south of North Conway. Modified American plan at inn omits lunch. European plan in cottages. Some rooms in inn with shared baths. Meals served to guests only. Closed Apr. and May, Nov. and Dec. No pets. Bicycles, square dancing, and xc skiing on the grounds. Golf, swimming, hiking, riding, tennis, and fishing nearby. The Stafford Family, Innkeepers.

Directions: Follow N.H. Rte. 16 north to Chocorua Village, then turn left onto Rte. 113 and travel 1 mi. west to inn. Or, from Rte. 93 take Exit 23 and travel east on Rtes. 104 and 25 to Rte. 16. Proceed north on Rte. 16 to Chocorua Village, turn left onto Rte. 113 and travel 1 mi. west to inn.

WOODBOUND INN
Jaffrey, New Hampshire

"In the summertime we have a very full program of activities for our guests." Jed Brummer and I were having dinner on Saturday night at the Woodbound Inn. Earlier, Jed had introduced the staff members to the assembled guests, including the cook, and the hostess, and everyone was made very welcome and all the activities for the coming week were carefully explained.

"During July and August, our minimum length of stay is one week, which starts on Saturday and ends the following Saturday, so that there is a constant program going on every day, including something for both adults and children. For example, on Monday we have craft courses in basket weaving and jewelry-making, and in the evening, a gentleman from the area comes in and runs a card party. There are games for children at night as well. Tuesday is beach-luncheon day. In the evening, there is outside entertainment, either a magician or a puppet show.

"On Wednesday, we always have a golf tournament, and a cookout, and a softball game at night.

"Thursday, we continue the crafts during the day and square dancing at night. On Friday, we have a farewell party and give commemorative plates to guests who have been returning to Woodbound each year for either 20, 25, or 30 years. We've had young people who came here before they were one year old, and now are bringing their children to Woodbound."

We talked more about the children's program, and Jed explained that their program actually goes on all day long, with time out for lunch in the summertime. There is an early supper for small children, and after-supper activities for the younger set, so the parents can be free to socialize.

He handed me a very attractive basket. "These baskets are made in West Rindge and decorated by a local artist. We fill them up with picnic lunches which our guests can take to their cottages or to the beach or hiking or even backroading. They were much enjoyed.

"In the winter we find the cross-country touring is very popular, especially since we have 50 miles of trails. We also have special rates which are attractive to families during the winter, and the program includes sleigh rides, cookouts during the day, and square dancing, and other such entertainment in the evening."

The Woodbound is a genial, family-resort inn. Ed and Peg Brummer started it all; their son, Jed, continued, along with his wife, Mary Ellen; and there is a third generation of Brummers doing the inn chores as well. For guests who like outdoor activities, it is a delight. The lake, the sailboat, canoes, and swimming are just a step away. The inn has its own golf course and tennis courts. Shuffleboard, hiking, and walking in the deep woods are other activities. I think the most significant thing that has happened in recent years are the handcraft classes which are very popular with guests.

"Come on," said Jed, "I will introduce you to some of our new guests."

WOODBOUND INN and COTTAGES, Jaffrey, N.H. 03452; 603-532-8341. A 40-room resort-inn on Lake Contoocook, 2 mi. in the woods from West Rindge or Jaffrey. Within walking distance of Cathedral of the Pines. American plan in summer and winter. Overnight European plan available in May, June, and late fall. Breakfast, lunch, and dinner served daily. Open from May 26 to 30; June 9 to Oct. 10; Dec. 26 to March 12, with some closed periods. Par 3 golf course, swimming beach, sailing, water skiing, tennis, hiking, children's program, ski area, touring trails, tobogganing, and skating on grounds. Ed and Peggy Brummer, Jed and Mary Ellen Brummer, Innkeepers.

Directions: From Boston, follow Rte. 2, then Rte. 119 to Rindge where there are directional signs to inn. From New York, follow I-91 to Bernardston, Mass. Proceed on Rte. 10 to Winchester, then Rte. 119 to Rindge and watch for signs to inn.

Vermont

BARROWS HOUSE
Dorset, Vermont

Charlie Schubert and his father and I were reminiscing about our first meeting in Stockbridge about seven years ago.

"I remember that you told us it was hard work, and that while it was very rewarding, at the same time we would really have to put our shoulders to the wheel." Mr. Schubert looked approvingly at Charlie and at Marilyn, his wife, who had joined us on the little patio under the Martini and Rossi umbrellas. "Well, Marilyn and Charlie have worked very hard and I think that it has been a success. At least, I seem to meet an awful lot of people who think that this is one of the best country inns they have ever visited."

Charlie's smile thanked his father, and then he went on to explain some of the additional factors:

"Dorset was the ideal community for us. It's a community that is oriented to both summer and winter activities. The people in the town are warm and responsive, and the Barrows House had an excellent reputation for a number of years under the previous owners. Also, we thought that our son, Charlie, would enjoy growing up here."

Marilyn joined in, "I think one of the significant factors, as I've told you several times, is the fact that Sissie came with us a few years ago and is really like one of our own family. She has complete charge of everything in the kitchen, and is always reaching out for new ideas. She really is a part of our family—we're going to take her, along with

123

our son Charlie, on a three-week trip to southern France and Spain. By the way, we're going to use your book on Europe."

"One of the really big things happening here for 1978," said Charlie, "are two paddle tennis courts we're putting on the grounds. There's been a tremendous interest in paddle tennis, and I think the new courts will fit right in with our tennis courts and swimming pool. And the changing rooms are available, as always, for our guests to use."

I think what Charlie said illustrates one of the reasons for the growing popularity of this very attractive village inn. In the time since the Schuberts took over the Barrows House, they have added considerably to the on-the-ground facilities, including a swimming pool and the tennis courts, and have entered into a vigorous cross-country ski program, which Charlie freely admits was greatly encouraged by the advice of Tony Clark at Blueberry Hill.

"I think we've become a sort of mini resort-inn," said Marilyn. "Many of our guests spend a great deal of time right here and when the spirit moves them, they go antiquing in the little villages up and down the valley and the Mettowe River, or drive into the mountains to see the further sights of Vermont. We can make recommendations for lunch or even pack a box lunch if they like. In the winter it is just a short drive to Bromley or Stratton Mountains for great downhill skiing."

Well, all of these factors certainly contribute to making the Barrows House an enjoyable place to visit — but in all fairness, I must say that it is both Charlie and Marilyn themselves who make it all work. Both of them, in spite of being very busy people, always have time to stop and talk to their guests, join with them after dinner in the living room with its big fireplace or out on the terrace during the warmer weather.

Yes, it took lots of hard work and lots of heart to make the Barrows House in Dorset, Vt. a favorite country inn for many people.

BARROWS HOUSE, Dorset, Vt. 05251; 802-867-4455. A 26-room village inn on Rte. 30, 6 mi. from Manchester, Vt. Modified American plan omits lunch. Breakfast, lunch and dinner served daily to travelers. Swimming pool, tennis courts, paddle tennis, bicycles, xc skiing facilities, including rental equipment and instruction, on grounds. Golf, tennis, trout fishing, and Alpine skiing nearby. Charles and Marilyn Schubert, Innkeepers.

Directions: From Rte. 7, proceed north on Rte. 30 to Manchester to Dorset.

BLUEBERRY HILL FARM
Goshen, Vermont

After closing in April, Blueberry Hill, an inn where the dominant theme is cross-country skiing, reopens in September of each year. However, I think it only fair to warn readers that guests in the fall are frequently, withal laughingly, pressed into service "clearing trails" as Tony Clark explains. Actually, it is a lot of fun and makes visiting Blueberry Hill in the non-cross-country ski season a real adventure.

In early November, 1977, I joined our group of innkeepers included in this book in paying a short visit to this mountaintop inn. Almost before I had gotten out of my car, two or three of them were telling me what a delightful place it was. "I love the bedrooms," and "those beautiful dining rooms," were typical of some of their comments.

I went through the familiar front door and found myself in a hubbub of conversation. I was literally surrounded by innkeepers. Some were in the small, book-lined library with the sporting prints. Others were in the dining room with its long oval table where Martha Clark was serving tea, coffee, and cakes to everyone and gave me a wave that said, "I'll talk to you later."

I found a good-sized group in the big fireplace room, where there are gay dried flowers hanging from the ceiling. This is the room where almost everybody gathers after a day on the ski touring trails. Perhaps the most exciting room on this visit was the Greenhouse, a new glassed-in section which has been built into the back part of the inn next to the kitchen. Tom Noonan, from the Bird and Bottle Inn, pointed out that it was a most unique and unusual way of adding additional space, and at the same time inviting the outdoors.

Later on, I had a chance to talk to Martha and she was very enthusiastic about the new ski touring facility which has been built across the road. "We'll have a lot more room," she said. "But the pot bellied stove and the tractor seats have all been moved from the old shop. This will eliminate the overcrowded conditions around the ever-bubbling pot of hot soup."

Our conversation turned naturally toward her domain—the kitchen. "We have one main dish for each meal, things like beef Bourguignon, chicken Cordon Bleu, leg of lamb, stuffed flank steak, pork roast with juniper berries, and the like. Everybody sits down around the dining room table at the same time and it's a real family affair. I love to cook and I love to experiment. It's just like having a dinner party every night except that I've got some very good helpers as well."

A few important observations about Blueberry Hill: There are no babysitting facilities for young children. Reservations for winter accommodations begin the previous winter, and the inn is often booked solid for weeks at a time.

BLUEBERRY HILL FARM, Goshen, Vt. 05733; 802-247-6735. A mountain inn passionately devoted to cross-country skiing, 8 mi. from Brandon. Modified American plan omits lunch. All rooms with private baths. Meals not served to travelers. Open from September to April. Closed Christmas. Swimming, fishing, and xc skiing on the grounds. Tony and Martha Clark, Innkeepers.

Directions: At Brandon, travel east on Rte. 73 through Forest Dale. Then follow signs to Blueberry Hill.

CHESTER INN
Chester, Vermont

One of the things I enjoy the most about revisiting country inns is to see what changes have taken place since my last visit, or what new plans are being made. On this particular day, I was on the second floor of the Chester Inn with Tom and Betsy Guido and we were having a firsthand look at all of the refurnishing and redecorating that was being done. "All of the second floor rooms will have new bathrooms," explained Betsy, "and we're putting in new carpeting and wallpaper as well. Each room will be individually decorated to bring out its distinctive, unique character."

Work had already been completed in the new Victorian suite which has authentic furniture and accessories of that period,

including heavy brocade swag draperies and frivolous grass reeds in gaudy vases. I noted a beautiful carved headboard, a little Victorian loveseat covered in a medallion-patterned fabric, a marble-top washstand, and a matching marble-top dresser. "We think it's the perfect setting for honeymooners," said Tom.

It is now about two years since Tom and Betsy Guido acquired this central Vermont village inn, and according to all reports they have made progress almost since the first day.

One of the most interesting developments got under way in the fall of 1977 with the Chester Inn Dinner Theatre. Dinner is served in the dining room, followed by a play "in the round." There was a favorable response from the first, and this was a continuing event throughout last winter.

"We probably won't continue it through the summer because of all the summer theatres in the area, but the way things look now, I'm sure we will pick it up again after their season closes," said Tom.

Chester is an old Vermont village with many 19th century homes and buildings, including a striking group of stone houses at the eastern end. Dominating the center of the town is a Victorian building that reflects many architectural influences. The porch runs across the entire first floor, and there is a second balcony over the center section. The block-long village green is directly in front of it. This is the Chester Inn.

First-time visitors are impressed with the very large lobby and living room. There is a big fireplace with several comfortable chairs and couches, and many bright watercolors add a distinctly airy feeling to the room.

The inn has an "L" shape which is not discernible from the front. In the shelter formed by the "L," a swimming pool has been built, surrounded by a sunny terrace. It is a short walk over the luxuriant green grass to some tennis courts, which are right next to the brook.

The Guidos came to Vermont from Cleveland, Ohio, and although neither of them had had prior experience in the inn business, they did come armed with a lot of nerve and determination to do well. Tom took a crash gourmet cooking course from Audrey Patterson, who with her husband Jim, had owned the inn for a number of years. Now, with a great deal more experience in the kitchen, he has added several of his own dishes to the menu. Betsy is frequently found as the hostess in the dining room, because as she said, "People especially like to have the personal touch of the owners."

This village inn is a busy place in all seasons. In winter it is convenient to several major ski areas. There is ample opportunity for cross-country skiing. Warmer weather guests use it as home base while exploring Vermont's back roads and antiquing. There is golf nearby as well.

"I think our guests like the idea of coming to a Vermont village that is unspoiled," said Betsy. "Here in Chester folks sit out on the front porch on a summer's evening and they might walk down to the store for a quart of chocolate ice cream."

CHESTER INN, Chester, Vt. 05143; 802-875-2444. A 30-room village inn on Rte. 11, 8 mi. from Springfield, Vt. Convenient to several Vt. ski areas. Lodgings include breakfast. Lunch and dinner served to travelers daily except Mondays. Closed from late October to mid-November and April to mid-May. No children under 4 in dining room. No pets. Pool, tennis, and bicycles on grounds. Golf, riding, Alpine, and xc skiing nearby. Tom and Betsy Guido, Innkeepers.

Directions: From I-91 take Exit 6. Travel west on Rte. 103 to Rte. 11.

EDSON HILL MANOR
Stowe, Vermont

Liz Turner had invited me to "meet the horses" and we were walking down the mountain from the main house at Edson Hill Manor, past the sunlit, terraced and flagstoned swimming pool, the putting green and the trout pond with the rowboat, and were now coming toward the stables. It was late September and the air at 1500 feet was clear and sharp. Robins and chickadees chatted noisily among the many varieties of trees to be found in the high Vermont

128

forest, most of which already had some brilliant autumn shades.

"I am so glad that you are here now," she said in her softly clipped English accent, as we stepped inside the gate of the corral. "This is one of our very best times of year, the fall colors are almost at their height. It's funny," she said, as we stepped inside of the barn, "most people wait until later in October but I think this is a much better time. Besides, there are far fewer people."

The barn was busy with horses stamping and snorting, and other guests getting ready for a morning ride. "We try to fit our riding program to the horsemanship of our guests. We can accommodate first-time riders or people who really want to improve their technique. I have been teaching advanced riding for quite a few years." Pointing to a map on the wall, she said, "A great many of our riding trails are also used for our cross-country ski program in the winter. In fact, this entire stable area is turned into a cross-country ski shop where our guests can rent all the equipment they need. We have miles and miles of trails on our own property and good instructors.

I learned that horseback riding and cross-country skiing are just two of the outdoor activities available at Edson Hill. There is golfing, tennis, fishing, and hiking nearby. For the guests who might be in a more contemplative mood, there is a beautiful wind-free terrace with a magnificent view of the valley and mountains beyond, dozens of places to curl up quietly with a book, and it takes just about thirty seconds to be on one of the walking trails in the woods. When I mentioned this to Liz, she said, "Yes, there are many things to do close at hand, or absolutely nothing at all, if that is the preference.

We are always available to help out with plans for the day. One of the nicest drives, especially for people with children, is to the excellent Shelburne Museum which makes a very interesting day trip. The granite and marble quarry in Barre and the cheese factory in Cabot make another pleasant journey. We have available a "roads and tours" map for all the northern back country roads. In the summertime, almost all of our guests ride up the Mt. Mansfield gondola. The view is just tremendous."

Walking into the living room at Edson Hill Manor is like entering someone's gracious and luxurious home—the beautiful oriental rug, the spacious fireplace flanked on either side by comfortable divans, the pine-panelled walls hung with paintings — some by owner Larry Heath's mother—the floor-to-ceiling windows with elegant draperies, the booklined shelves, the beamed ceilings; all somehow sum up the personality of this friendly, congenial place. The same sense of casual luxury is carried throughout in the bedrooms, many of which have fireplaces, private baths, and spacious closets, and all are attractively decorated.

Larry Heath and his wife, Gypsy, were much taken with this rather rustic, French Provincial, 20-odd-room "cottage" with such unusual design features as fireplace tiles from Holland, brass fittings and original shingles from Williamsburg, Virginia, and beams from Ira and Ethan Allen's barn.

Liz tightened down the girth on one of the saddles, and turned to me saying, "Why don't you take the morning ride with us? It is such a lovely day, I am sure you will enjoy it!"

I thought for a minute, weighing the remaining visits on my schedule for that day. Then I looked at the beautiful blue sky and the inviting prospect of a morning ride in the brilliant fall foliage. "Sure," I said. "Saddle up, I am ready to go."

EDSON HILL MANOR, Edson Hill Rd., Stowe, Vt. 05672; 802-253-7371. A 16-room resort-inn about 6 mi. from the center of Stowe, high in the Mt. Mansfield area. Mod. Amer. plan, winter; European plan, summer. Breakfast, lunch and dinner served to travelers, winter only. Open mid-December to mid-April; mid-June to end of October. Closed Memorial Day. No pets. Horseback riding, swimming, practice golf, xc skiing, fishing on grounds. Mountain climbing, downhill skiing, back roading nearby. Laurence P. and Dorothy Heath, Owners. Elizabeth Turner, Innkeeper.

Directions: Exit I-89 at Waterbury/Stowe. Follow Rte. 100 north to Stowe village, turn left on Rte. 108 north, turn right on Edson Hill Rd. immediately past Buccaneer Motel.

GREEN MOUNTAIN INN
Stowe, Vermont

Parker Perry had invented a game: "Identify five famous innkeepers in literature or history." That's the way Parker is — a man of infinite surprises. He usually has something bizarre and cogitative for me to ponder with each new visit to the Green Mountain Inn.

One time he took me down into the lounge which is called "The Whip" and said, "Okay, without counting, tell me how many actual whips we have here in this room." I took a look at all the various types of buggy whips and phaeton whips and old whips of countless other varieties and said, "129."

"Wrong again," he said, "there are two hundred and twenty-three." I felt somewhat relieved that he didn't ask me to estimate the number of bricks in the many fireplaces, or the square feet of wood panelling in the lobby. He could have asked me also how many pecks of fresh apples had been used for pies over a period of a year, or how many fresh muffins had been baked for breakfast. He might have asked me how many coach lamps were distributed throughout the inn!

Everyone has heard of Stowe for winter sports. What is perhaps not so well known is that Stowe is one of the most delightful places to visit in other seasons of the year.

It was mid-July, we were seated on the grassy terrace in the rear of the GMI enjoying a glass of iced tea and Parker was extolling the virtues of Stowe in the summer. "There are two important things," he said. "One, have you noticed there are no mosquitoes? The other one is the fact that air conditioning is not needed." He was right on both counts.

The afternoon sun was reflected from the red clapboards of the inn and the profusion of petunias, phlox, and other summer flowers contributed a New England feeling to the scene. When I remarked on it he replied, "Oh, we're as New England as the boiled dinners, baked beans, and fresh ice cream that we serve. After all, we're smack in the middle of Vermont, and I wouldn't know how to be anything else but New England."

Dottie Perry came out for a moment with a fresh pitcher of iced tea and a pair of garden shears. She was gathering flowers for the truly fabulous arrangements she makes in the inn. She also prepares dried arrangements to brighten up the winter, as well.

"What are you two up to," she asked.

"Well, I've been trying to persuade this erudite Berkshire Traveller to name five prominent innkeepers in literature and history, and so far he's managed to stall me off."

"You've got me stumped." I replied. "The only one I can think of now is that rascal who appears in the book *Country Inns and Back Roads — his name: Parker Perry.*"

GREEN MOUNTAIN INN, Main St., Stowe, Vt. 05672; 802-253-7301. A 61-room village inn on Rte. 100, 36 mi. from Burlington, 6 mi. from Mt. Mansfield, Vermont's highest peak. Modified American plan omits lunch. Breakfast, lunch, dinner served to travelers daily. Open mid-December to mid-April, late May to late October. Golf, tennis, riding, hiking, bicycles, Alpine and xc skiing nearby. Parker and Dorothy Perry, Innkeepers.

Directions: From I-89, take Exit 10, and proceed north on Rte. 100 to Stowe.

INN AT SAWMILL FARM
West Dover, Vermont

Ione Williams and I were walking down the gravel road toward the trout pond and I was reminiscing about the first year that Rod had put it in. "Oh, I remember it very well," she said. "We thought that it would never fill up. Now it's a delight to everyone. Next spring, we plan to move that old barn building back there down near the pond, and we'll extend it about ten to twelve feet over the water. Then we will build a deck out over the pond which will give us another living room suite with a fireplace, and two bedrooms."

We reached the edge of the pond, and went into the Spring House which is composed of a large studio suite on the first floor with a king-sized bed, sofa, two club chairs, and an old stone fireplace all

looking across the pond. It also has a small kitchen for snacks, a dressing room, and a private bath. The stairway from the studio leads to a landing and on into a twin-bedded room with a dressing room, and bath on the second floor.

"This originally was a spring house and ice storage building," she said.

Since my very first visit to the Inn at Sawmill Farm, which was included in the 1970 edition, I have reported continual progress and success. The inn is a group of elegantly restored farm buildings clustered around an attractive swimming pool on a slight elevation overlooking the village. The restoration started with the original barn which is now the living room and where the beams and barn siding make a marvelous contrast to both the antique and modern furniture. This particular brand of country sophistication is carried to the lodging rooms; each is different and has a character of its own, furnished in Victorian New England, country, or more formal, Colonial styles with touches of Chippendale.

There is much use of mellowed barnboard, shingles, old doors, beautiful aged brick and stone. The brass telescope in front of the picture window in the living room is aimed right at Mt. Snow.

"How's the cross-country skiing?" I inquired. Ione replied enthusiastically, "I'm sure that almost half of our guests each winter are really into it. By the way, we have snowshoes for people who want just to take a quiet walk. The ice skating is wonderful when we can get the snow off the pond."

Because Ione was for many years the only chef at the inn, our conversation quite naturally turned to food. "Brill, our son, is now the chef and is in charge of five young men who are fast-becoming good cooks. I'm really only allowed to make the desserts these days. Our menu changes by the season. We have a choice of about sixteen different appetizers from crabmeat on an artichoke heart to imported smoked Irish salmon. The entrees range from rack of baby lamb, steak au poivre, three veal dishes, and lobster Savannah, to good old country chicken. I still like to make apple pies, chocolate mousse, and things like that, and I put up 360 quarts of homemade tomato juice which I got from my grandmother's original recipe. We also have lots of frozen red raspberries, strawberries, and Jersey peaches."

Our walk led us to a small house with a deck overlooking the tennis courts. There were two people in one court playing a vigorous game. "Would you like to play some mixed doubles?" asked Ione.

"Just give me five minutes to change," I said.

INN AT SAWMILL FARM, Box 8, West Dover, Vt. 05356; 802-464-8131. A 17-room country resort-inn on Rte. 100, 22 mi. from Bennington and Brattleboro. Within sight of Mt. Snow ski area. Modified American plan omits lunch. Breakfast and dinner served to travelers daily. Closed Nov. 7 through Dec. 7. No children under 8. No pets. Swimming, tennis, and trout fishing on grounds. Golf, bicycles, riding, snowshoeing, Alpine and xc skiing nearby. Rodney, Brill and Ione Williams, Innkeepers.

Directions: From I-91, take Brattleboro Exit 2 and travel on Vt. Rte. 9 west to Vt. Rte. 100. Proceed north 5 mi. to inn. Or, take US 7 north to Bennington, then Rte. 9 east to Vt. Rte. 100 and proceed north 5 mi. to inn.

INN ON THE COMMON
Craftsbury Common, Vermont

There are so many exciting new developments at this inn since the 1977 edition that I had better provide an overview of it, and then go into details.

The village of Craftsbury Common was founded in 1789 and was for a long time the northernmost part of New England occupied by settlers. Many of the original buildings still stand around the Common. The buildings of the Inn on the Common which were constructed in the early 1800s are graceful examples of Federal architecture. There are antiques throughout, generously combined

with all the modern comforts. Each guest bedroom is individually decorated and is supplied with fresh flowers or plants, extra pillows and terry cloth bathrobes.

At dinner, guests sit at two oval tables, one hosted by Michael Schmitt, and the other hostessed by Penny Schmitt. Meals are served only to inn guests. Penny supervises the dinner, which sometimes includes fresh rainbow and brook trout, available only when the postmaster goes fishing! Breakfasts are quite elaborate with many types of omelets—cheese, herb, mushroom, onion, tomato, or an "everything omelet" which is all of the above.

A new swimming pool will be ready for summer of 1978, and there is an excellent tennis court; real "cutthroat" croquet is part of the fun, and plans are being made for lawn bowling. Many guests who originally came to this inn for one or two-night stays are now scheduling visits of four or five nights and even more.

So much for the overview. Now, here is what Penny Schmitt has to say about the exciting new developments: "In the building across the street which you saw in its early renovated state in June, 1977, we will have five guest bedrooms, a sitting room, and a kitchen which can be rented with one or two of the bedrooms as a housekeeping suite. We furnished it with both antiques and modern, and commissioned the stained glass windows on the first floor from a very talented craftsman from Hyde Park, Vermont. His wife made all our quilts and coverlets. Three of the new guest bedrooms are bed-sitting rooms, and two of these have Jotul fireplace stoves. The wallpapers are mostly traditional Williamsburg.

"We plan on opening our very posh craft shop in May, 1978. It will be called the 'Common Market'—Crafts. We have already lined up a group of very talented local craftspersons.

We will spend much of next spring grooming and beautifying our grounds, a chore which we adore. One of the greatest pleasures we have in the inn is surrounding people with beauty and watching them respond. After hours on your knees in the flowerbed you can feel pretty grubby, but it is all worth it when someone admires the flowers, the feeling of the place, and the care we put into it."

"Our good friend, Russell Spring and his family and employees have started a super, but low-key, touring center which will be our guests' facilities, and will certainly appeal to skiers of varying expertise from beginner to racer-in-training. The Center is about two miles from the inn and is the antithesis of the sort of fakery that is creeping into the xc business. I think that visitors will be able to learn what ski touring is really all about in quiet, wild, unspoiled nature. For the good-to-expert skier, there is a trail over Eden Mountain that is unforgettable — it literally seems to be out of this world."

There is much good news from The Inn on the Common.

INN ON THE COMMON, Craftsbury Common, Vt. 05827; 802-586-9619. An 11-room inn in a remote Vermont town 35 mi. from Montpelier. Shared baths. Modified American plan omits lunch. Breakfast and dinner served to houseguests only. Open from May 15 to Oct. 20 and Dec. 20 to Mar. 31. Attended pets allowed. Swimming, tennis, croquet, lawn bowling, xc skiing, snowshoeing, on grounds. Golf, tennis, swimming, sailing, horseback riding, canoeing, fishing, xc, and downhill skiing, skating, hiking, and nature walks nearby. Michael and Penny Schmitt, Innkeepers.

Directions: From Exit 7, I-89N, take Rte. 2 east to Rte. 14 north until 8 mi. north of Hardwick. Watch for marked right hand turn, go 2 mi. to inn. From Canada and points north, use Exit 26 on I-91 and follow Rte. 58 W to Irasburg. Then Rte. 14 southbound 12 mi. to marked left turn, 3 mi. to inn.

KEDRON VALLEY INN
South Woodstock, Vermont

"I was born right across the street," said Paul Kendall. "In fact, Barbara and I are two homegrown products who have never left home." We were sitting on the porch of the Kedron Valley Inn

waving at the occasional cars that make the big bend out in front. In the quiet we could hear the Kedron Brook blending with the sounds of the early evening bird calls. I got up to take a look at the box elder tree which is very rare even for that part of the country. Paul said that he was afraid that it only had a couple of more years.

We rocked our way through the twilight as the green of the mountains on both sides melted into the deep blue of the night sky.

The inn, as well as the annex, is built of beautiful dark red brick with very white mortar. Paul told me that the annex was for many years the store and post office in South Woodstock. The old safe is still built into the wall. The inn has operated continuously since 1822.

Paul and Barbara and their two active sons are living symbols of the new Vermont — young people with knowledge and spirit that see great opportunities in preserving the Vermont of yesteryear while at the same time providing modern, sensible conveniences which make it even more attractive. The KVI is tucked away in a mountain fastness near Calvin Coolidge's birthplace. However, Paul and Barbara are not content to get by on pastoral charm and Yankee reputation alone. They take pains to serve good food, keep spotless rooms and continually look for ways to improve the inn. I believe it works because some of their guests make close to a summer of it. I wish I could.

I wrote the above paragraphs in the 1968 edition of this book, and everything is true now except that there is a great deal more going on at the Kedron Valley Inn. Besides lounging near cozy firesides, the winter activities include paddle tennis, ice skating, cross-country skiing, and sleigh rides on the premises, and downhill skiing at several nearby ski areas.

Last year the inn became involved in a very old Vermont tradition, that of maple sugaring. Much of this is done in the old-fashioned way using a team of horses with a sled for gathering the sap. Chip Kendall, who is now 20, is in charge of the sugaring operation. Over 600 gallons were produced last year.

On my last visit, during the first snowfall of the season, the inn never looked better. The porches had been rebuilt and all the wood-trim painted, and the box elder tree still seemed to be doing very well. Besides the two sleeping rooms with fireplaces, there are three more sleeping rooms with old-fashioned woodburning stoves which add additional heat and more atmosphere. The inn is now open on a year-round basis.

The past ten years have seen continuing development of opportunities for summer time diversions: one is the acre-and-a-half pond with a sandy beach and diving board, and another is the Kedron Valley Stables, with mounts for beginners and experts, private lessons, wagon rides, picnic trail rides, and horse trekking.

Here's a comment from a most recent visitor: "This is the nicest inn we experienced on our trip east. Paul and Barbara Kendall are warm and gracious hosts and the spirit of the inn was lively and gay. There were people always about, playing the piano, singing, doing jigsaw puzzles, kindling a fire, and meeting other people. I especially loved the stables. The horses, all in fine condition, were well-behaved and delightful in every way. Our guided trail ride through the Green Mountains was one of the real highlights of our trip. Thank you for that recommendation."

KEDRON VALLEY INN, Rte. 106, South Woodstock, Vt. 05071; 802-457-1473. A 34-room rustic resort-inn, 5 mi. south of Wood-stock. Near Killington, Mt. Ascutney ski areas. European plan and Modified American plan offered. Breakfast, lunch, and dinner served daily. Closed Sunday evenings November to May. Closed Christmas Day. Swimming, riding, sleigh rides, carriage rides, paddle tennis, hiking, and xc skiing on the grounds. Tennis, golf, and bicycles nearby. Paul and Barbara Kendall, Innkeepers.

Directions: Take Exit 1 from I-89 and follow Rte. 4 to Woodstock. Proceed south on Rte. 106 for 5 miles. Or, take Exit 8 from I-91 and follow Rte. 131 for 8 mi. Proceed North on Rte. 106 for 12 mi.

NORTH HERO HOUSE
North Hero, Vermont

"Do you realize," said Caroline Sorg, "that you have been coming here every summer since 1972?"

I staggered back in mock surprise and nearly tumbled off the

end of the float boat which Roger, Caroline, and I were using for a short excursion in the bay waters of Lake Champlain in front of the North Hero House. "1972," I echoed, "it seems only a couple of years ago I drove up and found Lynn and David actually playing hide-and-seek with some of the guests' children."

David, who is now taller than his mother and almost as tall as his father, withered me with a glance. He is accomplished in all of the summer sports at the inn, including sailing, snorkeling, swimming, fishing, water skiing, bicycling, mountain climbing, and horseback riding. Both he and his sister Lynn, who works in the dining room, are very much involved with innkeeping.

The North Hero House is maintained for twelve weeks every summer by Roger, a dentist from Flemington, New Jersey and his family. Roger had spent several summers on the island as a boy, and even in those early days, dreamed of becoming the owner of the North Hero House.

Almost from the very beginning, I realized that the Sorgs were builders and renovators. In 1972, the main building of the inn had undergone a complete renovation and some bedrooms on the second floor had been converted into bathrooms. Each year I would find something new and exciting on the drawing board, and in the year following it would become a reality. Most recently, for example, waterside lodging rooms have been created in some beautiful old buildings across the road next to the lake.

For 1978, if all goes according to schedule, the newest reality will be a special addition to the dining room.

Caroline described it: "It will be a large open greenhouse area decorated with lovely plants, flowers, and sculptured copper fountains. We're not just adding more tables, we're trying to make everything more comfortable for our guests. It will be the "no smoking portion" of the dining room.

"Our summer garden has reached a new high in productivity. In addition to carrots, beans, lettuce, squash, spinach, Swiss chard, red and white cabbage, cucumbers, zucchini, beets, potatoes, corn, and radishes, we had a 'first' with eggplant; many guests enjoy helping with the picking."

At this point Roger, who had been unusually silent for the past ten minutes, announced he was going to go waterskiing. I remarked that we would probably have to go back to shore to get the launch, as I had seen Mr. Goodspeed towing some skiers around the bay earlier. "Oh, we won't have to get the speedboat, we'll use this boat," he retorted.

"You mean you are going to go waterskiing behind the float boat!" I exclaimed. "You'll barely get up out of the water."

"I'll tell you what, I've got two pairs of skis; why don't you put on a pair, and we'll see if you're any better at waterskiing than you are at tennis. Come on, I'll show you where we take all of our guests snorkeling."

Postscript: The boat went much too fast for me, and not only is Roger a better tennis player that I am, he is also a better waterskier. Then, to add insult to injury, he offered to give me lessons.

NORTH HERO HOUSE, Champlain Islands, North Hero, Vt. 05474; 802-372-8237. A 22-room New England resort-inn on North Hero Island in Lake Champlain, 35 mi. north of Burlington and 65 mi. south of Montreal. Modified American plan. Luncheon a la carte only. Breakfast and dinner served daily to travelers. Open from late June to Labor Day. No pets. Swimming, fishing, boating, water-skiing, ice house game room, sauna, bicycles, and tennis on grounds. Horseback riding and golf nearby. Roger and Caroline Sorg, Innkeepers.

Directions: Travel north from Burlington on I-89, take Exit 17 (Champlain Islands) and drive north on Island Rte. 2 to North Hero. From N.Y. Thruway (87 north), take Exit 39 at Plattsburg and follow signs "Ferry to Vermont." Upon leaving ferry, turn left to Rte. 2, then left again to North Hero. Inn is 15 min. from ferry dock on Rte. 2.

Just before going to press in 1977, John Carroll of Rabbit Hill Inn called to explain that he had just sold the inn to Ed and Nancy

Ludwig. "I know it is your policy to give new innkeepers a chance to find themselves," he said, "but they are lovely people, so do pay them a visit, please."

In the meantime, although Rabbit Hill was not included in the 1977 edition, I received several letters from readers traveling with the 1976 or even earlier edition of the book, who reassured me that the Ludwigs were indeed doing a wonderful job and that Rabbit Hill was still a splendid country inn experience.

I paid two visits to the Ludwigs; one in June, 1977 to get acquainted with Ed and Nancy, and a second in November to learn how things were progressing and what changes they have made. This is the story of my second visit.

RABBIT HILL INN
Lower Waterford, Vermont

What a wonderful late fall day to be visiting any New England country inn! It was the Saturday after Thanksgiving and as I turned off Route 5 in East Barnett and went over the Connecticut River into the birch woods, there was a light sprinkling of snow and the thermometer was in the 20's. After a short drive in the deepening dusk, I could see in the distance the lights of Pucker Street in Lower Waterford and there, once again, was the beautiful church spire pointing into the Vermont sky. Across the road, the Doric columns of Rabbit Hill Inn stood as stalwartly as they have since its construction in the 1830s.

I scurried up the slate walk and burst in the front door leaving the swirling snow behind me. "Welcome, to Rabbit Hill Inn," said Nancy Ludwig, and a fine welcome it was, with the wonderful aroma of the evening meal wafting from the kitchen, a crackling fire in the fireplace, and the hum of conversation among some of the guests who were already getting acquainted.

Ed Ludwig showed me up to my room which was spacious, with a melodeon in one corner and a fireplace. (There are five bedrooms with fireplaces.) The view of the Presidential Range of the White Mountains was spectacular.

I hurried downstairs as soon as possible to enjoy dinner and the rest of the evening with the Ludwigs and to share their enthusiasm about innkeeping.

"We've only been married about three years," said Nancy putting her hand on Ed's arm. "It was the second marriage for each of us, and we now have a total of ten children, including two Richards and two Lauras.

"Her Richard," said Ed, "has drawn the pictures on the menu and brochures, and my Richard is in hotel school. There are several assorted offspring, most of whom are involved in some way in the inn operation, working in the kitchen or waiting on tables. We are all having a wonderful time."

Rabbit Hill Inn has taken on some new dimensions in the past year. For one thing, cross-country ski and walking trails have been developed. The course includes six waterfalls and three bridges and winds in and among the hemlocks and other evergreens. "We have ten acres of our own," said Ed, "and have permission to use our neighbors' land. The trails go to the top of the mountain. By the way, another thing that we have done is to provide rental snowshoes. We think that this is an upcoming sport. The Briar Patch next door, which used to be a gift shop, is now used as our ski shop. We are also adapting it for parties and meetings. We put a Franklin stove in there which keeps it nice and warm."

I also learned that the Ludwigs have been spending a lot of time at antique shops and sales in pursuit of their refurbishing and redecorating program.

"I believe that one of the big changes your readers will note is that we have changed our buffet night from Saturday to Sunday," explained Ed, handing me a menu. "We will continue to have our Sunday brunch, which is always popular, and then serve from the menu the rest of the week with a special on each night. Steve Cobb is still our chef.

"Tuesday is something special," said Nancy. "We are closed to travelers for dinner, but during the winter we'll serve our own inn guests. We all sit down together. There is no menu, it's just family-style. We think it is a great deal of fun."

Among the hearty offerings on the regular menu are Barre Pike beefsteak, Vermont Drovers Journey End steak, veal Waterford, scallops Arcadia, Linden lemon sole and Comstock corn-cob smoked Vermont ham. Desserts include homemade gingerbread and a bread pudding with a strawberry hard sauce, which has been in Nancy's family for years. A neighbor makes the pies, so consequently they are known as "Gladys' Pies."

Yes, things are humming in every possible way at Rabbit Hill Inn. Ed, Nancy, and the ten assorted siblings are having a wonderful time and so, I am happy to report, are the guests.

RABBIT HILL INN, Pucker St., Lower Waterford, Vt. 05848; 802-748-9766. A 20-room country inn halfway between St. Johnsbury and Littleton on Rte. 18. Marvelous panoramic view of the Presidential Range of the White Mountains. Within convenient driving distance of many Vermont and N.H. natural and artistic attractions. European plan. Lodgings and meals available everyday to inn guests. Dining room closed to transients every Tuesday, December 24, 25. Snowshoeing, xc skiing, hiking, swimming on grounds. Picnicking, tennis, golf, hunting, nearby. Ed and Nancy Ludwig, Innkeepers.

Directions: From I-93, exit at Rte. 18, proceed north 7 mi. to inn. From I-91, exit at St. Johnsbury, follow Rte. 2 east 3 mi. to Rte. 18 south. 7 mi. to inn.

THE VILLAGE INN
Landgrove, Vermont

"We used to be called the J-Bar Lodge," said Kathy Snyder. "We changed the name to the Village Inn a number of years ago because we felt it was more like our real character. It is hard to realize that we have been here 17 years, although the inn has been here since 1939. The main activity used to be skiing. However, I think you could call us an all-season resort-inn. We just love families with children."

When I paid my first visit to this inn there were many active young people around, most of them in the Rafter Room, which has a big fireplace, log beams across the low ceiling, and plenty of games like ping pong, skittles, and bumper pool.

In winter, the outdoor-minded guests can enjoy downhill skiing at five major areas nearby, plus cross-country skiing, snowshoeing, and sledding in the woods and fields right behind the inn. There is also an ice skating pond.

Summertime activities at the inn include excellent tennis courts, a 9-hole pitch-and-putt golf course, a heated swimming pool, hiking trails, volleyball, and fishing.

"One of the most fascinating diversions is the Alpine Slide at Bromley," explained Jay. "It doesn't require any special skill and anybody can enjoy it, regardless of age. You take the chairlift up the mountain and then ride a sled with wheels on a chute that whizzes through hairpin turns and around curves. You can control the speed yourself."

"Families enjoy us because there are so many things to do in the mountains," said Kathy. "There is horseback riding, indoor tennis, lots of summer theatre, auctions, musical festivals, lots of country fairs, barn dances, and even church suppers."

Guest rooms at the Village Inn span a wide variety of tastes. Because the inn is family-oriented, the house has several rooms that would be adaptable for whole families as well as bunk rooms. There are also newer rooms in a recently completed new section which are furnished in a more contemporary style. Lodgings include a hearty breakfast.

To round out the family feeling, Jay and Kathy have two young daughters, both of whom are active participants in just about everything at the inn, and Jay's father and mother are also involved. Lois MacArthur has been in charge of the kitchen at the inn ever since the Snyders arrived on the scene and there is a great deal of emphasis on Vermont home cooking. There are dishes like baked potatoes, roast beef, strawberry shortcake, leg of lamb, summer salads, apple and blueberry pies, and the like.

I wrote about the Village Inn for the first time in the 1977 edition, and in August of that year, I received a letter from a man in Boston who said in part: "I recently spent several days at the Village Inn in Landgrove with my wife and three-and-a-half-year-old child.

The facilities, food, and accommodations were excellent. The setting was beautiful and the entire Snyder family was delightful. We appreciated the Village Inn because of all the inns we have visited, it proved to be one of the most hospitable and appropriate for both adults and children."

THE VILLAGE INN, Landgrove, Vt., 05148; 802-824-6673. A 21-room rustic resort-inn in the mountains of central Vermont, approximately 4½ mi. from Weston and Londonderry. Lodgings include breakfast. Breakfast, lunch, and dinner served to travelers during the summer except Wed. dinner. Open from Nov. 23 to April 15; July 1 to Oct. 17. Children most welcome. No pets. Swimming, tennis, volleyball, pitch and putt, xc skiing, fishing on grounds. Downhill skiing, riding, indoor tennis, paddle tennis, antiquing, backroading, Alpine slide, golf, summer theatre nearby. Jay and Kathy Snyder, Innkeepers.

Directions: Coming north on I-91 take Exit 2 at Brattleboro, follow Rte. 30 to Rte. 11 and turn right. Turn left off Rte. 11 at signs for Village Inn. Bear left in Village of Peru. Coming north on Rte. 7 turn west at Manchester on Rte. 11 to Peru. Turn left at signs for Village Inn. Bear left in Village of Peru.

Mid Atlantic

Grandview Farm, *Huntsville*

ONTARIO

TORONTO

LAKE ONTARIO

Clarkson House, *Lewiston*

Oban Inn, *Niagara-On-The-Lake*

Asa Ransom House, *Clarence*

Holloway Hou *East Bloomfiel*

Glen Iris Inn, *Castile*

LAKE ERIE

NEW

PENNSYLV

INTERSTATE 80

Tavern, *New Wilmington*

PITTSBURGH

PENNSYLVANIA TPK.

Century Inn, *Scenery Hill*

Hickory Bridge Farm, *Orrtann*

Fairfield Inn, *Fairfield*

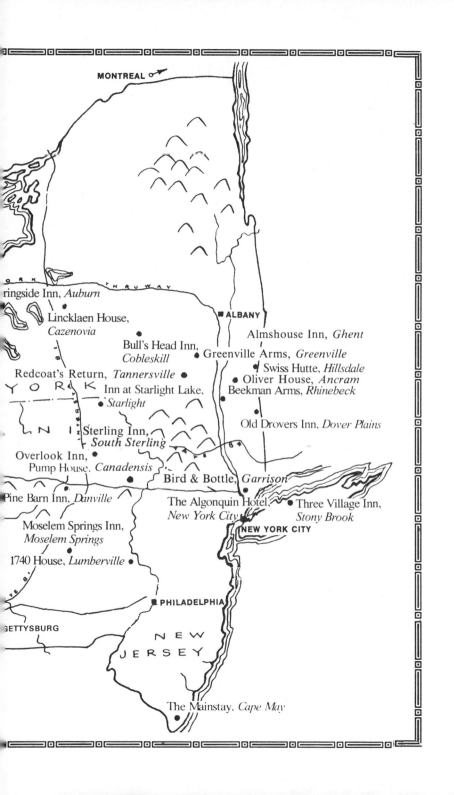

MONTREAL

ringside Inn, *Auburn*

Lincklaen House,
Cazenovia

ALBANY

Bull's Head Inn,
Cobleskill

Almshouse Inn, *Ghent*

Greenville Arms, *Greenville*

Swiss Hutte, *Hillsdale*

Redcoat's Return, *Tannersville*

Oliver House, *Ancram*

Y O R K   Inn at Starlight Lake,
Starlight

Beekman Arms, *Rhinebeck*

Old Drovers Inn, *Dover Plains*

Sterling Inn,
South Sterling

Overlook Inn,
Pump House, *Canadensis*

Bird & Bottle, *Garrison*

Pine Barn Inn, *Danville*

The Algonquin Hotel,
New York City

Three Village Inn,
Stony Brook

NEW YORK CITY

Moselem Springs Inn,
Moselem Springs

1740 House, *Lumberville*

PHILADELPHIA

GETTYSBURG

N E W

J E R S E Y

The Mainstay, *Cape May*

New Jersey

THE MAINSTAY
Cape May, New Jersey

The October weather in Cape May was mellow and soft. I was in the cupola, hidden away from the world, or at least hidden away from a very small portion of the world that was enjoying Sunday morning breakfast on the side veranda of the Mainstay. Sue Carroll promised me that the view from the top of the inn was well worth a climb up the stairs and the ladder. Here I was three stories above the town, but still not as high as some of the waving tree tops in the yard of this beautiful Italianate Victorian villa.

"It was built in 1856 by wealthy Southern planters as an elegant gambling club," explained Sue to the people who were on the daily house tour. "The first operator of the club, a Mississippi showboat minstrel, employed a lady to rock on the front porch to watch for the police. If she rocked violently, the gamblers inside would quickly stash their evidence and when the police arrived they would be having a harmless musicale."

After such a flamboyant beginning, the house was sold in 1896 to a sedate Philadelphia family who added the back wing and entertained some of the great and near-great of Philadelphia society during the many years that followed.

Today, the Mainstay is a lovely guest house in one of the most unusual remaining Victorian environments, the town of Cape May, New Jersey. Tom Carroll had pointed out to me that there were over 600 Victorian buildings in Cape May in various stages of restoration and preservation. He was well informed because he is Chairman of the Planning Board.

"Of course there is a lot more to Cape May besides Victoriana," he said. "Our summer population swells from 2500 to 60,000 and a great many of these people come here to enjoy the fine beaches and our amusement area."

The total Victorian aspect of the Mainstay has been exceptionally well preserved with the furnishings, many of which are original pieces custom-built for the house. There are also many hanging plants. "This was a real big fad back in the Victorian days," explained Sue. "They had plants everywhere."

The drawing room has much fringe, knickknacks and extra decorative touches. Upstairs there is a copper bathtub framed in wood like the one in Washington Irving's home. In addition to the ten-foot mirrors, ornately carved headboards, and marble-top dressers, there are some most unusual features. Under some of the beds are chamber pots that roll out on wooden trays, and other beds have the original mosquito nets which attached to small pulleys in the ceilings.

The only meal served at the Mainstay is breakfast, which is offered in warm weather on the broad veranda and on cool mornings in the Grand Dining Room. The house tour is conducted every day at 3:30 p.m. for both in-house guests and interested visitors. Everyone joins in for tea after the tour.

Overnight accommodations vary. Rooms are named for famous Americans who visited Cape May, and many of them are quite large and are furnished in ostentatious Victorian splendor. There are also several little cozy rooms in the new wing.

Well, I had whiled away the better part of an hour in the Mainstay cupola and now the Muse in me was being overcome by the thought of the quiche that I had seen Sue preparing for breakfast. So, I went back down the ladder and the circular staircase and out on the porch, where Tom was busy replenishing the coffee cups of his house guests and answering the innumerable questions that everyone has about this great house.

"You're just in time," he said. "I think we're down to the last piece."

"Oh, don't let him fool you," said Sue. "I have another one in the oven right now."

THE MAINSTAY INN, 635 Columbia Avenue, Cape May, N.J. 08204; 609-884-8690. A 10-room inn in a well preserved Victorian village just one block from the ocean. Modified American plan.

Breakfast served to house guests. Open every day of the year from March to December. No pets. Bicycles on grounds. Boating, swimming, fishing, riding, golf, tennis and hiking nearby. Tom and Sue Carroll, Innkeepers.

Directions: From Philadelphia take the Walt Whitman Bridge to the Atlantic City Expy. Follow the Atlantic City Expy. to exit for Garden State Pkwy., south. Go south on the Pkwy. which ends in Cape May. The Pkwy. becomes Lafayette St.; turn left at first light onto Madison. Proceed 3 blocks and turn right onto Columbia. Proceed 3 blocks to inn on right side.

New York

ALGONQUIN HOTEL
New York, New York

One of my greatest disappointments in recent years was the fact that I was in Italy visiting villas and country houses at the time that the Algonquin Hotel was given a 75th birthday party by their neighbors, the *New Yorker* magazine. This was most appropriate because legend has it that the *New Yorker* was actually brought to life in a room in the Algonquin during the 1920s. The *London Times*, when reporting this incident, said that "it was actually on the third floor during a poker game that Harold Ross, the first editor, borrowed money to start the magazine (after the game)."

I first mentioned the Algonquin in the 1971 edition when I explained that many CIBR readers had felt a real need for a place to stay in New York City. Almost simultaneously, I heard from Andy Anspach, the manager, who invited me to come down to meet him and see the hotel, because he felt it was really a country inn in the city.

Since that time I have received literally countless letters from people who have been kind enough to thank me for pointing out that this rather small hotel is really an ideal place to stay during sojourns in what O. Henry referred to as "Bagdad on the Hudson."

I must say I have had a great deal of fun writing about the Algonquin Hotel. I have described the famous lobby with its paneled pillars and comfortable chairs, where it is fun to sit and people-watch while enjoying a bit of refreshment. I've talked about the bedrooms many times, including my favorite, number 600. I have also told about the time I just couldn't get the television set to go on

and when I called the front desk, they sent up a very accommodating bellman who simply flipped the switch on the wall, and we both had a good laugh. I have even described the room service breakfasts with the most satisfying silver pot of hot chocolate this side of Vienna.

I have also talked about the individuals who make the Algonquin the real country inn that it is — the front desk clerk, doorman, assistant managers and even the friendly man at the magazine counter.

I guess I have told and retold the story of the famous Algonquin Round Table of the 1920s where the "in" literary crowd, including Edna Ferber, George S. Kaufman, Robert Sherwood, Dorothy Parker, Franklin P. Adams, Alexander Wolcott and Marc Connelly shredded everybody else in the literary and theatre world to ribbons almost every day.

I was delighted when the *London Times,* the *Los Angeles Times,* the *New York Daily News, Washington Post, Time Magazine,* "Punch," the London humor magazine not only paid tribute to its history and ambience, but noted that the Algonquin was a very comfortable, family hotel that was really entitled to put on airs, but never does. There was also wonderful coverage by both United Press and Associated Press, and several other distinguished journals. The *New York Daily News* quoted manager Andy Anspach as saying, "We try to be civilized, not just to Laurence Olivier who likes unsalted nuts, or to Daniel Patrick Moynihan, but to your mother when she is in from Dayton or Des Moines."

"Civilized" is one of the best words to describe the Algonquin Hotel today. I wish I had thought of it first.

ALGONQUIN HOTEL, 59 W. 44th St., New York, N.Y. 10036; 212-687-4400. A quiet, conservative 200-room country inn in the heart of Manhattan. Convenient to business, theatres and shopping. European plan. Breakfast, lunch, dinner and late supper buffet served to travelers daily except Sunday dinner. Open year-round. No pets. Very near bus, rail and air transportation. Garage directly opposite entrance, with complimentary parking for weekend visitors arriving after 3 p.m. Fri. or Sat. for minimum 2-night visit. Andrew Anspach. Innkeeper.

Directions: 44th St. is one-way from west to east; 43rd St. from east to west. Garage is accessible from either street.

THE ALMSHOUSE INN
Ghent, New York

The menu said, "The Almshouse Inn Thanksgiving Dinner, November 24th." It was indeed Thanksgiving, and I had made the short drive from the Berkshires to Ghent and was now joining the other guests at the Almshouse in celebrating this most American of holidays.

Two of the four owners, Dr. Cullen Burris and Robin Litton, made me feel welcome immediately and when I asked about Shirley Burris and Joe Leon, Cullen explained that Shirley was in the kitchen doing the finishing touches on the turkey and that Joe had seen me coming from the window and had gone to fetch something he wanted to show me.

Almost on cue, Joe returned, and said with a big smile, "Have you seen this?" He handed me a copy of the program from "The Merchant," a play in which he had taken over the lead role for Zero Mostel, and which had closed a few days earlier in New York. The playbill biography mentioned the fact that he was one of the four owners of the Almshouse, and that it is included in *Country Inns and Back Roads.* "They're reading about you all over Manhattan," he said.

It was great fun to be back at this rather elegant country inn which at one time was the county poorhouse. Groups of expectant diners were already gathering in the sitting rooms and parlors, and

there was a feeling of festivity in the air as we waited for the single sitting at 5 p.m.

The two dining rooms are quite different in character; the Oak Room is beautifully furnished and paneled with a traditional air, and the Garden Room is done all in black and white—very contemporary in design, with a wallpaper of exotic birds with long tails.

The dinner started with avocado Grand Duke which was a perfectly ripened avocado half, stuffed with crabmeat and small shrimp seasoned with lime juice, and served on a glass plate. Homemade corn muffins and a poppy seed roll came next.

I was then invited to go to the buffet, which was a horseshoe-shaped table in the Oak Room, where Cullen was carving a beautiful, delicately-browned turkey, and serving generous slices of white or dark meat. The table was laden with handsome bowls of both traditional bread dressing and a sausage and cornbread dressing, giblet gravy, mashed potatoes, and glazed sweet ptoatoes, creamed onions, and baby brussel sprouts, and my favorite chopped cranberry and orange relish, and a molded cranberry sauce. Joe and Robin were cordial hosts, urging us to return for second helpings.

But I was glad I'd saved room for dessert—pumpkin pie with a light touch of cognac in the whipped cream, mince tart with a hard sauce, or chocolate cake. I had at least two bites of each.

After dinner, Shirley, who had prepared all this, came out to greet her guests wearing a long gold and brown metallic knit dress looking very svelte and completely relaxed, as if she had been presiding at the head of the table. She and Cullen visited each table, shook hands with everybody and wished them a Happy Thanksgiving.

Following dinner, the guests dispersed to the various sitting rooms and parlors where there were continuing reminders of the holidays, including bowls of popcorn. In the front parlor a young man played the handsome grand piano which was stacked with sheet music, including the collected works of Scott Joplin, and a book of great songs from Broadway Shows.

Lodgings at the Almshouse include breakfast. Dinner is served at 8 p.m. by reservation only. There is one entree an evening and only thirty people are served.

The only bathroom I've ever seen with an open fireplace is in one of the three lodging rooms. These are frequently spoken for well in advance, so, as with dinner, reservations are not only advisable but usually mandatory.

I'd like to have Thanksgiving dinner at every one of the inns in this book, and now I only have 169 more to go!

THE ALMSHOUSE INN, Rte. 66, Ghent, N.Y. 12075; 518-392-5242. An elegant 3-room inn, 30 mi. southeast of Albany, N.Y., and approximately 30 min. from the Berkshires. European Plan. Lodgings include breakfast. Dinner served at 8 p.m. by reservation except Mondays and Tuesdays. (Inn is open for overnight guests on these days. Closed Christmas and probably during March. Sunday Brunch, 1 p.m. No pets. 7 mi. from Lindenwald, home of Martin Van Buren; 30 min. from Tanglewood, 90 min. from Saratoga, summer theatres in Chatham, N.Y., and Stockbridge, Mass. Tennis, swimming, riding, skiing nearby. Dr. & Mrs. B. Cullen Burris, Joseph Leon, Robin Litton, Innkeepers.

Directions: Follow Taconic Parkway to Rte. 203, Chatham. Stay on Rte. 203, 2 mi. to intersection with Rte. 66. Turn left on 66, proceed 2 mi. to inn.

ASA RANSOM HOUSE
Clarence, New York

The letter was typical of several I received during 1977 from readers who stayed at the Asa Ransom House: "A delightful surprise, we didn't realize that such a wonderful, old place existed near Buffalo. Here we were treated as personal guests. Our bedroom was really beautiful, furnished with old pieces and decorated with exquisite taste. The bathroom was one of the prettiest and cleanest I have ever seen. The dining room was crowded, but our table was kept for us until we arrived and then we sat down to one of the finest meals I have had for years. The next morning a complimentary breakfast

was served because we were remaining overnight. Everything seems to be homemade and from organically-grown produce. We intend to return."

As long as I am at it, let me quote still another reader's letter: "Driving down the main street of Clarence at dusk on a December day my spirit was brightened when I saw the warm glow of the lights of the inn reflected on the snow. I could see through the windows that everyone was thoroughly enjoying themselves. Upon entering I was greeted by Judy Lenz who showed me to my bedroom and gave me a bowl of fruit. My first night was a real treat at dinner with a most succulent smoked corn beef with a raisin applesauce. Lots of fresh bread and rolls were served by a pretty waitress, who turned out to be Judy's mother.

"An evening by the fire near the Franklin stove and a good book was a change of pace (without television) and most enjoyable. While I was reading one of the waitresses asked if she could bring me some tea or coffee."

There are four totally different bedrooms in this delightful inn in western New York State; each has a name to suit its own particular personality. An 1825 Cannonball double bed proudly presides in the Red Room, and the Blue Room with its canopied bed is very popular among honeymooning couples. The larger Gold Room is outfitted with twin iron and brass beds. This room has originally-designed stenciling on the upper walls, with coordinated patchwork coverlets whose theme is old-fashioned American hospitality.

The gift shop is literally a "village of gifts" in a single room, and the herb garden thrived its first year with over 50 herbs which are used in many of the inn recipes.

The unique menu also includes the Asa Ransom News, which provides interesting historical and gastronomic observations. Besides an impressive assortment of main dishes, such as fresh Boston schrod, seafood souffle, and country inn veal, the dinner includes steaming soup from the kettle, tossed garden greens, fresh vegetables, and freshly-baked bread, and muffins.

The Asa Ransom House is closed Friday and Saturdays because of the religious beliefs of Bob and Judy Lenz who are members of the World Wide Church of God. Incidentally, one of the dining rooms of the inn has been set aside for people who do not smoke.

ASA RANSOM HOUSE, Rte. 5, Clarence, N.Y. 14031; 716-759-2315. A 4-room village inn approximately 15 mi. from Buffalo near the Albright Knox Art Gallery, the Studio Arena Theatre and Niagara Falls. European plan. Dinner served Mondays through Thursdays, 4:30 p.m. to 9 p.m.; Sundays, 12:30 to 8 p.m. Closed Fridays and Saturdays. No pets. Tennis, golf, fishing and swimming nearby. Bob and Judy Lenz, Innkeepers.

Directions: From the N.Y. Thruway east (Exit 48A — Pembroke) Turn right to Rte. 5 and proceed for 11 mi. to Clarence. From the N.Y. thruway west (Exit 49) turn left on Rte. 78, 1 mi. to Rte. 5 and then proceed on Rte. 5 for 5½ mi. From the east via Rte. 20, just east of Lancaster, N.Y. turn right on Ransom Rd., go to end and turn left.

BEEKMAN ARMS
Rhinebeck, New York

"I've heard lots of explanations for the name Rhinebeck or 'Rynbeck'," said Chuck LaForge as we sat down for dinner in the low-ceilinged Tap Room of the Beekman Arms, "but recently I learned that on a ship coming to this country with Peter Stuyvesant, came a German, William Beckman, who originally came from the Rhine Valley. His son received a grant of land here from Queen Anne of England in 1703 and he named the property Rhinebeck. I guess the move from the word 'Beck' to 'Beckman' could have been the result of a clerical error in later years."

Sue LaForge, delicately balancing a succulent portion of veal marsala on her fork, took a different attitude. "You know, Chuck, there are quite a few discrepancies in that story, including the exact date of the arrival of Peter Stuyvesant in New Amsterdam. There are many people who say that 'Rhinebeck' literally means 'back of the Rhine'." I saw the twinkle in her eye and I knew that she was trying to get some kind of response from Chuck.

156

"Well, everything around here is so old and influenced by local versions that I suppose it is impossible to really pin it down," he countered. "We do know that an ancestor of this building was built in 1700, and that around 1766 Arent Traphagen built a two-story building here with walls three feet thick out of 8 x 12-inch oak beams and floor planks 14 inches wide and almost 2 inches think."

It is this kind of historical speculation, plus the well-preserved ancient building, that makes the Beekman Arms one of the most visited country inns in the United States. On this particular occasion, Chuck, Sue and I were celebrating the fact that the entire Tap Room and Lobby had been completely refurnished with handsome country furniture of carefully-seasoned woods, planed by hand and then joined with skill, and finished with natural ingredients. There were impressive chairs, tables, cabinets, hutches and smaller pieces which blended in beautifully with the panelled walls and ceilings. "These are made by the Waterwheel Woodworks," said Chuck. "They are located over the hill in Pine Plains, New York. They do beautiful work, and we feel that it helps to preserve the antiquity of the building."

I buttered a piece of the freshly-baked bread and continued to make inroads into my roast duckling, which is served in a Bing cherry sauce. While Chuck and Sue continued their exciting dissertations, I became preoccupied with a family of seven eating at a big table just across from us. There were two very attractive teenage daughters and some younger children obviously out for a family outing and having a wonderful time.

The village of Rhinebeck grew up around Traphagen's inn and today is one of the loveliest in the Hudson Valley within an easy driving distance of a great many restored homes and mansions. Today, one of the diversions is visiting the firehouse gift shop which is located right next door to the inn and, along with other shops, is housed in what used to be the old Rhinebeck firehouse.

As we finished our dessert, Chuck lit a corn cob pipe similar to those that have been hanging on the heavy beams since the mid-18th century, and said, "I'd like to say a few words in defense of William Beckman and Peter Stuyvesant. After all, so many arguments have been held in this inn we might as well continue the tradition."

BEEKMAN ARMS, Rhinebeck, N.Y. 12572; 914-876-7077. A 13-room village inn with an adjacent 4-room guest house, 1 mi. from Amtrak Station at Rhinecliff. Short drive to F.D.R. Library and Home in Hyde Park. European plan. Lunch and dinner served to travelers daily. Closed Christmas. Open year-round. Golf nearby. Charles LaForge, Innkeeper.

Directions: From N.Y. Thruway, take Exit 19, cross Rhinecliff Bridge and pick up Rte. 199 south to Rte. 9. Proceed south on Rte. 9 to middle of village. From Taconic Pkwy. exit at Rhinebeck and follow Rte. 199 west 11 mi. to Rte. 308 into village.

BIRD AND BOTTLE INN
Garrison, New York

It was an autumn dusk. I was crossing the Bear Mountain Bridge, a thin silver link over the Hudson where the mountains and the river join to make a moody Washington Irving atmosphere. A few minutes earlier, I had crossed this same river from Manhattan to New Jersey via the George Washington Bridge, and then turned north on the Palisades Parkway, stopping for a moment at one of the viewpoints to gaze at the New York side of the river. Tom Noonan had explained that this was really the fast way to come from Manhattan, although it involves crossing the river twice.

"The Palisades Parkway eliminates the traffic flow," he said, "and after you cross the Bear Mountain Bridge follow 9-D north into Route 403 and then up Route 9. You will see the Bird and Bottle sign."

Just a few minutes later I was sitting in the comfortable bay window seat at the B&B with Tom and Nancy Noonan and both of them were bursting with news.

"First, I am delighted to announce that Nancy and I are the sole owners of the Bird and Bottle."

"Yes," joined in Nancy, "I know exactly how Phil and Peggy Read at the Jared Coffin House felt when they bought their beautiful inn. There's something about being the owners that's such a great feeling."

"Our second bit of news," said Tom, "is something I know is going to make you very happy."

"Oh, let me tell him," said Nancy. "In your 1978 edition you'll be able to tell everybody that lodging rooms will be available. We will start with one, which I am sure will be ready by Memorial Day, and add others throughout the year. Eventually there will be four!"

"It's something we've wanted to do for some time," asserted Tom. "Things have been progressing so beautifully that we knew the time had come. Nancy and I are making plans to move out of the inn, and our apartment will be converted into bedrooms. There is a great deal for our overnight guests to enjoy here in the Hudson Valley. Right here in Garrison is the Boscobel Mansion which has been restored to its early 1800s splendor complete with furnishings, garden, and a carriage house. The military academy at West Point is just across the river and Van Cortland Manor at Croton-on-the-Hudson is only a few minutes away."

"Don't forget Phillipsburg Manor in North Tarrytown," said Nancy. "They have an early 18th century gristmill and a two-story stone house. The Franklin D. Roosevelt home and library at Hyde Park and the Vanderbilt Mansion are just to the north of us."

Tom excused himself for a moment and I asked Nancy about the Saturday night prix fixe dinners. "Oh, the've been very well received. The first course is usually a choice of shrimp paté or snails. This is followed by soup and a choice of about ten different entrees. We have several desserts, some of them flamed. I know you like that. It's a funny thing," she went on, "in the midst of all of this Continental cuisine and food preparation at the table, one of the most popular things we have is homemade pumpkin pie and banana nut bread."

It was a beautiful, long, and leisurely evening in the low-ceilinged dining room where the candlelight is reflected in the white napery, silverware, and highly-polished walls. It is interesting to realize that this old building may well have been the scene of some of the plots around Benedict Arnold's defection from the American Revolutionary War.

I bade a reluctant farewell to Tom and Nancy, once again congratulating them on all the new developments, but we all made plans to have a longer visit next time because I would certainly plan to stay overnight.

BIRD AND BOTTLE INN, Garrison, N.Y. 10524; 914-424-3000. A country restaurant rich in antiquity located on Rte. 9, a few miles north of Peekskill, N.Y. A short distance from Boscobel Restoration, U.S. Military Academy at West Point and Sleepy Hollow Restorations. Some lodgings available on Memorial Day 1978 and others throughout the year. Lunch and dinner served Monday through Saturday, dinner all day Sunday. Closed Mondays and Tuesdays during winter. Closed month of January. Thomas and Nancy Noonan, Innkeepers.

Directions: From N.Y.C., cross George Washington Bridge and follow Palisades Pkwy. north to Bear Mtn. Bridge. Cross bridge and travel on Rte. 9D north 4½ mi. to Rte. 403. Proceed on Rte. 403 to Rte. 9, then north on Rte. 9, 4 mi. to inn. From I-84, take Exit 13 and follow Rte. 9 south for 8 mi.

BULL'S HEAD INN
Cobleskill, New York

It was dusk and the clock in front of the Bull's Head showed five o'clock on an early December's evening. The red flame on the torch in front of the inn was already becoming more visible. There was the air of expectancy that seems to precede the Christmas holidays, as some of the Christmas lights were already lit in the Cobleskill stores and shops.

The big door opened as I ventured up the walk. There stood Monty Allen as dapper as ever, with a big smile of welcome. In the background I could see Shirley coming forward.

"Come on in," he said. "We have time before people start arriving to have a little visit. Where have you been traveling recently, Berkshire Traveller?"

It's a funny thing—I hadn't seen Monty and Shirley for almost a year, and yet both of them are so genuinely warm that we started talking as if we'd left off in the middle of a sentence. I explained that I was doing a tour of some of the New York State inns including the Asa Ransom House in Clarence, the Glen Iris in Castile, the Springside Inn in Auburn, and the Lincklaen House in Cazenovia.

"Oh, we've got to get over and see Helen," said Shirley. "It's such a pretty drive on Rte. 20."

Things hadn't changed much at the Bull's Head, except for a few more old farm implements and artifacts, which the Allens' friends had presented to them since my last visit. There was a new hay rake, a lantern and another picture of early Cobleskill. Another thing that brought me right back was the marvelous aroma from the open hearth in the back of the dining room, where Chef Schaeffer was already starting on the beef specialties of the evening. Monty said that the tenderloin with Bordelaise sauce, the filet mignon and the ribs continue to be what people ask for again and again. He indicated these and other beef dishes on the clever wooden menu which has been a feature of the inn.

"I hope you make it clear to your readers that we don't have lodgings here," he said. "We're happy to direct people to where there are some clean, adequate accommodations nearby."

The Bull's Head is a hearty restaurant in the heartland of the rich central New York State farming country. Many visitors find it an interesting experience to visit nearby Howe Caverns as well.

People were now coming in for dinner, and Monty suggested that we order. After all these years of ordering the tenderloin with Bordelaise, I broke precedent and ordered the charcoal broiled filet.

BULL'S HEAD INN, 2 Park Pl., Cobleskill, N.Y. 12043; 518-234-3591. A country restaurant, 5 mi. west of Howe Caverns and 30 mi. from Schenectady. No lodgings. Lunch served Tuesdays through Fridays; dinner served Tuesdays through Saturdays and Sundays from 1-8 p.m. Closed Christmas Day. Monty and Shirley Allen, Innkeepers.

Directions: Restaurant is 40 mi. southwest of Albany on N.Y. Rte. 7.

CLARKSON HOUSE
Lewiston, New York

"American historians," said Marilyn Clarkson, "tend to underscore naval victories and play down the several unsuccessful attempts of the Americans to invade Canada during the War of 1812. The fact is that the English and French united in repelling the invaders from the south, and Canada held the ground across the Niagara River which includes Queenston and Niagara-on-the-Lake."

I was getting this lesson in history at the Clarkson House, a country restaurant, in Lewiston, which is just a few moments from the Lewiston-Queenston Bridge, leading into Canada. I was enjoying one of my most favorite dishes—lamb chops. These were two good sized rib chops, cut in the French style and served with a chilled green salad, baked potato with chives and butter (I could have had sour cream, if I so desired), and chunks of homemade bread.

"On the night of December 19, 1813," Marilyn explained, "Lewiston was burned to the ground by the British; there was only one building left standing. Therefore, I think you can see why the oldest houses in Lewiston date from that event. Our building was one of the first to be constructed after the British left. It was started around 1818.

"The timbers in the original building are mortised and pinned and you will notice that there were no nails used. Those that we have found have square heads and are handmade. These are the original posts and beams, hand-hewn of oak and chestnut. Look at the little adz marks and wormholes. By the way, the chimney is the original chimney."

Bob and Marilyn Clarkson have succeeded in creating a pleasant and historically-oriented atmosphere in which to enjoy good food, here at the Clarkson House. The artifacts and decorations are all part of the aura of New York State during the past 170 years. Paintings on the walls depict local countryside scenes of long ago. The collection of lamps out of western New York State antique shops took me back to the 19th century. On the tables and booths there are old-fashioned kerosene lamps. Among the many fascinating wall trappings, I saw a glove ironer, a mouse trap, a soap mold and several antique implements that I could not identify.

The talk shifted from the War of 1812 to the always agreeable subject of food. Bob explained that he and Marilyn have discovered it is best for them to have a small number of entrees on the menu, prepared in the best possible way. "I think it's interesting that we're so famous for our baked potatoes. I can see that you are enjoying yours.

"Although we have only 22 tables you'd be surprised to know the number of people who dine with us. Reservations are needed almost every evening."

By this time it was the magic moment for the dessert, and I'll admit the choice among cherries jubilee, baked Alaska, a cream puff with hot fudge sauce and hot Dutch apple pie was a severe test.

I chose the apple pie and the War of 1812 faded into the past.

THE CLARKSON HOUSE, 810 Center St., Lewiston, N. Y. 14092; 716-754-4544. A country restaurant, 7 mi. from Niagara Falls and Olde Fort Niagara. No lodgings. Dinner served daily except Mondays. Closed Christmas. Bob and Marilyn Clarkson, Innkeepers.

Directions: From I-90, exit at Lewiston and follow Rte. 104E for 1½ mi. Turn right on Rte. 18F and travel 2 blocks west to restaurant.

GLEN IRIS INN
Castile, New York

Just for the fun of it I checked through back issues of CIBR to see what year I first visited the Glen Iris Inn. It was in the 1972 edition where at this time I learned that Castile really rhymed with "smile" and not "steel." Since that time I have paid many happy visits to this inn which is located in Letchworth State Park in western New York on the 107-foot middle falls on the Genesee River. The wonderful, lyrical sound of the river is ever-present. The nearest point to view the falls is a terrace about 25 steps from the front of the inn. There are several paths leading to other lookout points, however, this is only the beginning.

Letchworth State Park is about 18 miles long and about two miles wide. It follows the course of the Genesee River in what is best described as a miniature Grand Canyon. The full length is traversed by an auto road. There are several different turn-off points with spectacular views that the river has carved in a path through the land on its way north to Lake Ontario. There is not a single bit of commercialism to mar this enchanting experience.

The inn was the former home of William Pryor Letchworth and was built in the early 1800s. The bedrooms are very comfortably furnished and are reached by a twisting, turning staircase of dark chestnut wood that leads all the way to the third floor. Instead of having room numbers, the rooms have the names of trees found in the park. All are furnished in the 19th century style. A modern motel unit is located in a nearby grove for additional overnight guests.

Cora and Peter Pizzutelli, sensitive, nature-loving people, are the innkeepers. Each is deeply devoted to this beautiful inn. The feeling has run in the family, because both their son Peter Jr., and their daughter Paula are very much involved in the inn-keeping business.

Peter is a chef with many years of experience, and the many different dishes that come out of the kitchen are always prepared under his watchful eye.

Cora's area of interest is the ever-growing gift shop within the inn.

The unusual combination of a beautiful country inn located next to a spectacular waterfall in a totally protected state park in an historical section of western New York State attracts large numbers of visitors to the area and to the Glen Iris Inn. Consequently, I cannot emphasize too strongly the advisability of having reservations in advance for either breakfast, lunch, or dinner, and also for lodgings. Cora tells me that every summer they regretfully have to tell people that there is no room in their inn.

I receive much mail from many delightful readers, and one card tells the story very succinctly. It was a color photograph of the Glen Iris Inn with its stately white columns and huge trees. The falls were visible in the background. On it was written, with no signature: "Beautiful place, beautiful scenery, great food."

These are the six words that tell the story of the Glen Iris Inn.

GLEN IRIS INN, Castile, N.Y. 14427; 716-493-2622. A 20-room country inn located at the Middle Falls of the Genesee River in Letchworth State Park. European plan. Breakfast, lunch and dinner served to travelers daily. Open from Easter Sunday to Nov. 6. Footpaths, swimming, and bicycles nearby. Historical sites in Park and spectacular views within walking distance. Peter and Cora Pizzutelli, Innkeepers.

Directions: Inn is located off Rtes. 436, 19A and 39 in Letchworth State Park, 55 mi. from Buffalo and Rochester.

GREENVILLE ARMS
Greenville, New York

The more I thought about it the more I realized there were actually two different aspects to the Greenville Arms. Approaching it from the street in Greenville, it is a typical Victorian country mansion, with several interesting porches, cupolas, gables, and corners. It is well-shaded with tall trees, and beautifully landscaped with bushes and shrubs. I learned that it was built by the Vanderbilts during the 19th century, and that Ruth Stevens is only the third owner. The interior reflects a great deal of this country Victorian feeling. There is a handsome red brick fireplace that runs clear to the ceiling of the sitting room and several different clocks are scattered throughout the inn, each of them with its own history. I also noticed a beautiful chest from eastern Massachusetts with a 1790 date on it.

There are several lodging rooms above stairs. All of these things combined to create a feeling of "hominess." The kitchen is readily accessible from the dining room, and Ruth Stevens is quite apt to be making pies or preparing some of the country dishes for which the inn is well-known.

However, there was a surprise connected with all of this, because behind the inn, beyond a hedge and over a tiny footbridge, is a very large carriage house which has more bedrooms, some with porches, and a recreation room. There is a large, beautiful lawn with a swimming pool, shuffleboard, pingpong, horseshoes, badminton, and lawn bowling.

"Oh, yes, there are all kinds of things to do here," said Ruth. "In the winter there is skiing at Hunter and Windham Mountains, and in the spring we have trout fishing and hiking. There are many historical houses and historic places nearby. In the summer and fall guests can go horseback riding, play golf or spend the day in the mountains if they like."

I could imagine that many of the guests also would enjoy sitting quietly on the front porch or next to the pool, reading a good book, watching the birds or just resting.

Incidentally, in the tradition of the Catskill Mountains, the Greenville Arms has weekly rates which include two meals per day as well as the use of all the sports and recreational equipment on the premises. "The difference in rates is based solely on the type of accommodations desired," explained Ruth. She particularly emphasized the necessity for calling ahead for dinner reservations. During the off season, Ruth will consult with the caller about the main dish.

I had a long conversation with Ruth at a special innkeepers' meeting which was held at the Redcoat's Return in Tannersville, New York which is a relatively short distance from Greenville. At that time I asked her about the guests that were coming from *Country Inns and Back Roads.*

"They are just delightful," she said. "A great many of them come for one night and spend two or even more. They are usually on their way from inn to inn and are so excited about the idea of finding inns like ours in other places. We fill them up on zucchini squash, scalloped potatoes, meat loaf, cabbage salad, cheesecake and our homemade breads and rolls. Most of them leave vowing to come back for a longer stay. We just love Berkshire Travellers!"

GREENVILLE ARMS, Greenville, N.Y. 12083; 518-966-5219. A 20-room country inn with many resort features 20 miles from Catskill, N.Y., on Route 32. Modified American or European plans. Breakfast and dinner served to travelers by reservation only. Open every day; no meals served Thanksgiving and Christmas. Children most welcome; cribs, cots and highchairs available. Pets accommodated in nearby kennels. Pool and lawn sports on grounds. Riding, golf, skiing, hiking, backroading, antiquing nearby. Ruth Stevens, Innkeeper.

Directions: Exit N.Y. Thrwy. at 21B. (Coxsackie-New Baltimore). Turn left on 9W South 2 mi. to traffic light. Turn right on Rte. 81W 13 mi. to Greenville. Turn left at traffic light. Inn is second house on right. Via Taconic Pkwy., exit at Ancram on Rte. 82W over Rip Van Winkle Bridge and follow Rte. 23 to Cairo. Turn right on 32N, 9 mi. to Greenville.

HOLLOWAY HOUSE
East Bloomfield, New York

It was a beautiful sunny day in western New York. The corn was up, covering the rolling hills off Route 20. The sky was blue without a cloud, and the silos and barns of this beautiful farming country were constant reminders of its rich yield.

This time, I was coming east after paying an overnight visit to the Asa Ransom House in Clarence, and entered East Bloomfield just about noontime. East Bloomfield is a village of elms, maples, and oak trees and lovely old homes. It is a relatively short distance from Rochester. Doreen Wayne explained that Jonathan Child, who

was elected in 1834 as Rochester's first mayor, had opened a store in 1812 in part of Peter Holloway's tavern. In 1818 he married Sophia Eliza, the daughter of Colonel Nathaniel Rochester, who lived a mile west of the tavern when he established his city at the falls of the Genesee.

"In those days, of course, the road was just thin ruts created by stagecoaches and farm carts," said Wayne. "now Route 20 moves along the northern edge of what we call in these parts the 'Bristol Valley.' A great many people find their way to our door, just as they did when Peter Holloway, the village blacksmith, built this as a tavern in 1808."

The inn was doing a very brisk business for lunch, but Fred and Doreen promised to visit with me as soon as things got quieter, and showed me to a corner in the Peter Holloway Room, which has a view of the village through the beautiful trees. The waitress recited the lunch menu for me and brought a wonderful variety of hot fresh breads for which the inn is quite famous. Doreen was able to visit for just a few moments and to tell me about the buffet dinner which is served on Friday nights during July and August.

"We have seafood, shrimp, scallops, oysters, creamed mushrooms, and various types of Newburg dishes. Everybody always 'oohs and aahs' over the way the big table is decorated. It is very popular with the people who live in the area. On Saturday night we have a prime roast beef dinner.

"Incidentally, we have two kinds of dinners, either a complete dinner or a plate dinner. The plate dinner includes the entree, two vegetables, a salad, beverage, our well-known Sally Lunn bread and homemade rolls. The complete dinner includes a choice of appetizers, entree, choice of potato, two vegetables, a choice of salad and salad dressing, the Sally Lunn bread, homemade rolls, beverage and a choice of dessert."

In previous editions, I have mentioned the fact that the Waynes have been here at the Holloway House Inn for 18 years, but this time I had the opportunity to meet their two sons. One is Steve, who runs the grill and is also sometimes a host. He is a Cornell graduate and is going to continue in the inn business. David works in the kitchen helping the chef, and I understand he is an excellent goalie on the local high school soccer team. So, I learned that once again we have family participation in a real country restaurant.

Speaking of the kitchen, it is absolutely immaculate, and I hope that all of our readers will take advantage of the opportunity to take a peek inside and meet the head chef, Harold Draper. Everyone is welcome.

HOLLOWAY HOUSE, Rtes. 5 & 20, East Bloomfield, N.Y. 14443; 716-657-7120. A country restaurant 8 miles west of Canandaigua, N.Y. No lodgings. Lunch and dinner served daily except Mondays. Open April 1-Dec. 1. Sonnenberg Gardens, golf courses and Finger Lake Racetrack nearby. Fred, Doreen and Mildred Wayne, Innkeepers.

Directions: From N.Y. State Thruway take Exit 45, follow Rte. 96E 3 mi. to Victor N.Y. Go south on Victor-Holcomb Rd. 5 mi. Turn right at light in Holcomb then second left to Rte. 5 & 20.

LINCKLAEN HOUSE
Cazenovia, New York

I moved over on the couch in the Hogarth Room at the Redcoat's Return to make room for Helen Tobin. The two of us, along with several other innkeepers mentioned in this book, had been enthusiastic onlookers as Tom Wright, the innkeeper at this Catskill Mountain inn had demonstrated the preparation of our evening meal, and we were now going to enjoy a short visit.

"What's new at the Lincklaen House?" I said.

"Well, the best news I have is that Barbara is going to return to the inn in May. You remember she was married in April of 1977—you couldn't be there because you were in Germany. It was a beautiful wedding. So many of my friends are now asking for a wedding just the same as Barbara's. I had one just a few weeks ago and the uncle of the bride came to me and said that his daughter was to be married and he wanted exactly the same thing." I should explain here that Helen Tobin has, since the late 1960s, been the innkeeper of the Lincklaen House in Cazenovia, New York, and Barbara is her daughter.

Cazenovia is one of the attractive towns along Route 20 in the central part of the state, and its situation on a beautiful lake is an added attraction for Lincklaen House guests. In fact, Helen has a new beach house where she supplies her guests with picnic lunches and cold drinks, and there is a place for them to swim and row on the lake. It is just a few miles from the location of the inn in the center of town.

The inn has been called the best example of early 19th-century

170

architecture. It was built in 1835 as a stopover for travelers, and named after the founder of the village. Over the years many famous guests have enjoyed its hospitality, including Franklin D. Roosevelt, Grover Cleveland, John D. Rockefeller, and John Dewey. Fortunately, the interior and exterior embellishments have remained untouched and visitors are delighted with their discovery of the intricate carving and paneling.

"A lot of exciting things have happened this year," she said. "On Christmas Day, Trudi Hill comes over and we have a cafe Brulote. She is the daughter of Mrs. Munson at the Lamothe House in New Orleans from whom I got the idea to make my outdoor terrace. Trudi is a guide at the Lorenzo Museum and loves to do things for people who are from out of town.

"Cazenovia has come out with a new book on the town, and the Lincklaen is in it in three different places. There is a picture taken in 1891 that is identical to the appearance of the inn today.

"We've had band concerts every Thursday night all summer and a Franklin car meet was held in Cazenovia for one week in August. There were also carriage races on the grounds of the Lorenzo Mansion during the first week in August.

"Main Street in Cazenovia looked like 5th Avenue, New York, in December. The merchants opened the shops for a 'shopper's walk' on the first Friday of December and we lent our services by offering refreshments in the tavern. People came from all over—whole families; I've never seen the main street of Cazenovia with so many people at one time. We all had the most enjoyable experience imaginable.

"You know that Cazenovia is really a wonderful central point for people to visit many things in New York State. We have a public swimming area, the inn beach house, and you can drive to so many different places like the Harden Furniture Factory, the wine country, and the Steuben Glass Company in Corning, and it is a very nice trip to the Baseball Hall of Fame in Cooperstown."

The Lincklaen House is a very well-organized, friendly village inn. It is a community meeting place, as well as a convenient stopover for travelers and vacationers. Among the menu specialities are eggs Benedict, beef Bourguignon, popovers, filet mignon with Bordelaise sauce, and chocolate mousse.

I've never had a conversation with Helen Tobin in which she didn't report something new and exciting.

LINCKLAEN HOUSE, Cazenovia, N.Y. 13035; 315-655-3461. A 27-room village inn, 20 mi. east of Syracuse. Near several state parks, the Erie Canal Museum and the Canal Trail. European plan. Modified American plan upon request. Breakfast, lunch and dinner served to travelers daily. Open year-round. Tennis, golf, bicycles, Alpine and xc skiing nearby. Helen Tobin, Innkeeper.

Directions: From west on N.Y. Thruway, take Exit 34A, follow Rte. 481 south, take Exit 3E and follow Rte. 92 east to Cazenovia. From east on N.Y. Thruway, take Exit 34 and follow Rte. 13 south to Cazenovia. From Rte. 81, take Exit 15 (LaFayette) and follow Rte. 20 East, 18 mi. to inn.

OLD DROVERS INN
Dover Plains, New York

Menus are some of my favorite reading, particularly menus from country inns. This time I was reading the portable menu at the Old Drovers Inn. It was hanging on one of the low beams next to the fireplace, but innkeeper Trav Harris is prepared to move it to any corner of the dining room so that everyone may contemplate the culinary marvels awaiting his choice. There are the famous Old Drovers cheddar cheese or cold lemon soups, also onion or Russian cabbage soup.

A second course could be, among others, a paté of duck livers, Portuguese sardines, or a shrimp cocktail. Choosing an entree involves deciding between dishes like roast duckling, curry of turkey or lamb with chutney, sauteed calves liver, beefsteak and kidney pie, shrimps rarebit, rainbow trout, or julienne of veal served Zurich style (that's veal sauteed in butter and white wine with mushrooms, shallots and sour cream served over rice).

The desserts that evening included one of the inn's famous sweets: fresh key lime pie. There was also strawberry meringue glacé, peach Melba, pecan pie, and apple cheese cake. This last is apple pie with cheese cake on top garnished with walnuts and coconut.

I've gone into some detail about this menu because luncheon and dinner are the main reasons why most people visit Old Drovers Inn. The atmosphere in the dining room is romantic, to say the least, with red leather benches, low wood ceilings, and a wonderful combination of rough beams and stone walls. Lining the walls, just below the ceiling, is a collection of glass, copperware and brass. An old musket hangs over the fireplace. Oversized glass hurricane lamps protect the candles on the tables, and it is great to come in on a chilly day to this beautiful room with a cheery fire crackling in the fireplace. The atmosphere reminds me very much of English country inns I've visited.

The three somewhat sumptuous lodgings on the floors above are reached by a box-like staircase hung with marine prints. A most comfortable sitting room on the second floor has a fireplace, deep-cushioned chairs, and plenty of books and magazines. An elegant room where breakfasts are served is decorated with some interesting Hudson Valley murals.

There is a handsome, double-sized sleigh bed in the corner bedroom which also has its own fireplace and is wood-paneled. Another bedroom has twin beds with beautiful quilts, more handsome paneling, a tall chest of drawers and a fireplace. The curved ceiling in one room indicates that before its conversion into a spacious bedroom, it must have been part of the ballroom. These rooms, by the way, are usually booked considerably ahead.

Dining at the Old Drovers Inn is an elegant, luxurious experience, and the prices reflect the skilful preparation of top-quality food and drinks, the fine tableware, and expert service. Innkeeper Harris says, "Guests spending the night and taking dinner and a full breakfast should plan on sixty to seventy dollars each."

A dining experience like this must be savored in the most leisurely and unhurried fashion. But imagine, with all of this, I can still order browned turkey hash served with mustard sauce and delicious, crispy, crunchy-on-the-outside-and-soft-on-the-inside popovers!

OLD DROVERS INN, Dover Plains, New York 12522; 914-832-9311. A 3-room authentic 18th century luxury country inn midway between New York City and the Berkshires just off New York Rte. 22. European plan. Breakfast available to house guests.

Closed on Tuesdays and Wednesdays and for 3 weeks prior to Dec. 30 each year. Luncheon served weekdays from noon to 3 p.m. Dinner served weekdays from 6-9 p.m., Saturdays and holidays from noon to 9:30 p.m., Sundays from 1-9 p.m. Located in historic Dutchess County in the scenic foothills of the Berkshires. Travis Harris, Innkeeper.

Directions: From New York follow Saw Mill River on Hutchinson River Pkwy. to I-684 which leads into Rte. 22 at Brewster. Go north to Dover Plains.

THE OLIVER HOUSE
Ancram, New York

It looked like Vienna, it felt like Vienna, it sounded like Vienna —but it wasn't Vienna. It was the Opera House in Ancram, which had been transformed into an elegant ballroom, and the string and piano trio playing the lilting strains of a Viennese waltz, the sparkling crystal chandeliers, the polished floor where waltzing couples whirled, set the scene for another Twelfth Night Frolic held by John-Peter Hayden and Donald Chapin, the innkeepers of the Oliver House and originators of the Ancram Restoration. It was a gala evening, indeed, and as John-Peter reminded me, only one of the many evenings of entertainment offered throughout the year by these young entrepreneurs.

They were both full of enthusiasm for the Gotham Light Opera Guild's continuing program for the Opera House of "Viennese

Nights 1978," which will feature a full production of a grand opera, an operetta, and a variety of other musical events, such as string ensembles, song recitals, and brass quartets over the year. "Tell your readers," John-Peter suggested, "to write us at the Oliver House for a complete schedule of events if they would like to make plans in advance to be here for the kind of event they prefer."

Historic preservation is in full swing in the restoration of Ancram, a small eastern New York State village midway between Salisbury, Connecticut, Hudson and Rhinebeck, New York, and Great Barrington, Massachusetts. My original interest was because of the Oliver House, a restored 19th century country inn which along with the Vauxhall, a restored Greek-Gothic villa, provides food and lodgings for visitors. Between them they have ten bedrooms decorated in period furnishings and shared bathrooms.

Lunches and dinners are served in the elegant Palm Room at the Oliver House with its potted palms and lovely crystal chandeliers. Dinners are prix fixe and offer a choice of two entrees such as a choice of roast leg of lamb Bordeaux, or breast of chicken roasted in champagne. John-Peter's soups are always delicious. I particularly enjoy the cream of carrot. There is always homemade bread, and the cakes offered on a tea cart are wickedly luscious. Dinners are by reservations only.

However, on my first visit I perceived that the Oliver House shares the center stage with other stars in the Ancram galaxy. Besides the Opera House there is the Johann Strauss Athenaeum where there is a collection of operetta memorabilia, (the only one in America and perhaps the only one in the world,) including posters, playbills, and photographs from both European and American productions of famous operettas. An ongoing program of outstanding film musicals is held here on weekends.

Most recently restored is an 1855 church, the Oratory of the Holy Spirit, which will have services on a regular basis with Eucharistic services in the morning or early afternoon and vespers in the late afternoon. Simon's General Store, which has been in operation since 1874, is now full of such choice items as German silk flowers, fine china, very special jams and jellies, homemade sweet breads such as apple, blueberry, and date nut, good cheeses, and excellent candies.

All of these jewels are presented in a very gentle, almost European environment which encourages strolling and meandering in all seasons of the year.

Innkeepers Hayden and Chapin have many more plans up their collective sleeves. They expect to expand the lovely gardens and are working on a plan to have light refreshments such as sandwiches and pastries available in the gazebo in the garden to give summer sojourners an even more delightful stay at their country inn in the Ancram Restoration.

THE OLIVER HOUSE, Columbia County, Route 7 and N. Y. Rte. 82, Ancram, N. Y. 12502; 518-329-1166. A 5-room restored Victorian village inn with an additional 5 rooms available in the restoration's Vauxhall (manor house) midway between Salisbury, Conn., Hudson and Rhinebeck, N. Y., and Gt. Barrington, Mass. European plan includes Continental breakfast. Breakfast, lunch, afternoon tea served daily to travelers. Dinner by reservation only. Closed from 3rd Mon. in Jan. to Thurs. before Lincoln's birthday. Not especially for children Small well-trained pets welcome. Ice skating and fishing on grounds; swimming, horseback riding, skiing, golf, antiquing, and backroading nearby. J. P. Hayden, Jr. and Donald Chapin, Innkeepers.

Directions: From New York City: exit Taconic Parkway North at Jackson Corners, turn east and follow the signs 7 mi. to Ancram. From Massachusetts: turn west from Rte. 22 into Copake and turn right at the village clock following signs to Ancram.

REDCOAT'S RETURN
Tannersville, New York

I was taking a few moments to sit quietly in the small sitting room behind the fireplace at the Redcoat's Return. It had been a beautiful day and the drive over from the Berkshires to the Catskills on one of the most "fall" afternoons of the year had been glorious. Interestingly enough, it happened at a time when I didn't expect the fall foliage to be at its height, but here in the Catskills there was a marvelous muted combination of russets, yellows, reds, and greens, and the Redcoat's Return, nestled among the trees, looked extremely romantic against the backdrop of the mountains and the western sky which was already streaked with gold at the end of the day.

I had arrived in time to join a small group of innkeepers included in this book who were all seated in Tom Wright's kitchen as he conducted the first of what proved to be many cooking demonstrations at different inns during the next few months. It is part of a continuing plan for the innkeepers in CIBR to exchange viewpoints and ideas. Tom was particularly well-qualified to explain the preparation of the evening meal of which we were all soon to partake, because he has been an expert chef for quite sometime. After an apprenticeship at the Dorchester in London, he was a chef on the

Cunard Line for a number of years. He kept us very much involved, explaining each of the dishes that he was preparing and even supplied us with recipes.

Helen Tobin from the Lincklaen House in Cazenovia, New York joined me for a moment, and she was most enthusiastic about Tom's ideas and the fact that there were several more of these cooking demonstrations and get-togethers in the future. We decided to take a walk through the inn and look at some of the newly-decorated rooms. "Oh, it is so homey here," she said, "and the wallpaper fits very well with the types of furniture in the bedrooms and the patchwork quilts."

When we returned to the first floor there were a group of people clustered around the fire and Peggy Wright lit some of the candles on the dinner tables. As the light waned and the stars started to come out, the parlor and living room took on a new feeling. Rex, the Irish setter, came in and curled up on the sofa with Rover, the collie, and we started talking about how country inns have resident pets.

Ramona Stafford from Stafford's-in-the-Field in New Hampshire, herself an expert cook, joined us, full of admiration for Tom's ability as a chef and as an entertaining instructor. "I'd like to have one of these meetings at our place," she said. I immediately scheduled one with her for mid-spring.

The menu at the inn includes prime ribs with Yorkshire pudding, poached filet of sole, roast duck and orange sauce, steak and kidney pie, and English-style fish and chips. Desserts include sherry trifle, cheesecake, and chocolate mousse, just to name a few.

There are twelve rooms at this inn, all of them with wash basins—and the changes have now provided private bathrooms for several more rooms. The inn is located high in the Catskills, near the Hunter Mountain and Cortina Valley ski areas for some great downhill skiing, and cross-country skiing is right at the door.

Our dinner and get-together was a huge success and many of our innkeepers, on a kind of holiday, do what they do quite naturally in their own inn, started talking to the other inn guests.

Although the others would remain overnight, I had to return to the Berkshires late that evening. But before I left we all rose and toasted Tom and Peggy Wright and the Redcoat's Return, "an ideal country inn."

REDCOAT'S RETURN, Dale Lane, Elka Park, N.Y. 12427; 518-589-6379. A 12-room English inn approx. 4 mi. from Tannersville, N.Y., in the heart of the Catskill Mts. Within a short drive of several ski areas and state hiking trails. European Plan. Lodgings include breakfast. Dinner served daily except Thursdays. Open from Memorial Day to Easter. No pets. Hiking, nature walks, trout fishing, croquet, skiing, swimming, ice skating, riding, tennis nearby. Tom and Peggy Wright, Innkeepers.

Directions: Exit 20 or 21 from N.Y. Thwy. Follow 23A to Tannersville; turn left at traffic light onto County Road 16. Follow signs to Police Center 4½ mi. Turn right on Dale Lane.

SPRINGSIDE INN
Auburn, New York

Bill and Barbara Dove, the innkeepers at the Springside, and I were having a "breakfast in a basket" in one corner of a little lounge where the house guests at the inn eat breakfast. My eye caught an unusual watercolor portrait and when I remarked about it, Bill explained that it had been done by Barbara and that she was dissatisfied with it and was going to throw it away. "I bought if from her," he said, "and since it was my painting I decided to hang it on the wall in here. We get quite a few comments about it."

This complimentary breakfast is a very pleasant treat for travelers at this mid-New York State inn. The first one down in the morning plugs in the coffee pot. I managed to consume an unusual amount of the blueberry muffins with sweet butter that are served with fresh fruit.

In the 1977 edition, I spoke about my tour of the lodging rooms on the second floor which had been considerably redecorated. One was in shades of pink with a pink bedspread and matching curtains, another had twin Victorian bedsteads and lamps with red bows. Still another room with twin beds on the top floor was done in shades of tan and yellow with a formal valance on the window, a tiffany-type lamp, and hooked rugs.

This time, Barbara and I talked about the redesigning and decorating done on the first floor. For example, the Garden Room has been changed, and the newest feature is a raised fireplace with two owl andirons. Matching wallpaper and curtains had transformed the front porch into a dining room and one of the inside dining rooms had a new Scotch plaid carpet and lots of comfortable furniture that created a sort of living room feeling.

I also had an opportunity to look over the playbill for the Springside Inn dinner theatre which is featured for several weeks during the summer. "We've been doing it for a number of years," explained Bill, "and it has been a very gratifying success. We usually have a different special dinner with each presentation. For example, during the run of 'Mame' we featured prime rib (which we do for every show) and a second choice of Long Island duckling. For 'Carnival' the second choice was Alaskan King Crab legs, for 'Cabaret' it was Coq Au Vin, for 'Six Rms Riv Vu' it was lobster Newburg, and for 'Applause' it was sole Bon Femme."

Incidentally, this inn which is at the northern end of Owasco Lake, one of the New York Finger Lakes, actually began as a boys' school in 1851. Tradition says that it was at one time part of the Underground Railroad for runaway slaves during the War Between the States.

After a series of owners, it was opened as a summer resort in the 1920s, and in 1930, it became a year-round hotel-restaurant. Today the inn is operated by the second generation of Barbara's family.

Here is an excerpt from a letter I received from a couple living in Upper Black Eddy, Pa. about their visit to the Springside Inn: "We wish to tell you that the Springside Inn at Owasco Lake is everything a country inn should be in our opinion. It was a pleasant surprise to come upon such an attractive, well-groomed, comfortable place at the end of a difficult day's drive. The food was good and the management most helpful with a couple of unforeseen problems which arose. This is the kind of a place one hopes for and all too seldom finds."

Our tour of the dining rooms and the redecoration completed, we returned once again to the breakfast room for a final few moments.

"You know, the more I look at the painting," said Barbara, "the more I think that I didn't charge him enough for it."

"It's too late now," said Bill.

SPRINGSIDE INN, 41 West Lake Rd., Auburn, N.Y. 13021; 315-252-7247. A 7-room country inn, 1 mi. south of Auburn with a view of Owasco Lake. In the heart of the historical Finger Lakes. Lodgings include Continental breakfast. Some rooms with shared baths. Dinner served to travelers daily except Mondays and Tuesdays. Closed Memorial Day, July 4th, Labor Day, Christmas and New Year's Day. Boating, swimming, bicycles on grounds. Golf, riding, Alpine and xc skiing nearby. Bill and Barbara Dove, Innkeepers.

Directions: From N.Y. Thruway, take Exit 40 and follow Rte. 34 south through downtown Auburn to Rte. 38. Follow Rte. 38 south to traffic circle at Lake and take 2nd exit right at West Shore of Owasco Lake. Drive ¼ mi. to inn.

SWISS HUTTE
Hillsdale, New York

It was a very bright, very cold, blowy Saturday afternoon in January. I was at the Swiss Hutte for a spot of lunch and a chat with Tom and Linda Breen.

I sat in a warm, sunny corner with the panorama of the Catamount Ski Area spread out before me. It was a little too cold to ski, and there were quite a few people who stopped for lunch. There was a great deal of kidding about going back on the slopes in the afternoon.

This same scene is quite different in the middle of the summer with the rushing brook gurgling its way down the mountain and both the artificial and natural swimming pools out in front of the inn with people sunning themselves.

Oddly enough, the people who were here today were almost as tan and ruddy as the summer guests.

The Swiss Hutte is a Continental-type inn in a hidden Berkshire valley right on the New York-Massachusetts line. It is actually in Hillsdale, New York, but I can't help but think of it as being a Massachusetts inn.

There are two types of accommodations available. One is in the main inn where there are country inn-type rooms. The other 15 rooms are in chalet-type motel units, each with its own balcony and excellent view of the mountains. In the summer, everything feels sequestered among the trees.

Catamount ski area

Coming up the Taconic Parkway from New York, it is an ideal distance for leaving late in the afternoon and arriving in time for dinner. Even today there was a variety of license plates in the parking lot, including one from California and one from West Virginia.

In spite of all the natural beauty, perhaps the Swiss Hutte is best known for its food. Both lunch and dinner are leisurely affairs with individually prepared dishes. That particular day I ordered French pancakes filled with chicken. The cool, fresh salad was delicately bathed in a perfect combination of oil and vinegar and condiments. The fresh French bread was hot to the touch. Among

181

the other entrees are sweetbreads in Bernaise sauce, Weiner schnitzel, sauerbraten, and veal chops Normande.

Desserts which are included in the price of the main dish, include creme carmel, French apple torte cheesecake, and a super delicious raspberry cream pie.

At the Swiss Hutte guests can enjoy tennis, swimming, hiking, skiing, cross-country skiing, and many other seasonal attractions. In summer, Tanglewood, Jacob's Pillow, and Berkshire Playhouse are just a few miles away. Berkshire backroading is famous, you can start right at the front door using dirt roads that lead through the forest.

That's the Swiss Hutte. A little bit of the Austrian alps in the Berkshires.

SWISS HUTTE, Hillsdale, N.Y. 12529; 518-325-3333. A 21-room Alpine country inn overlooking Catamount ski area, 6 mi. from Gt. Barrington, Mass. Modified American plan omits lunch. Breakfast, lunch and dinner served to travelers daily. Closed month of April and from Nov. 15 to Dec. 15. Pool, tennis, putting green, Alpine and xc skiing on grounds. Tom and Linda Breen, Innkeepers.

Directions: From Boston, travel on Mass. Tpke. and take Exit 2. Follow Rte. 102 to Rte. 7. Proceed on Rte. 7 to Rte. 23. From New York City, follow Taconic Pkwy. and Rte. 23. From Albany, follow N.Y. Thruway and Taconic Pkwy. Inn is 10 mi. east of Pkwy. on Rte. 23.

THREE VILLAGE INN
Stony Brook, New York

It was about 9 p.m. on a very soft summer's night. I walked through the low doorway of the inn to the terrace with its white wrought-iron furniture and decided to take a short stroll before retiring. Through the wonderful old trees there was a cluster of lights which proved to be the marina with a great collection of cruisers, speedboats, luxury yachts, outboards, and sailboats. They gleamed white in the floodlight, and what was passive and quiescent tonight would be back in action tomorrow. I happened to meet other guests at the inn and we sat down on a handy bench and started comparing notes.

"We expected something good," they said, "but I don't think we expected to be so removed and serene. It is like a little country village. Imagine a clapboard colonial built by an old sea captain. Low ceilings, green shutters, geraniums, and ivy climbing up the trees.

"Something that surprised us is the Long Island seafood. I have

always known that there was fish in Long Island Sound, but I never expected such a variety."

They plunged on. "I'll tell you what impressed us tremendously besides the paintings, prints, antiques, and old Long Island atmosphere . . . it's the history of the whole area. The Robertses, particularly Whitney, gave us a touch of it today but I think we could stay here for at least three days and not experience it all. I just love that sweet little Caroline church with its ancient greystones and white picket fence."

The Three Village Inn is located in one of the most interesting and well-preserved towns on Long Island, about 60 miles from New York City. In recent years, very attractive cottages have been built facing the Yacht Club and marina, bringing the total number of rooms available for guests to 22.

Besides walking the sandy beach behind the inn and watching the boats in the marina, there is a great deal to do in this part of the north shore of Long Island, which is very rich in colonial history. A most interesting afternoon can be spent at the Suffolk Museum and Carriage House which contains a fine collection of horse-drawn vehicles.

From my very first visit I realized that Nelson and Monda Roberts (he's the head chef) have placed a great deal of emphasis on the food. They are very particular about some things including not using foil for baked potatoes and baking them in rotation through the evening. Vegetables are fresh whenever they are available. The menu is quite extensive and includes a great deal of beef, pork, veal, and lamb as well as the fresh seafood. The extra touch of serving sherbet with the main meal is something I have always enjoyed. Desserts include things such as apple crisp, homemade cakes, Indian pudding, and delicious fruit pies and tarts. They are all made in the inn's kitchen.

I've seen quite a few interesting improvements at the inn over recent years. One thing, a small parlor with a very inviting fireplace, has been turned into a Common Meeting Room for inn guests. A great many people from New York City found that the inn and this section of Long Island provide a very marvelous opportunity for a weekend vacation. As Monda Roberts was telling me, "Many professional people just simply can't take the time to get away and so we have been discovered by people who would like a change of pace and yet not get too far away from the city."

As we walked back to the inn, I asked them whether or not they had seen the drama at the post office at 12 o'clock noon each day, where the wooden eagle with the 20-foot wingspread flaps his wings? They replied, "Not as yet." So we all agreed to meet there the next day. It is just a few steps across the green from the inn.

THREE VILLAGE INN, Dock Rd., Stony Brook, L.I., N.Y. 11790; 516-751-0555. A 7-room village inn with 15 adjacent cottage/motel accommodations, 5 mi. from Port Jefferson, N.Y., on Long Island's historic north shore. Near Suffolk County Museum, Craft Center and Carriage Museum. European plan. Lunch and dinner served to travelers daily. Closed Christmas. No pets. Golf, swimming and boating nearby. Nelson and Monda Roberts, Innkeepers.

Directions: From L.I. Expressway, take Exit 62 and travel north on Nichols Rd. to Rte. 25A. Turn left on Rte. 25A and proceed to next light. Turn right on to Main St. and travel straight ahead to inn. Available from New England via L.I. ferries from Bridgeport during the summer. Ferry reservations advisable.

Pennsylvania

CENTURY INN
Scenery Hill, Pennsylvania

I moved the rocking chair on the front patio of the Century Inn so that the big tree would screen the direct rays of the mid-afternoon sun. Settling down for a few moments of reflection, I realized that the aspect from this vantage point was probably much the same as it had been when Lafayette stopped at the inn on a trip across the National Pike in 1825, and during Andrew Jackson's two stays during the same period.

The Century Inn, I mused, was built before 1794 and is the oldest continuously operating tavern on the National Pike, most of which is today's U.S. Route 40. The public and lodging rooms of this handsome old inn are filled with rare antiques, most of them gifts to its restoreers and innkeepers for many years, Gordon and Mary Harrington.

My mind drifted back to 1969 or 1970, I believe, when I paid my first visit. The Harringtons were delightful. I remember staying up until almost daylight talking history and inns with Gordon who was a marvelous raconteur. Mary gave up on us about 2:30 a.m.!

He told me the history of almost every piece of furniture at the inn, including the grandfather clocks, paintings by David Hanna, the exquisite end tables, the Chippendale highboy brought from the east by Conestoga wagon, platform rockers and the beautiful collection of china in the many different cupboards. We pored over photographs of the inn in various stages of its career. It was from Gordon that I first learned of the Whiskey Rebellion and its famous flag which still hangs in the front parlor.

I was to visit with Gordon one further time before his passing and enjoyed many, many long talks with Mary Harrington who passed on during the spring of 1977.

Today, their daughter Nancy, whom I have known for a number of years, and her husband, Bob Sheirer, carry on in the footsteps of the Harringtons. The first thing she showed me was the newly-decorated Stencil Room. "I am so happy that Mother saw it in its completed state," said Nancy. "She cut the stencils for the design."

The inn is being kept with the same meticulous attention to detail that characterized the senior Harringtons. The menu still continues to feature roast turkey, golden fried chicken, stuffed pork chops, Virginia ham, chicken croquettes, ham and asparagus roll and an absolutely fantastic hot turkey sandwich.

Desserts include temptations like fresh strawberry shortcake, pecan balls with buttersauce and a variety of homemade pies.

I felt a hand gently shaking my shoulder and Nancy's voice saying, "Would you like a glass of ice tea?" I opened my eyes and realized that a generous lunch, plus the warm sunshine and gentle action of the rocker, had carried me from reverie into the vestibule of the land of nod. She pulled another rocker over closer to mine and said, "It is so lovely out here I think I will join you for a few minutes."

It was wonderful to be back in Scenery Hill and know that I would be visiting the Century Inn for many more years to come.

CENTURY INN, Scenery Hill, Pa. 15360; 412-945-6600 or 5180. A 10-room village inn on Rte. 40, 12 mi. east of Washington, Pa., 35 mi. south of Pittsburgh. European plan. Breakfast served to house guests only. Lunch and dinner served to travelers daily. Closed approximately Dec. 21 until April 1. Contact inn for exact opening and closing dates. No pets. Nancy and Bob Scheirer, Managers, Mary W. Harrington, Innkeeper.

Directions: From the east, exit the Pa. Tpke. at New Stanton. Take I-70 W to Rte. 917S (Bentleyville exit) to Rte. 40E and go 1 mi. east to inn. From the north, take Rte. 19S to Rte. 519S to Rte. 40E and go 5 mi. east to inn or take I-79S to Rte. 40E and go 9 mi. east to inn. From the west, take I-70E to I-79S to Rte. 40E and go 9 mi. east to inn.

Fairfield, a small Pennsylvania town in the farming land west of Gettysburg now has not one, but two, country inns. Both of them are the inspiration of the Hammett family — Doctor Jim, his wife Nancy Jeane and assorted Hammett offspring. I had been entranced with the Fairfield Inn on my first visit there in 1975, at which time Nancy Jeane was spearheading the restoration work that involved all the Hammetts. Parts of the inn had been built in 1757, and in the summer of 1977, the restoration was still in progress.

Ever-mindful of the challenges of life, the Hammetts have now sold the Fairfield Inn to David Thomas, the young man who was the manager of the inn for a great portion of the past two years. In turn, she has converted an old farm nearby into a country restaurant called The Hickory Bridge Farm.

The two places complement each other very well. For example, the Fairfield Inn is closed on Sundays, whereas that is one of the big days at Hickory Bridge Farm. The Fairfield Inn is open year-round and Hickory Bridge Farm is closed during the winter months.

FAIRFIELD INN
Fairfield, Pennsylvania

How is David Thomas, the new, young innkeeper at the Fairfield Inn progressing? Well, I spent a considerable amount of time there on my visit to Fairfield, and I concluded that he was enjoying great success. Of course, he had already had some considerable experience as manager of the inn, and merely changed aprons to become the owner.

David was sharing some of his considerable enthusiasm about innkeeping with me as we sat in one corner of the newest of the restored dining areas.

"As you know, we just have two lodging rooms, so the main reason for people to stop here is the food. We serve three meals a day except on Sundays when we suggest that our guests go to Nancy Jeane's Hickory Bridge Farm. Everything that we serve is made from scratch. However, we are not only continuing with all of the things that made the Fairfield Inn a great success, such as chicken and biscuits, country ham steak, the salty kind, a 'frizzled city ham' and our family-style meals which include everything from appetizer to dessert, but also I am introducing new main dishes as well. The desserts will always include deep dish apple pie served with a pitcher of cream or a wedge of cheese or other seasonal "goodies."

"People also come here for a total experience. They don't just come for the food—they come to see what we have done, to see what we have restored or rearranged, and the new antiques we have added. We have to be careful about moving the antiques, even the small pieces, because our guests frequently search me out to ask why something was moved from one corner to another. Even a small item like a pewter teaspoon is important, as we have had ladies here for lunch who have been told by their friends that they must come into the parlor and see the collection in the corner cupboard. I have heard them mention that this plate or that bowl wasn't there the last time they came.

"There are many things here in the inn that have been loaned to us by people here in the area. We have discovered that there is a great community pride in this inn, and most of the credit belongs to Nancy Jeane Hammett and the rest of the Hammett family who really saw its possibilities and put so much into restoring it."

Here's part of a letter I received in November, 1977:

"My husband and I used CIBR last year to plan a trip in eastern Pennsylvania and we were delighted to discover the Fairfield Inn. It is our favorite. We were so smitten that we changed our schedule to return for a night at the end of our trip, and asked Mr. Thomas to please reserve one of the two rooms in the spring at apple blossom time. When I learned that he was now the owner of the inn I was so pleased, because if the Hammetts wanted to see the inn in the hands of someone who would carry on with what they had begun, they couldn't have made a better choice. The food is delicious as ever and I am looking forward to a return visit."

Congratulations David Thomas; Nancy Jeane Hammett is a hard act to follow and it is very obvious that you are getting rave reviews.

FAIRFIELD INN, Main St., Fairfield, Pa. 17320; 717-642-5410. A country restaurant near Gettysburg with 2 lodging rooms available. Breakfast, lunch and dinner served daily. Closed on major holidays, Sundays and last week in August. Dinner reservations advised. No pets. Nearby region is rich in history including Gettysburg Battlefield. David W. Thomas, Innkeeper.

Directions: Fairfield is 8 mi. west of Gettysburg on Rte. 116.

HICKORY BRIDGE FARM
Orrtanna, Pennsylvania

In the 1976 edition of CIBR I noted that the then-owner of the Fairfield Inn, Nancy Jeane Hammett was a 'believer'. She has the wonderful kind of optimism that seems to overcome all obstacles and feels that hard work is the answer to all of life's problems.

In mid-summer 1977, I visited Fairfield not only to congratulate David Thomas the new owner of Fairfield Inn, but also to see the Hammetts' newest undertaking. This time they had acquired the old Deardorff Farm, just a few miles north of the town at Orrtanna, and turned it into a farmhouse restaurant. It even has two cottages available for overnight guests.

When I asked Nancy Jeane how it happened, she said:

"It all started to fall into place when David indicated that he would like to purchase the Fairfield Inn. Then we knew that Hickory Bridge Farm could be the Hammetts' next project. We'd been looking at it for years. Incidentally, I'm so pleased with the way things are going at the Fairfield Inn. David is such a fine person and we've had a great many people say that he is doing a marvelous job."

So now, on a mid-afternoon in August, Nancy Jeane and I were catching up on the lastest "inn news" and I was seeing this farm restaurant for the first time.

As soon as I walked into the big barn where the meals are served and saw the wide floor boards, massive beams, and rustic pillars, I just felt good all over. The long harvest tables had six or eight settings on each side, and the entire atmosphere was made more appealing

189

with a splendid collection of old farm tools hung on the walls and interspersed with seed posters and other agricultural artifacts from an earlier day. Horse-drawn sleighs of all sizes and shapes are also on display, with one of them doing double duty as a salad bar.

Still another low-ceilinged dining room has been created out of what once were stables. The highly-varnished, knotty pine walls are decorated with a plate rail displaying the familiar country agate ware. Several old-fashioned highchairs are pressed into service for the younger generation at almost every meal.

Nancy Jeane was most enthusiastic about the food: "There is always a choice of two entrees, home-baked bread and rolls, many different vegetables and fruits, most of which come from right here on the farm, and desserts with all the trimmings. The meals usually begin with an apple shrub or apple juice, and then the guests are invited to help themselves at the salad sled. A typical Sunday dinner would have both roast turkey and baked ham with sweet potatoes, apple fritters, applesauce, and anything else we can get from the garden. We also have chicken corn soup, Dutch lettuce, stewed apples, corn fritters, apple butter, schmier kase, apple pan-dowdy and shoo-fly pie. Everything is made entirely from scratch in our farm kitchen. We keep our own bees and blueberry patch.

"Wednesday through Saturday, the farm is open for dinner from 5 to 8 p.m. Sunday dinners are served from 12 to 6 p.m. Reservations are advised."

Each of the two cottages at Hickory Bridge Farm have two rooms, making a total of four lodging rooms. These cozy cottages are in the forest overlooking a little brook, a short distance away from the main buildings. These are available for lucky people who have reservations.

Yes, Nancy Jeane Hammett is still a believer, and she and Hickory Bridge Farm have convinced me once again.

HICKORY BRIDGE FARM INN, Orrtanna, Pa. 17353; 717-642-5261. A country inn on a former farm 3 mi. from Fairfield and 8 mi. from Gettysburg. Near Gettysburg Battlefield National Park, Totem Pole Playhouse. Farm dinners served Wed. thru Sat., 5 to 8 p.m.; Sun. from 12 to 6. Open from Mar. 1 to Dec. 20. 4 lodging rooms available in 2 cottages nightly from Mar. 1 to Dec. 20. Breakfast available to guests. Hiking, biking, hayrides, square dancing, fishing, hunting on grounds; golf, swimming available nearby. The Hammett Family, Innkeepers.

Directions: From Gettysburg take Rte. 116 west to Fairfield and follow signs 3 mi. north to Orrtanna.

INN AT STARLIGHT LAKE
Starlight, Pennsylvania

I walked out to the end of the dock where a very handsome woman with blonde hair was sunning herself. There were five rowboats and a Sunfish tied up and a July sun was sparkling on Starlight Lake, creating interesting shades of green through the surrounding trees.

"Isn't it beautiful," said the handsome blonde. "And I've got to leave in just a few minutes because we have to go back to the city."

I asked her how long she had been there and what she had been doing.

"We came for one night and decided to stay for three, and we've been mostly just sitting in the sun. My husband likes to sail, and we've also been doing some walking in the woods, and a little back roading. We have our youngest son with us, and he is just about the same age as Will McMahon, so the two of them have been riding bikes and playing ping pong and getting acquainted. It makes quite a difference to have someone for younger children to play with."

There are quite a few things that make the Inn at Starlight Lake different. For one thing, I think the best way to describe it is "rustically informal"—guests cannot help but become acquainted with the various members of the inn staff who are mostly local country people and have an open friendliness that invites conversation. While I was there, the front of the inn was being painted and the painter stopped occasionally to share a few words with the guests.

The guest bedrooms are very much out of the early 20th century with flowered wallpaper, old prints, and have been redecorated in a country style reminiscent of yesterdays. There are a few cottages immediately adjacent to the main building, and some of these have been winterized for additional use by the cross-country ski crowd which seems to be coming to Starlight in great numbers.

When I mentioned the cross-country skiing to Judy McMahon, she said, "Last winter was delightful and we had a great many people. You know, we have all these trails and people can also use the lake to ski on to get their ski legs. Cross-country skiing is a very important part of what we are doing here, and I think the people like to come into our big living room and just sort of relax and be themselves after a day in the snow."

In the summertime, there are rows of rustic rockers on the front porch which overlooks the lake. The guests enjoy rocking and talking, and at the same time keeping an eye, if necessary, on their children who can enjoy the swings and other playthings along the lake shore.

In addition to being a resort-inn where guests stay for quite a few days, the inn also has a brisk trade with people from the surrounding countryside who drop in for lunch and dinner. The food, I guess, is best described as "country cooking with a dash of gourmet." I wish I could say I invented that phrase, but it is actually a quote from the lady I met on the dock.

Another reason why the Inn at Starlight Lake is different is because Judy and Jack McMahon were for many years in show business. As Jack says, "Running an inn is like being 'on' all the time. In the old days, people in vaudeville and show business dreamed about retiring to a chicken farm. We always wanted to have an inn, and Judy and I have had the time of our life with our four children here. It is not all taking bows and encores. It keeps us busy a great deal of the time, but we really love it. I think that when we were in the theatre, we both developed a sense of timing that helps us to understand our guests' responses and needs."

Food at the inn also has a difference. There are a number of German specialties, including a Jager schnitzel and a weiner schnitzel. Some of the dishes I sampled were cream of cauliflower soup, Hungarian goulash, sauerbraten, buckwheat cakes, and blueberry pie. There is a great deal of emphasis on serving only fresh meats and vegetables and homemade breads. Even the coffee is freshly ground before each pot is brewed.

The McMahons may no longer be in show business, but they are a smash in Wayne County, Pennsylvania.

THE INN AT STARLIGHT LAKE, Starlight, Pa. 18461; 717-798-2519. A 35-room resort-inn (25 rooms in winter) located 5 mi. from Hancock. N.Y. Modified American and European plans available. Breakfast, lunch, dinner served daily between May 15 and April 1.

Closed Easter if it falls within above dates. Swimming, boating, canoeing, sailing, fishing, hunting, tennis, hiking, bicycling, xc skiing, and lawn sports on grounds. Canoeing, hunting, fishing, golfing nearby. Judy and Jack McMahon, Innkeepers.

Directions: From N.Y. Rte. 17, exit at Hancock, N.Y. Take Rte. 191S over Delaware River to Rte. 370. Turn right, proceed 3½ mi., turn right, 1 mi. to inn. From I-81, take exit 62 and go east on Rte. 107. Turn left on Rte. 247 to Forest City. Turn left on Rte. 171, go 10 mi. to Rte. 370. Turn right, proceed 12 mi. Turn left, 1 mi. to inn.

MOSELEM SPRINGS INN
Moselem Springs, Pennsylvania

"Are you feeling 'countrified' or elegant tonight?"

There was a twinkle in Madeline Stoudt's eye as she asked this question. At first I thought it might be a bit of her Pennsylvania Dutch humor coming to the fore, but then I realized that she was expecting an answer.

"If you're feeling informal and sort of 'countrified,' then I'd suggest that you have dinner in the Golden Eagle Room. But if you're feeling a little more dignified, then I think you'll find the formal atmosphere of the Presidential Room to your liking."

This is the kind of good-natured joshing I expect from Madeline and Walter Stoudt. I'm happy to number them among the innkeepers that I've known the longest.

Madeline did make a good point, however. The Golden Eagle

Room has a big fireplace, heavy wooden chairs with red leather upholstery, a pegged floor and shutters at the window. The Presidential Room has high arched windows, formal draperies and portraits of American statesmen.

A third dining room—the Blue Willow Room—strikes a happy medium between casual and formal dining with antique china displayed on the fireplace mantle and a corner cupboard with a carved cornice. There's a blue jardiniere in the middle of each table and white captain's chairs. This room has been completely reserved for non-smokers.

The menu in Moselem Springs is as varied as the dining rooms. For example, there are braised short ribs of beef country style, prime ribs, stuffed boneless breast of chicken, pan-fried baby calves liver, and delicious smoked corned beef with raisin sauce.

The list of regional dishes is extensive. Among them are smokehouse beef sausage with horseradish and apple fritter, fried cheese, breaded fried mushrooms, beef and sausage pie, Dutch country scrapple, lemon butter and cinnamon crackers, and delicious round loaves of homemade bread served with whipped tub butter.

"We are very much involved in serving natural things," explained Madeline. "We don't use any perservatives at all. We have three kinds of tea and we don't serve instant iced tea. Our coffees include a natural dandelion coffee which is delicious, and Sanka. Everything is served with real cream if the guest prefers."

"There is one thing I hope you will try while you are here," said Walter. "It's called a 'Tavern Plank'. It's really a big chef's salad which has ham, cheese, tomatoes, chicken, beef, and horseradish on the side, along with pickled eggs, cheddar cheese and makes a very full meal."

Nobody ever accused me of not being able to take a hint. "Put me in the Willow Room." I said, "and I'll have a Tavern Plank."

MOSELEM SPRINGS INN, R.R. 4033. Box 10, Fleetwood, Pa. 19522; 215-944-8213. An historic country inn restored to 19th century opulence on U.S. 222, 13 mi. from Reading and 18 mi. from Allentown. No lodgings. Lunch and dinner served daily except Fridays and Saturdays. Full dinners served all day Sundays. Closed Christmas and special holy days. Open year-round. Walter and Madeline Stoudt, Innkeepers.

Directions: From I-76 and U.S. Rte. 22, exit at Pa. Rte. 100 and travel south to U.S. Rte. 222. Follow Rte. 222 south to Pa. Rte.662. Inn is located at this junction.

OVERLOOK INN
Canadensis, Pennsylvania

May I share a portion of a letter with you from two readers in Harrisburg, Pennsylvania? I think it tells us all something very special about the Overlook Inn.

"Last week we spent three days at the Overlook Inn in Canadensis. Lolly Tupper was so nice and made us feel at home the minute we walked in the door. The food was delicious, Sunday breakfast especially. Delicious pastry, pancakes that tasted as if they were made with cream! Saturday morning when we went to breakfast we were only out of our room for about 45 minutes and when we got back our bed was made, and fresh towels were in the bathroom. Wonderful!

"This was the first time that we had ever stayed anywhere except at a motel, and now we are going to stay in country inns at every opportunity. Once again thank you so much. Your book opened a whole new world for us."

Well, thank you very much for the compliment. May I say that this is quite typical of letters that I receive continuously from people who enjoy country inns, and it is one of several that I have received in 1977 about the Overlook in particular.

I've always maintained that one of the things that sets country inns apart from other accommodations and restaurants is "people," people who keep country inns, and guests who enjoy being in country inns. Bob and Lolly Tupper at Overlook not only have experience as

195

innkeepers, but also a tremendous amount of concern and involvement with their guests, as we can see from the above letter.

On a trip the fall of 1977, Bob and Lolly showed me how several of the lodging rooms are going to be changed to accommodate new bathrooms. "The net effect will be to reduce our total rooms from 28 to 23," said Bob, "but we think that many people appreciate a private bathroom."

These lodging rooms are all furnished in true country inn style with shades and bedspreads and hooked rugs.

I also admired the paintings done by Bob and Lolly's son, Rick, including one print showing 85 varieties of fresh and salt water fishes. There was another, a moving, emotional North Carolina beach scene, a blending of sun, sand and sky. "Rick is a commercial fisherman," said Bob, "but he really enjoys painting. We have several of his prints and originals. He has a gallery in Hillsdale, North Carolina."

As I sat down in the dining room, I noticed the handsome new service plates, of which the Tuppers are justly proud. After my dinner of marinated breast of chicken, Chef Joe Vibercik joined us for a few minutes on his nightly rounds with the guests. He is an Americanized Czechoslovakian, who speaks five languages, and was particularly interested in my recent trips to Germany, France and Italy. "How's the cheesecake?" He asked "I'll bet you didn't get anything like that in Munich, did you?" I agreed.

Incidentally, I always receive several telephone calls and letters in the late fall from people who are looking for a place to spend the Christmas holidays. I am happy to say that among others, the Overlook is open every day of the year. During the last two years, there has been an ample covering of snow, providing a real holiday feeling at this inn in the Pocono Mountains.

OVERLOOK INN, Dutch Hill Rd., Canadensis, Pa. 18325; 717-595-7519. A 23-room resort-inn in the heart of the Poconos, 15 mi. from Stroudsburg, Pa. Mod. American plan. Dinners served to travelers. Open every day of the year. Not ideal for children. No pets. Pool, archery, shuffleboard, bocci, hiking on grounds; golf, tennis, Alpine slide, ice skating, downhill and xc skiing, indoor tennis, antiquing, backroading, summer theatre nearby. Bob and Lolly Tupper, Innkeepers.

Directions: From New York City take George Washington Bridge to I-80, west to Pa. Exit 52, follow 447 north to Canadensis at traffic light. About ¼ mi. past traffic light, turn right on to Dutch Hill Rd., 1½ mi. up hill to inn.

THE PINE BARN INN
Danville, Pennsylvania

I couldn't believe it. Here I was in the middle of Pennsylvania enjoying a fresh flounder Mornay stuffed with crabmeat and shrimp. Furthermore, the menu had many fresh New England seafood items including deviled crabcake, filet of haddock, Cape Cod scallops, Boston scrod, lobster, filet sole. "It is delivered fresh twice a week," explained Shube Walzer. "We never have any frozen seafood items on our menu."

I was in the main dining room of the Pine Barn Inn country restaurant in Danville, Pennsylvania and, among other things, we were talking about the proximity of several colleges. Shube's son, Marty, chimed in, "We see a great many parents, students, and alumni from Bucknell, Susquehanna, and Bloomsburg. I went to Cornell and Dad went to Penn State. We feel surrounded by colleges. They supply us with cute and pleasant waitresses, and the best-educated dishwashers and kitchen help."

The dining room of the inn has handsome reproductions of Pennsylvania Windsor chairs, candles on each table, and a scattering of country furniture. One room has wooden shutters on the inside, polished stone floors and heavy wooden pillars and posts to continue the Pennsylvania barn theme.

The motel-type accommodations here are quite unusual. The rooms are furnished with attractive cherry reproductions. There are many homey, thoughtful touches in these rooms, including magazines, books, and hanging plants. The latter are the result of Barbara Walzer's influence, as she is in charge of the indoor decorations. Plants abound in the dining room and Gift Shop, and dried flowers, antique baskets, and lithographs provide a pleasant clutter to the walls, ceilings, and tables.

197

Shube Walzer is in charge of outdoor flowers and landscaping.

Marty Walzer was quick to credit Pine Barn's growth to the friendly staff: "Arlene and Mary spark the dining room and are quick to identify CIBR visitors," he said. "Susan Dressler, who really runs the place, and I , both celebrated our tenth year by taking a deep breath for the next ten. The men in the kitchen are Roger and Larry, who have done such a marvelous job with homemade pies, breads and rolls." I also noted country favorites such as roast beef, roast leg of lamb, and salads that are large enough to be an entire meal.

"Some of our most memorable evenings come on Sundays," said Marty. "We discovered an unusually talented Dixieland band residing in our area and they really bring down the roof once a month. Everybody has a great deal of fun and I guarantee that Dixie is not dead along the Susquehanna. We're hoping to continue with it indefinitely."

PINE BARN INN, Danville, Pa. 17821; 717-275-2071. A picturesque country restaurant with 45 attractive motel rooms in central Pennsylvania. European plan. Breakfast, lunch and dinner served daily except Christmas, July 4th and Memorial Day. Pets allowed in some rooms. Near several colleges and historic sites. Golf, tennis, water skiing, sailing, and canoeing nearby. Martin and Barbara Walzer, Innkeepers.

Directions: From Exit 33 of I-80, go south 3 mi. to Danville. Take a left at the first traffic light. Proceed 10 blocks and follow signs to Geisinger Medical Center. Pine Barn adjoins the Center.

PUMP HOUSE INN
Canadensis, Pennsylvania

In looking through the list of beautiful relais and chateaux that I visited in France in 1977, I found several that had much in common with the Pump House Inn which is located high up in the Poconos in Canadensis, Pennsylvania.

For example, the menu reminded me of a great many French inns that also serve roast rack of lamb Persille, roast tenderloin Chasseur, duckling Normande, and of course, many dishes prepared at the tableside.

The setting and location recalled to my mind Chateau d'Ige, which is in the wine country near Lyon, and the Hotellerie du Bas Breau, which is on the edge of the Barbizon Forest, south of Paris.

Both of these are included in the revised edition of *Country Inns and Back Roads, Europe.*

"I'm not surprised at the similarity," said Todd Drucquer, "Dad is French, and we feel a definite affinity for French cuisine. Our chef, Mark Kaplan is very much at home with French cooking, both classical and modern."

Just before this edition went to press, I telephoned Todd who, with his father Henri, is the innkeeper at the Pump House. "Oh, it is beautiful here this morning," he said. "We have about 14 inches of new snow and we expect to have skiing until the middle of summer. These mountains are just beautiful when the sun shines on the new fallen snow. We're going cross-country skiing now!"

"Dad, Penny, and I are very excited about the new addition on the back of the inn. We needed some office space, so we added on a section which has a 28-foot-high curved window. It is really very impressive and when it is lit up at night it is gorgeous. We are designing a little room in it where our guests can enjoy looking out over the landscape and perhaps have a cup of tea or something similar. I think our guests have become accustomed to something new happening here every year, and this is what is new this year."

It is quite true that something new has been happening at the Pump House almost every year since my first visit in the late sixties.

In 1977, it was the innovation of Thursday Epicurean evenings, where only twelve people are served and bookings have to be made by the previous Sunday night. There are two hors d'oeuvres one hot and one cold, followed by a soup course which is sometimes lobster bisque or a pumpkin soup, and then a fish course which Todd explains is usually something simple like filet of sole. The meat course can be a steak, tournedos of beef, or one of the other many Pump House specialties. The vegetables might include pommes de terre noisette which are nut-shaped potatoes, and baby peas. Salad frequently is white asparagus served with an herb, oil, and vinegar dressing. Homemade bread from chef Mark Kaplan's kitchen, and dessert and coffee completes the dinner. This meal is more expensive than the average country inn dinner.

Much originality is displayed throughout the dining rooms of the inn, one of which has its own indoor waterfall! There is a side dining room with a beautiful view of the forest and lots of old books on the shelves, a great many of which have grown up with the Drucquer family.

The Pump House has four very pleasant country inn bedrooms on the second floor, some of which are suites with baths. These are booked well in advance and reservations are most necessary.

As I was writing about the Pump House it occurred to me that there was still another French inn that has many similar features. It is Auberge de Noves, just a few miles south of Avignon in Provence. I'm sure Mr. Lalleman, the proprietor, would agree.

THE PUMP HOUSE INN, Canadensis, Pa. 18325; 717-595-7501. A 4-room country inn high in the Poconos, 1½ mi. north of Canadensis village and 16 mi. northeast of Stroudsburg. European plan. Sophisticated country dining. Dinner served to travelers daily. Closed Mondays in summer and Mondays and Tuesdays in winter. Closed Christmas and New Year's Day. Bicycles and golf nearby. The Drucquer Family, Owners. H. Todd Drucquer, Innkeeper.

Directions: From the north, follow I-84 to Rte. 390 south. Inn is located 13 mi. south on Rte. 390. From the south, follow I-80 to Rte. 191. Travel north on Rte. 191 to Rte. 390 north. Follow signs to Canadensis. Inn is 1½ mi. north from light in Canadensis.

1740 HOUSE
Lumberville, Pennsylvania

Harry Nessler, relaxed in grey flannels and sport coat, and accompanied by his two dogs, was waiting for me at the front door of the 1740 House. "Good morning," he said, "I see you've been taking a constitutional."

I had indeed. I'd awakened about 6:00 a.m. and decided not to lose a moment of my working holiday. My room in the inn was originally an old stable and the walls were made of heavy stone. There were massive beams overhead. Through one window I could see unspoiled woods on the far side of the Delaware River and Canal, and I could see the southern tip of Bull's Island. The swimming pool was visible through the other window. Each of the lodging rooms here either opens onto a terrace or has its own balcony.

I decided that this would be a good morning to take a stroll over the footbridge from Lumberville to Bull's Island. In the growing light of the morning, the oak, walnut, and sycamore trees around the inn

were beginning to take shape, and I noted with approval the arrangement of plantings that Harry had made including laurel, forsythia, rhododendron, and myrtle.

After enjoying fresh, clear quietness of the country morning, I walked back along the canal towpath, I think you can see why the the cardinals, grosbeaks, and doves were already busy searching out their morning meal.

That thought sent me back to the inn at a faster pace, and Harry suggested that we go right in and have breakfast.

We made our own toast from homemade bread and enjoyed delicious jams, fruit juice, croissants, pastries, cold cereal, and Pennsylvania Dutch, hot hard-boiled eggs. This breakfast is included in the room tariff. Other guests came in, and one of them asked Harry about the exact place where Washington crossed the Delaware.

"It's about ten miles south of here," he said. "And Valley Forge is only about 45 minutes away." He reached into his pocket and said, "I hope you'll take a copy of this brochure. It's called 'Highways of History' and it's the best thing to take with you if you're touring Buck's County. There are well over a hundred historic sites and buildings within an easy drive. The best way is to take the three tours, one day at a time."

There are a few unique features of this country inn that reflect its "one-of-a-kind" innkeeper. For one thing, weekend reservations must include two nights. Usually these are booked well in advance. Another feature worth noting is that dinner is served between 7:00 and 8:00 p.m. in the small dining room, and it's necessary for everyone—even house guests—to have reservations.

Harry also has definite ideas about the ambience of his inn. "It's an extension of the things I hold dear—good taste, good food, and good manners. We welcome everyone who shares these enthusiasms. I like to think of all the people who come to this inn as my house guests."

1740 HOUSE, River Rd., Lumberville, Pa. 18933; 215-297-5661. A 24-room riverside inn, 6½ mi. north of New Hope, in the heart of historic Bucks County. Lodgings include breakfast which is served to house guests daily; dinner served daily except Sundays and Mondays, by reservation only. Open year-round. Pool and boating on grounds. Golf and tennis nearby. Harry Nessler, Innkeeper.

Directions: From N.Y.C., travel south on N.J. Tpke., and take Exit 10. Follow Rte. 287 north to Easton exit. Proceed west on Rte. 22 to Flemington, then Rte. 202 south over Delaware Toll Bridge. After an immediate turn onto Rte. 32N, drive 5 mi. to inn. From Pa. Tpke., exit at Willow Grove and proceed north on Rte. 611 to Rte. 202. Follow Rte. 202 north to Rte. 32 and turn north to inn.

STERLING INN
South Sterling, Pennsylvania

The ducks at the Sterling Inn were crossing the road single file. They had just completed their constitutional from the pond next to Wallenpaupack Creek, across the putting green and shuffleboard courts, past the Lodge, and Meadowlark guest house, through the picnic area, and on to the lake. I think it's their daily ritual.

It was late May, and spring in the Poconos was approaching its peak. It was a little early for the laurel, but a great variety of flowering shrubs were showing delightful blooms. Robins and hummingbirds were building nests, and the one hundred acres of woodlands and lawns of the inn were decked out in green.

The Sterling Inn is one of the few full American plan inns remaining in northern Pennsylvania. It is possible to spend days at a time enjoying all of the varied activities and facilities without ever leaving the grounds.

The old bell from the South Sterling elementary school was rung to announce dinner. I walked through the card room and took a moment to note that there were literally hundreds of books. Four people were finishing up a rubber of bridge and one of them waved "hello."

Carmen Arneberg showed me to a table and I immediately fell into conversation with two delightful people from Philadelphia who said that they had been married for fifty-three years and had been coming to the Sterling Inn for a long, long time. They were

most enthusiastic.

"It really is hidden away in the mountains, isn't it? I don't think that you could find it if you didn't know where it was.

"Do you know why we like it here? It's because there are a lot of young people. Mr. and Mrs. Arneberg realize that people like us whose families have grown up and left home, are still very active and enjoy doing many, many things.

"Another reason is that the menu offers hearty dishes such as roast beef and roast pork and turkey—something that two people wouldn't often prepare for themselves at home. We especially like the blueberry hot cakes.

"Do you know that they have some kind of entertainment here almost every night of the week? There are activities like singing, movies, and lectures. Mr. Arneberg told me this afternoon that when the inn opens up in the spring of 1978 there will be a new, all-weather tennis court. Next year we will remember to bring our rackets!"

It may sound corny, but I'd say that the Sterling Inn is a place to stay young.

STERLING INN, Rte. 191, South Sterling, Pa. 18460; 717-676-3311. A 67-room secluded resort-inn in the Pocono Mountains, 8 mi. from I-84 and 12 mi. from I-380. American plan. Reservation and check in office closes at 10 p.m. Breakfast, lunch and dinner served to travelers daily. Breakfast served 8-9 a.m.; lunch served 12:30-1:30 p.m.; dinner served 6-7:15 p.m. No liquor served. Open weekends only beginning May 5 (Friday to Monday a.m.) until May 25; open every day thereafter until October 24 closing date. No pets. Swimming, putting greens, shuffleboard, all-weather tennis court and woodland walks on grounds. Golf courses and horseback riding nearby. Henry and Carmen Arneberg, Innkeepers.

Directions: From I-80, follow I-380 to Rte. 940 to Mount Pocono. At light, cross Rte. 611 and proceed on Rte. 196 north to Rte. 423. Drive north on Rte. 423 to Rte. 191 and travel ½ mile north to inn. From I-84, follow Rte. 507 south through Greentown and Newfoundland. In Newfoundland, pick up Rte. 191 and travel 4 mi. south to inn.

THE TAVERN
New Wilmington, Pennsylvania

*"The sheltered cot, the cultivated farm,
The never-failing brook, the busy meadow,
The decent church that topped the
    neighboring hill,
The Hawthorn bush, with seats
    beneath the shade,
For talking age and whispering lovers made."*

These words from Oliver Goldsmith in many ways express the beautiful countryside and ambience of New Wilmington, which is in the rolling country of northwest Pennsylvania. I was here to visit Cora Durrast, who for more than 45 years has been the innkeeper of The Tavern.

I enjoyed my trip down from the Berkshires, especially the drive through the beautiful farm country of Pennsylvania. The early corn was up, and farmers were harvesting the wheat and oats. The first cutting of hay was baled and waiting to be collected and put in the barns. As I drove, I kept my eye peeled for Amish buggies, and before long I spotted two or three.

At one farm an entire Amish family, dressed in the traditional clothing of their sect, was outside. Next to the road were tables piled high with the fresh eggs and produce they were selling to passersby. The corn on the cob looked particularly tempting, but I reminded myself that in just a few minutes I would be at The Tavern enjoying some wonderful country food.

And country food aplenty there was. The luncheon menu included chicken salad, chicken pie, ham loaf, pork chops, liver, flounder, ham, shrimp and scallops. The appetizers were homemade chicken noodle soup or potato soup, fruit cup, a variety of juices and white grape, cranberry or pineapple fruit shrub. A tossed green salad and a pear salad with a strawberry-pineapple whipped topping were also on the menu.

While I was making up my mind, two warm honey buns with whipped butter were placed in front of me. It took all of my resolve

not to eat them both immediately.

The people at the adjoing table were being served chicken pie. It looked delicious. Two waitresses passed bowls of vegetables; there must have been four or five different kinds. I decided on the smoked pork chops which came with a side order of very crisp pork dressing. The desserts included cherry crisp, butterscotch pie and all different kinds of ice cream and sherbet.

Meanwhile the expected guests had arrived and Cora was hurrying about, making certain that everything was just right. After they finished lunch and their bus departed, Cora and I had a chance for a little chat. She said that she just loved "Berkshire Travellers," that they were her kind of people, and that she frequently wished she had a few more rooms in the small lodge across the street because there were "more Travellers coming all the time."

New Wilmington is just a few minutes from I-80, the east/west highway that crosses northern Pennsylvania. I am happy to report that there is another Pennsylvania country inn, the Pine Barn Inn in Danville, further east on I-80. "That means they can be here for lunch and over there for dinner," said Cora.

"Or even vice versa," said I.

THE TAVERN, Box 153, New Wilmington, Pa. 16142; 412-946-2020. A bustling country restaurant on the town square with 5 sleeping rooms in a lodge directly across the street. European plan. Lunch and dinner served daily except Tuesdays. Reservations required. Closed Thanksgiving and Christmas. Sports and cultural events at Westminster College nearby. Mrs. Ernst Durrast, Innkeeper.

Directions: From I-80, take Exit 1-S, and follow Rte. 18 south to Rte. 208. Proceed east on 208 to town square. From I-79, follow Rte. 208 west for 14 mi. to New Wilmington.

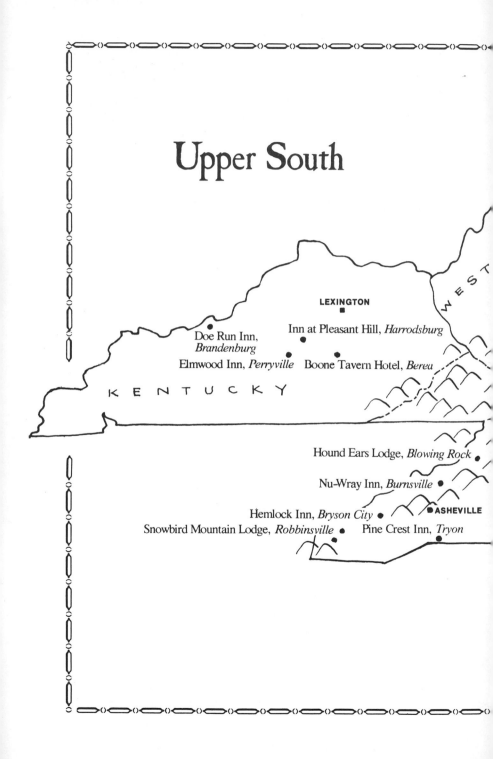

Upper South

WEST

LEXINGTON

Inn at Pleasant Hill, *Harrodsburg*

Doe Run Inn,
Brandenburg

Elmwood Inn, *Perryville* • Boone Tavern Hotel, *Berea*

K E N T U C K Y

Hound Ears Lodge, *Blowing Rock* •

Nu-Wray Inn, *Burnsville* •

Hemlock Inn, *Bryson City* • **ASHEVILLE**

Snowbird Mountain Lodge, *Robbinsville* • Pine Crest Inn, *Tryon*

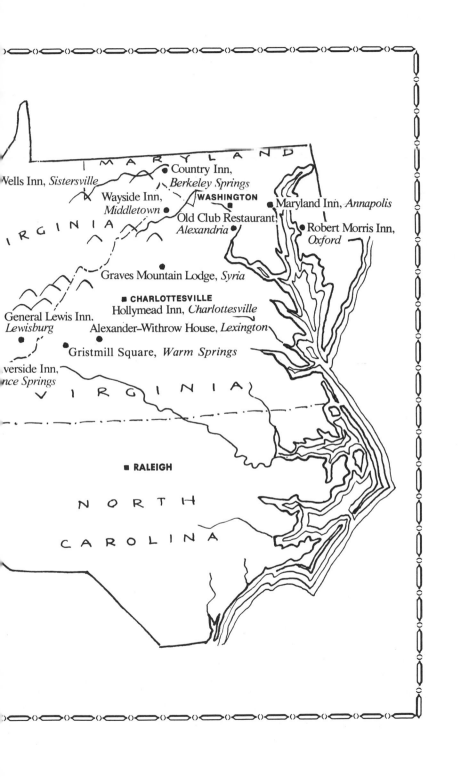

Kentucky

Berea College in Berea, Kentucky is undoubtedly one of the most unique institutions of higher learning in the U.S., if not the world. It has a 10-hour-weekly student work program involving 64 different departments of the college, and students are expected to prepare their schedule to work in this program which includes many arts and crafts. The college serves the youth of 230 mountain counties in the region known as Appalachia. Eighty percent of the students are from this region and are chosen on the basis of financial need, high scholastic standing, and character. The other twenty percent come from other states, as well as Europe, Asia, and Africa.

The Boone Tavern Hotel is owned by the college and the students have the option of working there as part of their work program. A tour of the college includes visiting many of the student work areas such as the woodworking and weaving shops. The tour leaves several times a day from the lobby of the Boone Tavern Hotel.

BOONE TAVERN HOTEL
Berea, Kentucky

From time to time during the past few years I have shared with you some of the letters I have received from Clare and Lucy DeeDee who live in Grand Rapids, Michigan, and who have been dear friends for many years. They have also recommended country inns in out-of-the-way places that I have then visited and included in subsequent editions.

This time as I was headed for the Boone Tavern in Berea, Kentucky, I reread the letter I received from them early in April, 1977, which told about their adventures in visiting this place for the first time. Here are a few excerpts:

"On our way home from Florida we had the pleasure of stopping at Boone Tavern for a night and just had to tell you that being here is like an oasis in the desert. Not that Kentucky is a desert, it is one of the most beautful places we have ever visited. We were driving north on the Interstate, and decided to stop off in Berea and found that they had a charming room available for us. We dressed for dinner as gentlemen are expected to wear coats, and then just plain relaxed. It was beautiful. In other words, 'we love this place'. We bought some beautiful pottery here and the food is delicious. Clare had extra helpings of the spoon bread."

Berea College Campus

I smiled at Lucy's ebullience, but it is that wonderful expectation of good that has made them such excellent Berkshire Travellers.

I couldn't help but remember my own first trip to the Boone Tavern in 1968. It was a very damp day at the end of two weeks of rain, and when I arrived I was delighted to find a fire in the sitting room fireplace and Dick Hougen, then the innkeeper, greeting me with a broad smile and a friendly welcome.

Now, many such trips later, stepping out of the bright August sunshine into the comparative coolness of the inn, I felt the welcome in 1977 from Curtis Reppert and Cecil Connor was every bit as enthusiastic as Dick's had been in 1968. They share the managerial duties and were themselves former students at Berea, completing the course in hotel management. Dick Hougen has retired to Cape Cod, after many years of service to the college and the hotel.

First order of the day was the touring of several of the newly-redecorated lodging rooms, and I found them both attractive and spotless. Most of the furniture has been made in the college woodworking shop and as always, about ninety percent of the staff is a part of the student work program or enrolled in the hotel management course.

"Many of our first-time guests stop here because it is on the main road to and from Florida," said Curtis. "But they return year after year for other reasons." One of these reasons, I couldn't help but reflect, is the food at the inn. For example, for lunch I enjoyed chicken served in a bird's nest. In this case the "bird's nest" was a basket of shredded potatoes with a little spot of cinnamon-berry jelly to add spice. Also on the menu were several other of Dick Hougen's highly original dishes which are still being used at the inn. These include southern fried chicken with hush puppies, roast leg of lamb in a caper gravy, and minced chicken patty with a supreme sauce and served with fresh cranberry relish at all seasons of the year. For dessert I had the Jefferson Davis pie which is also in one of the Boone Tavern Cookbooks. In addition there was banana cream pie, cherry cobbler a la mode, and several others. The evening meal has the same basic menu as the one offered at lunch except that there are some additional first courses. Incidentally, anyone intending to have lunch or dinner should phone ahead for reservations.

BOONE TAVERN HOTEL, Berea, Ky. 40403; 606-986-9341. A 60-room village inn in a unique college community on I-75, 40 mi. south of Lexington, Ky. European plan. Breakfast, lunch, dinner served daily to travelers by sittings only. Dinner and Sunday noon coats required for men, dresses or pant suits for ladies. Open every day of the year. All campus activities open to guests; campus tours twice daily except Saturdays and Sundays. Tennis on grounds. Golf, pool and bicycles nearby. Berea is on Eastern Time. Curtis Reppert and Cecil M. Connor, Innkeepers.

Directions: Take Berea exit from I-75. One mi. north to hotel.

DOE RUN INN
Brandenburg, Kentucky

It was dusk. I had walked down the path across the wooden footbridge to the island which is formed by two branches of the Doe Run Creek. There was a light mist rising from the waters which were swollen by the recent rains. It wasn't hard to imagine Indian canoes shooting over the rapids and into the dark forest. Now the sky overhead was filled with swallows that were making a few last circles before disappearing into the night.

Doe Run Inn is just about as "pioneer America," I believe, as it is possible to get in the latter part of the 1970s. It was built as a mill about 165 years ago out of huge limestone blocks four feet thick, made to repel Indian attacks. The tremendous front door could withstand any attempt to break in, and the huge fireplace still sends warmth radiating throughout the room.

Earlier that afternoon I had arrived during a warm spell, and I found that the big fans in my bedroom were a welcome change from conventional air conditioning. Although my room happened to have

210

a private bath, "down the hall" in this inn actually means that many rooms have separate showers and bathrooms off the hallway. The atmosphere is rustic, and the floors have a definite slant.

I love to wander through the upper hallways and see the collection of emblems, banners, and old prints. It is possible to look at some of the bedrooms through hallway windows, and I noticed that while some of them are very small, one bedroom had four beds, and still another had five! "It was simply impossible to divide them up," explained Curt Brown later on at dinner.

The doorway to my bedroom, Number 5, which was the honeymoon suite, had to be cut at an angle at the top in order to accommodate the angle of the door frame. My big comfortable bed had belonged to Lucille Brown's grandmother.

During the warm weather, the porch overlooking the creek and the island is very popular for all three meals. It was here that I had a nice long talk with Lucille and Curt, and they told me several extremely amusing anecdotes about Kentucky innkeeping. "The inn had been in the family for many, many years and we have been here since the mid-1930s." I asked about the most popular menu items.

"Chicken and ham are really the most popular here. We actually serve 450 chickens a week and about four hams a day. Curt illustrated his enthusiasm by ordering a second piece of Lucille's lemon pie. "I make at least five a day," she said.

The next morning, about as dewy a one as I have seen, I had a country breakfast of Kentucky ham, fried eggs and grits, and became acquainted with Tom and Marilyn Good of Michigan. This was the last stop for them on what had been a trip to many inns in CIBR. We all agreed that there was no place anywhere quite like the Doe Run Inn.

DOE RUN INN, Rte. 2, Brandenburg, Ky. 40108; 502-422-9982. A 17-room country inn reminiscent of the backwoods on Rte. 448, 4 mi. south of Brandenburg, 38 mi. south of Louisville. Near Fort Knox. European plan. 5 rooms with private bath; 12 rooms with shared baths. Breakfast, lunch, and dinner served to travelers daily. Closed Christmas Eve and Christmas Day. Hiking, fishing and swimming nearby. Curtis and Lucille Brown, Innkeepers.

Directions: From Louisville take 64W through Indiana to 135S. Cross the toll bridge to Kentucky and follow 1051 to the dead end. Turn right on 448 and follow signs to Doe Run Inn.

ELMWOOD INN
Perryville, Kentucky

I had a most enjoyable ride, using the Kentucky back roads from Berea to Perryville, and now approaching this central Kentucky town, I found that Perryville, according to the sign, has 800 people. Route 150 goes right through the town, and there are several signs indicating the proximity of the famous Perryville battlefield.

I arrived after a good cooling-off rain and the trees in front of the inn, where the lawn slopes down to the river, had more than their share of birds. The majestic Doric columns on the front were beautifully set off by the handsome dark brick of the building and by the house shutters. I stepped inside to find a picture of Colonel Sanders enjoying, what I understand, was one of his many visits here each year. I must be sure to ask Gladys Coyle what he orders.

The Elmwood Inn can only happen in Kentucky. It is located in the residential section of Perryville in a grove of maple and sweet gum trees alongside the Chaplin River. The building was constructed in 1842 and became a field hospital following the battle of Perryville during the Civil War. The inn has been carefully furnished with antiques and Kentucky and Civil War memorabilia. Each of the six serving rooms has been named for some worthy individual well-known to the region or to the community.

Innkeeper Gladys Coyle and I were walking through the inn once more, which included a visit to a very spotless kitchen. "What's new and exciting?" I asked. "Well, I think the most exciting thing that has happened was that Governor Reagan and his staff dined here a short time ago. He was in Kentucky to speak to the Young Republican Party and we had a lovely party for him."

I stopped for a moment to sit down in the graceful living room and she showed me several letters from people who had enjoyed

lunch or dinner (no lodgings available here) at the inn. There were commendations from Minnesota, Florida, Michigan, Utah, Washington, California and New Hampshire.

She also reported that the restoration program in Perryville is moving along at a great rate. Several buildings are in the process of being restored and she felt that in a very short time Perryville would take its place among the other historical cities in the South.

One of the luncheon offerings I have enjoyed in the past is fresh fruit arranged around a generous scoop of sherbet, served with hot biscuits and Kentucky fried ham.

We also took a few minutes to look at the menu for that evening, which included sweet breads, fried shrimp, Florida pompano, and other tempting dishes.

"Gladys, tell me truthfully, what does Colonel Sanders order when he eats here?"

"Well, he loves the chicken, hot biscuits, small new potatoes, a big salad and the peas," she said. "I have to tell you that he says our chicken is the best he has ever eaten."

ELMWOOD INN, Perryville, Ky. 40468; 606-332-2271. A country restaurant in an historically important Kentucky town on Rtes. 150 and 68, 9 mi. from Harrodsburg and Danville. Near the Perryville Battlefield State Shrine. No lodgings. Lunch and dinner served daily except Mondays. Closed Christmas Eve and Christmas Day. Open year-round. Gladys Coyle, Innkeeper.

Directions: Exit Bluegrass Pkwy. at Bardstown and take Hwy. 150 into Perryville. From Harrodsburg take Rte. 68 to Perryville.

It was in the late 1960s that I first visited Shakertown at Pleasant Hill, Kentucky, and since that time it has been one of the continuing joys of my life to revisit it. I am delighted to say that I receive a steady stream of letters from readers who have visited Shakertown for the first time and have been introduced to the Shaker way of life.

The Shaker colony at Pleasant Hill began in 1805 and grew to become a unique and active community. It is reflected in the restored village today. The Shakers were a religious group whose formal name was the United Society of Believers In Christ's Second Appearing. They were termed Shakers by witnesses to their trembling and frenzied devotional dancing. Their basic tenets were celibacy, confession of sins, separation from the world, and common ownership of property. Industrious and inventive, they made lasting and important contributions to agriculture and technology. And their furniture, although considered "plain" in its time, is now recognized as classic in early American design.

After a century of prosperity, the Pleasant Hill adventure came to an end when the last member died in 1923. Throughout their history the gentle Shakers of Pleasant Hill were always hospitable to "the world's people," as they termed outsiders, and the village is once again welcoming travelers.

A non-profit preservation group is re-creating a total Shaker environment by carefully restoring the 27 original buildings, and by providing a sensitive interpretation of the Shaker way of life for visitors. Eating and sleeping in the atmosphere of Shaker tradition, and in original buildings, lend a totality to the Pleasant Hill experience, making it a unique way to grasp a remarkable segment of the American past.

INN AT PLEASANT HILL
Shakertown, Kentucky

On this visit in the summer of 1977, I had a room on the third floor of the Trustee's Building, again looking at one of my favorite views down through the gardens and fields past the old road of the original village. I could see several of the distinctive red brick buildings of restored Shakertown.

My room was unusually large with two twin beds, and underneath each of these were two trundle beds, which could be pulled out for young people to use. There were Shaker pegs for clothing, a handy built-in closet, and a distinctive chest of Shaker drawers. Shaker rockers and straight chairs, as well as a candle stand, completed the picture.

Since the inn at Shakertown was first established, every effort has been made to keep the Shaker ambience, and at the same time maintain an inn where everyone would be comfortable and happy. As a result, there are good modern bathrooms at this inn, and also television sets for those who prefer them. There is even air conditioning which is most welcome during the warm Kentucky weather. However, all in all, it is a very acceptable compromise with Shaker austerity.

In my bedroom, which was typical, the walls were white; an interesting contrast to overhead beams, chair rails and pegs which were colored "Brethren Shop Red," an authentic Shaker color. Ordinarily, I would like to have watercolors and prints on such pristine walls, but I found this most pleasant. The furniture was all reproductions of Shaker pieces. (Incidentally, many of these pieces can be found in Ejner Handberg's three books—*Shop Drawings of Shaker Furniture and Woodenware,* which is published by The Berkshire Traveller Press and available at the Pleasant Hill Gift Shop.)

As I stepped outside my bedroom, one of four on the front part of the fourth floor, I could see the window used in earlier times by "watchers" who made certain that the rules of celibacy were being kept by the members of the village. A circular staircase took me down to both the second and first floor. This is one of the features of the Trustee's House and a terrible temptation for any young person, including myself, to slide all the way down. It's much too steep.

On the first floor is the dining room where waiters and

waitresses are dressed in Kentucky-style clothes. There is a sitting room off the hallway which has a collection of at least 12 highback Shaker rockers and when they are empty in this very simple room it presents a most interesting picture.

The Shakers at Pleasant Hill were farmers, and this is reflected in the food with hearty offerings such as country ham, cheddar cheese pie and fruit tarts.

Shakertown is open year-round providing food, lodging, and a marvelous opportunity to step into the American past. There are some special weekends during January and February, and I would suggest contacting Ann Voris, the new innkeeper, about some of the events. There is also a harvest festival during the last three weeks in September.

Shakertown is a marvelous experience for everyone in the family, and it is made doubly exciting by the excellent Inn at Pleasant Hill.

INN AT PLEASANT HILL, Shakertown, Ky., P.O. address: Rte. 4, Harrodsburg, Ky. 40330; 606-734-5411. A 63-room country inn in a restored Shaker village on Rte. 68, 7 mi. northeast of Harrodsburg, 25 mi. southwest of Lexington. European plan. Breakfast, lunch, dinner served daily to travelers. Open year-round. Suggest contacting Inn about winter schedule. Closed Christmas Eve and Christmas Day. Ann Voris, Innkeeper.

Directions: From Lexington take Rte. 68 south toward Harrodsburg. From Louisville, take I-64 to Lawrenceburg and Graeffenburg exit (not numbered). Follow Rte. 127 south to Harrodsburg and Rte. 68 northeast to Shakertown.

Maryland

MARYLAND INN
Annapolis, Maryland

The night was filled with rain, pelting enormous drops that clouded my windshield instantly and made the lights of the Maryland Inn even more welcome than usual.

I parked my car and splashed across the brick streets, up the wooden stairway and through the big doors into the lobby of the inn feeling like a Colonial wayfarer. Innkeeper Peg Bednarsky was behind the main desk with her usual warm greeting.

"Well, what room would you like?" Peg asked. "We can give you

a view of St. Anne's Church and the Circle, or the old town and the bay."

I chose one facing the harbor, and found myself in a newly-decorated room with colonial blue trim in pleasant contrast to white plaster walls.

Rain or no, it was good to be back in Annapolis, because I knew that the rain would pass and, hopefully, tomorrow I would be able to renew my walking tour of the historic section of the town. This time I would visit Hammond-Harwood House not far from the inn, and also take a guided tour of the U.S. Naval Academy.

Dinner that evening was in the Treaty of Paris Restaurant, named to commemorate the document offically ending the Revolutionary War. It was signed by representatives of nine states in 1784 in the Maryland State House which is just across the square.

Proprietor Paul Pearson joined me for a few minutes, and explained that there has been an extensive amount of restoration in recent months. "We've restored the main lobby and other parts of the inn to its Victorian period which was a very important time for the inn. We've replaced the iron railings on the porch outside the main entrance with the original wood banjo boards, and you will see that we replaced the main entry door with a reproduction of the original Victorian period entry door. We have a cabinetmaker fabricating wooden shutters for the great windows in the Duke of Gloucester Room which will be installed very shortly. In fact, the entire Duke of

Gloucester dining room will be returned to its Victorian splendor as an intimate ballroom."

Paul was very enthusiastic about the fact that the inn had received substantial matching funds, grant-in-aid from the National Park Service, recognizing the historic importance of the inn and enabling the preservation efforts to continue.

The Maryland Inn's location on Chesapeake Bay means that there is a great deal of very succulent seafood on the menu. This includes crab Imperial, flounder stuffed with oysters, whole baby flounder stuffed with crabmeat, as well as cream of crab soup.

Thomas Hyde built this inn which was erected on a "lot of ground" originally set aside for the use of the town drummer. Early advertisements typified it as "an elegant brick house in the dry and healthy part of the city ... one of the first houses in the state for a house of entertainment."

Entertainment today is being carried on in a very exciting way as a result of Paul Pearson's energetic efforts, and I would imagine Ordinary Keeper Hyde would approve of such festive occasions as Dickens' Christmas, Thanksgiving, Bastille Day, Heritage Weekend, and the Freaker's Ball on Halloween.

Furthermore, today's entertainment features weekly appearances of great jazz artists of the caliber of Charlie Byrd (who makes the inn his second home), Ethel Ennis, Earle "Fatha" Hines, and Dizzy Gillespie. These artists are all part of the continuing successful program of the Maryland Inn Jazz Club.

The next morning the rain had stopped, and white sails were once again sparkling on Chesapeake Bay. Some of the skipjacks were on their way out to the oyster beds. Perhaps I would rent a sailboat and do a little exploring myself, savoring by sea even more of the magic of Annapolis..

MARYLAND INN, Church Circle, Annapolis, Md. 21401; 301-263-2641. A 44-room 18th century village inn in a history-laden town, 20 mi. from Baltimore and Washington, D.C. Near U.S. Naval Academy and Chesapeake Bay. European plan. Breakfast, lunch, and dinner served to travelers daily. Sunday brunch served year-round. Jazz Club, music nightly except Mondays in the King of France Tavern. Tours arranged to historic and scenic points of interest. Tennis and sailing school available. Paul Pearson, Proprietor; Peg Bednarsky, Innkeeper.

Directions: From Baltimore, take Rte. 2 south to first directional turnoff "Washington/Annapolis." From Washington, take Rte. 50 east to exit "Annapolis, Naval Academy."

Captain Bill Benson's Oxford-Bellevue ferry

ROBERT MORRIS INN
Oxford, Maryland

In the 1977 edition, I mentioned the fact that Benjamin and Kent Gibson, the sons of Wendy and Ken Gibson would be going to school, and Wendy felt she would have more time to herself. "Whether to play tennis or work at the inn remains the question," she said.

I am now ready to report that Wendy's tennis game made little progress in 1977, because it was a very busy year at the Robert Morris Inn. I feel she has captured some of the ideals of this lovely place on the Chesapeake Bay, and I am going to share a few lines from a letter I received from her early in December 1977:

"The Robert Morris Inn is in the process of becoming an Historic Trust. It has been one year in the making and we are all very excited about it. We had some marvelous articles written about us in *Holiday, Good Housekeeping, Maryland,* and *Baltimore Magazine.*

"I also did my complete bed check on every room in the inn. It is a great treat to go bouncing from one bed to another messing up the spreads and making wrinkles. As a result of this testing, we bought some new mattresses and box springs. Another major improvement was chairs. After a two-month search I finally found the style I liked, so now all the rooms in the Lodge have two new chairs. I also put a gorgeous antique chair in Room 2. I picked up some colonial prints in Connecticut, and have since had them framed and placed in ten of the rooms.

"I now have 'Wendy's Corner'; it is a small antique china closet where I display my canisters, some homemade items, and nautical jewelry. This has been a real success.

"Ken and I have been able to role switch now and then, so that I can work for him and he can be with Kent and Benjamin. There are two qualifications for this — a great husband and a close proximity to work. The nights I work, he picks up the boys at school, spends the evening with them and puts them to bed. The nights he works, I do it. It has really given us both the chance to appreciate what the other goes through.

"We have acquired a basset hound named Morris. I must admit I have mixed feelings about him, but the kids love him and Ken never had a dog as a boy, so he is rather happy about him, too. The biggest problem is that this summer Morris would go down to our beach and bring me the guests' towels and shirts."

The Robert Morris is a cozy, old waterside inn on the banks of the Tred Avon River. It dates back to 1710 and was named for one of the town of Oxford's most distinguished early citizens. Ships' timbers were used in the construction, and ballast stones can be seen in the fireplace. The original murals in the main dining room were copied from wallpaper samples used 135 years ago. They depict four American scenes of the early 19th century.

The sizes of the lodging rooms in the main building vary, and several of them have some unique touches, such as a closet with a window in it, or a bed that is so high a small set of steps is needed to reach it. Rooms are also available in the Lodge which is located on the Point, just a few paces away, with a marvelous view of the scope of Chesapeake Bay.

Oysters prepared in many ways, as well as a wide variety of Chesapeake Bay seafood dishes, are the specialties of the menu. A seafood platter includes crabmeat, shrimp, small crab imperial, rockfish, clams, and oysters. Local fishermen say that the oysters a la Gino are some of the best. Incidentally, breakfast includes scrapple and homefries, as well as omelets and blueberry pancakes. I don't know how it manages, but Oxford is still one of the most lovely, unspoiled villages on the eastern seaboard. It is not "touristy" in any fashion, and it is a real pleasure to walk the tree-lined streets and see the old houses and the view of the Tred Avon from the Strand.

Anyone stopping at the Robert Morris should say "Hi" for me to Ken, Wendy, Kent, and Benjamin and tell Morris, the basset hound, that I will be along soon.

ROBERT MORRIS INN, Oxford, Md. 21654; 301-226-5111. A 31-room village inn in a secluded colonial community on the Tred Avon, 10 mi. from Easton, Md. European plan. 6 rooms with private baths; 25 rooms with shared baths. Breakfast, lunch and dinner served to travelers daily. Open year-round except Christmas Day. No pets. Tennis, golf, sailing, swimming and bicycles nearby. Kenneth and Wendy Gibson, Innkeepers.

Directions: From Delaware Memorial Bridge, follow Rte. 13 south to Rte. 301 and proceed south to Rte. 50, then east on Rte. 50 to Easton. From Chesapeake Bay Bridge, follow Rte. 50-301 to Rte. 50 and proceed east to Easton. From Chesapeake Bay Bridge Tunnel, follow Rte. 13 north to Rte. 50 and proceed west to Easton. From Easton, follow Rte. 333 to Oxford and inn.

North Carolina

HEMLOCK INN
Bryson City, North Carolina

I try to visit almost every inn in this book every year, but sometimes my plans go awry. Instead of traveling to the Great Smokies in the fall of 1977 to visit John and Ella Jo Shell at the Hemlock Inn, a last minute change of plans took me to Italy. However, perhaps excerpts from Ella Jo's letter will bring all of our readers up to date, and at the same time provide further insight into this beautiful inn high in the western mountains of North Carolina.

"We opened early (April 24th) this year with a full house: a group of wild flower enthusiasts to hear Arthur Stupka, the first Smoky Mountain Park Naturalist, who is a friend of ours. Arthur shared his slides, his books, time, and took folks on nature walks. His wife, Margaret, is a creative person who relates her slides of wild flowers to different fabric media. The Stupkas are wonderful to share their wealth of knowledge through the years with Hemlock Inn guests.

"In June we had a little activity added to our routine. Our daughter, Diane, and our two beautiful granddaughters, Jenifer, 5 and Laurel Ann, 3, came for three weeks. Up goes the swing in the front yard and immediately the older folks become playmates and a lot of giggles and fun are shared by all. This scene helps to prove that children add spice and life to Hemlock Inn. It encourages young parents to bring their children and grandparents can share the place they found years ago with the rest of their family.

"Our staff was super-great this year. Unfortunately, the day we opened, our beloved cook, Myrtle Mask, passed on. She had been here 16 years and was our stabilizing force, not only as an employee with local contacts as she was a native of our area, but also, she was a real friend to all of us. No problem was ever too great for her to have an answer, whether it was feeding ten more people at the last minute or getting a car out of a ditch. We miss her very much and will always love her.

"So many interesting guests come with CIBR and we were delighted to see them in May and September when our weather is so beautiful. The book brings us people from other parts of the country that are so much fun.

"Hemlock Inn continues to operate at its measured pace. We are a mile off the main highway at the top of the mountain. Breakfast is served at 8:30 a.m. and dinner at 6 p.m. There is no TV or telephones in the rooms, no swimming pool and we probably wouldn't suit a lot of people. Yet there are so many busy folks in our rush-rush world who need a break from golf and country clubs and want seclusion—a quiet walk in the pretty woods, a good book to read on a private screened porch, to hear the brown thrush's beautiful song in the morning, to stroll by the waters of the deep creek or ride a tube down it, to not have any decisions to make, even in choosing the meals. As you know, we serve from Lazy Susan tables; or as a friend who wrote a nice article about us after a visit last summer, says, 'Rock and Roll—North Carolina style. You rock on the front porch in one of the many big rockers all day, eat the delicious homemade yeast rolls served at the meals and go to sleep with the symphony of crickets.'

"After nine years as innkeepers we still love it and so do most of our folks."

I'm happy to say that my plans are already made for a spring visit to the Hemlock Inn this year.

HEMLOCK INN, Bryson City, N.C. 28713; 704-488-9820. A 25-room Smoky Mountain inn 4 mi. from Bryson City and 60 mi. from Asheville. Near Fontana Village, Cherokee, and Pisgah National Forest. Modified American plan omits lunch. Breakfast and dinner served to travelers by reservation only. Sunday dinner served at noontime. Open from early May to early November. No pets. Shuffleboard, skittles, ping pong, hiking trails on grounds. Tubing, rafting, and golf nearby. Ella Jo and John Shell, Innkeepers.

Directions: Located 1 mi. off Rte. 19 between Cherokee and Bryson City, N.C. Take paved road to top of mountain.

HOUND EARS LODGE AND CLUB
Blowing Rock, North Carolina

There are few places mentioned in this book which may seem as far removed from the concept of a New England country inn as Stockbridge is from Sydney, Australia. These include the Inn at Rancho Santa Fe, California, the Bay Shore Yacht Club in Florida, and Hound Ears Lodge in Blowing Rock, North Carolina. I was persuaded that, although these places were not all that quaint or particularly ancient, they did have some of the qualities for which I search in a country inn. These included warmth, involvement, and the opportunity to meet and enjoy myself with other people.

It is my assumption that there are several different kinds of country inns and resort inns. I enjoy myself at all of the inns featured in this book, and from the volume of my correspondence, apparently there are a number of people who share my enthusiasm.

Hound Ears is a full American plan resort-inn. The emphasis is on some great golf, marvelous scenery, and in the winter, some excellent skiing both on the grounds and nearby. It is an inn for adults with an active interest in outdoor activity such as golf, tennis, swimming, and walking in the peaceful woods. Because there are so many activities nearby such as the Tweetsie Railroad and the Land of Oz, the younger generation finds it to their liking as well. I met and talked to quite a few families on my visits. They enjoyed climbing Grandfather Mountain.

Hound Ears is tucked away in a valley of the high country of North Carolina's Blue Ridge Mountains. Many people who visit there eventually buy houses which dot the surrounding mountainside.

All of the furnishings and appointments, both interior and exterior, are carefully thought out and harmonized. For example, my room was done in compatible shades of brown with yellow sheets on my bed. All of the buildings were set among rhododendron and evergreen trees. In many places, huge boulders were allowed to remain where they rested, and the road was built around them, curving, twisting, and ever-climbing.

It is difficult in mid-summer, when experiencing the verdant greens and fairways punctuated by the clear white, menacing sand traps, to realize that everything is covered by many inches of snow in the winter, and that the other face of Hound Ears is one that includes spectacular alpine and cross-country skiing, roaring fireplaces, and the exhilaration of pure winter air.

HOUND EARS LODGE and CLUB, P.O. Box 188, Blowing Rock, N.C. 28605; 704-963-4321. A luxurious 25-room resort-inn on Rte. 105, 6 mi. from Boone. Near natural attractions. American plan. Meals served to houseguests only. Open year-round. 18-hole golf course, swimming, skiing, and tennis on grounds. Bill Jeffcoat, Innkeeper.

Directions: From Winston-Salem, follow Rte. 421 west to Boone, then travel south on Rte. 105 to inn. From Asheville, follow Rtes. 19 and 19E to Pineola, then Rte. 181 to Linville and Rte. 105 north to inn. From Bristol, Va., and I-81, follow Rte. 421 east to Vilas (mountainous), then Rte. 321 east to Boone. In Boone, pick up Rte. 105 and turn on Shulls Mills Rd.

NU-WRAY INN
Burnsville, North Carolina

There was a noise. An insistent urging, cajoling clang of a bell. I awakened from a sound sleep in my somewhat austere bedroom on the third floor of the Nu-Wray Inn and realized that Rush Wray, the innkeeper, was informing all of his house guests that it was 8 a.m., and exactly thirty minutes before breakfast.

About 29½ minutes later I stumbled down the stairway into the main living room where I found the other house guests seated on the various Carolina antique furniture that Rush has scattered around informally, all shaking their heads and saying the same thing:

"I don't know how he does it. This is the only place I've ever stayed where they wake you up with a bell." In just a few moments the bell rang once again, this time with our host standing in the hallway at the entrance to the dining room.

Upon that signal we all ventured forth like a group of hungry hippopotami, to be greeted in the main dining room by the most magnificent sight that I could imagine at that hour of the morning — great long tables with white tablecloths covered with platters of scrambled eggs, steaming pancakes, warm syrup, country ham, grits, applesauce, hot biscuits, apple butter, great compotes of honey, and tubs of fresh country butter.

Rush introduced all of the newcomers, and we sat down to pass the food, talk, laugh, and eat.

What a fantastic way to start the day in the North Carolina mountains!

There are two meals a day served at the Nu-Wray; the other is dinner. It is at six-thirty and reservations are necessary. There is just one sitting, and if you are not there when the bell rings, you've missed it.

225

At the Nu-Wray there are old-fashioned door keys, and every guest returns his to the old-fashioned key rack in the lobby. There is a big fireplace at one end, and many, many antiques, including rockers. There is an old Regina, like the one at the Botsford Inn in Farmington, Michigan, which is an old-fashioned music box that has metal discs. On the second floor they have a most charming drawing room furnished with family antiques.

Burnsville is located 3000-feet above sea level in the North Carolina mountains just a few miles from the highest peak in the east, Mt. Mitchell. The Parkway Playhouse Summer Theatre, which has been operating for thirty years, offers a new play every week during July and August, and the Burnsville Painting Classes, a fine art school which has been operating for thirty-one years, is also in session during those months. "Music in the Mountain" presents lovely concerts every Sunday night during the summer. The area is rich in beautiful drives and walks, and is ideal for photographs, botany, bird watching and back roading. Although Rush indicates that the inn is open every day of the year, it will close January, February, and March of 1978, so anyone traveling at that time better telephone ahead.

NU-WRAY INN, Burnsville, N.C. 28714; 704-682-2329. A 35-room village inn on town square on Rte. 19E, 38 mi. north of Asheville. A few miles from Mt. Mitchell. Modified American plan omits lunch and Sunday night supper. Breakfast and dinner served every weekday to travelers. Noon dinner served on Sundays only. Open every day of the year. Golf, swimming, hiking and skiing nearby. Rush T. Wray, Innkeeper. Mrs. Annie Wray Bennett, Hostess.

Directions: From Asheville, go north on Rte. 19-23 for 18 miles, then continue on 19. Five miles from Burnsville, 19 becomes 19E. From the north via Bristol or Johnson City, Tenn., take Rte. 19-23 to Unicoi. Turn left on 107 to N.C. State Line. Take 226 and turn right on Rte. 197 at Red Hill to Burnsville.

PINE CREST INN
Tryon, North Carolina

The telephone rang about 9:30 p.m. It was Jim Mellow from St. Louis and he was full of enthusiasm.

"I'm here at the Pine Crest and it is really beautiful," he said. "You know, as soon as I drove in to the parking lot, a gentleman approached me and said 'you must be Jim Mellow from St. Louis.'

I guess my Missouri license plate gave me away." I laughed and said, "That must have been Bob Hull."

Jim went on. "The weather is really terrific, but then it is most of the time, because it is in a thermal belt. I have a room in one of the cottages called 'Stone House', and it even has a fireplace. In fact, the fire was all laid for me when I came in."

I told him I remembered the cottage because I had stayed there myself. Many of the cottages have fireplaces.

I asked him about dinner. "It was delightful," he said. "We had a buffet dinner by candlelight. I found out that many of the waiters have been here for twenty years. In fact one of them, Theron Barton, who is 76 years old, has been at the Pine Crest for 63 years. They told me that he just won an award for being the third oldest waiter in the United States!"

The Pine Crest is in the foothills of the Blue Ridge Mountains near Asheville, in the town of Tryon, which in itself is a very interesting place. Many artists and writers have moved there over the recent years, finding inspiration in these mountains where nature has been so generous. Because of its advantageous location and its healthful climate, Tryon is an ideal place to spend vacation. Many guests return to the Pine Crest year after year and make arrangements to meet each other on the next trip.

The rooms in the individual cottages are furnished in Carolina furniture which is handmade locally, and many of them have splendid views of the mountains. One of them by the way is called

"Swayback" and was at one time occupied by F. Scott Fitzgerald.

The innkeepers at Pine Crest are Fran and Bob Hull who say of themselves, "We left Fairfield County, Connecticut, and corporate living about six years ago, and have found a completely different way of life here keeping a country inn." Fran does all of the cooking which is often a great surprise to the guests, because she manages to look so cool and chic, in spite of the rigors of the kitchen.

Apparently the new way of life agrees with Bob and Fran, and with their guests as well. "We do like to do things in our own way," says Bob. "We like jackets and ties on gentlemen at dinner, although ties can be eliminated in the warm weather. We think it is important to have the morning paper at your table at breakfast, and a delivery of ice to your room late in the afternoon. Most of the time we have a single entree at dinner, although some nights we might have two."

Back to the telephone call from Jim Mellow: I thanked him very much for calling me, and told him I was delighted he was having such a good time. "I certainly am," he said, "and I will be back again next spring."

PINE CREST INN, P.O. Box 1030, Tryon, N.C. 28782; 704-859-9135. A 34-room resort-inn midway between Asheville, N.C. and Greenville/Spartanburg, S.C. Breakfast, lunch, and dinner served daily to travelers. Closed January. Attended leashed pets allowed. Golf, tennis, and swimming at nearby country clubs. Riding, nature walks, rock hunting nearby. Reservations required. Robert and Fran Hull, Innkeepers.

Directions: From Asheville, take I-26 to Tryon exit, then 108 to Tryon. Go through town. Do not cross railroad tracks but bear left to Pine Crest Lane. The inn is at the end of the lane. From Spartanburg/Greenville take I-85 north to I-26. Exit at Columbus, N.C. Take Rte. 108 toward Tryon—go through town. Do not cross railroad tracks but bear left to Pine Crest Lane. The inn is at the end of the lane.

SNOWBIRD MOUNTAIN LODGE
Robbinsville, North Carolina

Ed Williams handed me a card that listed 314 birds of the Middle Atlantic states. "I've been able to identify about 70 of these," he said, "but I'm still in the learning stage. Some of our guests can go as high as 110. We are really a focal point for people who love birds."

We were sitting where everyone sits at Snowbird Mountain Lodge—on the terrace which almost hangs over Lake Santeetlah, at

least a thousand feet below. Gazing over the railings we could see a tiny automobile on the thin, winding sliver of road climbing the adjacent mountain. Directly in front of us, almost close enough to touch, were at least fifteen majestic mountain peaks, with heights from 4,000 to 5,500 feet.

Mary, Ed's wife, joined us and the talk turned to the changing colors of leaves and flowers with each of the seasons.

"In the springtime," Mary informed me, "the trailing arbutus, all of the violets, the laurel and dogwood are indescribably beautiful. We go into midsummer with the crimson Bee Balm, cardinal flowers, Turk's cap, Carolina lilies, and of course, the rhododendron which reaches its peak bloom about the Fourth of July.

"What can we say about fall? Can you imagine all of these trees in full color in October?"

Ed started to talk about the birds that have been sighted at or near Snowbird, but Mary announced that lunch was ready. I noticed that there were quite a few people missing whom I had met at breakfast, and Ed explained that there were many hikers and 'back roaders' at the inn. Box lunches were provided because people preferred to be out in the great woods. The Joyce Kilmer Memorial Forest is just two miles away.

Along with the fact that the inn is located literally on the top of a mountain, there are a great many activities to enjoy in the daytime — shuffleboard, horseshoes, skittles and of course, all of the great hiking and walking trails. There's also some stream and lake fishing nearby. I'm happy to report that along with the books which are on the tables in the natural wood-paneled lodging rooms, there is a huge library that affords a lot of good vacation reading.

The glorious, nature-filled days at Snowbird result in hearty appetites. Among the tempting main dishes are fresh mountain trout Almandine, roast beef, fresh ham, and steaks. All of the baking is done in the spotless kitchen. Breakfasts also are a highlight with delicious coffee made with spring water and marvelous sausage.

That evening after dinner I was seated next to the fireplace enjoying the welcome warmth against the cool mountain air, when Ed came over to introduce one of the guests. "This gentleman," he said, "is sure that he sighted a bird here today that hasn't been reported in some time. He calls it a blue-eyed, speckle-bearded Berkshire Traveller."

SNOWBIRD MOUNTAIN LODGE, Joyce Kilmer Forest Rd., Robbinsville, N.C. 28771; 704-479-3433. A 16-room inn on top of the Great Smokies, 12 mi. from Robbinsville. American plan. Lunch and dinner served to travelers by reservation only. No children under age 12. No pets. Open May 19 through October 29. Swimming, fishing, hiking, nearby. For nature lovers. Mary and Ed Williams, Innkeepers.

Directions: Approaching from the northeast or south, take U.S. 19 and 129; from the northwest, take U.S. 129.

Virginia

WAYSIDE INN
Middletown, Virginia

The flickering candlelight in the Slave Kitchen cast our shadows on the smoke-blackened beams overhead and was reflected in the pewter plates, pitchers, and old windows. The fireplace radiated a warm glow and two cast iron pots on the crane gurgled and boiled.

"This room was hidden," explained Cathy Castro, innkeeper of the Wayside Inn. "It was discovered by accident, and restoring it was a great deal of fun. Those are the original brick walls, and I see you've already noticed the adz marks on the beams. All of the tools are from the colonial period."

The Wayside Inn dates from at least 1797. It is correctly referred to as an historic restoration. It was carefully restored to its present form after 1960 when Leo Bernstein, lawyer and banker from nearby Washington happened to drive through the main street in Middletown and recognized the inn's tremendous possibilities. The inn is an antique lover's paradise. Its rooms are packed with

a mind-boggling collection of tables, chests, paintings, and *objets d'art*.

The menu includes some very old country recipes, such as spoon bread and peanut soup, as well as whole, baked tomatoes, Virginia country ham with red-eye gravy, and both smothered and pan-fried chicken. Homemade bread and real whipped butter accompany every dinner. Young people wearing the costume of the era serve these tempting dishes.

Three meals plus afternoon tea are served seven days a week in dining rooms decorated in accordance with their names: the Front Room, Lord Fairfax Room, President's Room, and Senseney Room. In earlier days the Wayside Inn served as a way station where fresh teams of horses waited to harness up to arriving stagecoaches traveling the Shenandoah Valley Turnpike. Soldiers from both the north and the south frequented the inn, then known as Wilkinson's Tavern, seeking refuge, comfort, and friendship during the War Between the States.

Later on, it became known as America's first motor inn—and who could have foreseen the trend which was to follow?

Rooms at the inn are decorated in many different styles, because Leo Bernstein, an avid collector, has an eye for antiques of any kind. Hence, each lodging room is quite apt to be a potpourri of anything from Byzantine to Victorian.

In the summertime, Middletown also enjoys the Wayside Summer Theatre with a professional company of actors. Dinners are served earlier in order to provide guests ample time to walk the two or three blocks to the theatre.

The newest of the many enterprises connected with the Wayside Inn is the Hotel Strasburg, which is located a few miles south on Route 11. I have not seen it since its restoration, but I understand it has a most impressive history which started in the latter part of the 19th century.

Middletown actually provides the traveler with an introduction to the northern Shenandoah Valley. It is a short drive to the northern terminus of the Skyline Drive, and there is ample skiing, hiking, fishing, swimming, horseback riding, and golf besides the wealth of history to be found on the back roads.

WAYSIDE INN, Middletown, Va. 22645; 703-869-1797. A 21-room country resort-inn since 1797 in the Shenandoah Valley. About 1½ hrs. from Washington, D.C. European plan. Breakfast, lunch, and dinner served daily to travelers. Open every day of the year. Professional summer stock theatre and arts center, Belle Grove, Cedar Creek Battlefield, Blue Ridge Parkway, Crystal Caverns, Hotel Strasburg, and Shenandoah Valley historical sites nearby. Bill and Cathy Castro, Innkeepers.

Directions: Take Exit 77 off I-81 to Rte. 11. Follow signs to inn.

HOLLYMEAD INN
Charlottesville, Virginia

The most startling innovation at the Hollymead Inn, in the last 18 months, is that in addition to being open Tuesday through Saturday for dinner, this country restaurant is also open Tuesday through Friday for lunch.

"Joe and I thought it out very carefully," explained Peggy Bute when she and I were seated in the Hessian Room on a recent visit, "and we decided that there was a definite need for a good place for lunch. I'm very glad that we did."

"How did this particular dining room get it's name?" I inquired.

"After the defeat of Gentleman Johnny Burgoyne at Saratoga in 1777, many Hessian mercenaries were sent to Boston and then to Charlottesville. The march took 90 days and 4300 prisoners covered 600 miles. This included many women and children. A lot of them had deserted by the time they arrived at their new home, the Albemarle Barracks located nearby. Albemarle soon became over-crowded and additional quarters were built to house the prisoners, and this is the room they built — it's the earliest part of the building.

"The timber in this room dates back to about 1780. The center

part of the house was constructed between 1810 and 1820 and was used for a period of time as a private boys' school. The Wedgewood Room is located in that portion. About ten boys lived in the two rooms on the third floor; their lessons were held in what is now one of our private dining rooms.

"The bricks in our front walk were taken from the old Monticello wine cellar in Charlottesville, which was constructed by Italian masons brought to the area by Thomas Jefferson to build his university."

There is a great deal of American history in this part of Virginia. Monticello, the home of Thomas Jefferson, is just a few minutes from the inn, as are Ash Lawn, the home and gardens of James Monroe; the University of Virginia, with its famous serpentine walls and beautiful Georgian architecture; and Castle Hill, a Virginia landmark built in 1765.

Where the Hollymead really shines is in offering exceptional Virginia hospitality and good food. Peg does most of the cooking herself and supervises everything in the kitchen. "We are very particular about many things here," she said. "For example, we believe in serving the food while it is still piping hot. There is nothing more distressing than cold rolls or lukewarm Beef Wellington. We take a great deal of time and care with dishes like our trout stuffed with crabmeat, flounder stuffed with shrimp, boneless breast of chicken in sauce, and other house specialties. We want nothing less than perfection."

One of the truly unique features about this central Virginia inn is the fact that it contains a country butcher shop, the Hook and Cleaver, which is located in the basement where Virginia hams, beef, and other succulent meats are sold. I ordered a Virginia country ham and I am still enjoying the marvelous taste of fried ham and eggs, and grits occasionally, for breakfast.

The Hollymead is aptly named because it sits in a grove of holly trees which are plainly visible from the windows of the dining room. The rolling Virginia hills with maple, magnolia, and oak trees stretch out in all directions. The building is a white clapboard Colonial with the distinctive red brick walk leading up to the front door.

HOLLYMEAD INN, Rte. 8, Box 367A, Charlottesville, Va. 22901; 804-973-8488. A country restaurant a few minutes north of Charlottesville on Rte. 29. Near Monticello, Ash Lawn, University of Virginia and Skyline Drive in Blue Ridge Mts. No lodgings. Dinner served Tuesdays through Saturdays. Lunch served Tuesday through Friday. Open year-round. Closed Christmas Eve, Christmas Day and New Year's Day. Mr. and Mrs. Joseph Bute, Innkeepers.

Directions: Proceed 6 mi. north of Charlottesville, Va., on Rte. 29 North.

OLD CLUB RESTAURANT
Alexandria, Virginia

For me the Old Club is a gateway to the South. I try to stop as often as possible to renew my taste for southern cooking. Take ham, for example; on my last visit, Innkeeper Lee Palmer and I were discussing the subject. He explained his hams are "real country" hams from Culpeper, Virginia. "We soak it overnight, boil for about nine hours, cool it and then put in the oven with vinegar, brown sugar and cloves and let glaze for two hours.

"Country ham is best served thinly sliced and salty. Our guests like it warm over bread with black-eyed peas and candied sweet potatoes."

The oldest part of this Colonial mansion in Alexandria was built by George Washington and his friends as a private club, hence the name. The little brick building on the north was said to have been young Washington's office while he was surveying this area. There are dozens of stories connected with this sedate restaurant, including the fact that during the War of 1812, when the British were at the gates of Alexandria, all the handsome wooden furniture was buried in what is now the vegetable garden.

The Old Club has been included in CIBR since the late 1960s and as on that first visit, I have always led off my meal with a cup of peanut soup, which is a feature of this historic restaurant. I find that a cup is sufficient, because there is still enough appetite left for the

choices on the menu, which have changed very little during my tenure. Besides the Virginia country ham served over cornbread, covered with maple syrup, there is Allegheny mountain trout, which is boned and stuffed with mushrooms and rice, and topped with tartar sauce. I have also enjoyed chicken Laura Lee, which is a chicken breast on hickory ham served with a mushroom sauce.

The Old Club is located in the historic section of Alexandria where there are many buildings dating back to Colonial days. In recent years, Alexandria has had an excellent program of restoration and preservation, which includes at least twenty-seven historic sites and buildings that are really architectural jewels. There is an excellent walking tour available with an explanation of such landmarks as Christ Church, Captain's Row, Gadsby's Tavern and Carlyle House. Mount Vernon is just a few miles away by car.

I had finished my helping of country ham on cornbread, and Lee suggested I top it off with some deep dish apple pie. "It is made with a little apple wine and a little whipped cream. Our guests sing its praises all the time."

We finished dinner and walked out on the flagstone patio and Lee explained that the Old Club is becoming a popular place for rehearsal dinners and wedding receptions. "As a matter of fact," he said, "we have had six marriages at the Old Club this year."

We said good-bye and Lee said, "Come back real soon."

I certainly would.

OLD CLUB RESTAURANT, 555 So. Washington St., Alexandria, Va. 22314; 703-549-4555. Just across the river from Washington, D.C. in one of the country's best preserved Colonial cities. No lodgings. Lunch and dinner served daily except Mondays and Christmas. Convenient to Christ Church, Robert E. Lee House, Gadsby's Tavern, Old Apothecary Shop, and Potomac River. Mt. Vernon and Gunston Hall nearby. Lee Palmer, Innkeeper.

Directions: North and south bound traffic on 495 take Exit #1 North to Rte. 1. Turn right on Franklin St. and left on Washington St., 1 block to inn. (Mount Vernon Memorial Hwy. is Washington St. in the city.)

GRAVES MOUNTAIN LODGE
Syria, Virginia

Dinner was over. It happened to be on a Tuesday which is one of the Potluck nights at Graves Mountain Lodge. In addition to huge platters of pot roast bathed in delicious gravy, there was a steady stream of string beans, corn, hot bread, mashed potatoes, peas, lima beans, relishes and jams. Pitchers of milk were passed from one end of the long harvest table to the other.

After a generous helping of apple cobbler I realized that the placemat served a double purpose, because it provided the guest with an excellent overview of the considerable scope of the mountains and forests which are part of the total experience at this very popular resort-inn.

Jim Graves happened to be passing through the dining room and saw me tracing out one of the many trails which lead from the Lodge into the Blue Ridge Mountains.

"Yes, there are trails everywhere," he said. "This one goes through apple and peach orchards and follows the Rose River up past the Upper Cabin and joins the fire trail leading up to the Franklin Cliffs Overlook.

"The Cedar Run Trail, here, will take you up to the Hawksbill Shelter, and the White Oak Canyon Trail goes through some very pretty country on the way to Skyland. Our guests use this map all the time for their hikes into the mountains."

I remarked to Jim that there seemed to be quite a few lively children around on that particular evening.

"Well, just about the average number," he said. "Many families come here with young children who actually have their first experience on a working farm. It is an opportunity for them to get acquainted with horses, cows, geese, ducks, and chickens in a very natural setting. You know a lot of youngsters have never been in a hay barn or seen farm equipment actually being used.

"Families also enjoy the horseback riding and the junior-size Olympic pool. We have a sports camp in the summer with instruction in basketball and other sports. In fact, many people visiting us for dinner for the first time learn about the facilities and either return as a family or send their young people to the sports camp."

There is a wide variety of accommodations. The several different rustic lodgings located in what were at one time farm outbuildings are popular with the younger generation. These include farmhouses, cabins, and cottages many with their own fireplaces. There are also lodgings available in two modern motel units located on the side of the mountain above the Main Lodge.

The Main Lodge, as is the case with all the buildings, is built out of lumber taken right out of the hills. It contains the big country dining rooms where food is served family-style on long tables, a large recreation room and gift shop, and the W.C. Bader Room, named for the man who does the beautiful wood inlays of all kinds of birds and outdoor scenes which adorn the walls. There is a welcome apple barrel in one corner of the room as well.

Graves Mountain Lodge is really a very unusual experience. It is actually much more like the ranches I have visited in Arizona than other eastern country inns included in this book. As Rachel Graves remarked later on that evening, "Well, we certainly aren't luxurious and we don't look like a New England country inn, but I think we must be making a good impression on a lot of people, because most of them seem to come back."

GRAVES MOUNTAIN LODGE, Syria, Va. 22743; 703-923-4231. A 38-room secluded resort-inn on Rte. 670, off Rte. 231, 10 mi. north of Madison, Va., 38 mi. N.W. of Charlottesville, Va. American plan.

Rustic lodgings including 11 cottages and cabins and two modern motel units. Breakfast, lunch, dinner served to travelers by reservation only. Closed Dec. 1 to late March. Swimming, tennis, riding, fishing, basketball on grounds. Golf nearby. Jim and Rachel Graves, Innkeepers.

Directions: Coming south from Wash., D.C., take I-66 to Gainsville. Follow Rte. 29 south to Madison, turn right onto Rte. 231 West, go 7 mi. to Banco, turn left onto Rte. 670 and follow 670 for 4½ mi. to lodge.

ALEXANDER-WITHROW HOUSE
Lexington, Virginia

Patty and Carlson Thomas were full of good news. "We're just having the most wonderful time with the guests from your book," she said enthusiastically. "Do you know that they leave us little notes before they depart? I brought some with me today so that you can see for yourself."

We were all having a very enjoyable breakfast in the bakery which is just around the corner from the Alexander-Withrow House in Lexington. From the very first edition in which I shared my experiences in visiting this unusual guest house, I have pointed out that there is an arrangement with this shop to deliver pastries, breads, sticky buns and coffee to guests of the AW House in the morning. This time, instead of having this light breakfast delivered, the three of us were seated around one of the tables, and Patty and Carlson were busy saying hello to their many friends who dropped in for a cup of coffee or a donut.

"Having the antique shop on the first floor has been a real joy," said Carlson. "Many of our guests spend a great deal of time browsing."

"Yes, it gives us a chance to chat more with our guests," joined in Patty.

The AW House was built in 1789, just two years after the original founding of Lexington. It has four corner chimneys and most elaborate brick work known as "diapering." Another unusual feature is the Italianate roof. I don't believe I saw another one similar to it in the area.

It was in the mid-sixties that historic preservation began coming into its own in Lexington. In 1966 the Historic Lexington Foundation, a non-profit organization was established. Alexander-Withrow House was the first property to be restored, and the Thomases

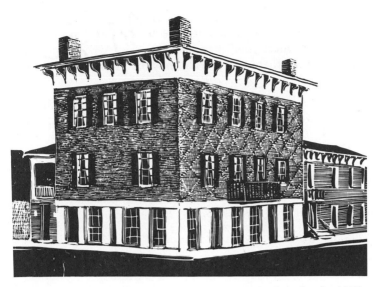

bought the house, redesigned and restored the interior in 1971.

Furnished with beautiful antiques and reproductions, each of the five suites has its own sitting room-bedroom, small refreshment center and private telephone.

I would like to explain something for prospective guests at the AW House. There isn't a 24-hour desk, and arriving guests sometimes find written instructions on how to obtain keys, and directions to their suites. The Carlsons live on the top floor of the inn, and if they are not in evidence when the guest arrives, they certainly will be during his or her stay.

"Well, just about the most exciting thing that has happened since you were here was the fact that we had a visit from Ladybird Johnson," exclaimed Patty. "She was just lovely and she enjoyed the porch overlooking the courtyard. She is so interested in preserving the beautiful things in this world."

Breakfast finished, we walked out on the bustling street of Lexington to see some of the students from Washington and Lee University and Virginia Military Institute trouping by between classes. The colleges are part of a 26-stop walking tour of the town, information about which the Carlsons are very happy to supply for their guests.

Back at the AW House, Patty showed me the scrapbook that has a great number of the "thank you" notes from their guests. Here are a few excerpts:

"We thoroughly enjoyed our stay, this has been one of the nicest inns that we visited through *Country Inns and Back Roads*"; "Fond

Regards—thanks for letting us occupy such beautiful rooms"; "I'm certainly glad that we were able to take an additional day to stop at your inn and to meet you."

Yes, indeed, there was much good news on the Alexander-Withrow House.

ALEXANDER-WITHROW HOUSE, 3 W. Washington St., Lexington, Va. 24450; 703-463-2044. An elegantly restored, 5-suite guest house. Lodgings only. No meals served. Room service continental breakfast available. Advance reservation recommended. Open year-round. No pets. Within walking distance of Virginia Military Institute, Washington and Lee University, and the George C. Marshall Research Library. Natural Bridge, Blue Ridge Parkway nearby. Carlson and Patty Thomas, Innkeepers.

Directions: Any Lexington exit from I-64 or I-81.

GRISTMILL SQUARE
Warm Springs, Virginia

The ornamental clock at one end of the Gristmill Square courtyard said, "Four minutes before 8 a.m." Once again I stood on the bridge next to the old water wheel and took advantage of the morning quiet to review some of the events of the past twelve hours.

For one thing, it was wonderful to see Cathy and Philip Hirsh once again. Each of them is so filled with enthusiasm and energy. All around me I could see evidences of this energy. Philip had promised me when I visited there in the fall of 1976 that quite a few changes would be made during the winter months, and all of these, indeed, came about. There were three brand-new, all-weather tennis courts just across the road from Gristmill Square, in addition to a beautiful new swimming pool. "Now we are something of a resort-inn," said Philip, "and the major part of our projects has been accomplished."

"Yes, and we also moved some of our shops to make room for new accommodations," said Cathy, with her eyes shining. "The new Board Room is complete and we used old barn boards for the walls. The Dinwiddie Mantle Room is also being used as an accommodation. That's the one where Philip has put the famous Dinwiddie carved mantle that we found in one of the buildings on our farm."

My reverie about the events of the previous evening was momentarily distracted by the wiggly gyrations of at least 153 minnows which had found a sandy section of the brook next to the bridge. Every so often they would all move at once as if frightened by the same thing. Perhaps it was the presence of turtles underneath the

waterwheel. Out in the mainstream of the brook there were a few larger fish.

There are two brooks which border Gristmill Square: one that supplies some of the power for the waterwheel, and another coming at right angles down the hill. Both of them meet on the other side of the road, and then gurgle their way through the hills, eventually finding their way to the sea. Along the banks of the brook across the road there is a profusion of beautiful late-spring and early-summer flowers—sweet peas, wild roses, forget-me-nots, and daisies.

Hella Armstrong, the manager of Gristmill Square, took me to see the new sauna and we talked about other developments at the inn. "I'm sure you know," she said, "we serve a Continental breakfast in the lobby for our inn guests. Guest privileges are available for the Bath and Tennis Club. We have horseback riding, fishing, hunting, and hiking, and in winter, there is skiing just an hour away. Golfers are just a few minutes away from the famous Cascade and Lower Cascade courses at Hot Springs."

Gristmill Square is a hub for getting acquainted with the surrounding mountains by way of local country roads which lead through the breathtaking vistas of the Alleghenys. Warm Springs Mountain is over 3000 feet high. I sometimes wonder how vacationers of one hundred years ago ever got here.

Lunches and dinners at Gristmill Square are served in the Waterwheel Restaurant which is an authentic gristmill dating from the 19th century. There is a marvelous aroma of ground meal, and the patina of the natural wood is enchanced by the exposed beams, millstones still in their wooden housings, and much of the original

241

locust wood flooring. The menu includes fresh rainbow trout from the nearby hatcheries, vine-ripened tomatoes, and crisp zucchini from Philip and Cathy's own garden.

As we stood on the bridge, townspeople were now arriving at the village post office and a shaggy-haired, old country dog came by and sniffed at my ankles. He seemed to find me acceptable.

GRISTMILL SQUARE, Warm Springs, Va. 24484; 703-839-2231. An unusual restoration which includes a restaurant, accommodations, small shops, and many resort attractions, in a small country town approx. 19 mi. from Covington in the Allegheny Mts. European plan. Lunch and dinner served daily Tuesday — Saturday. Sunday brunch only. Closed Mondays. Many different types of accommodations available. Suggest telephone for details. Children welcome. Pets allowed but not permitted loose on grounds. Tennis, swimming pool on grounds. Golf, skiing, skating, riding, hiking, fishing, hunting, antiquing, back roading nearby. Philip and Catherine Hirsh, Innkeepers.

Directions: From Staunton, Va., follow Rte. 254 to Buffalo Gap, Rte. 42 to Millboro Spring, Rte. 39 to Warm Springs. From Lexington, take Rte. 39 to Warm Springs. From Roanoke, take Rte. 220 to Warm Springs.

West Virginia

THE COUNTRY INN
Berkeley Springs, West Virginia

I was looking at the special Thanksgiving menu from the Country Inn. The cover had been done in a very homey fashion with some cut-outs of a Canada goose and a ruffled grouse pasted on the orange paper and the words, "The Country Inn" written in crayon. Inside, carefully lettered out, was the menu, and everything was held together with a piece of blue yarn.

The menu led off with turkey noodle soup which the guests were invited to follow by a visit to the salad bar. Cranberry relish, and stuffed celery, along with dishes of apple chutney, pickles, olives, raw cauliflower, and mixed nuts were passed around. Roast turkey with stuffing was the main course, but there was also Country Inn baked ham, and top round of beef. Homemade bread and pastries from the inn kitchen, and hot mince pie rounded out the meal.

All of this was served in the dining room overlooking a mountain stream which follows the road through the center of the town of Berkeley Springs. The floors have a high polish, and the furniture is all West Virginia country style.

I first became acquainted with innkeepers Jack and Adele Barker in the fall of 1972, when my son Keith and I were on an "inn trip" through Maryland, West Virginia, and Pennsylvania. They were, for years, the operators of a very successful school near Washington, D.C. During many of those years, they dreamt of owning a country inn. A few years ago, this inn in Berkeley Springs, which is a somewhat sequestered community in the northwest panhandle of West Virginia, became available, so they gave up their school and embarked upon a new and exciting career.

Almost from the start, the Barkers made new friends in this venture and I have received many letters of praise over the years. However, they were not content to stand still and many new, exciting things have always been happening there.

This time, it was the addition of three fireplace-model, Fisher woodburning stoves. "We have placed them in front of our first floor fireplaces," said Jack. "They burn all day and all night, and best of all, our guests wake up to a toasty-warm building. They like that and so do I."

Besides the new woodburning stoves at the inn, Jack was very enthusiastic about the annual Apple Butter Festival which started four years ago. "This year the festival drew about 6000 people who enjoyed seeing apple butter made in the middle of the street by our friends wearing Colonial costumes. About 60 booths lined the street and the park, demonstrating broom-making, ceramics, wood, and leather art, and other ingenious crafts. All this amidst the smell of smoke, food, cooking, and live blue grass music, made it quite a day for Berkeley Springs and a very busy one for the Country Inn."

At one time Berkeley Springs was the closest "spa" to Washington, and many trains came back and forth on the B&O. The springs were here long before the white man. George Washington paid a visit and, legend has it, planted a tree. The springs, however, are still here and it is possible to enjoy a vapor bath, a hot tub, and a massage at most reasonable rates. These baths are maintained by the State, and are just a few paces from the inn.

This entire section of West Virginia is known as the Potomac Highland, and many guests who stay at the Country Inn enjoy taking one of the literally innumerable circle tours which take them to dozens of places with natural and historical interest. The 6000-acre Cacapon State Park is just a few minutes from the inn where there are hiking, bridle, and cross-country ski trails. There is also a new Robert Trent Jones 18-hole championship golf course and opportunities for picnics, tennis, swimming, boating, and fishing.

THE COUNTRY INN, Berkeley Springs, West Va. 25411; 304-258-2210. A 37-room resort inn on Rte. 522, 34 mi. from Winchester, Va. and 100 mi. from Washington, D.C., or Baltimore, Md. Berkeley Springs Spa adjoins inn. European plan. Most rooms with private baths. Breakfast, lunch, dinner served to travelers. Open every day of the year. Hunting, fishing, hiking, canoeing, antiquing, championship golf nearby. Jack and Adele Barker, Innkeepers.

Directions: Take I-70 to Hancock, Md. Inn is 6 mi. south on Rte. 522.

GENERAL LEWIS INN
Lewisburg, West Virginia

I asked Mary Hock and Larry Little whether many people had stopped at the General Lewis because of reading about it in *Country Inns and Back Roads*.

"Oh, yes. We've had dozens of people here because of the book," explained Mary. "All of them would like to have the bedroom with the canopy four-poster and fireplace."

"The thing that's most enjoyable about the Berkshire Travellers," said Larry, "is that they know exactly what to expect before they arrive. There can be misunderstandings about country inns. Some people expect to find ultra-modern places, but we're rather unpretentious with the accent on hospitality and good food. A great

many of them love West Virginia country food, such as chicken, pork chops, country ham, sweet potatoes, and apple butter."

I could certainly number myself among that group because the memory of a West Virginia country dinner was still fresh in my mind.

We were seated on the spacious lawn of the inn with its oaks and maples interspersed with hemlock, dogwood and redbud trees.

On a walk through the garden, Mary pointed out the many varieties of flowers. "There's always something in bloom," she said. "We have iris, poppies, pansies, jonquils, hyacinths, phlox, lilies, and, oh, at least a half a dozen more." I also spotted a number of cardinals and bluejays.

Mary then took me on a tour of the inn, as she does with so many of her guests. I learned that the old part of the building, where the dining room is located, was built in 1798 as a private dwelling. In 1929 it was opened as an inn by Mary and her husband, Randolph. They carefully collected all the antiques that can be found at every turn.

There seemed to be no end of utensils, spinning wheels, churns, chairs, tables, oils, water colors, prints, and literally dozens and dozens of different types of old-fashioned tools, firearms, and weapons. Mary pointed out that every room in the inn is completely furnished with antiques, and this includes the bedrooms as well. Particularly impressive was the large collection of china and the wide variety of rocking chairs scattered throughout the inn.

Later that afternoon I took another walk through the old streets of Lewisburg and once again browsed around the Old Stone Church with its shuttered windows and ancient cemetery. It was quiet and peaceful with the confidence that comes with age. Built in 1796, it's said to be the oldest unrestored church in continuous use west of the Alleghenies, and was used as a hospital after the Civil War battle fought in Lewisburg.

Before we retired for the night, I asked Larry if there had been any changes at the inn. He said, "Oh, no. Not to speak of. We're really interested in remaining the same."

GENERAL LEWIS INN, Lewisburg, W. Va. 24901; 304-645-2600. An antique-laden 30-room village inn on Rte. 60, 90 mi. from Roanoke, Va. European plan. (Modified American plan only during W. Va. State Fair) Breakfast and evening meal served daily with an additional meal on Sundays at noon. Dining room closed Christmas Day. Famous golf courses nearby. Laurence Little, Innkeeper.

Directions: Take Lewisburg exit from I-64. Follow Rte. 219 south to first traffic light. Turn left on Rte. 60, two blocks to inn.

RIVERSIDE INN
Pence Springs, West Virginia

Jamestown still lives at the Riverside Inn! Kelly Berkley, wearing a fetching Early American costume, handed me a pewter plate with some delicious cheese and a ripe pear. "I trust Sire, that your dinner was satisfactory."

She was joined by her husband, Ashby Berkley, wearing a leather vest and knee britches, and sporting a well-trimmed beard. I felt as if I had stepped into Jamestown, Virginia in the early 1600s, which is exactly the period that has been created. Here is the intimacy of an old English variation of the raodside tavern where travel-weary guests refresh themselves with the table fare of their hosts. The interesting aspect is that this inn is in the beautiful mountains of West Virginia.

My dinner had begun with an appetizer and English mulled cider, followed by bean and bacon soup. A salad came next, made from an old English recipe called "Hot Slaw" which is hot cabbage salad served with a dressing of bacon, sugar, and vinegar.

The entrees presented the problem of making a choice. There was Pantry Pie which consists of chicken, duckling, and giblets served in a white wine sauce with vegetables all in a flaky crust, or roast fruit-stuffed duckling for two, roast goose on wild rice with glazed

grapes, pork loin stuffed with prunes and apples and roasted with an apricot glaze, a colonial game pie, and oysters stuffed with filets of beef and cooked in a burgundy sauce.

The desserts included rum pie, fresh fruit cobblers served with ice cream; the final course was the cheese and fruit plate.

Kelly explained that almost everything is made from the basic ingredients and this includes the bread which is baked by Ashby's mother. "Vegetables come from either our own garden or from other farms right here in the valley," she said.

The building of the Riverside Inn is a log cabin with porches, a large fireplace, and a splendid view of the Greenbrier River. It can best be described as an elegant West Virginia country tavern. This year there are two rental cottages available from Memorial Day to Labor Day, but please make reservations or risk being disappointed.

The six-course menu which I have described above is also augmented by a la carte offerings. Dinners are served in the low-ceilinged main dining room, which was for many years a private house where the cooking was done in the fireplace. There are pewter serving plates, pistol-handled knives, heavy oaken tables, and a candelabra fashioned out of tin by local craftsmen. In 1978, the dining room capacity will be increased by enclosing the porch overlooking the countryside and the river.

My visit to Kelly and Ashby also included visiting the Pence Springs Water Company which is an old mineral spa where naturally-carbonated spring water bubbles up out of the ground. One of the main buildings has been turned into an old-fashioned ice cream parlor where more casual meals are served every day from 9 to 5.

A Sunday flea market now the largest in the state, often attracts as many as 2000 people offering everything from junk to antiques.

"We will be hosting the national John Henry Folk Festival here on Labor Day Weekend in 1978," said Ashby. "I grew up with that legend and we think it will be one of the biggest events in the state."

RIVERSIDE INN, Rte. 3, Pence Springs, W. Va. 24962; 304-445-7469. A country restaurant 12 mi. from Hinton, W. Va., located in the beautiful West Va. mountains on the Greenbrier River on Rte. 3 between Hinton and Alderson. 12 mi. from Lake Bluestone. Limited lodgings. Dinner served daily except Mondays. Lunch served by special reservation only. Open from February through Dec. 31. Closed Thanksgiving, Christmas, and Easter. Skiing, boating, hiking, swimming, spelunking, white water canoeing nearby. Ashby and Kelly Berkley, Innkeepers.

Directions: From the east, take Alta exit off I-64, follow Rte. 12-S to Alderson then Rte. 3-W 8 mi. to Pence Springs. From the west, from W. Va. Tpke. follow Rte. 3 from Beckley through Hinton to Pence Springs. The inn is located in Pence Springs on Rte. 3 between Hinton and Alderson.

THE WELLS INN
Sistersville, West Virginia

"Here is your old friend, Victoria" said Max Taylor. "She hasn't spoken a word during your absence."

I must say Victoria, an alabaster statue in the lobby of the Wells Inn was very much in style. Her pristine whiteness showed up very well against the gold velours of the walls, the rich, "gay nineties" carpeting, and the velvet cushions on the circular bench where we were seated.

Visiting the Wells Inn is a flashback to days of late 19th-century opulence, with its Victorian parlor, where there is a Tiffany lamp, striped wallpaper, mahogany wainscoting, marble-top tables, and handsome settees. On the wall is an oil portrait of Ephraim Wells, the builder of the hotel and the grandson of the founder of Sistersville.

The main dining room has original gas chandeliers, now converted, hanging from an old-fashioned ceiling of molded metal. The walls are covered with rich, flocked paper in a red and gold pattern and that presents a most interesting contrast to the green velvet uphostered dining room chairs.

My bedroom had a brass bed, thick carpeting, and a kerosene-type lamp suspended gracefully on a draped chain from the ceiling.

As Max pointed out, "The original Wells Hotel was built in 1894 but faded into obscurity about 1912. It was remodeled in 1929 and had a second grand opening. In 1965, Wells Kincaid, a grandson of the original builder, bought the hotel at auction and by this time it had fallen into a state of some disrepair. He and his son, Jack, made the happy decision to make it a turn-of-the-century hostelry. Period furniture was obtained, some of the 1894 furnishings were donated by townspeople, and major reconstruction took place with one thing in mind: providing modern conveniences in an authentic gay nineties style of decor. So, there was third grand opening."

I have been visiting the Wells Inn since 1970 and on each visit I have found something more to share with our readers. On this particular visit, it was the arrival of Max Taylor, who has had a considerable background in the innkeeping business, and his very attractive wife, Diana. Since Max's new association with my good friend, Jack Kincaid, some most interesting things have been happening to the Wells Inn menu. Because Max has had a great deal of experience as a maitre d' hotel and is training the dining room staff in the European art of preparing food at the table, the menu of this inn has taken on new dimensions. In 1970, I never would have expected to see frogs legs Provencale, oriental pepper steak, Sukiyaki, turkey Tetrazzini, veal Cordon Bleu, bananas Foster, peaches Melba, cherries jubilee, and flaming coffees. Those are some of the inspiring, new offerings.

"There has been a complete change in our dining policy," explained Diana. "One of the most popular has been our salad bar where there are twelve different types of salad ingredients and several different dressings!"

So I have observed yet another development at the Wells Inn, and it appears to be a favorable step forward.

However, I am sorry to say that none of this has had any effect on the obdurate immovability of Victoria. Again, she refused my invitation to dinner, and not even mentioning the rainbow trout amandine had any visible effect on her. However, there was one ray of hope when I offered to drape my jacket around her Praxitelesian shoulders, I fancied I saw a faint twitch of her lips and a flicker of an alabaster eyelid!

WELLS INN, 316 Charles St., Sistersville, W. Va. 26175; 304-652-3111. A restored Victorian 36-room village inn, 50 mi. south of Wheeling, 38 mi. north of Parkersburg. Sistersville is a former oil boom town of the '90's. European plan. Breakfast, lunch, dinner served daily. Open year-round. Skiing nearby. Max Taylor , Innkeeper.

Directions: From the south, leave I-77 at Parkersburg and proceed north on Rte. 2. From the north, leave I-70 at Wheeling and travel south on Rte. 2.

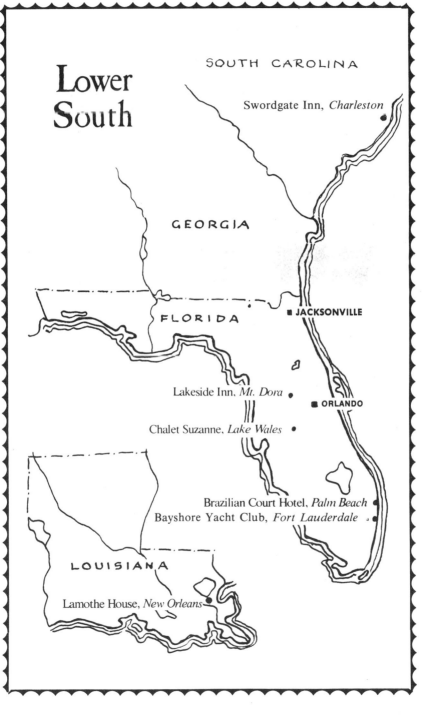

Lower
South

SOUTH CAROLINA

Swordgate Inn, *Charleston*

GEORGIA

FLORIDA   ■ JACKSONVILLE

Lakeside Inn, *Mt. Dora*

■ ORLANDO

Chalet Suzanne, *Lake Wales*

Brazilian Court Hotel, *Palm Beach*
Bayshore Yacht Club, *Fort Lauderdale*

LOUISIANA

Lamothe House, *New Orleans*

Florida

BAY SHORE YACHT CLUB
Fort Lauderdale, Florida

A country inn in Fort Lauderdale, Florida? Don't even smile. I've discovered warm, hospitable inns with a feeling of personal involvement in such metropolitan areas as New York, Palm Beach, and St. Louis. The emphasis is on the "inn" rather than the "country." But what really makes such a big difference to me are the innkeepers, Janet and Bert Carvalho. They are sort of aunt and uncle to everybody who stays there, and they are such good fun to be with.

It was in late winter of 1976 when I finally made it to Fort Lauderdale, and the BSYC proved to be everything that I had been told and even more.

Being located on the Intracoastal Bay Shore provides three docks for convenient mooring of visiting yachts and cruisers. Although not a yacht club per se, as a fun, tongue-in-cheek gesture, the guests are presented with membership cards signed by the "Commodore" which entitle them to the rights and privileges of the "Club."

The BSYC is a white, four-story building facing the blue waters of the Intracoastal Waterway which traverses Fort Lauderdale. A great many of the accommodations have a very impressive view of the continuous water traffic. There are over 200 feet of landscaped waterfront gardens. The tropical gardens include gardenias, ixora, crotons, dieffenbachia, schefflera, coconut and Christmas palms, fern palms and many others. In this beautiful, warm climate near the ocean there are cardinals, bluejays, woodpeckers, mourning and ground doves, and spot-breasted orioles who make their homes in the trees.

Most of the accommodations are efficiencies or apartments with kitchens, so it is possible for guests to prepare their own meals or take advantage of the many restaurants in the Fort Lauderdale area. The guests' comforts are well provided for in tastefully decorated apartments furnished with fine furniture and carpeting. The cabinets are stocked with china and silverware, and the facilities include central air conditioning, heating, sheltered parking (most important with that Florida sun), and maid service.

Janet and Bert make all of this beautiful atmosphere and sunshiny ambience really come to life—they're the big difference that makes the BSYC an inn. I think it is a fair statement that they consider each guest to be their friend and do everything they can to make everybody as comfortable as possible. They introduce all the guests, and join them at the pool.

While I was there, there was a reunion between one of the guests, who had been at the BSYC for quite awhile, and her son who had driven down from Washington to spend a couple of days. The boy arrived while his mother happened to be out, and Janet made him feel at home immediately and took care of things until his mother returned.

Fort Lauderdale is a city that frankly awes me. Naturally, being on the sunny tip of Florida where the famous beach just stretches out for miles, there are thousands of people who visit during the cold weather in the north. I asked Bert about the best time to visit Fort Lauderdale and he said, "February and March are the popular months, but Janet and I think that April, May, September and October are ideal because it is very comfortable, not nearly as many people, and prices on everything are really much lower."

The BSYC is not Henniker, New Hampshire, but it is a place where people, from Henniker, Bellows Falls, Great Barrington, and Litchfield meet to thaw out.

BAY SHORE YACHT CLUB, 341 N. Birch Rd., Ft. Lauderdale, Fla. 33304; 305-463-2821. A comfortable homelike environment with many types of accommodations, including 4 efficiencies, 2 hotel rooms, 31 apartments with kitchens and baths located on the Intracoastal Waterway. Tennis, golf, sailing, ocean swimming nearby. Shuffleboard, fishing from dock, heated pool on grounds.

Open year-round. Children welcome from April thru Dec. No meals served. Kitchen facilities with efficiencies and apts. No pets.`Janet and Bert Carvalho, Jr. Innkeepers.

Directions: From Florida Tpke. exit at MacArthur Interchange, turn left (east) to Sunrise Blvd., go approx. 7½ to ocean. Turn right on Atlantic Blvd., turn right at second light to Bay Shore Drive. Proceed one block to Birch Rd. and turn left to Bay Shore Yacht Club. From I-95 S exit at Cypress Creek Rd., follow to Sunrise Blvd., then east for 7 mi. Turn left at ocean to Atlantic Blvd. and follow directions above.

BRAZILIAN COURT
Palm Beach, Florida

Let's talk about a country inn in Palm Beach, Florida. In a way this reminds me of the tempest in a teapot that arose when I first chose to put the Algonquin Hotel of New York City in this book. Within a year we were getting letters of thanks.

When I first visited the Brazilian Court in 1972, it struck me as being just the kind of resort-inn that I would hope to find in Palm Beach. Maybe not the kind I would find in Michigan or Arizona or Maine, but for Palm Beach it was perfect. The letters of agreement reaffirmed my instinct.

I've often said that country inns are people. People who own, staff, and manage them, as well as people who visit them. When there is communication, consideration, and friendliness expressed on both sides of the front desk, we have the makings of a country inn.

And this is what has been happening at the Brazilian Court for quite a number of years. For most of those years, almost forty in fact, Bright Johnson, the innkeeper, has been on hand. Because so many people return each year, he's developed a firm friendship with many of his guests, and this in turn is reflected by the staff.

Another characteristic that we look for is uniqueness. Certainly, the Brazilian Court is unique. It is the *other* side of Palm Beach, not the socially-conscious aspect, but the genuine, real Palm Beach.

The Brazilian Court was erected back in the 1920s, and the residential district grew up around it. The building is a two-story Palm Beach Mission design built around two completely enclosed patios. One contains a profusion of trees, flowers, bushes, and plants and has a most decorative fountain in the middle. This is the outdoor dining area. Weather permitting, morning, afternoon and evening

meals are served here, and each has its own mood. For example, in the evening, small lights twinkle inside umbrellas which are discreetly placed around the patio, and indirect color lighting highlights the exotic tropical plants and palm trees.

The lights take on more beautiful hues with the coming of semi-tropical darkness. Well-tanned guests gather for dinner and conversation after a pleasant day on the beach, the nearby golf courses, or a charter fishing trip. The whole scene is enchanting.

Lodging accommodations at the "BC" resemble living rooms and bedrooms in a beautiful home. They're larger than one usually finds. They overlook the patios of the inn, or face the attractive private homes of Palm Beach.

Finding a country inn in the city is always fun.

BRAZILIAN COURT HOTEL, 300 Brazilian Ave., Palm Beach, Fla. 33480; 305-655-7740. A 125-room hotel in the heart of Palm Beach. A secluded patioed garden spot just a short walk from the ocean and Worth Avenue shops. All plans available. Breakfast, lunch and dinner served to travelers daily. Open from mid-December to early April. No pets. Swimming, boating, fishing, tennis, golf and bicycles nearby. Bright Johnson, Innkeeper.

Directions: From Sunshine State Pkwy., take Exit 40 to Okeechobee Blvd. Turn left and proceed 6 mi. to Royal Palmway Bridge. Cross bridge and take first right, then turn left after 1 block on to Brazilian Ave. Hotel is two blocks east on Brazilian Ave.

255

CHALET SUZANNE
Lake Wales, Florida

I sat next to the swimming pool at Chalet Suzanne among the fabulous flowers and trees, wondering where to begin describing this place.

I decided to start with the Great Depression of the 30s. At that time Bertha Hinshaw was a new widow with two children, $1700 from a cancelled insurance policy, two old cars, and a six-room house about a mile and a half from the main highway. She decided to open a restaurant. For ten days no one came, and then finally a family of five arrived and stayed for Christmas. Chalet Suzanne was in business.

A fire in 1943 turned out to be a blessing because Bertha started all over again — this time with some pretty unique ideas. She created an atmosphere that looked like a set from a movie. There is a conglomeration of little houses, lodges and chalets that could belong in nearby Disney World. It's Oriental, Persian, Bavarian, Swiss, and chocolate layer cake. There are little bridges, penthouses, cupolas, balconies, minarettes, peaked roofs, flat roofs, and here and there, little tiny windows that lack only a Snow White peeking through them. Just to make it more fun, these strange places contain lodging rooms!

These are all connected by brick walls and cobblestone paths. Guests can choose accommodations for their moods — Byzantine or medieval, carpenter gothic or *Erehwon*.

Truly exceptional food is served at Chalet Suzanne in five different dining rooms, all in a sort of Hans Christian Andersen setting. The late Clementine Paddleford tasted the soups and wrote in her column in the *New York Herald Tribune,* "It's good! good! good!" In fact, the soups led to still another business and now Chalet Suzanne Soups, including at least nineteen different kinds, are available in food specialty shops and supermarkets all over the country.

Besides the soup, the cannery in 1977 added six new citrus sauces which are delicious as an accompaniment to all meats, poultry, and hot or cold entrees. Chalet Suzanne products are available in the gourmet pantries of local supermarkets, and in gourmet-type shops.

Bertha's son, Carl, is the major-domo of the kitchen, and the opening course for dinner at Chalet Suzanne is always an invention by Carl's wife, Vita, a chicken liver canapé centered in the original Chalet baked grapefruit. Among other specialties is their famous Chicken Suzanne, glazed with its own natural juices to a beautiful amber color. Other main courses are lobster Newburg, lump crab and shrimp curry. Crêpes Suzanne are served just before the dessert. These are rolled-up tiny pancakes topped with one of the new sauces. Incidentally, Carl is also operator of the Chalet Suzanne air field, which is immediately adjacent to the inn.

One important further thought — children love Chalet Suzanne. After all, why not? All those funny buildings, a lake, a swimming pool, airplanes arriving and taking off, and even a little golf cart to ride around on. It "out-Disneys" Disney World.

CHALET SUZANNE, P.O. Box AC, Lake Wales, Fla. 33853; 813-676-1477. A 30-room phantasmagoric country inn and gourmet restaurant, 4 mi. north of Lake Wales, between Cypress Gardens and the Bok Singing Tower near Disney World. European and Modified American plans available. Dining room open from 8 a.m. to 9:30 p.m. daily. Closed Mondays June through October. Pool on grounds. Golf, tennis, riding nearby. The Hinshaw Family, Innkeepers.

Directions: From Interstate 4 turn south on U.S. 27 toward Lake Wales. From Sunshine State Pkwy. exit at Yeehaw Junction and head west on Rte. 60 to U.S. 27 (60 mi.). Proceed north on U.S. 27 at Lake Wales. Inn is 4 mi. north of Lake Wales on Rte. 17A.

LAKESIDE INN
Mount Dora, Florida

It was just after dinner at the Lakeside Inn. One of the guests sitting on the porch invited me to play some shuffleboard, and another new acquaintance asked me to be a fourth at bridge. Those were fun prospects, but I was in the mood for an early evening stroll.

As I walked through the gardens leading to a pool on the edge of the lake, I inhaled the heavy aroma of tropical blooms. There were camphor trees, azaleas, sabal palms, and orange blossoms. A light breeze swept through the trees which were literally filled with singing birds. There are well over two-hundred and fifty varieties in Mt. Dora.

If I felt a little homesick for New England, Mt. Dora could certainly relieve it. This is the most New England of Florida towns. I needed only a sign saying "Lower Waterford, 14 miles" to convince me. A great many of the houses would be at home in Norfolk, Connecticut or Lyme, New Hampshire. Even the tropical foliage is interspersed with oaks and fir trees on a hilly terrain.

I left the lakeshore and walked a few paces over to the lawn bowling area. There are superb courts here, well lighted for night play, and several guests in the traditional lawn-bowling whites were enjoying an evening of sport. I remembered seeing quite a few of them on the Mr. Dora golf course that morning.

If the community of Mt. Dora is a bit of New England, the Lakeside Inn puts frosting on the cake. Many people on the staff are from Vermont and Massachusetts and quite a few are employed in Maine during the summer. The guest list is generously sprinkled with people from the New England area.

Dick Edgerton, the owner of the Lakeside Inn was telling me earlier at dinner, "We don't have tourists — we have winter visitors. People come and stay as guests, and many stay for quite awhile. Our houseguests are on the American plan, but we serve all three meals to travelers.

"We've been very popular with retired people, but in the last few years there has been a steady increase in the number of younger guests who frequently come with their children. I think part of this is because we have so many activities available here or around the inn. Along with the two pools and a wide variety of outdoor games and we have great fishing and boating. Last winter, the Mt. Dora Golf Club built two beautiful tennis courts so that there are four excellent courts nearby where our guests can play.

"It is possible to reach the inn on the Florida Inland Waterway system. Our lake can handle boats with a draft up to 3 feet and about 28 feet long."

I left the lawn bowlers to their game, and took the long way back through the village streets with their many attractive shops. I still have two brass candlesticks that I purchased at one of the antique shops several years ago.

I arrived back at the Lakeside Inn just in time to make a fourth for bridge.

LAKESIDE INN, P.O. Box 175, Mount Dora, Fla. 32757; 904-383-2151. A 110-room resort-inn on Lake Dora in central Florida, 30 mi. northwest of Orlando. American plan. Breakfast, lunch, and dinner served to travelers daily. Open from Dec. 15 to April 15. Swimming pool, fishing, waterskiing, putting green, and shuffleboard on grounds. Golf, tennis, bicycles, lawn bowling, and sailing nearby. Marie and Dick Edgerton, Innkeepers.

Directions: Follow I-95 south to Daytona Beach, then I-4 to Rte. 46 west to Mount Dora. Or, follow I-75 south to Wildwood, then Rte. 44 east to Rte. 441. Proceed on Rte. 441 to Mount Dora. After passing Lakeside Inn billboard on Rte. 441, turn south at first paved road (Donnelly St.) and proceed to Lakeside Inn.

The Lamothe House is one of my "country inns in the city." In large urban centers, one usually does not expect to find an inn with a sense of personal concern for the comfort of its guests — this kind of personal involvement is more often associated with country places. I have found a few "country inns in the city," among which are the Algonquin in New York City; The Cheshire in St. Louis; the Brazilian Court in Palm Beach; the Botsford Inn in Farmington Hills near Detroit; Sword Gate Inn in Charleston.

LAMOTHE HOUSE
New Orleans, Louisiana

I first visited the Lamothe House in the fall of 1972 where I met that most unforgettable personality, Mrs. Gertrude Munson. She told me all about the Lamothe House and its marvelous history, and we became good friends. A few years later, Mrs. Munson had to retire from direct participation in the inn and her daughter, Mrs. Mimi Langguth, took over the more active management. During that time none of the charm of this unusual guest house on the edge of the French Quarter was lost and, in fact, the many letters I have received from readers has indicated that the spirit of Mrs. Munson lives on.

Now to bring everything up to date, let me share with you a letter I received from Mrs. Munson just before this book went to press.

"Greetings to a world traveler! It is always good to have news from you and particularly so when we have good news in return, and that is that I am growing stronger each day and am now taking up some of my former duties. It is great fun to see some of our old friends and welcome them each day.

"Lamothe House opened September 1st and we have rarely had a vacancy since. During the period the Lamothe House was closed this summer, we did much redecorating of our bedrooms, preparing for the influx of visitors. We are looking forward to seeing

Jim and Mary Virginia Mellow when they arrive for a short visit next month.

"New Orleans has changed quite a bit. You would never recognize the River Front, so many skyscraper hotels; and the old U.S. Mint at the end of Esplanade Avenue is now being gradually restored—and the Lamothe House is still tucked away in its little nook which everyone seems to find."

Jim and Mary Virginia Mellow told me that Mrs. Munson is back at her usual station, serving coffee at the petit dejeuner every morning from a 200-year-old Sheffield urn, and advising people about the many wonderful experiences to be had in New Orleans.

I am happy to report that visitors to Lamothe House will have the pleasure, not only of warm hospitality and unusually gracious rooms, but also the delightful opportunity to have a chat with Mrs. Gertrude Munson.

LAMOTHE HOUSE, 621 Esplanade Ave., New Orleans, La. 70116; 504-947-1161. A small, elegant, 14-room inn in the French Quarter within walking distance of many fascinating New Orleans restaurants and attractions. European plan with complimentary petit dejeuner. No other meals served. Closed mid-July to Sept. 1. No pets. Near Lake Pontchartrain, Mississippi River, bayou and river cruises, plantations and mansions on the Great River Road. Golf, tennis, fishing and bicycles nearby. Mrs. Gertrude Munson and Mrs. Kenneth ("Mimi") Langguth, Innkeepers.

Directions: From the west or east on I-10, take the Orleans Ave. exit to Claiborne Ave. which runs under I-10 at that point. Proceed east for 7 blocks or until the intersection of Esplanade Ave. Turn right on Esplanade and proceed 10 blocks. Or take Esplanade Ave. exit from I-10.

South Carolina

SWORDGATE INN
Charleston, South Carolina

"We have several events in Charleston every year," said Kerry Anderson, the innkeeper at the Swordgate Inn. The first is in March and April, the House and Garden tour. Our own gardens have been replanted using the 'old timey' plants . . . silver bells, ladies' slippers,

Indian daisies and sweet williams. Along with the azaleas and camellias we already have, spring will be even more colorful."

I was having breakfast in the morning sunshine on the patio. The muffins were hot from the oven, the Charleston grits that had been cooking overnight were tasty and nutlike, the jam and homemade bread continued to tempt me. Our conversation about upcoming events in Charleston interested other guests, so Kerry went on.

"The next big season comes in the middle of May. The Miss U.S.A. Pageant hosted by Charleston in 1977 was such a success that it is planned here again for 1978. The nationwide TV coverage of the city and the low country acquainted many more people with the really unique qualities of this area. I guess the secret of Charleston is being discovered.

"Probably the most exciting event of 1978 will be the Spoleto Festival in May and June. 1977 was the first year Spoleto was held outside of Italy and was a real outpouring of music and art. Spoleto '78 will be an event never before matched in the U.S.

"The fall tour season sponsored by the Preservation Society of Charleston will be held again in October 1978. Our inn was highlighted on one of the two 'historic buildings' candlelight tours, which featured a group of five musicians playing recorders in the ballroom. The old melodies and the candlelight really transported the five hundred or so visitors back in time. It was a breathtaking experience for us all."

Kerry's family is very much involved with the inn; his 22-year-old brother, Steven, has been working summers as assistant manager since May, 1977, and his parents are always shopping for just the right antique pieces to further enhance the five guest rooms. A recent note from him adds the news that they had just acquired a lovely antique Kerman rug for the ballroom.

It is evident that much care and thought has gone into the furnishing of their five rooms. In addition to the distinctive bed linens and accessories (different for each room) and the beautiful antique pieces, there are always fresh fruit and flowers in each room, and a newspaper at the door every morning.

Hospitality and comfort is the keynote at the Swordgate Inn, and Kerry Anderson knows they have succeeded when, as he says, "Our guests feel so at home that they appear for breakfast in their robe and slippers!"

I can just imagine that "robe" is some little number run up by Givenchy or Halston—anything else would be out of place in this stately Charleston mansion!

SWORDGATE INN, 111 Tradd St., Charleston, S.C. 29401; 803-723-8518. A quiet 5-room elegant inn located in the center of an historic area of the city, amidst distinguished 18th and 19th century homes. Within walking and biking distance of most of Charleston's cultural and historic landmarks. Bicycles furnished without charge to guests. Lodgings include informal breakfast. No other meal served. Open every day of the year. No children or pets. Beaches, sailing, and fresh water and deep sea fishing nearby. Kerry Anderson, Innkeeper.

Directions: Take I-26 to Meeting St. South Exit. Turn right on Meeting St., 12 blocks to Broad St.; turn right on Broad, two blocks to Legare St. Turn left on Legare for one block; turn left on Tradd St. Look for small sign on right that says Swordgate Inn.

Old Charleston Mansion

One of the best times to go to Charleston is during the period when many of these old houses are open to the public. In 1977, this house festival took place between March 17th and April 11th. It is at approximately the same time each year. For full information write to: The Historic Charleston Foundation, 51 Meeting Street, Charleston, S.C. 29401.

263

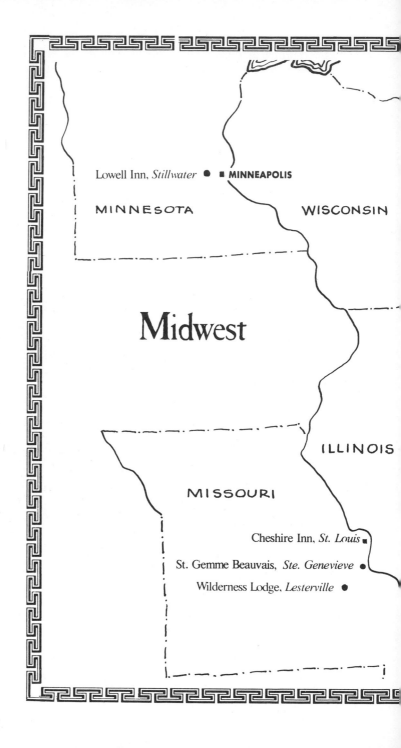

Midwest

Lowell Inn, *Stillwater* ● ■ **MINNEAPOLIS**

MINNESOTA

WISCONSIN

ILLINOIS

MISSOURI

Cheshire Inn, *St. Louis* ■

St. Gemme Beauvais, *Ste. Genevieve* ●

Wilderness Lodge, *Lesterville* ●

Stafford's Bay View Inn,
Petoskey

MICHIGAN

DETROIT

Botsford Inn, *Farmington*

National House, *Marshall*

CLEVELAND

The Patchwork Quilt,
Middlebury

Welshfield Inn, *Burton*

OHIO

COLUMBUS

Buxton Inn, *Granville*

INDIANAPOLIS

Durbin Hotel, *Rushville*

INDIANA

Golden Lamb, *Lebanon*

CINCINNATI

New Harmony Inn,
Red Geranium,
New Harmony

EVANSVILLE

Indiana

HISTORIC NEW HARMONY

Ralph Schwarz and I were standing at the topmost point of the superstructure of the new Atheneum in New Harmony. It was early fall 1977 and the official opening of this most unusual structure designed by Richard Meier was scheduled to take place in the summer of 1978. What made it all so fascinating was the hour: it was approximately midnight.

After enjoying a good dinner at the Red Geranium, we had walked through the quiet, tree-shaded streets of the town to his home and while we were talking over the progress of New Harmony, in a burst of his usual enthusiasm, he suggested that we "walk over to the Atheneum to see what it all looks like by moonlight."

Now we stood looking out over the town of New Harmony where the swaying trees made the street lamps seem to twinkle. The harvest moon had turned from a deep orange to a bright silver, and the entire countryside was bathed in its effulgence.

"I think you can see most everything from here," he said. "Over there is the Roofless Church and to the right is the log structure of 1775, the earliest building in the area. We can see the roof of the Opera House, and if you look a little to the right, there are the outlines of the Murphy Auditorium.

Atheneum, New Harmony

He swung his arm in a complete semi-circle and said, "one of the things that makes this so terribly exciting is that the plan of the village is the same as it was from the very beginning — only now we can see how well thought-out and disciplined it was."

On my first visit to New Harmony in the early '70s there was only a vague hint of the developments which would take place in the next few short years. There has been great progress in the restoration of this most unique environment.

New Harmony began in 1814 when a group of Lutheran Separatists from Germany led by Father George Rapp purchased thirty thousand acres of heavily forested lands on the banks of the Wabash. They created a unique, planned community in what was then a new frontier. They prospered and offered many practical innovations including "new town" development. It was indeed a forecast of 20th century methods.

When Father Rapp came to the conclusion in 1824 that his community seemed to be less concerned with matters of spirit and more with temporal things, he sold the entire town, lock, stock, and barrel to Welsh-born industrialist Robert Owen. Owen was one of the great dreamers of his day. He hoped to create a model community where education and social equality would prosper. Although his Utopian dream remained unrealized, his venture did a great deal toward spurring on the Golden Age of innovation in American science and education.

Some of the impressive ideas which came to fruition during the short span of the Owenites' era were the establishment of the first free public school system, the first free library, the first kindergarten, the first civic dramatic club, and the first geological survey in the United States. All children in New Harmony had equal access to education which was most unusual for that time. Among the aims of this society were "equality of rights uninfluenced by sex or condition in all adults; community of property; freedom of speech and action; courtesy in all intercourse; preservation of health; acquisition of knowledge; and obedience to the laws of the country in which we live."

One of the most beautiful and lasting contributions of the Owenites was not in the intellectual or scientific field, but was the importation of seeds for the Golden Rain Tree. New Harmony has been made exceptionally beautiful each spring by the blooming of these gorgeous trees.

Ralph continued, this time on the subject of the Atheneum. "There are five terraced levels. We are at the highest. Standing out here, I am reminded of the days when Father Rapp guided visitors to the gallery on the roof of his mansion to view the planned town with its impressive buildings and formal arrangement. The Atheneum will really be the pulse of New Harmony. It will have many conference rooms and halls and an open air theatrum for dance, symphony, and musical drama.

"We consider New Harmony a continuing experience and not a museum village. New Harmony is as vital as it always has been. Our goal is to capture a sense of continuity and quality. The ultimate plan is to preserve all of its unique historical periods and trace them through the architecture of the individual buildings. What is most important, we are putting all of them to excellent use today. There are many shops, galleries, that have given new life to the beautiful Victorian business buildings. The Murphy Auditorium, which was built in 1914, schedules a series of programs with the finest facilities for visual and performing arts.

Opera House, New Harmony

"We had the Eddy Brown Baroque Ensemble, a children's film festival; Tommy Dorsey's and Woody Herman's orchestras; pianist Zadel Skolovsky; and the New Harmony Jazz Festival this year. The series for '78 is more of the same. We also use the Opera House for plays, lectures, and the like.

"Throughout the year we have band concerts, art shows, dance workshop, mini-craft vacations, and a continuing group of archaeology studies."

Beginning in the summer of 1978 the visitor to Historic New

Harmony will be directed to the Atheneum and then, after a view from the top level, can follow a planned walking tour which will include dozens of houses, residences, and other buildings from both the Harmonist and Owenist days.

To date, success in the New Harmony restoration has stemmed from careful planning, thorough research, meticulous accuracy, the development of significant new restoration techniques, and above all, the generosity of many individuals and foundations who have made it possible.

Of course there was something in New Harmony to restore and preserve. Until a few short years ago, the idea of such a conservation was a vision of Jane Blaffer Owen, who had married a descendant of Robert Owen. She saw what it had been and what it could become.

Her enthusiasm was shared by some of the citizens of the town, such as Helen Elliott, whose family goes back to the time of the arrival of the Rappites, and who has worked tirelessly for the town's restoration.

A turning point in the development of New Harmony came with the arrival of Ralph Schwarz, a former consultant to the president and founder of the National Historic Preservation Fund. He took the reins of the New Harmony program in 1972, and currently serves as president of Historic New Harmony, Inc., a private nonprofit organization formed to advance the historic preservation and restoration of the community.

From New Harmony, other communities may learn to lift themselves by their own bootstraps and create new working and living environments that are more meaningful and inspirational. City planners and other civic-minded citizens, take heart. Visit New Harmony and then go back to your own community and see how much there is to preserve and restore.

NEW HARMONY INN
New Harmony, Indiana

Like all the other arriving guests, I checked in at the Entry House and then walked a few paces to the main building to take the elevator to my lodging rooms on the second floor at the New Harmony Inn. When I walked in the front door I was greeted by a wall plaque with a most unusual message taken from a medieval guest house:

"If any pilgrim monk comes from distant parts, if with wish as a guest to dwell in the monastery and will be content with the customs which he finds in the place, do not perchance by his lavishness disturb the monastery but

*is simply content with what he finds, he shall be received
for as long a time as he desires. If indeed he find fault with
anything and expose it reasonably and with the humility
of charity, the abbot shall discuss it prudently, less
perchance God has sent him for this very thing. But if
he had been found gossipy and contemptious at the time
of his sojourn as a guest, not only aught he not be joined
to the body of the monastery, but also it should be said
to him honestly that he must depart. If he does not go,
let two stout monks in the name of God explain the
matter to him."*

When I mentioned this to Gary Girard, the innkeeper, we both
laughed and he said, "Well, we don't have any problems with our
guests, so therefore, there are no stout monks for us to call upon to
explain anything!"

My room was one-and-a-half stories high with a twisting iron
staircase leading to a balcony where there was a double bed. This
would be fun for children. On the main level there was an attractive
sofa that converted into another bed, and complete kitchen conveniences including a two-place electric stove, a toaster, china for
six people, flatware, and a refrigerator. Adding to the homelike
atmosphere was a fireplace and a balcony overlooking a small lake.

The furniture was Scandinavian with a blond finish and quite
in harmony with the somewhat restrained design.

The overall design of this new inn reflects contemporary
influences. There is a generous use of stone and plaster blended with
the red brick walls of the rooms, hallways, and reception areas. The

exterior of the inn, including the surrounding grounds, is landscaped with evergreens, firethorn, and Oregon holly.

On that particular warm Indiana afternoon, I was delighted to plunge into the indoor swimming pool with its glass ceiling and walls open to let in the fresh air.

There are no meals served at the New Harmony Inn; however, there is a substantial Continental breakfast offered in the Entry House. Luncheon and dinner are available at the Red Geranium Restaurant which is just a few steps from the inn, and the Shadblow Restaurant which is located a few blocks away in the restored business section of New Harmony.

At the present time, still another inn is being planned and I shall no doubt be visiting New Harmony and reporting on it in future issues.

NEW HARMONY INN, New Harmony, Ind. 47361; 812-682-4491. A 45-room village inn on the site of Harmonist and Owenite restorations. No meals served; some rooms with kitchenettes. No pets. Open every day. Year-round swimming pool on grounds. Golf, boating, tennis and riding nearby. Gary Gerard, Innkeeper.

Directions: Located 30 mi. northwest of Evansville. Approximately 18 mi. on Rte. 460, south of I-64.

RED GERANIUM AND SHADBLOW RESTAURANTS
New Harmony, Indiana

During recent years I have enjoyed visiting two restaurants in New Harmony. One is the Red Geranium, which I first visited in 1972—it is right next to the New Harmony Inn, the Paul Tillich Park, and the Roofless Church. The other is on the main street in the Mews and is called The Shadblow, after the tree of the same name, which has brought so much joy to residents and visitors to this area.

In the Red Geranium the service is leisurely and the menu is quite extensive. The Shadblow is a "homey" type of place, built more recently around an open courtyard in the center of which stands a living Shadblow tree. This restaurant provides quick service, particularly for people who are touring historic New Harmony and wish to stop for soup, a sandwich, or something light. The Shadblow also features several salad specials, which I prefer in the middle of a busy day. There is one sandwich which I found particularly tasty made with Canadian bacon, tomato, and a creamy cheese sauce on an English muffin. Salisbury steak, chicken livers, and deep fried shrimp are typical of the limited menu.

The Shadblow also has the advantage of being located directly adjacent to the Red Geranium Bookstore which has a most comprehensive collection of books about the early development of New Harmony. Its light and airy atmosphere is most conducive to browsing.

At the Red Geranium, the eight-page menu reflects the products of the Indiana farmlands surrounding the town. There are an unusual number of beef dishes including char-prime steak which is prepared by cooking an entire prime rib in the oven and then putting slices of it on the grill at the last moment. These slices are succulent and thick, and the gravy is so good that everybody dips their homemade bread in it. Ham is another specialty of the house, including ham steak served with red-eye gravy, and Shaker ham steak which is baked in apple cider. Desserts include fresh strawberry pie (honest), coconut Bavarian pie, baked Alaska, and German chocolate cake. The old-fashioned Shaker lemon pie is heavenly.

The Red Geranium is a restaurant in which to enjoy a long, leisurely meal and reservations are most necessary.

RED GERANIUM RESTAURANT, New Harmony, Ind. 47361; 812-682-4431. No lodgings, guests accommodated at adjacent New Harmony Inn. Open 11 a.m.-11 p.m. Tuesdays-Saturdays; 11 a.m.- 8 p.m. Sundays. Closed Mondays. Closed July 4th, Christmas and New Year's Day. Gary Gerard, Manager.

SHADBLOW RESTAURANT, New Harmony, Ind. 47361; 812- 682-4463. No lodgings. Breakfast served from 5:30 a.m.; lunch from 11 a.m.; dinner 4-8 p.m. Open every day except Christmas.

DURBIN HOTEL
Rushville, Indiana

The Durbin Hotel is the essence of Midwest America. It is like corn on the cob, fried chicken, and James Whitcomb Riley's poetry. The Durbin family tradition of innkeeping has been going on for 52 years. It began when Leo Durbin, a traveling salesman from Ohio, and Mary Kane of Indianapolis, were married and went into the hotel business. They had seven children, a great many of whom, inspired by their upbringing in the hotel, went into the business in other places. The present innkeeper, their son David, has continued in Rushville and many of *his* seven children have been employed at various times in the family hotel.

I really enjoyed my most recent visit during the summer of 1977. David immediately took me in tow to see some of the interesting changes that had been made recently. "We used to call this room the Gay Nineties Room, but after we uncovered the brick walls, exposing the beams, and made it into a reproduction of an old tap room, the rest of my family began to call it 'David's Folly'—the name has apparently stuck. By the way, we have live music here every night except Sunday and Monday."

I followed him into a newly-decorated corner dining room with very bright colors and an air of gaiety. "We call this room the Strawberry Patch," he said. "You know we are pretty homey folks out here, and everyone feels comfortable with familiar names."

Our tour continued through many of the newly-decorated and refurnished bedrooms. Each of them has its own theme, and all are very attractive. I asked him whether or not some of the beds still had the "Magic Fingers" mattresses. He smiled and said, "Well you don't find them in very many hotels or inns, but our guests tell us that they love them." By the way, it was in the Durbin Hotel that I first got the idea about having green plants growing in the lodging rooms. This is something that many other inns in CIBR are also doing now.

We returned to the lobby again, and while David went to get a menu, I sat down and just enjoyed being here in this friendly atmosphere. There is a main counter with all kinds of post cards, old-fashioned stick candy in jars, books, maps, and even some crafts from that section of Indiana. The grandfather clock tolls every fifteen minutes, and the penny scale still works. There is an arrangement of comfortable furniture in one corner, which is appropriately decorated with many photographs of Mr. Wendell Willkie, the Republican presidential candidate during the early 1940s who made the Durbin Hotel his campaign headquarters.

David returned and we immediately launched into a discussion of home-cooking at the hotel which is noted far and wide.

"To begin with," he said, "everything is made from scratch. We make our own pies, cakes and breads right here in the kitchen. The menu is just good farm food, things like scalloped chicken, noodle casseroles, fried chicken, candied yams, baked beans, Danish lobster tails, filet mignon.

"Our menu changes with the season and, of course, we have fresh vegetables whenever they are available. One of our most popular dishes is a homemade ham loaf. We also serve lots of liver, either broiled or pan fried. Do you know that we serve 700 for dinner on many Sundays? By the way, in this part of Indiana when someone says 'dinner' it usually refers to the midday meal. Supper is served at night."

We had a great time at lunch (dinner) that day, as David had invited several of his friends whom I had met on a previous visit. I was delighted when his mother also was able to join our big table.

When I said good-bye to David, once again I was filled with good food, loaded down with the warm wishes of new friends, and delighted with all that had been happening at the Durbin Hotel. The way things are going I am sure it will be there for 52 more years!

DURBIN HOTEL, 137 W. Second Street, Rushville, Ind. 46173; 317-932-4161. A 28-room country hotel in a bustling town, about one hour from Indianapolis. European plan. Breakfast, lunch, dinner served daily except Christmas and New Year's. Leashed pets allowed. Rushville is the home of Wendell Willkie, the 1940

Presidential candidate. Several round barns and covered bridges in the area. David Durbin, Innkeeper.

Directions: From the Indianapolis Beltway take I-74 south to Rushville-Shelbyville exit. Or follow Rte. 52 from the Beltway directly to Rushville.

PATCHWORK QUILT
Middlebury, Indiana

Here I was, back again at the Patchwork Quilt, and glad to be here. It was the same as before, the broad fields, the white house and the trim out-buildings of a real working farm.

Arletta Lovejoy handed me a glass of mulled cider and introduced me to the other guests awaiting the dinner bell. We were indeed a "mixed bag." There were quite a few people from such nearby Indiana towns as Elkhart and South Bend. There were also Chicagoans, people from Cleveland, and New England.

The signal was given and we all took our places in the Keeping Room. My seat was placed so that I could see into the remarkable kitchen with its Danish oak cabinets. The ladies of the neighborhood, many with cooking specialties, were each busy with some phase of preparing our meal.

Now, one of them came out to the salad-and-relish buffet table and made an announcement. "This evening we have applesauce, kidney bean salad, potato salad, pecan cheese roll, a five-bean salad, corn relish, pickle relish, ham salad, Waldorf salad, Hawaiian franks, pumpkin bread, Swedish fruit soup, and five different dressings." I could just feel the "ooh" go through the room. After all, this was really a prelude to the main event. I tried to use discretion in sampling all of these, although the Swedish fruit soup was too tempting. The U.S. Senate Bean Soup was served from a steaming caldron hanging on a crane in the blazing fireplace.

Next, another pretty lady from the kitchen announced the main dishes, which were all served family style and changed about every day. There were ham, steak Robert, and, of course, the prize-winning Buttermilk Pecan Chicken. The plate with the meats was garnished with parsley and small red tomatoes. There were also green beans served with mushrooms and almonds, and corn served with bits of red pimentoes.

The only meal served at the Patchwork Quilt, which is a real working farm, is dinner, and it is always necessary to reserve in advance. It is closed on Sundays and there is a fixed-price dinner on

Fridays and Saturdays. There are no guest rooms available, but the upstairs bedroom displays extremely attractive furnishings, including beautiful quilts that are for sale.

At dinner that evening Arletta told me the good news that her daughter, Michele, who was just a young girl when I first visited the inn a number of years ago, and her husband, who was a veterinarian, had decided to move from California back to Middlebury where Michele could take a more active interest in the inn. "She's taught several cooking schools, so I am sure she will have much to offer," said Arletta.

Finally, a large serving cart brought blueberry pie, pecan pie, candied violet cake, grasshopper pie, apricot chiffon pie, cherry cake, cherry walnut torte, and my eye caught the coffee toffee pie made with butter, eggs, chocolate crust, nuts, and chocolate filling.

Would you believe that the whole table actually stood up and applauded!

PATCHWORK QUILT COUNTRY INN, 11748 C.R. #2, Middlebury, Ind. 46450; 219-825-2417. A working farm restaurant in the tradition of midwestern hospitality, about 20 mi. east of Elkhart. No lodgings. Dinner served daily by reservation only. Closed Sundays, Mondays, Thanksgiving, Christmas and New Year's. Arletta Lovejoy, Innkeeper.

Directions: From east or west, exit Indiana Toll Road at Middlebury (Exit 10) and go north ¼ mi. to County Rd. #2 and proceed west 1 mi. to inn. From Middlebury follow Indiana Rte. 13 for 8 mi. north to County Rd. #2 and west 1 mi.

Michigan

BOTSFORD INN
Farmington Hills, Michigan

It was a late, lovely summer afternoon in Farmington and after taking one of the crossing roads from the Detroit Airport I was on Grand Avenue headed toward Farmington and turned into the parking lot of the Botsford Inn to see a number of people enjoying the pool. A welcome breeze had come up, breaking the hot weather in Detroit, but I was still glad to know that my room at the Botsford would have air conditioning if I needed it.

I go back with the Botsford Inn — not way back to 1836 when it was first built or when the famous Innkeeper Botsford had it — but for quite a few of the more recent years. I can remember when I first heard of it, my reaction was, "Who would expect to find a country inn in Detroit." Well, the Botsford Inn isn't exactly a New England country inn, however, some of the 19th-century atmosphere has been preserved; first in the 1930s, with the help of Henry Ford, and continued by the present owner and innkeeper, John Anhut, who has a penchant for country inns.

He joined me for dinner in the main dining room with its oaken beams and broad picture window. This time the conversation led naturally to some of the innovations that were being made at the inn.

"For one thing," he said, "the next time you visit here we will have an addition to this dining room. We will be able to accommodate more people, but will have an even better view of the garden.

"We are going to continue to have dinner theatre each Thursday and Sunday in the Coach House. The emphasis is on light comedy. For instance, this year we played 'I Do, I Do,' 'The Last of the Red Hot Lovers,' 'The Mousetrap,' and things like that."

While we were talking some strolling violinists walked through the dining room, pausing for a moment at each table. John explained that they played on Tuesday, Wednesday and Thursday and were a great hit.

We talked for a moment about the menu at the Botsford Inn and he had this to say: "We believe in serving predominantly American food; we aren't a French restaurant and have never tried to be one. Consequently, we have a lot of things on the menu that people come to associate with country living here in the Midwest."

This idea of country food was certainly reflected in the salad bowl of crisp lettuce, pea beans, a sprinkling of carrots and celery and tomato sections. The dressing was something that reminded me of my grandmother's, back in central New York State, a little on the vinegary side with bits of bacon in it. The short ribs that night were delicious. Each came in its own casserole and the sauce was excellent. I poured it over both the meat and potatoes; it was exactly what I wanted.

In 1836, Farmington was a day's journey from the banks of the river where Detroit was a burgeoning city. Today it is just a short drive from the hustle and bustle of the Motor City. As many things as possible have been preserved, particularly in the main building where there are a variety of reminders of other times in Michigan.

Many of the bedrooms, furnished with reproductions, have the conveniences that American travelers often find not only helpful but necessary. Best of all, the spirit of country innkeeping and community service is very much alive.

BOTSFORD INN, 28000 Grand River Avenue, Farmington Hills, Mich. 48024; 313-474-4800. A 62-room village inn on the city line of Detroit. European plan. Dinner served daily except Monday. Breakfast and lunch Tuesday thru Saturday. Sunday brunch. Closed Christmas and New Year's Day. Pool on grounds. Greenfield Village, skiing and state parks nearby. John Anhut, Innkeeper.

Directions: Located in Farmington Hills on I-96 which is easily accessible from major highways in Michigan.

Marshall, Michigan was a complete and pleasant surprise to me. Letters from readers recommending the National House Inn also included some teasers such as "and the town is beautiful," or "you will love the beautiful homes." However, I had no hint as to just how beautiful and unusual the town really is.

The fact is that Marshall was such an interesting experience I returned in the summer of 1977 for a second walking tour and a longer visit.

Marshall should certainly take its place, along with Cape May, New Jersey and Port Townsend, Washington, as one of the most significant centers of Victorian restoration in the world. There are dozens and dozens of gorgeous Victorian homes being lived in by the good people of Marshall today. Fifteen have been designated as state historic sites and six are in the National Register. The residential sections of the town all have beautiful, tall shade trees and sidewalks bordering carefully trimmed lawns and hedges. Everywhere are evidences of civic pride.

The most significant individual in Marshall's restoration and revival is Mr. Harold C. Brooks, a former mayor and true benefactor of the community. He became involved in the preservation more than fifty years ago. He bought several of the important vacant Victorian homes in Marshall and held them until an owner arrived on the scene who was interested in preserving and restoring the building. It appears that very stringent zoning laws and building restrictions have been enacted by the wise citizens of the town in order to preserve this truly magnificent reminder of America's

Honolulu House, Marshall

opulent building period. Aided by a very explicit brochure, visitors to Marshall can enjoy a walking tour of the entire community.

The highlight of Marshall's year comes on the first weekend after Labor Day. It is the Annual Historic Home Tour in which Marshall homes are open for visitors. Over 35 organizations and 1400 volunteers work on this project and this is astonishing when we consider that the city has a population of only 7400. Thousands of people are in Marshall during these two days.

Some buildings, including the famous Honolulu House Museum, which has a fantastic collection of Victorian furniture and artifacts, are open May through October. The name "Honolulu House" stems from the fact that it was built by a former U.S. Consul to the then Sandwich Islands who decided to live "Hawaiian style" in Marshall.

For lovers of all Victoriana including the Italianate, Greek Revival, Gothic Revival, Queen Anne, and Italian-villa-style houses, Marshall is indeed a feast. Perhaps more than that, it is an inspiration for all communities to recognize, preserve, and use the irreplaceable reminders of the past.

THE NATIONAL HOUSE
Marshall, Michigan

"The Marshall Historic Home Tour—oh it is just marvelous. Everybody in town seems to get involved. It has grown so much. We already have full reservations for 1978 and 1979 for the first weekend after Labor Day."

Norman Kinney, the innkeeper at the National House Inn was helping me to assimilate the experience of this unusual town. "Mr. Brooks was the most important factor," he said. "He was the man who had the vision of Marshall. But everybody in town has joined in. We are proud of the homes and the museums and we all work together. I am sure that we could not have restored the National House if it hadn't been a community effort. People helped out in so many ways."

Our conversation turned toward the National House itself. "This is probably the oldest remaining hotel building in Michigan," he pointed out. "We learned that it was open in 1835 and undoubtedly was the first brick building of any kind in our county. We do know that it was the scene of a Grand Ball on January 1, 1836, which helped transform the frontier village into a bona fide town. It was a hotel for many years, frequently called the National House, Mann's Hotel, National Hotel, the Acker House, and the Facey House. At one time it was a windmill and wagon factory, and more recently an apartment building." Norman continued, "My good friend, Hal Minick and I, along with his wife Jacqueline and my wife, Kathryn, decided to restore the building and return it to its original purpose.

"It has really been hard work, but underneath the dirt and grime of dozens of years, we found the solid, beautiful structure of the original brick as well as the irreplaceable woodwork. We converted the apartments into 14 bedrooms and baths. We have named all the rooms after significant Marshall citizens. Your room was named for Sidney Ketchem, a land surveyor from Peru in Clinton County, New York who had the original idea of creating Marshall as a political and mercantile center. He founded Marshall's first bank."

I asked Norman about the unusual and frequently elegant furnishings. "As you can see, Marshall is very much a Victorian restoration. We searched everywhere — culled all the antique shops and removed furniture from our own homes. We and the Minicks both live in restored Victorian houses. Many of our friends contributed some of their beloved pieces in order to help us recreate the atmosphere of Marshall before the turn of the century. We are always searching, restoring, and refinishing authentic pieces."

One of the most striking features of the National House is the passionate attention to detail. There are dozens and dozens of small things that make it a gem. For example, each bedroom has its own ambience and there are colorful comforters, old trunks, marble top tables, bureaus, dried flower arrangements, electric lamps that are reproductions of gas lamps, candle sconces with reflectors, little corner sofas, special care with door knobs, and special attention is given to the linens. These furnishings have all been combined to provide a great deal of comfort and color. The bedroom windows overlook either the residential part of town, or a beautiful fountain in the town center park.

Breakfast is the only meal served and is offered every morning in the dining room which has a most fetching collection of chairs and tables from great-grandfather's day. The color tones are warm brown and beige. The breakfast offerings include homebaked coffee cakes and muffins, nut breads, and the like. I spent an hour and a half at breakfast talking with many different people.

The Kinneys and Minicks have devoted a great deal of loving care, pride and considerable investment in restoring this beautiful building to its original state. The people of Marshall can well be proud of the National House Inn.

NATIONAL HOUSE INN, 102 South Parkview, Marshall, Mi. 49068; 616-781-2494. An elegantly restored 14-room Victorian-period village inn. Marshall is the finest example of 19th-century architecture in the Midwest. It has 15 State historic sites and 6 National Register sites. European plan includes Continental breakfast. No other meals served. Open year-round. Closed Christmas Eve and Christmas Day. Tennis, golf, swimming, boating, xc skiing nearby. Norman D. Kinney, Steve Poole, Innkeepers.

Directions: From I-69 exit at Michigan Ave. in Marshall and go straight 1½ mi. to inn. From I-94 use exit 110, follow old 27 south 1½ mi. to inn.

STAFFORD'S BAY VIEW INN
Petoskey, Michigan

Janice Smith and I were seated in one corner of the Blueberry Hill Inn having our first real talk in quite a few years. "Do you remember," she asked, "when you and I took a little back-roading tour and saw some of the Lake Michigan shoreline a few years ago?" I remember that day very well. Along with her son, Reginald, and her daughter, Mary Kathryn, we had set out from Stafford's Bay View Inn, and I gained a marvelous overview of that entire section of Michigan.

Now we were at a mountaintop inn in Vermont, along with several other innkeepers, enjoying the chance to get together once again.

"First of all, Kathy sends her best and is sorry that she couldn't be with us on this trip." (Kathy Hart is the manager of Stafford's Bay View Inn.) "Speaking of Kathy, I do wish you could be with us at Christmas time. The inn looks prettier than ever then. There are over

400 white lights decorating the outside of the inn, and the Victorian cupola looks like a giant Christmas tree. As you enter the front door, you are greeted by Kathy's beautiful gingerbread village, which actually takes about two months of loving care to prepare. We have families stopping all the time to show the children the trees and the village.

"Christmas is when we have our gala buffet. We have been doing it for 11 years, so I guess it is a tradition. Even now, in early November, we have reservations. There is a lot of activity at the inn during Christmas week and lots of young people. Each evening we put out popcorn and munchies, and we set aside the Sun Room as a playroom so that they can play skittles, checkers, and things like that. It is a very healthy setting for young families who are mostly from large cities."

Janice and Stafford Smith have a really great story. In 1960, Stafford was fresh out of college and employed at Bay View. Janice was hostess there that summer and the two young people found many things in common. The following year they were married and purchased the inn all within two weeks. Since that time the inn has continued to flourish.

This reminder of Victorian days is on the edge of the Bay View section of Petoskey, a summer resort community which has grown up around a program of music, drama, art, and religious lectures and services. The early residents built fine Victorian homes which are still standing. The cultural and religious programs which started then are still going on, and guests at Bay View often find them most enjoyable.

The inn, with its wide, broad porches is located just a short distance from the shores of Little Traverse Bay, where water skiing, sailing and other summer sports abound.

One of the factors that contributes greatly to the inn's popularity is the fact that senior citizens are made to feel most welcome. I found it to be a comfortable place for all ages. There are a lot of children around during the summer, and some of the older guests seem to take naturally to entertaining them. I think the best term for them is "surrogate grandparents."

"We're quite active during Christmas week and other long weekends in the winter," said Janice. "The Nub's Nob Ski Area is only six miles from the inn and it is undergoing some significant improvements. We're open only on long weekends during the winter sports season, and besides the downhill areas in the region, we have much cross-country skiing.

I'm not certain about my Christmas plans for 1978, but my summer plans include a visit to Stafford's Bay View Inn.

STAFFORD'S BAY VIEW INN, Box 3, Petoskey, Mich. 49770; 616-347-2771. A 23-room resort-inn on Little Traverse Bay in the Bay View section of Petoskey. Modified American plan omits lunch. Breakfast, lunch and dinner served daily to travelers. Open daily Memorial Day to mid-October, Christmas week and long weekends during the winter sports season. Lake swimming and xc skiing on grounds. Golfing, boating, fishing, hiking, and Alpine ski trails nearby. Kathleen A. Hart, Manager. Stafford and Janice Smith, Innkeepers.

Directions: From Detroit, take Gaylord Exit from I-75 and follow Mich. Rte. 32 to Rte. 131, north to Petoskey. From Chicago, use U.S. 131 north to Petoskey.

Minnesota

LOWELL INN
Stillwater, Minnesota

The headline on the *Stillwater Evening Gazette* said, "Lowell Inn To Celebrate 50th Anniversary, Monday, June 27th." Innkeeper Arthur Palmer handed me another edition commemorating the Lowell Inn's anniversary, which was entirely devoted to the activities in the town 50 years ago when the inn was originally opened. "It

replaced the old Sawyer House which had been standing since the middle of the 19th century," said Arthur.

One of the things that surprised and fascinated me from the instant I saw the Lowell Inn in the summer of 1975 was its Williamsburg architecture. The roof with its gables and dormers recalls the roofs of the best buildings of colonial times. The stately, two-storied portico with its thirteen slender columns reminded me very much of George Washington's home in Mt. Vernon. I never expected to find this reminder of Virginia's tidewater in the middle of Minnesota.

In the 50-year history of the Lowell Inn there have been several important events. Perhaps the most important took place on Christmas Day in 1930, when Arthur and Nelle Palmer took over the stewardship of the inn, which has continued to be a family enterprise through their son, Arthur, and his wife, Maureen, and their many grandchildren.

"Mother and Dad had spent a great deal of their youth and young adulthood 'on the road'," said Arthur. "She was an actress and he was a pianist. They had met and were married while working with Nelle's sisters who produced shows and traveled in the Midwest. They were playing Stillwater, and the opportunity to manage the inn arose, so they stayed on, and it eventually became their inn in 1945.

"I'm sorry you couldn't have been here for the anniversary. We had two of the original shareholders who sat down to the inn's first meal, and William Ingemann, the Lowell Inn's architect and his wife, who were the first honeymoon couple at the inn, and observed their golden wedding anniversary with us."

Today, the Lowell Inn, which has had as many as seven Palmers working in it at one time, is an outstanding country inn. It is recognized among keepers of country inns as exceptional. There are three dining rooms, each with its own theme. The George Washington Room shows an appreciation and love for the antiques of the Williamsburg Colonial period. The Garden Room was conceived as an outdoor garden court, and even has an outdoor trout pool from which guests may select their own trout. The Matterhorn Room would be unique even in Switzerland: the room is filled from floor to ceiling with authentic Swiss wood carvings. The staff is dressed in Swiss costumes, and they feature a five-course, fixed-price dinner that includes fondue Bourguignonne.

"I'm sure that our patio area on the south side is going to be open in the spring of 1978 as a sidewalk cafe," said Arthur. "We plan on specializing in French crepes and a light, modestly-priced lunch." We walked to the front patio, and he showed me where all of the outdoor tables would be placed and how it would all be accomplished.

It was on this visit, too, that I viewed all of the guest rooms in the inn which had been redecorated. One of the most ambitious features was a different set of decorator sheets and pillow cases set aside for each of the guest rooms.

Truly there is much more to be said about this unusual inn in such an attractive town on the banks of the beautiful St. Croix River. I would like to add my congratulations to the many already received by Arthur and Maureen, and tip my hat to Nelle and Arthur Palmer whose spirit and originality still persist.

THE LOWELL INN, 102 N. Second St., Stillwater, Minn. 55082; 612-439-1100. A 22-room village inn 18 mi. from St. Paul, near all the cultural attractions of the Twin Cities. European plan. Lunch and dinner served daily except Christmas Eve and Christmas Day. Open year-round. No pets. Canoeing, tennis, hiking, skiing and swimming nearby, including 4 ski resorts within 15 mi. Arthur and Maureen Palmer, Innkeepers.

Directions: Stillwater is on the St. Croix River at the junction of Minn. 95 (north and south) and Minn. 36 (east and west). It is 7 mi. north of I-94 on Hwy. 95.

Missouri

CHESHIRE INN & LODGE
St. Louis, Missouri

This is the story of two inns: One is one of the most prestigious and ancient hostelries in the Old World and the other is located in the

heartland of the United States. One has centuries of history behind it, and the other was created for the most part within the past decade. Each is an excellent example of how good taste, good management, and dedication to serving guests can mean success. The first inn is the Lygon Arms in Broadway, England, an inn which I have written about in the European Edition of *Country Inns and Back Roads*. The second is the Cheshire Inn on the outskirts of St. Louis, Missouri.

The Cheshire Inn was constructed in Tudor style with half-timbers embedded in the plastered outer walls. The Lygon Arms, which incidentally has had several additions to it over the years, is for the most part made of red sandstone.

I have never asked Stephen and Barbara Apted whether they have visited the Lygon Arms, but since they did visit so many other English inns, manor houses, and castles, I can't help but feel reasonably certain that some of the ideas which they have incorporated into the Cheshire Inn were inspired by decorations, wall hangings, and furniture that is typical of the Lygon Arms.

Some of the lodging rooms are quite similar although there is a wide variety in both inns. I can well imagine awakening in one of the king-sized, canopied beds of the Cheshire Inn and believing, at least for a moment, that I was in the heart of the Cotswolds. The hallways and lodging rooms have furniture, prints, and portraits that would be equally at home in the Lygon Arms. The rooms at the Cheshire have been named after prominent English literary figures such as Galsworthy, Dickens, and Tennyson. As I recall, the rooms in the English inn had been named for prominent English figures as well.

Certainly the menu at the Cheshire could be served in its British cousin's dining room without causing a single eyebrow to be raised. There are main courses such as roast prime ribs of beef with Yorkshire pudding and horseradish mousse; another is roast duck, which according to the menu is served in the manner "preferred by Charles Dickens." There are also glazed pork chops Buckingham with sweet and sour sauce, topped with a grilled pineapple ring. There are many more offerings including trout stuffed with crab-meat, short ribs of beef, fish, lobster tails, and, of course many types of steaks. In this last respect, I would imagine that the steaks at the Cheshire would probably be greater in variety because of the proximity to the great American beef of the Midwest.

Even the desserts are similar and I am sure that in St. Louis, as in England, the most popular dessert is the English trifle. However, at the Cheshire it is possible to get Missouri apple pie served with warm cheese and/or ice cream.

Speaking of cheese, there is a new cheese and wine shop at the east end of the restaurant building at the Cheshire, known as the "Cheshire Cellars." There is a large selection of imported and domestic cheeses, sausages, whole bean coffee, teas, and much more. I'm sure that this would include some hearty Stilton, one of the cheeses for which the Lygon Arms is famous.

There is one interesting difference between these two inns. One of them has two double-decker, red, London buses which are used to transport guests to various points of interest in the immediate vicinity. Is it the Lygon Arms which has these friendly means of transport? No, it is the younger American cousin, the Cheshire.

CHESHIRE INN and LODGE, 6300 Clayton Rd., St. Louis, Mo. 63117; 314-647-7300. A 110-room English style inn, 1 block off Hwy. 40 near Forest Park. European plan only. Breakfast, lunch and dinner served to travelers daily. Accommodations available every day of the year. Restaurant closed on New Year's Day, Memorial Day, July 4th, Labor Day, and Christmas Day. Pool, bicycles on grounds. Boating, golf, tennis and riding nearby. St. Louis Art Museum, zoo, Gateway Arch and opera nearby. Mike Parker and Jim Prentice, Innkeepers.

Directions: Just off Hwy. 40 at Clayton Rd. and Skinker Blvd. on southwest corner of Forest Park. From the east, take Clayton Rd. exit. From the west, take McCausland Ave. exit, north two blocks to Clayton Rd.

ST. GEMME BEAUVAIS
Ste. Genevieve, Missouri

I love waking up in a country inn. Here in Ste. Genevieve I had set the alarm for an early hour because I wanted as much time as

possible to get a full tour of the Inn St. Gemme Beauvais, and to learn all I could about Ste. Genevieve, the first white settlement in Missouri.

My bed had a large, carved back in polished mahogany. The marble-topped bureau also had an impressive mirror with a 19th century carved frame. The flowered wallpaper, draperies, carpets, and other furniture made it an authentically Victorian experience. I learned subsequently that each of the eight suites has at least two rooms completely furnished with antiques.

My day really started with breakfast in the dining room, which had walnut ladder-back chairs, Belgian lace curtains, a marble fireplace, fine china, and graceful stemware — all reminders of elegant bygone days.

I discovered that two meals a day were served at St. Gemme Beauvais: breakfast and lunch by advance reservation. Anxious to preserve the true French heritage of the town, Frankye and Boats Donze, the innkeepers, put great emphasis on French cuisine for both meals. My eggs Benedict were very tasty, but I found that there was something different each day, such as French crepes, French mushroom omelettes, and French toast with ginger fruit sauce.

The luncheons favored Quiche Lorraine, broccoli casserole, and other French specialties, such as stuffed chicken breast.

After breakfast Frankye took me on a tour of each of the eight 2-room suites of the inn. I was particularly impressed by the bridal suite with its elaborate crystal chandelier, some handsome antique pieces, and two windows overlooking the Main Street. She also explained to me that each of the numbers on the lodging room doors were painted recently by her daughter-in-law. One of the rooms had an unusual bridal picture from at least a hundred years ago. The inside of the filigree frame was decorated with material obviously from the bride's gown and preserved flowers from her bouquet.

Frankye said that she and Boats have carefully collected as many regional antiques as possible for the inn.

Ste. Genevieve is one of the most pleasant surprises in the Midwest. It was the first permanent settlement in Missouri established around 1732, and the town has an impressive number of existing buildings from 150 to 200 years old. Quite a few of them have been restored as tour homes and museums, and most of these 18th and 19th century structures are occupied today and maintained with pride by their owners.

Among these is the Amoureaux House which is one of three major restorations by the Donzes. The Keeping Room dates back to 1770, and the furnishings mix various styles and modes, indicating that a house does not really remain static. Another of their restorations is the Beauvais House, which was also built around 1770, and moved from an old village. It has huge ceiling beams, and a great fireplace divides the two rooms. The third restoration was completed in 1978, and is the Green Tree Tavern which was built around 1790. It was the first inn in Ste. Genevieve.

Back downstairs in the tiny office, Boats, who grew up in the house, explained that the old-fashioned cubbyholes came from a post office in Illinois. I noticed a little sign which best expressed the real philosophy of this home-like inn:

"There are no strangers here, just friends we haven't met."

ST. GEMME BEAUVAIS, 78 N. Main St., Ste. Genevieve, Mo. 63670; 314-883-5744. An 8-room village inn about 1½ hrs. from St. Louis. Modified American plan includes breakfast only. Breakfast served daily. Lunch served Mon.-Sat. Open year-round. Closed Thanksgiving and Christmas Day. No pets. Golf, hunting and fishing nearby. Frankye and Boats Donze, Innkeepers.

Directions: From St. Louis, south on I-55 to Hwy. 32. Exit east on 32 to Hwy. 61 to the Ste. Genevieve exit.

WILDERNESS LODGE
Lesterville, Missouri

Friday evening at Wilderness Lodge. All of the guests were gathered next to the Black River for the get-acquainted barbecue which starts off the weekend activities. The spareribs on the fire were already sending forth their magic aroma, mixed with the marvelous scents of autumn in the Ozarks and fresh mountain air.

Big platters of potato salad, slaw, corn muffins, and relishes were brought down to the riverside and everybody was sitting on benches around the fire. Most of the talk was in anticipation of the next day's activities.

"We've already got our morning tennis game booked," said one man. Another replied: "Well, I don't know what the rest of you are going to do, but I am going to start the day with a two-hour float."

"Oh, you don't even know how to paddle a canoe."

"Well, I am going to learn how in just a few minutes because they have canoeing demonstrations here, and besides, the Black River is the safest river in Missouri."

Sure enough, the Lodge does offer demonstrations of the various canoeing strokes, and a short course in canoe safety. Also, a wrangler demonstrates how to handle the horses from the Lodge stable and how anybody can get on a horse and have fun for the first

time. "As long as you don't try to do too much the first day," he said. "You use muscles you never knew you had when you ride a horse!"

Here in the forest just two hours from St. Louis there are many activities including tennis, hayriding, trail rides, fishing, canoeing, platform tennis — all in the beautiful Ozark setting. And, of course, the good food served family style. It is a wonderful place for kids and grown-ups since everybody can have a good time, either together or separately. Families especially enjoy the hearty, generous meals.

The newest, most exciting addition to activities at Wilderness Lodge is the construction of a private airplane landing strip. As Barbara Apted explained, "There is nothing available for private planes in the area and now guests can come right to the lodge." For landing instructions, I would suggest a telephone call to the inn.

She also said that a new husband-and-wife team are managing the lodge, Glen and Kathy Shepard. "Glen is an engineer and a pilot, and will be supervising the construction of the landing strip and the nearby new campgrounds we are putting in. Kathy will manage the office and kitchen. She is very attractive and I am sure our guests will like her very much."

There are various kinds of accommodations. My room, in a rustic cabin made of native wood, had a big fireplace with the wood already laid in the grate. A rear balcony was perched high in the trees on a hillside overlooking the river. The varnished floors, along with the furniture, were all country made. This is not an ordinary hunting lodge, but something very special with conveniences built right in.

Floating, of course, is part of the fun here, and guests are taken upstream along with their canoes so that they can coast downriver at their own rate of speed. For all trips, box lunches are made available to the guests.

Another very popular activity is trail riding. There are several horses and wranglers to guide guests around the 1200 acres of woodlands and riverside trails. You can even bring your own horse.

About an hour after the Missouri barbecue began, everybody had eaten his fill, and a big bonfire was crackling away. I heard a guitar tuning, and I knew we were in for an evening of hill country stories and good fun.

WILDERNESS LODGE, P.O. Box 87, Lesterville, Mo. 63654; 314-296-2011. A 24-room resort-inn located in the heart of the scenic Ozarks approximately 2½ hrs. from St. Louis. Modified American plan. Breakfast and dinner to travelers. Closed from Christmas to the day before New Years. Box lunches available. No pets. Tennis, platform tennis, bocci, horseback riding, canoeing, float trips, walking and nature trails, fishing, archery, and many other sports on grounds. Stephen and Barbara Apted, Innkeepers.

Directions: From I-244 take Hwy. 55 south and just past Festus, take Hwy. 67 south. After the junction of Hwy. 32, Hwy. 67 becomes two lanes only. Follow 67 and very shortly look for a sign: "W," Farmington. Take this exit and turn right. You'll be on W west. Remain on W for approximately 8 mi. and there will be a sign, Jct. V. Turn left onto V for 9 mi. and it ends at Hwy. 21 in Ironton, where you turn left. Follow 21 and 1 mi. past town of Hogan be careful. This is Jct. of 21 and Hwy 49. 49 will continue straight ahead and 21 will swerve to the right. No big thing if you look for it just be sure to go right toward Lesterville. As you approach Lesterville, you'll pass Lake Taum Sauk signs. ¼ mi. further, on the left, are a Dairy Queen and an old package store (both small white buildings), and a group of resort signs. Turn left, before the signs, follow the hard surface road. You'll cross over the Black River bridge and follow the road turning left at the next set of signs, and just a little further, on the right, is Wilderness Lodge.

Ohio

BUXTON INN
Granville, Ohio

Five of us were in the downstairs tavern at the Buxton Inn playing "Gone With The Wind." It seemed like a natural game, because we already had a Melanie, who was 14 years old during my last visit in the summer of 1977. It was an obvious choice for Amy, who is 11½, to play Scarlett. Orville, tall and handsome, had to be Ashley Dukes and Audrey, mother of Amy and Melanie, we decided, should continue that role in our game, except that nobody could remember the first name Margaret Mitchell gave her. (If anyone does remember, please tell Audrey, we can't have her wandering around without a name.) Amy, for some reason or other, said that I would be the perfect Rhett Butler. I never quite understood that.

All the Orrs, as well as the waiters and waitresses were dressed in costumes worn in 1812, which is the date that an inn was first opened here.

It was a great treat to be back at the Buxton Inn once again for a really wonderful reunion with all of the Orrs by whatever names. I made my first visit there in 1975 and was completely captivated. Apparently, a great many of our readers felt the same way, because in the past three years Orville has reported a steady stream of "Berkshire Travellers" visiting his inn, which is in one of the most attractive towns in central Ohio.

If first impressions are the longest and most important, then

Granville should be remembered by everyone who has visited it. The main street is broad and lined with trees, the sidewalks are clean, and here and there are little fences in front of homes. There are very attractive-looking shops; the library, bank building, and other public buildings are all most handsome—and best of all, the Buxton Inn is just a short walk away.

The five of us had lunch together in the front dining room which has low ceilings, candelabra-type fixtures, and deep windows overlooking the street. There is an old-fashioned fender in front of the fireplace, prints of Martha and George Washington, and a cabinet with a collection of very fine chinaware.

The menu is in the form of a newspaper and not only lists the famous Buxton bean soup, eggs Benedict, quiche du jour, and "croques" (sandwiches dipped in eggs and sauteed), but also had some of the history of early Granville and the Buxton Inn, and also the beginnings of Denison University which is located in Granville.

On that particular day, Amy had to be excused after lunch because she was feeling a little out of sorts, and I promised to stop for a final good-bye before going on to the Golden Lamb in Lebanon.

Hence, it was Melanie who became my guide, and this very attractive young lady, like her sister, seems born to the innkeeping business. We walked into the back dining room which has a fantastic old chandelier which is let down with a pulley, and once must have held candles. She pointed out the oil painting of young Abraham Lincoln. "His eyes just seem to be looking right through you, don't they?" she said. I agreed.

Melanie introduced me to one of the waitresses at the inn who was a famous cook in Africa. "She even goes to Columbus and does TV shows."

We went upstairs to look at the guest bedrooms with their antique beds, old quilts, old chests of drawers, Victorian prints, and chandeliers. All of the floors were beautifully finished. There is a sitting bathtub in a corner of one of the rooms.

Back downstairs once again, she was very proud to show me through the really excellent gift shop which has some attractive glassware, tinware, pewter, candles, small china pieces, figurines, and many rings, jewelry.

Of course, I did stop to bid Amy a regretful farewell, and she apologized for not being able to join me for our annual walk. She was entering the 6th grade in September, and promised to send me a sample of her artwork, which she loves. As I left, Major Buxton, the cat, gave me a purring good-bye, and Amy kissed me and said, "Come back soon." I would.

BUXTON INN, 313 E. Broadway, Granville, Ohio 43023; 614-587-0001. An 8-room inn in a college town in central Ohio near Dennison University, the Indian Mounds Museum and the Heisey Glass Museum. European plan. Lunch and dinner served daily. Closed Christmas Day. No pets. Golf, tennis, horseback riding, cultural activities nearby. Orville and Audrey Orr, Innkeepers.

Directions: Take Granville exit from I-70. Travel north 8 mi. on Rte. 37 into Granville.

GOLDEN LAMB
Lebanon, Ohio

Sandra Reynolds and I were seated in the lobby of the Golden Lamb waiting for Jack Reynolds to finish a telephone call, and then we were all going to walk up the street to the Warren County Museum.

Just to be in this lobby is to partake of a generous helping of the American past. Among other things, there was a lamp, the base of which was made out of a candle mold, and a curly maple table. An old coal stove that was used 100 years or more ago, is still in use today. Always on hand is a big punch bowl where guests and friends may enjoy a modicum of refreshment. There are quite a few examples of Shaker crafts in the lobby and elsewhere in the inn, including Shaker boxes, dowels, chests, and Shaker-style furniture in the dining room.

"The Shakers came to this section of Ohio during the 19th century and attracted buyers from all over the country for their fine farm stock, medicinal herbs, furniture, and other household essentials," explained Sandra. "Their community Union Village

Fireplace, Warren County Museum

295

was sold by them over a half century ago, but we have a lot of local interest in their culture, and the Warren County Museum has a considerable area devoted to Shaker memorabilia."

If Ohio could be called the "mother of Presidents," the Golden Lamb might be called the "mother of country inns," because it is a significant force in providing inspiration for many innkeepers to preserve the best of the old, and at the same time to back it up with good innkeeping. Throughout the inn are found artifacts, furniture, and furnishings that have been collected from America's past which in a sense give us a real feeling of appreciation for what our forebears thought was beautiful, useful, and promising.

The building dates back to 1815 and was built on the site of an original log cabin erected by Jonas Seaman, who was granted a license in 1803 to operate "a house of public entertainment." Even before roads were built many guests came on foot or horseback to the inn. Here in the warmth of the tavern's public rooms they exchanged news of the world and related their own experiences. Many famous people have stopped here, including ten United States presidents as well as Henry Clay, Mark Twain, and Charles Dickens. Overnight guests may stay in rooms that are named for some of the great and near-great, both national and international, who have enjoyed accommodations here in the past.

"This section of Ohio is really quite a holiday and vacation focal point," said Sandra. "We have the Little Miami, Ohio's first scenic river, with fishing, canoeing, hiking, and riding, as well as the Glendower State Museum which is in a restored Greek-revival mansion. I think one of our most popular things, however, is King's Island, which is a fantastic place for everyone in the family to enjoy lots of fun. It is centered around a 33-story replica of the Eiffel Tower and has a variety of rides, attractions, and entertainment. Jack Nicklaus has a golf center there too."

Jack came out of his office and handed me a letter. "Here is something I think you will enjoy reading," he said. "It is a letter from a lady who said she enjoyed having Sunday dinner here and makes a point that no matter how busy it may seem, it never loses its special feeling of friendliness. She said she also enjoys the gift shop, and all of the reproductions of 19th century rooms on the third floor."

We had a very pleasant visit at the museum and a lovely dinner at the Golden Lamb. I remained all night and joined Jack the next morning at the village ice cream parlor, since the inn does not serve breakfast. It is a kind of morning village meeting place and nicely augments the Golden Lamb.

*GOLDEN LAMB INN, 27 S. Broadway, Lebanon, Ohio 45036;
513-932-5065. A historic 20-room village inn in the heart of Ohio
farming country on US Hwys. 63, 42 and 48. European plan.
19 rooms with private bath. No pets. Breakfast served only on
Sundays. Lunch and dinner served daily except Christmas. Golf and
tennis nearby. Jackson Reynolds, Innkeeper.*

*Directions: From I-71, exit Rte. 48 N, 3 mi. west to Lebanon. From
I-75, exit Rte. 63 E, 7 mi. east to Lebanon.*

WELSHFIELD INN
Burton, Ohio

I reached into my pocket and pulled out a five cent piece,
dropped it in the slot, heard it clink and clank its way through some
mysterious mechanism, and then suddenly the machine started to
play. I recognized the tune immediately, "Barney Google." It was, to
say the least, a triumph for my memory of trivia as I sang along with
it: "Barney Google, with the goo, goo, googlie eyes; Barney Google
with a wife three times his size."

Brian Holmes chuckled, "You'd be surprised how many people
know the words." We were standing in the dining room of the
Welshfield Inn in Burton, Ohio, and I felt almost as if a newsboy
would come in momentarily with the tidings of Dewey's victory at
Manila Bay! Here was a part of mid-America at its nostalgic best,
and only 25 miles from Cleveland.

I first visited the Welshfield Inn in 1972 and each subsequent
visit convinced me that Brian and Polly Holmes have as neat and
fetching a country inn as I have seen anywhere. Furthermore, the
inn has a rather interesting history. It was built, so Brian told me, in
the 1840s and was originally known as the Nash Hotel. This was the
center part of the building. The front addition was made by a later
owner named Dr. Foster, and the name was changed to the Troy

297

Hotel. The proprietor at that time was also the village postmaster. Once again, I've discovered an inn that, during the American un-Civil War, was used as an underground station where slaves were cared for on their escape to Canada.

Polly explained that during the 19th century, social affairs were held at the Nash, including spelling matches, a singing school, and a dancing school. A ballroom was added under Captain Marcy, as well as several other alterations.

My visits to inns always include an extended stay in the kitchen, and I have seldom seen such a well-organized and executed food-preparing and serving area as at the Welshfield. As Brian explained: "This type of thinking allows time to be spent on such things as preparing the arrangement of food on the plate, about which I'm most particular." It also provides opportunity to do other special things such as homemade preserves, pickles, soups — including a New England clam chowder, which is as tasty a clam chowder as I have ever had.

As usual, I could go on at considerable length about the menu, but suffice it at this time to say that features such as the fresh country-fried chicken, which is done in an old-fashioned iron skillet and then put in the roaster, makes eating a pleasure. The menu also has prime ribs of beef, baked ham, and crab Supreme. Vegetables are served in family-style casseroles, along with bowls of mashed potatoes, gravy, relishes, and salads.

Desserts include such goodies as freshly-baked rhubarb, apple, and lemon chiffon pies. There is also a Galliano mousse which has a special apricot sauce to enhance it.

Adding to the atmosphere are the pretty young waitresses who are wearing traditional country costumes right down to the white dusters on their heads.

Then, there is that crazy nickelodeon which makes sounds like a piano, violin, mandolin, and flute. That alone would be worth a trip half-way across the country. I'm glad I made it.

WELSHFIELD INN, Rte. 422, Burton, Ohio 44021; 216-834-4164. A country restaurant on Rte. 422, 28 mi. east of Cleveland. No lodgings. Lunch and dinner served weekdays. Dinner only served on Sundays and holidays. Closed the week of July 4th and three weeks after Jan. 1. Closed Mondays except Labor Day. Near Sea World and Holden Arboretum. Brian and Polly Holmes, Innkeepers.

Directions: On U.S. 422 at intersection of Ohio 700, midway between Cleveland and Youngstown, Ohio.

James House,
The Farmhouse,
Port Townsend   Captain Whidbey, *Coupeville*

■ SEATTLE

Far
West

● Lake Quinault Lodge, *Quinault*

WASHINGTON

Partridge Inn, *Underwood*

■ PORTLAND

● Benbow Inn,
  Garberville

A R I Z O N A

● Heritage House, *Little River*
● Harbor House, *Elk*

Rancho de los Caballeros,
● *Wickenburg*

■ PHOENIX

Wine Country Inn,
  St. Helena   ■ SACRAMENTO

Lodge on the Desert,
Tanque Verde,
● *Tucson*

AN FRANCISCO ■   Sutter Creek Inn, *Sutter Creek*

Normandy Inn,
Vagabond House,
Carmel

● Ojai Valley Inn, *Ojai*

LOS ANGELES ■

The Inn, *Rancho Santa Fe*

■ SAN DIEGO

Arizona

THE LODGE ON THE DESERT
Tucson, Arizona

"Schuyler," I asked, "what kind of bird is that out in the cactus garden?"

"That," replied Schuyler Lininger, "is a ferruginous owl which breeds here in southern Arizona. If you are really interested in birds," he said, "you have come to the right place. We have bird tours directed by field-experienced ornithologists from the University of Arizona graduate school. There have been over 435 species of birds recorded here. The tours are conducted with advance notice on Monday, Wednesday, and Friday of each week."

I must confess that I really didn't believe that Schuyler knew the name of that bird, but when he told me about the tremendous birding program here at the Lodge on the Desert I was quite impressed. That is only one of several things that impressed me during my visit here.

Schuyler and Helen Lininger joined me for breakfast on the little patio adjoining my room. The sun was high, and we were talking about things to do in Tucson and vicinity.

On this subject, Helen provided a wealth of information. "There are so many things to do in Tucson that I don't know where to start," she said. "We have a marvelous new Art Center, the San Xavier Mission, the Arizona-Sonora Living Desert Museum, Old Tucson, the Kitt Peak National Observatory which is only 60 miles away,

Colossal Cave, and, well, so much more," she said. "Mexico is only an hour away, and did you know that Tucson is one of the oldest cities in the United States? We've already had our bicentennial."

The Lodge on the Desert is a sophisticated country inn that started over 40 years ago out in the desert. Gradually the city of Tucson grew to surround it. Its six acres are separated from the city's residential area by a great hedge of oleander. The lodge is a series of one-and-two-story adobe buildings built in the manner of the Pueblo Indians. The lodging rooms are tastefully designed with the small touches that mean so much, such as very good linens and towels. Most rooms have fireplaces, and each has its own patio area. The rooms are unusually large as are the closets. Helen explained that this is because a great many of the guests stay from two weeks to three months to enjoy various seasons of the year in Tucson.

The center of inn activity is the pool area which is flanked by three great palm trees. Here guests can sit in the sun and enjoy the magnificent view of the mountains. The adjoining lounge area has a large library where many of the guests gather in the evening to play cards and socialize.

Bettie Gilbert, the former innkeeper at Colby Hill Inn in Henniker, New Hampshire, told me about her stay at the lodge and was particularly enthusiastic about the fact that the guests can order breakfast sent to their lodgings. "It was truly luxurious to have breakfast on my own patio," she said.

All around the inn are evidences of Helen Lininger's interests in furniture, art, and music. There is no one particular style of decor. "If it works, we use it," she explained. "We mix traditional and modern, Indian and Colonial, although my first preference is for things of the Southwest.

All this and a ferruginous owl, too.

THE LODGE ON THE DESERT, 306 N. Alvernon Way, Tucson, Ariz. 85733; 602-325-3366. A 35-room luxury inn within the city limits. Near several historic, cultural, and recreational attractions. American and European plans available in winter; European plan in summer. Breakfast, lunch and dinner served to travelers every day of the year. Attended, leashed pets allowed. Swimming pool and lawn games on grounds. Tennis and golf nearby. Schuyler and Helen Lininger, Innkeepers.

Directions: Take Speedway exit from I-10. Travel east to Alvernon Way, turn left (south) onto Alvernon. Lodge is on left side between 5th St. and Broadway.

RANCHO DE LOS CABALLEROS
Wickenburg, Arizona

"The idea of a winter vacation on a guest ranch in Arizona never occurred to us," said the letter from Michigan. "Wickenburg seemed like such a long way and we weren't quite sure what kind of people would be there. We certainly weren't horseback riders and we thought we might feel out of place. However, we were reading your book about how much you enjoyed the noon buffet around the pool at Rancho de los Caballeros and getting some horseback riding tips from Buford Giles, and we began to think that maybe we would enjoy it too.

"The trip from Detroit to Phoenix was quite short and the ranch car met us at the airport. When I talked with Ann Giles on the telephone she assured me that we'd feel right at home and that we should bring our tennis rackets. She mentioned that golf clubs could be rented if we didn't want to carry them. We literally dragged our two early-teenage sons with us, and did their faces light up when almost as soon as we arrived they saw some other young people. I don't believe we saw them for the rest of the two weeks.

"You were right about Buford Giles, and by about the third day I began to feel as if I had almost been born on a horse. We decided to spend Christmas there next year."

Rancho de los Caballeros ... "The ranch of the gentlemen on horseback." Just the name alone has an unusually romantic, melodic sound, and its location in the high country is equally romantic. As my correspondent from Michigan said later on in her letter, "The mountains and the desert literally grow on you."

I love to sit on the terrace at sunset and watch the changing colors and dimensions of the Bradshaw Mountains far across the valley.

Rancho de los Caballeros is a rather elegant ranch-inn. A continuous program of watering and irrigation makes it a green jewel in the desert. Many of the lodging rooms and suites are built around a carefully planned cactus garden and oversized putting green, and are decorated in Arizona desert colors with harmonizing hues of tan, yellow and brown. Each accommodation or "casita," as they are called in this part of the world, has a private patio and many of them have fireplaces.

A program of planned activities for younger people is one of the reasons this ranch experience is so popular with families. "We feel that it is a good balance," says Innkeeper Rusty Gant, "because children of all ages have several activities every morning, and in the afternoon they can join their parents with more trail riding, the

pool, or tennis. At dinner the children's counselor gathers them all together, and they even have their own dining room. They are kept occupied until bedtime. This has proven to be an excellent idea for both children and their parents alike."

I've visited Los Caballeros several times since my initial visit in 1971, and have always had a marvelous time, so I am not at all surprised at the experience of my friends from Michigan.

RANCHO de los CABALLEROS, Wickenburg, Ariz. 85358; 602-684-5484. A luxury 62-room ranch-resort, 60 mi. north of Phoenix in the sunny dry desert. American plan. Rooms with private baths. A few with shared baths. Breakfast, lunch and dinner served to travelers daily. Open from mid-October to early May. No pets. Pool, corral of 75 horses, hiking, skeet shooting, airstrip, putting, tennis on grounds. Golf nearby. Dallas Gant, Jr., Innkeeper.

Directions: Rtes. 60, 89 and 93 bring you to Wickenburg. Ranch is 2 mi. west of town on Rte. 60 and 2 mi. south on Vulture Mine Road.

TANQUE VERDE
Tucson, Arizona

A gorgeous plumed male cardinal got a good hold of Bob Cote's finger and clamped down in earnest.

"Oh boy, that stings. These are the worst kind." He went on carefully untangling the light net that had entangled the bird, and after three more bites, popped him into the little net bag to carry him back to be banded.

Banding birds takes place every Thursday morning at Tanque Verde. It's under the direction of Chuck Cochran. He does it as a hobby, but makes a very careful record of the species, length of the wing and tail feathers and the weight of each bird. The records are sent to Washington from stations like this all over the country, as he explained: "We can tell a great deal about the migratory habits of the birds that we love. Since 1970 we've banded over 11,600 birds, these include the Black-capped Vireo, the Hooded Merganser, Eared Greb, and the Golden-Crowned Sparrows."

Bob and I walked back toward another net, and he was saying that there is a great deal of interest in birds among the guests at Tanque Verde. "It's growing each year. Guests come with notebooks, cameras, and binoculars and really enjoy themselves.

"We are, as Mel Becker, the Head Wrangler says, a 'riding ranch'. There is a lot of interest in the birds, plant, and animal life, and tennis, and swimming, but by-and-large our guests really come from all over the country for the riding."

We had arrived at the next net at the same time the morning ride was leaving from the Corral. About fifteen or twenty guests from New England, the Midwest, and the Far West, many of whom were as inexperienced on a horse as I am, were setting out enthusiastically. In about thirty seconds they would be out of sight in the tall brush which is dotted very dramatically by the giant Saguaro Cactus, Arizona's state tree.

Tanque Verde holds a very special place in my memory because it was the first ranch that I ever visited, and I have been back a number of occasions. I spent New Year's eve there in 1975. I always find people who have been returning for twenty or twenty-five years without a break. Bob's mother and father were there before him, and they have many old friends who have brought children and now even grandchildren back to Tanque Verde for family reunions.

Meanwhile, Bob and Dee Dee, with their children Brett and Carra, are continuing to create at Tanque Verde the same wonderful, friendly place that was started so many years ago.

In recent years there have been some changes made at Tanque Verde to meet the desires of the guests that come from all over the United States, as well as 18 foreign countries. Four tennis courts, a complete indoor health spa, a fully-automated exercise room that has all the modern health equipment necessary to maintain a trim physique, as well as an indoor swimming pool, against the chance of inclement days or cool nights.

Tanque Verde has a one-hundred-year-old history as one of Arizona's pioneer guest and cattle ranches, and even has stories about Indian raids. One such story is that the Indians hung a previous owner from the rafters of the ranch gun room in an attempt to have him divulge where he kept his gold and valuables. Bob remarked, "I bet he certainly could have used the whirlpool bath!"

TANQUE VERDE RANCH, Box 66, Rte. 8, Tucson, Ariz. 85710; 602-296-6275. A 65-room ranch-inn, 10 mi. from Tucson. American plan. Breakfast, lunch and dinner served to travelers by reservation. Open year-round. Riding, indoor and outdoor pool, tennis, sauna, exercise room and whirlpool bath on grounds. Robert and Dee Dee Cote, Innkeepers.

Directions: From U.S. 10, exit at Speedway Blvd. and travel east to dead end.

California

BENBOW INN
Garberville, California

The bid was four hearts. My partner did not double, and as I had no count in my hand I passed. The dummy laid down his hand, the lady from Red Bank, New Jersey began to play.

We were in one corner of the sumptuous lobby of the Benbow Inn, which is located in the heart of the big redwood country of California. Other guests were also playing cards; some were enjoying an interesting game of cribbage, and a father was teaching his son how to play chess. Our table was a few feet from a large fireplace which had a cheery blaze, and we had a chance to say hello to many people who came to share the warmth in late October.

My partner was a man from Sacramento whom I had met on the inn golf course earlier that afternoon. He and his wife had visited the Benbow quite a few times. "I like this golf course," he said, "because it is seldom crowded and the scenery is fantastic. We both love the food here at the inn."

The lady from Red Bank, who was busy making six hearts instead of four, paused for a moment to tell me that she was touring the west coast with a copy of CIBR. "It is the only book that has inns all over the United States," she said.

She made game and that was the rubber, so I excused myself and joined Dennis Levett who, along with Conny Corbett, is the innkeeper of the Benbow. I mentioned the fact that there were guests from so many places and he said, "We're both a destination inn and an overnight traveler's inn. People come and stay because they enjoy our golf course, the swimming, fishing, and walking in the forest. We're essentially informal; we don't require gentlemen to wear coats in the dining room — but I think we have as many coats as non-coats. People are inclined to be a little more casual here in the Northwest than they are in the East, have you noticed?"

The Benbow was designed and built in the early 1920s by Albert Farr, a well-known San Francisco architect. The Tudor style was enjoying a very popular revival during those years. Today, the inn has furnishings that are reminiscent of those times with stone work and carved wood that would be virtually impossible to duplicate today. The many wrought iron lamps and massive tables are also characteristic of the period.

Distances are sometimes rather long in this part of northern California, so many guests arrive at the Benbow with big appetites. Fortunately, the portions are generous and there are hearty dishes such as beef Stroganoff, pork chops, and Shish Kabob. Two of the most popular choices are mushrooms Normande and lobster Mornay. Abalone is frequently on the menu. With an eye toward convenience for travelers, there is also a young people's menu.

It is nice to have another opinion, and this is what John Philip Sousa, the travel editor of the *San Diego Union,* said after a visit in August, 1976: "For a moment, for a brief and magic spell, you feel as if you are transported to some sparkling corner of Tudor England."

I'll bet Henry VIII would have loved the Benbow Inn!

BENBOW INN, Garberville, Calif. 95440; 707-923-2124. A 70-room inn in the heart of redwood country on Rte. 101, 2 mi. from Garberville, near Benbow State Park. European plan. Breakfast, lunch and dinner served to travelers daily. Open from April 1 through Dec. 1. Golf and swimming on grounds. Hiking and bicycles nearby. Cornelius Corbett and Dennis Levett, Innkeepers.

Directions: From San Francisco, follow Rte. 101 200 mi. north and exit at Benbow.

HARBOR HOUSE
Elk, California

"How do you answer all of the questions that guests must ask you about this place?" Handing me a small brochure entitled "Your Tour Guide of the Harbor House (Living and Dining Areas)," attractive innkeeper, Pat Corcoran, replied, "This answers most of the questions, but we love to explain the more intricate details to our guests."

Harbor House, an inn by the sea, was built in 1916 as an executive residence by a lumber company. The construction is entirely of redwood taken from nearby forests. It's an enlarged replica of the redwood model house at the 1915 Pan American Exposition in San Francisco.

The hand-carved and hand-fitted redwood ceiling and wall in the living room were coated with hot beeswax in 1916. The process preserved the color and quality of the wood for over 60 years. From the dining room windows, sundeck, and oceanside rooms, there is an incredible view of the Pacific, including two large rocks with natural tunnels and bluffs which shield Harbor House from wind and weather.

There is a private sandy beach for guests which is reached by a winding path from the inn. It is from this beach that I found a closeup view of two carved tunnels that are actually out of sight from the sundeck of the inn. One of the tunnels is shaped like a Y; the waves roll in the two ends of the Y, crash together in the tunnel and then roll out on the beach. It is nothing short of spectacular.

Four of the five rooms at the inn have fireplaces, and there are four additional cottages on the south side of the main building. All of these rooms have private baths. Furnishings are nicely complemented with antiques.

"We've been doing lots of things here," said Pat. "We've installed new hot water heaters, purchased new linen, recovered lots of furniture, and rewired and replumbed. Of course, chopping away the brush is something that goes on all the time because we try to keep the view of the ocean unimpeded."

That night, after watching a typically magnificent sunset, we were happy to stoke up the fire in the living room fireplace, and Pat summed everything up quite succinctly: "Basically what we try to provide is a respite from telephones, television, kids, and professions. Speaking of kids, many of them under 16 years of age would really not be happy here.

"Our menu has homemade soups, salad dressings, breads, and desserts. Our main courses are broiled things like salmon, pork chops, or red snapper. Mocha-toffee pie is a dessert favorite. I enjoy making shirred eggs or eggs Benedict for breakfast. It is all very leisurely."

Yes, indeed, it *is* all very leisurely at the Harbor House in Elk. The guests I talked to said they have been back three or four times. They all felt very possessive about their own personal hideaway on the Mendicino coast.

HARBOR HOUSE BY THE SEA, Hwy. #1, Elk, Ca. 95432; 707-877-3203. An 8-room seaside inn, 16 mi. south of Mendocino, overlooking the Pacific. Modified American plan omits lunch. Breakfast and dinner to house guests served daily. Open year-round. Ocean swimming, abalone and shell hunting, fishing and hiking on grounds. Biking, boating, deep sea fishing, golf, canoeing nearby. Pat Corcoran, Innkeeper

Directions: Take Rte. 128 from I-101 to Coast. Turn south on Hwy.#1, 6 mi. to Harbor House.

HERITAGE HOUSE
Little River, California

It might have been the Maine Coast. The sixty-foot cliffs looked out over an ocean disarmingly calm. The sloping lawn led to an ivy-covered, white Colonial that could have graced Kennebunkport. Behind it was a low hill covered with evergreens that reminded me of Bar Harbor. Taken all together, the guest houses looked like a village near Bucksport, seventy-five years ago. Even the names have the flavor: "Firehouse," "Schoolhouse," "Chart Room," "Ice Cream Parlor," "Apple House," "Barber Pole," and "Stable."

However, I was sitting in a rustic chair on the edge of the Pacific at Heritage House in Little River, California.

"There's good reason for you to feel as if you're in Maine," explained Innkeeper Don Dennen. "Many 'down easters' came out here over 125 years ago, lured by the big timber. Naturally, the homes they built were similar to those they left behind. There are many along the Mendicino coast."

The guest houses were inspired by the early-day buildings. Mine was the "Country Store," and like most of the others it had many antiques and its own fireplace. There were a few with sod roofs, something I've never seen in New England.

The New England influence is quite strong in this lovely little seaside inn. However, I believe the Dennens have blended the best of both coasts, because there is a reaching out for new ideas, a willingness to try new things that is typical of California.

This is reflected in the menu and the service as well. To illustrate: this is the only place where I've had corned beef spiced with ginger, or where I was asked how crisp I wanted my breakfast bacon, and where I could make my own toast at the breakfast table. Meanwhile, through a clever communications system, my bed was being made and the room freshened. "We think that our guests should return to a civilized-looking room," Don explained. Later in the day, there is a complete cleaning.

From San Francisco, 140 miles away, I believe the fastest way to Little River is via Rte. 101 to Cloverdale. The Coastal Highway #1 through Bodega Bay, Jenner and Point Arena sometimes seems to hang by its fingernails on the cliffs over the ocean. It takes 45 minutes longer. Both are scenic routes.

Heritage House is different. It has a pleasant, intimate atmosphere without room telephones or television. There are no planned activities. There are beautiful drives and walks along the ocean, and in the forests and mountains and valleys nearby. Like the Drovers Inn in New York State and other elegant places mentioned in this book, and at the risk of a double negative, it is not inexpensive. Anyone planning to visit for a weekend should reserve months in advance. It might be a little easier in the middle of the week, but even then, reservations should be made. The good food, peace and quiet, and the Pacific Ocean right outside the door make it something very special.

HERITAGE HOUSE, Little River, Ca. 95456; 707-937-5885. An elegant 50-room oceanside inn on Coast Highway #1, 144 mi. north of San Francisco, 6 mi. south of Mendocino. Modified American plan omits lunch. Breakfast and dinner served to travelers daily by reservation. Open from February through November. Don Dennen, Innkeeper.

Directions: From San Francisco, follow Rte. 101 to Cloverdale, then Rte. 128 to Coast Highway #1. Inn is 5 mi. north of this junction on Hwy. #1.

NORMANDY INN
Carmel, California

It was an icy, cold Sunday afternoon in January in the Berkshires. The wind was from the north rattling the panes of my library, and even my sturdy fire didn't seem to warm up the room. "Where," I asked myself, "would I like to be if I could press a button and be there instantly?"

The answer came through loud and clear ... the Normandy Inn in Carmel, California. I was sure that the Carmel sun would be so warm that I would be sitting in my shirtsleeves in the garden or by the swimming pool. Such quiet and tranquility.

In imagination, I breathed deeply the aroma of the bougain-villea and other blooming flowers. In my mind's eye, I looked through the archway from the pool area into the courtyard of the inn with many hanging galleries and wooden stairs. I would be surrounded by the potted flowers that are changed twelve times a year.

The Normandy Inn is a symbol of gracious living conceived by owners, architect Robert Stanton and decorator Virginia Stanton, who was party editor of *House Beautiful* a few years ago. Everything has been done with taste and comfort in mind, such as over-sized twin, and extra-long beds with down-filled pillows. Some of the bathrooms are particularly spacious, and some suites have dressing rooms and fireplaces.

To talk of the Normandy is also to talk of Carmel, which is a community of fascinating shops. Innkeeper Mike Stanton was telling me that the ratio of shops to people was about three to one. Every possible kind of shop is here, not just apparel shops and boutiques — but what's even more important, at least ninety percent are attractive and well worth a visit.

To make it more appealing, Ocean Avenue, the main street, has an aisle of green running through the middle with palm trees and flowers in profusion.

Carmel is also a town of courtyards. There are tiny shops inside of these courtyards, and many of them have coffee shops and small restaurants. Incidentally, at the Normandy, the only meal served is a continental breakfast in the French Provincial kitchen just off the lobby.

"With so many excellent restaurants here in Carmel, we thought another one would be redundant," explained Mike.

I am sure that someone has visited all of the restaurants in Carmel and nearby Monterey, but the task is an eminently prodigious one, since there are almost one hundred.

The scenery, nearby ocean beaches, shops, and the famous golf courses attract visitors to Carmel throughout every month of the year. I personally prefer to visit there from October through April when the pace is a little slower. But, whenever I go, it is always a delight to return to the quiet elegance of the Normandy Inn.

NORMANDY INN, Carmel, Ca. 93921; 408-624-3825. A 48-room French Provincial inn in the heart of Carmel, on Ocean Ave. between Monteverde and Casanova. Within walking distance of beach, shops and restaurants and near Point Lobos State Park. European plan includes Continental breakfast served to inn guests only. No other meals served. Open year-round. No pets. Tennis, golf, fishing, bicycles nearby. Mike Stanton, Innkeeper.

Directions: Follow Rte. 101 to Salinas, then Rte. 68 into Monterey Peninsula. Or, follow Coast Hwy. #1 which travels through Carmel.

OJAI VALLEY INN
Ojai, California

I well remember my first trip to the Ojai Valley Inn. It was in the late '60s, in February, when the sun was shining brightly on the beautiful mountain-ringed valley. My telephone call back to the Berkshires disclosed that there were at least 14 inches of fresh snow on the ground and it was still snowing.

At that time the only decision I had to make was whether to play golf or tennis or go horseback riding. What a shame to miss all the snow-shoveling and traffic tie-ups!

This country inn is a place where sports and the weather get together. Innkeeper Bill Briggs explained to me that the mountains provide a year-long shelter from fog, smog or dampness. "Temperatures are moderate, from 70 to 90 degrees in summer," he explained, "and from 60 to 85 degrees in winter. You know, we are 1000 feet up so the air is quite dry."

These factors make it perfect for sports enthusiasts since golf, tennis, riding and swimming can be enjoyed year-round. The Club has its own 6800 yard par 70 golf course with a natural rolling terrain that is beautifully maintained. Ray Reitzel is the tennis pro, and each time I have visited he's managed to scare up a game of singles or fit me into some doubles.

On my most recent visit, I had enough time to go horseback riding in the mountains. The inn has its own stable, and there are hundreds of miles of trails through the valley and into the adjoining ranch country.

I also enjoy having lunch out on the terrace. It is really a delightful experience. I pointed out to Bill that the beautiful tree in the middle of the terrace was missing. "Yes," he said, "we hated to take it down, but it had finally reached the point where it had to go. However, we've replaced it with some new young trees that will soon be as beautiful as our old friend. In fact the birds are beginning to nest in them already."

Birds, flowers, beautiful sunshine and clean fresh air abound here. Bill explained that the word Ojai, which is pronounced O-hi, is

313

the Indian word for "the nest." I wasn't surprised when I realized that it actually nestles in the vast amphitheatre of Sierra Madre mountains, about 14 miles from the shores of the Pacific. "It's really quite different from the rest of California," Bill said. "Many of our visitors love it so much they come back and buy some land."

At the Ojai Valley Inn gentlemen are requested to wear jackets and ties to dinner, and ladies usually wear dresses or pants suits in the evening. When I commented on this to Bill, he said, "Our guests tell us that they prefer it this way."

OJAI VALLEY INN & COUNTRY CLUB, Ojai, Ca. 93023; 805-646-5511. A 100-room resort-inn with its own championship golf course, 12 mi. northeast of Ventura on U.S. 33. American plan. Breakfast, lunch and dinner served to travelers daily. Open year-round. No pets. Tennis, riding, heated pool, golf and bicycles on the grounds. Bill Briggs, Innkeeper.

Directions: From the Ventura Freeway, exit at Hwy. 33.

SUTTER CREEK INN
Sutter Creek, California

It was 1967 when I first flew to the West Coast in search of country inns. I had been persuaded by Jane Way at the Sutter Creek Inn to visit the gold fields of California. She was sure that I would love it. Well, Jane was right, and I have been visiting California and writing about the Sutter Creek Inn ever since.

It is, in fact, an inn with its New Hampshire heritage much in evidence in the porches and high pointed roof. There are grape vines, tomato plants, gardenias, trumpet vines, Virginia creepers, hollyhocks, chrysanthemums, gooseberries, zinnias, and roses in abundance.

On that first visit and every time since, I have joined the other guests on the porch at the end of the day to watch the huge, old white owls that live in the barn circle over the backyard and fly off to the redwood trees to spend the rest of the night.

The only meal served at this inn is breakfast, but it is really an experience. When the bell rings at 9 a.m., everyone sits at long, family-style tables. "Our breakfasts are big and hearty," says Jane. "It's a good basis for a full day of exploring the Mother Lode country."

In the evening, Jane is apt to join her guests at dinner across the street at a restaurant which serves delicious Mexican food. There are also Italian restaurants and Serbian boarding houses nearby which have very special dishes.

Seven of the several bedrooms of the inn have fireplaces and four have swinging beds that hang from the ceiling on chains. These, by the way, can be stablized. Jane fell in love with the idea while traveling in the tropics. They are the most popular rooms at the inn. "Very romantic, indeed," says Jane.

I should caution our readers that reservations in advance are almost always necessary in order to avoid disappointments. There is a two-day minimum stay on weekends, either Friday and Saturday or Saturday and Sunday. "Sometimes," said Jane, "we do have last minute cancellations." With this in mind, a telephone call to Jane on a Thursday might provide a very pleasant surprise.

"You might also point out to your readers," explained Jane, "that we are rather small and so children are not encouraged as guests. In addition, pets and cigar smoking are a 'no-no'."

At the Sutter Creek Inn, deep in the Mother Lode country, fireplaces blaze in cold weather and there are warm lazy summer days to be spent in hammocks, or out exploring the Gold Rush country. Sutter Creek, Volcano, Murphy's, Angel's Camp and Sonora are all part of the great living legend of gold in California and they are all on or near Route 49 which runs along the foothills of the Sierras.

By the way, the next time you visit the Sutter Creek Inn, ask Jane to tell you the story about Old Abe, the cannon, delivered to the gold fields by a horsedrawn hearse during the Civil War.

SUTTER CREEK INN, 75 Main St., Sutter Creek, Ca. 95685; 209-267-5606. A 16-room New England village inn on the main street of a historic Mother Lode town, 35 mi. from Sacramento. Lodgings include breakfast. No meals served to travelers. Closed all of January. No children under 10. No pets. Water skiing, riding, fishing and boating nearby. Mrs. Jane Way, Innkeeper.

Directions: From Sacramento, travel on the Freeway (50) toward Placerville and exit at Power Inn Rd. Turn right and drive one block, note signs for Rte. 16 and Jackson. Turn left on Fulsom Rd., approximately ¼ mi., follow Rte. 16 signs to right for Jackson. Rte. 16 joins Rte. 49. Turn right to Sutter Creek. From San Francisco, follow Freeway (80) to Sacramento and take previous directions or drive via Stockton to Rte. 49.

THE INN
Rancho Santa Fe, California

If the east coast has such distinguished resort-inns as the Black Point, the Asticou, Hound Ears, and the Brazilian Court, the west coast has The Inn at Rancho Santa Fe. They all have at least one common denominator: they're inns with tradition, beauty, and grace.

I sat at breakfast in the Garden Room overlooking the swimming pool and the broad lawns which lead down to the business block of Rancho Santa Fe village. It was a balmy, February morning and I could see from the dress of the other guests that many would be teeing off at a nearby country club, while others in tennis whites would spend the day at the courts. There were badminton players, lawn bowlers (there's a beautiful lawn bowling area), and horseback riders. On this kind of day there would be a sizeable group gathering

around the pool, or off for a day at the inn's own cottage at nearby Del Mar Beach on the warm shores of the Pacific.

But, whatever the main activity of the day, everyone was sure, at some time or other, to browse among the really impressive and individualized shops of the village.

The town Planning Commission has strictly enforced a code to prevent commercialism from creeping in. I actually stood in front of the supermarket for a full minute without realizing that it was there! This village is an example of architectural planning and civic foresight that might be emulated by communities everywhere.

Our west coast readers may be familiar with this inn, but I feel certain that it will come as a surprise to people in other parts of the country to know that tucked away in a corner of southern California, not far from San Diego, is an elegant inn with such unusual touches as triple sheets, turn-down service and finger bowls.

The inn is made up of attractive cottages spaced out over twenty-two acres of woodland and landscaped grounds. Each cottage has from two to ten individual bedrooms. Many of the rooms and suites have fireplaces and some have kitchens. Each has air conditioning and a private sun terrace.

There is a great deal of emphasis on maintaining the beautiful grounds, dominated by lush eucalyptus trees and acacias. Birdsongs in the morning are almost a symphony.

The inn is still a family-run operation, originally started by Steve Royce, who was well-known as the former owner of the Huntington Hotel in Pasadena. Now his son Dan continues the tradition with help from other members of the family. One of the ongoing traditions of the Royce family is that the innkeeper makes it a point to visit individually with guests during their stay.

Although there is plenty of outdoor activity, I found the main living room with its spacious windows and high ceilings most restful.

There are quite a few original paintings on display. I was also delighted with the 4,000 book library.

A gentle place — the Inn at Rancho Santa Fe.

THE INN, Rancho Santa Fe, Ca. 92067; 714-756-1131. A 75-room resort-inn, 27 mi. north of San Diego Freeway #5, 5 mi. inland from Solana Beach, Del Mar. European plan. Breakfast, lunch and dinner served to travelers daily. Open year-round. Pool, tennis, putting green and bicycles on grounds. Golf and ocean nearby. Airport transportation provided. Daniel Royce, Innkeeper.

Directions: From I-5, take Exit S8 and drive inland about 6 mi.

VAGABOND HOUSE
Carmel, California

I first visited the Vagabond House in 1975 and when Chuck Watts met my plane at the airport, he explained that it was part of the inn service to supply transportation back and forth. "We encourage people to leave their cars at home when they come to Carmel. The walk down to the Carmel beach is quite short from the inn and the shops are just a few steps away."

My most recent visit was in the summer of 1977, and I joined Chuck and Patsy when Muffin took all three of us on an early morning walk on the beach. Muffin is a blonde Afghan hound and everyone makes a big fuss over her. Patsy explains to everyone that Muffin is really one of the family. "We are very particular about pets," she said. "They must always be leashed and never left inside the room unattended. We love Muffin and we believe we know how to treat a dog."

The walk on the beach in the early morning is one of the most attractive aspects of visiting Carmel, and Muffin proved to be an expert guide. It was a morning of gentle surf and Chuck said that there were times when the sound and action of the Pacific is positively thrilling.

"We've been so happy here at the Vagabond House," said Patsy. "This has been ideal for us. Our guests, many of whom return every year, really appreciate the basic qualities which we think are so important."

The inn is made up of 12 rooms which border three sides of a square. Most of them have woodburning fireplaces and each room has a completely individual feeling about it. During my visit, the Watts were planning the final phase of redecorating, and they have had great fun finding the antiques with which every room is

furnished. There were attractive overstuffed swivel rockers in almost all the rooms. Among other amenities, morning papers are delivered to all of the rooms, and each lodging has many different clocks. Chuck, like Karl Jokinen at the Mountain View House in Norfolk, Connecticut, is also an enthusiastic clock collector and repairer.

On the other hand, Patsy's deftness with needlepoint can also be seen in every room with her many pillows. Each of the lodging rooms is almost like a bedroom and study combined, with many books and periodicals.

A simple Continental breakfast in a basket is provided each morning; however, I usually join the more hearty eaters at Donel's Restaurant about two blocks away for griddle cakes or eggs.

Here is an excerpt from a letter I received in the fall of 1977: "We couldn't agree more with your praise about the Vagabond House Inn in Carmel. This is the 'Tiffany diamond of country inns.' It is immaculate, beautiful, sweet-smelling, cozy, charming, comfortable, homey, quiet (but not dead), moderately priced, superbly located, and is run by two most hospitable and friendly people ... Chuck and Patsy Watts. We had the pleasure of staying there for three nights last Halloween. What a treat! Pumpkins lined the courtyard, wood-burning fireplaces, and crackling leaves flavored the crisp autumn air, our own natural hearth bathed us in warmth and the whole atmosphere glowed with life and love.

"This is our first experience in using *Country Inns and Back Roads* and we hope the following ones will be as great. The Vagabond Inn looked like a tough act to follow."

VAGABOND HOUSE INN, Fourth & Dolores Streets, P.O. Box 2747, Carmel, Ca. 93921; 408-624-9988. A 12-room village inn serving Continental breakfasts to house guests only. No other meals

319

served. Open every day of the year. Not ideal for children. Attended leashed pets allowed. Bike renting, golf, natural beauty nearby (see notes on Carmel-Monterey region). Chuck and Patsy Watts, Innkeepers.

Directions: Turn off Hwy. 1 on Ocean Ave. in Carmel. Turn right off Ocean to Dolores St. Go 2½ blocks to inn.

THE WINE COUNTRY INN
St. Helena, California

The story of this inn is inspirational. It goes back a few years when Ned and Marge Smith visited me in Stockbridge, Massachusetts, and we talked about the ideals and objectives of innkeeping. They live in St. Helena, in the beautiful Napa Valley, where Ned is a prominent real estate broker. They were looking for the qualities that they most admired in country inns because they were interested in having an inn of their own. I was delighted that they stopped off to share some of their experiences with me.

After visiting about 15 New England inns they returned to California and began to give form to their ideas. A perfect site was found and the Smith family, all of them, began to work on building their inn.

In June of 1975 I called them to say that I was planning to come to California in late August. "Wonderful," said Marge. "We'll be open by that time for certain." The day arrived and I drove down from Elk on the coast and approached St. Helena from the north on Rte. 128. At the outskirts of St. Helena, following directions, I turned down Lodi Lane and in about thirty seconds I saw a spanking new sign, "The Wine Country Inn."

After our reunion, we set off on a complete tour of every nook and cranny of the new inn. Ned explained that the building was carefully designed to fit the site which overlooks the upper part of the Napa valley in full view of Glass Mountain.

"We tried to arrange for every room to have a view. So some have intimate balconies and others have patios leading to the lawn. The natural wild mustard, lupin, poppies and live oak trees have been blended with plantings of oleanders, petunias and Chinese pistachios to accent the scenery."

Each room is individually decorated with country antique furnishings refinished and reconstructed by members of the family. Many of the rooms have fireplaces, canopied beds, tufted bedspreads and handmade quilts. There are no televisions or radios, but a generous supply of magazines and books and big, comfortable, fluffy pillows encourage the lost art of reading.

To top everything off there is a generous Continental breakfast served every day with fresh California fruit and muffins or delicious caramel pecan rolls served warm. When it comes to the evening meal the Smiths can make many helpful suggestions for they know every restaurant in the valley. In 1978, the Smiths plan on adding six more rooms in the Brandy House—a completely separate building with what Ned calls a "nifty" view and complete privacy.

On my trip to California in June, 1977, I invited other northern California innkeepers in CIBR to join me for the day at the Wine Country Inn. We had a wonderful time on the outdoor deck in the sunshine talking over innkeeping problems, and we were all very much impressed with the Smiths' son, Jim, and his wife, Nita, who are now managing the inn, greeting the guests, and making them feel at home in the Napa Valley.

THE WINE COUNTRY INN, 1152 Lodi Lane, St. Helena, Ca. 94574; 707-963-7077. A newly built 15-room country inn in the Napa Wine Valley of California, about 70 mi. from San Francisco. Continental breakfast served to house guests, no other meals served. Open daily except December 22-27. No children, no pets. This inn is within driving distance of a great many wineries and also the Robert Louis Stevenson Museum. Golf and tennis nearby. Ned and Marge Smith, Innkeepers.

Directions: From San Francisco take the Oakland Bay Bridge to Hwy. 80. Travel north to the Napa cutoff. Stay on Hwy. 29 through the town of St. Helena, go 1¾ mi. north to Lodi Lane, then turn east ¼ mi. to inn.

321

Washington

CAPTAIN WHIDBEY INN
Coupeville, Washington

"Coming about," John Stone swung the rudder hard over and the boom moved to the starboard side of our trim sailboat; I fumbled for a moment or two with the jib as we set out on a new tack.

The morning was the kind that inspires poetry. The blue waters of Penn Cove in front of the Captain Whidbey Inn were ruffled by a slight breeze. Overhead there were just enough white clouds to accent the tremendous expanse of azure skies. To the east, the Cascades, dominated by Mt. Baker at more than 10,000 feet, were glistening in the sunshine. On the western side, the Olympics, with Mt. Olympus at almost 8000 feet, also had a white blanket. It was early June and Captain Whidbey Island, already blessed with dozens of varieties of spring flowers, was basking in the warm sunshine. John Stone, the manager of Captain Whidbey Inn, and I were taking advantage of the opportunity to do a little sailing.

"I'm sorry that Mother and Dad are not here this weekend," he said, "but they have already told me they will see you in the fall at the Middlebury Inn in Vermont at the Innkeepers' meeting."

"Mother and Dad" in this case were Steve and Shirlie Stone who purchased the Captain Whidbey Inn a number of years ago and have made it into as fetching a piece of New England as you can find west of Cape Cod. It is an old-fashioned inn and the New England touches come quite naturally, because Steve Stone is a native of Nantucket Island and a good example of the old saying "you can take the boy out of Nantucket but you can't take Nantucket out of the boy"; the tweedy look, the unmistakable accent and the corn cob pipe are all there.

The exterior of the inn is, however, pure northwest, built in 1907 of the distinctly regional madrona logs. The interior remains just about the same as it has always been, with highly polished log walls decorated with antiques and bric-a-brac.

The natural center of the inn is the living room with a very big fireplace made out of round stones. Here everybody, house guests and dinner guests alike, sit around talking and leafing through the dozens of magazines. There is a fire almost every evening, because as John says, "It really does draw people together."

Some of the lodging rooms are upstairs in the main house. It is here that a relaxing area with comfortable chairs has been set aside especially for house guests, with floor-to-ceiling shelves jam-packed with books. It is also decorated with Stone Family heirlooms, including rare chairs and chests, an old Navy uniform and a spinning wheel.

In 1975, an additional number of rustic lodgings called Lagoon Rooms were built in the woods across the road from the main house. They overlook their own private lake.

John and I continued our sail and the talk quite naturally turned to things historical. "Joseph Whidbey, for whom the island was named, was the master of the H.M.S. Discovery which sailed here in 1792. He discovered Deception Pass and proved that Whidbey Island really was an island and not part of the mainland."

By this time the sun was high and I knew John had to return to the inn to help with lunch, so we headed back to the Captain Whidbey dock. Furthermore, it seemed like a long time since breakfast; some baked Dungeness or Alaskan crabmeat sounded very good to me. I mentioned this to John and he said, "Yes, and don't forget some of our homemade French bread and biscuits."

THE CAPTAIN WHIDBEY, Rte. 1, Box 32, Coupeville, Wash. 98239; 206-678-4097. A 25-room country inn, 50 mi. north of Seattle, 3 mi. north of Coupeville. European plan. 4 cottages with private bath; 12 rooms with private bath. Breakfast, lunch and dinner served daily to travelers. Open year-round. Pets allowed in cottages only. Boating and fishing on grounds. Golf nearby. Steve, Shirlie and John Stone, Innkeepers.

Directions: Whidbey Island is reached year-round from the south by the Columbia Beach-Mukilteo Ferry, and during the summer and on weekends by the Port Townsend-Keystone Ferry. From the north (Vancouver, B.C. and Bellingham), take the Deception Pass Bridge to Whidbey Island.

THE FARMHOUSE
Port Townsend, Washington

John Ashby Conway and I were walking along the grassy height of land overlooking the Strait of Juan de Fuca. It was high noon and I could plainly see the hills of Victoria, British Columbia, in the distance. On clear nights, the lights of that city are a shimmering nimbus.

"We are going to make some changes in 1978," he said. "This has come about through requests of many of our guests who are celebrating anniversaries with us. Each year they say they have the same food. Since they cannot change their anniversaries, we have decided to change our schedule.

"We are closed in December and January. In February we will continue with the Mandarin food from North China. In March we are returning to German, including sauerbraten, red cabbage, spaetzle, rouladen and Schwartzwaldenkirschenkuchen.

"In April we'll switch to classic Greek food, including our marinated lamb broiled over charcoal, as well as pastitzo, moussaka and Queen's cake.

"In May '78, we are doing the northern Indian food including curry and sambals. Do you know that we have had Indians ask for our recipes?

"Easter and Mother's and Father's Day we will have two sittings at 3 p.m. and 6 p.m. In June, July, and August we will go back into our summer schedule with dinners on Thursday, Friday, Saturday, and Sunday. In September, it's back to the weekends again with an Italian menu. In October, it will be Hungarian food including gulyas, strudel and all the rest.

"In November we will be serving classic Japanese food omitting the restaurant cliches and concentrating on beautiful, delicious, and unusual items little-known outside of Japan. By the way, Thanksgiving Day we also have two servings at 3 and 6 with traditional holiday food."

I first visited The Farmhouse in 1972, and in the intervening years I have had several letters from many parts of the world commending the food, the view, and the unusual atmosphere. John does all of the cooking which is an interesting occupation for a retired professor of drama.

Dorothy Conway, an expert photographer in her own right, is on hand to greet and seat all of the patrons. I have returned several times and it has always been a pleasure.

"It's such a relief to have finished remodeling our kitchen," he sighed. "I think that completes our projects, because we cannot add on to the house since we are in a residential zone. By the way, I'm still learning — I'm taking six sessions with the leading pastry chef in Seattle. On desserts!"

Remember, one set menu each month. There are no choices. It is true gourmet cooking. I hope that all our readers will telephone or write in advance. Please do not "drop in" on The Farmhouse. While it is not an arduous trip from Seattle, it would be a disappointment not to be served. It might be convenient to reserve rooms at the nearby James House which returns to CIBR in this edition.

THE FARMHOUSE, North Beach, Port Townsend, Wash. 98368; 206-385-1411. A unique gourmet country restaurant, 50 mi. from Seattle. Meals by reservation only. Dinner served Thursdays through Sundays in June, July and August; dinner served Fridays, Saturdays and Sundays from September through May. Closed months of December and January. Dorothy and John Ashby Conway, Innkeepers.

Directions: From Seattle take Edmonds-Kingston Ferry and follow Rte. 104 over Hood Canal Floating Bridge to Rte. 101 N. Exit at Port Townsend and make inquiries for The Farmhouse before driving into town.

JAMES HOUSE
Port Townsend, Washington

"Here's the way we feel about innkeeping," said Lowell Bogart. "We enjoy sharing our home with folks who are coming from a hurried world and busy lives, and perhaps are weary of travel and look-alike impersonal accommodations. We like to bring all their senses into good working order, because we feel it is easy in this day to have one's senses dangerously numbed. For instance, this lovely old place is so pleasing to the eyes, we feel it offers a homey atmosphere in the midst of 19th century elegance."

We were sitting on the front porch of the James House in Port Townsend overlooking the bay, with the Cascade Mountains to the east and the Olympic Mountains to the west. Lowell and Barbara were explaining that they actually discovered the James House in 1976 in the pages of *Country Inns and Back Roads*.

"Yes, it was your book that led us to this beautiful place and its lovely surroundings," said Barbara. "After our first visit we decided to change our entire way of life, so we bought the inn from Bill and Ethel Eaton and moved out here. It has been a wonderful experience.

"We don't have television and there is only the ticking of the old clocks, the howling winds, the whistles of the ferries, and quiet music to disturb the peace," said Lowell. "To continue with those senses I was talking about: smell and taste are tantalized with the aroma of the fresh-baked breads and the homemade jams and jellies.

326

Touching is great, also. The wood in this house, the bannisters and bureaus, get much loving and caressing."

The James House is a Victorian jewel and I am certain that the innkeepers of two other significant centers of Victoriana, Tom and Sue Carroll of the Mainstay Inn in Cape May, New Jersey and Norman Kinney of the National House in Marshall, Michigan would find Port Townsend and the James House a great experience. It is most attractively and authentically furnished throughout, except for the mattresses which are new and wonderfully comfortable.

There are actually four floors with bedrooms and suites, each one with its own distinguishing characteristics. Three of the bedrooms have fireplaces or stoves, and there are three sitting rooms; two with fireplaces and the other filled with books and games. As Lowell has already hinted, a Continental breakfast is served in the kitchen daily, next to a woodburning range, and includes homemade baked breads and jams.

Barbara was very enthusiastic about Port Townsend. "It is rapidly becoming an art and cultural center with a summer season of art featuring workshops, festivals, and special events including chamber music, orchestras, poetry, dance, master painting classes and even a science fiction workshop. There are many art galleries and antique shops."

Besides these cogitative diversions, guests at the James House, which by the way is now open every day of the year, can enjoy sailing, hiking, fishing, scuba diving, cycling, and soaring nearby. It is great fun to take ferry boats over to Whidbey Island or even to Vancouver in Victoria, British Columbia. In this respect the entire area reminds me of the Norwegian fjords.

I was delighted to meet the Bogarts and their daughter, Jennifer, and to see the interesting things that they are accomplishing in this lovely old Victorian mansion. I am delighted also to welcome the Jame House back to the pages of *Country Inns and Back Roads*.

JAMES HOUSE, 1238 Washington St., Port Townsend, Wash. 98368, 206-385-1238. A 10-room village inn, 50 mi. from Seattle on the Olympic Peninsula. Some rooms with shared baths. European plan with sit-down breakfast served to house guests. No other meals served. Open daily including holidays. No children under 12; no pets. State parks and beaches nearby. Lowell and Barbara Bogart, Innkeepers.

Directions: From Seattle take Winslow or Edmond-Kingston ferries. James House is adjacent to the post office on the bluff overlooking Port Townsend Bay.

327

I've walked in many forests in New England, Pennsylvania, the Great Smokies, and in other places in North America, and Europe, but the Rain Forest of the Olympic Peninsula in Washington is a unique experience. Supported by ideal moisture and temperature conditions, this area supports a living, dying, continuously evolving environment. There are elk browsing in the forest shadows, salmon jumping in waterfalls, and moss, ferns, and saplings growing on decaying logs. There is enough timber growing in a single acre to build over 40 average houses.

There are great giants of the forest standing so high that I could barely see the sun shining on their tops. There were western red cedars from which the Indians made their canoes, stately Douglas firs which are the largest and oldest of the trees, nearly 300 feet high and 500 years old, and western hemlocks, the Washington state tree. On the shadowy forest floor where the sun seldom penetrates, lay several trees felled by high winds.

I may have expected silence, but I found that there were continuous sounds in the rain forest. The snapping of twigs, the flutterings of wings, the chirping of birds, and almost always the low muttering of the wind.

LAKE QUINAULT LODGE
Quinault, Washington

It was ten o'clock on a summer evening and the big living room of the Lake Quinault Lodge was filled with a number of guests reading, talking, doing puzzles, and playing bridge. In one corner some people were singing softly to the accompaniment of a guitar. The moon had risen over the lake and a light breeze was stirring the great trees on the mountains.

One of the guests who had been there about a week, dropped a couple of aromatic birch bark logs on the fire. Although it was a mild night, a small fire was quite welcome.

"Well," he asked me, "what did you do all afternoon?"

I replied that I spent most of the time just walking in the woods, getting the feel of the great trees. "Yes," he replied, "I think that's what almost every newcomer does. It takes time to get used to these two- and three-hundred foot giants that surround us."

This is indeed big tree country with cedars, redwoods, spruces, Douglas firs, hemlocks, and pines in profusion. My afternoon walk in the woods was an inspiring experience.

"It's interesting to watch people come into this relaxing atmosphere for the first time," my new friend continued. "They arrive tired and tight from city living and I can see them unwind.

Finally they're sitting around like all of us without a worry in the world. I think that the saunas, jacuzzi, and indoor swimming pool help out a great deal, too," he added.

In 1890, two brothers of the pioneer Olson family built a crude log hotel which served as the only haven for travelers coming to Quinault. Another temporary structure was built to provide additional shelter for travelers in 1923, and finally, in 1926, the site for Quinault Lodge was selected in a natural clearing, and the lodge was constructed with great care and the finest materials.

The present innkeepers, Marge and Larry Lesley, have worked very hard to preserve the best of the old and, of course, to incorporate it with some of the improvements of today's conveniences. The result is a growing lodge in which the new rooms look out over the lake and command an excellent view of the mountains.

The Lake Quinault Lodge is a year-round resort-inn about three hours from Seattle and Tacoma. Frankly, I feel totally inadequate to describe the tremendous scope of the trees and the entire forest, mountain, and lake experience.

Everything about the lodge is homelike and comfortable, and is clearly a source of pleasure to the many families staying there. The irrepressible younger set spends many an enjoyable evening in the dandy recreation room with its variety of games.

With so much time spent out of doors, it was easy to see why the dining room is an important part of the inn experience. I found homemade baked bread, Yankee pot roast of beef, and many other typical country inn items interspersed with things that are found only in the Northwest, like alder-smoked Quinault salmon.

As the evening moved on, I strolled over to the corner where the people were singing to a guitar and joined the widening circle. About thirty minutes later, the great old grandfather's clock in the corner tolled eleven. With this, the group started to break up and say good-night, all of them headed for another deep sleep here in the woods.

LAKE QUINAULT LODGE, Southshore Rd., Quinault, Wash. 98575; 206-288-2571. A 56-room resort-inn in the Olympic National Forest of the State of Washington, about 40 mi. from Aberdeen. European plan. Breakfast, lunch and dinner served daily to travelers. Open every day of the year. $3 fee for pets; must be attended. Indoor swimming pool, chipping green on grounds. Hiking, mountain climbing, fishing, nature walks nearby. Marge and Larry Lesley, Innkeepers.

Directions: Use Quinault exit from Rte. 101. Proceed 2 mi. on south shore of Lake Quinault to inn.

THE PARTRIDGE INN
Underwood, Washington

For two years before my short visit to the Partridge Inn I had a lively correspondence with Mrs. Nora McNab. Her letters described the view of the Columbia River from the dining room windows, the pear and apple orchards surrounding the Partridge Inn, and how her baked Columbia River salmon was purchased in season right out of the Indians' nets.

She went into some detail also about the little villages of White Salmon and Bingen, whose buildings reflect a Rhineland influence.

Being a small country restaurant, she explained she was open only at 5 p.m. on weekdays, and noon on Sundays and holidays. "Although," she said, "if people are coming from a distance and call ahead, we can open a little earlier to accommodate them, or we might even serve lunch, and most certainly breakfast, if they were spending the night."

After many delays I was finally able to schedule a trip to the Partridge Inn and the entire experience was a memorable one.

Nora prevailed upon the good services of a neighbor, Mrs. Sharon Harmsen to pick me up when I arrived at the Portland airport, and I had the pleasure of her company and her knowledge of the Columbia River country as we drove to Underwood.

Unfortunately, I was visiting on the first rainy and overcast day in weeks, so that my view of the Columbia River and the mountains

was obscured most of the time; however, I found Mrs. McNab's warm-hearted generosity and good food well worth the visit. Her letters were entirely accurate, and everything was in spic-and-span condition.

She had invited a reporter from a local newspaper to have lunch with me while she, in turn, took care of a large special luncheon party. She was kind enough to introduce me to her other guests, and I became re-acquainted with a gentleman I had known slightly when he lived in the Berkshires.

Everything on the luncheon had a real "homemade" taste, and I was doubly sorry that my travel schedule prevented me from remaining for dinner. As Nora says, "We strive to keep the prices reasonable with consistently good food. We offer just plain country cooking. Besides baked salmon, another speciality is barbecued Cornish hen. We also have Swiss steak, seafood Thermidor, our popular Underwood Mountain meatloaf, and usually roast beef, and roast pork with bread dressing. Our bread is always warm, and our own specialty, pear butter, is part of every meal. Pies, of course, are homemade."

The Partridge Inn is a modest, unassuming restaurant with rooms available for guests' convenience. Representative of the Columbia River area, it is a pleasant, homey stop for travelers, and well worth a side trip from the Coastal Highway. But please, please call ahead for reservations, local weather, and lodging information from Nora.

THE PARTRIDGE INN, Box 100, Underwood, Washington 98651; 509-493-2381. A country restaurant with two lodging rooms located

60 miles east of Portland, Oregon or Vancouver, Washington. Dinner served every night, year-round, weather permitting. Breakfast served to houseguests only. Hiking trails and camping nearby. Free huckleberry picking in season. Pears and apples for sale most of the year. Nora McNab, Innkeeper.

Directions: On Washington Highway 14, 60 miles east of Ft. Vancouver turn left on to Cook-Underwood Road at the confluence of the Columbia and White Salmon Rivers. (This road has 2 ends, do not turn off at Cook). Follow yellow line up the hill for 2 miles. When the Columbia River is on the left begin to look for inn sign on the right. Coming from the Oregon side along Interstate 80N, 60 miles east of Portland cross the interstate bridge at the town of Hood River. Turn left and drive 2 miles to Cook-Underwood Road directly after crossing the White Salmon River. Follow directions up the hill as above. From coastal region take any highway leading to Portland, Oregon, then pick up 80N going east.

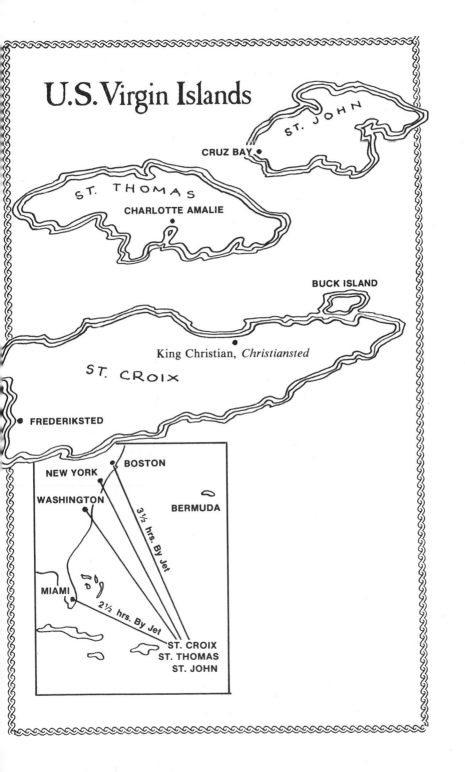

U.S. Virgin Islands

U.S. Virgin Islands

St. Croix has mountains and gorgeous beaches as well as excellent swimming, snorkeling, and scuba diving. It has two communities, Christiansted and Fredericksted. Each of these has picture book charm.

For further and more detailed information about both the American and British Virgin Islands I recommend Margaret Zeller's book, The Inn Way . . . Caribbean, *$4.95, Berkshire Traveller Press, Stockbridge, Massachusetts 01262, or your bookstore. It contains her adventures in searching for country inns on all the islands in this sunny part of the world.*

KING CHRISTIAN HOTEL
Christiansted, St. Croix, Virgin Islands

"I think we are very fortunate here on St. Croix," said Betty Sperber. "In addition to the King Christian, there are several excellent accommodations on many different parts of the island. More and more people are coming to St. Croix every year. I think it's because of the beaches, the tranquility, the golf course, and the fact that it is such an entirely different atmosphere."

Betty and I had been walking through the hotel and had stopped momentarily on a balcony overlooking the harbor. I remarked that the Kings Wharf seemed to be the center of a great deal of activity.

"Yes, it's fun right here on the waterfront," she said. "You know this is a working harbor, and in addition to the pleasure craft and boats that are available for rent, there are also fishermen who go out every day. Our guests seem to like the feeling of being near the water. We are within walking distance of museums, many art galleries, and shops. The beach is just 300 yards away. Did you know that Alexander Hamilton spent his boyhood in Christiansted and worked within two blocks of where we are now?"

Since my last visit, I received a letter from Betty bringing me up to date. She writes in part: "We are doing many exciting things with the hotel. The swimming pool has been resurfaced and looks gorgeous. The entire building has been painted in a cream color and the shutters in deep blue. The restaurant outside patio area has been redecorated. The lounge is all done, with built-ins and super graphics using Marimeko prints on the cushions. It really does look lovely. If I should sound enthusiastic, it's because I'm watching my dreams come true one by one."

KING CHRISTIAN HOTEL, King's Wharf, Christiansted, St. Croix, U.S.V.I. 00820; 809-773-2285 (N.Y. reservations 212-661-7990). A 38-room waterfront hotel in town. Open year-round. No pets. Restaurant, fresh-water pool, duty-free stores, dive shops on premises. Sailing, snorkeling, scuba diving, glass-bottom boat rides, Hertz car rental all arranged by the inn. Dine-around plan. Tennis and golf nearby. Betty Sperber, Innkeeper.

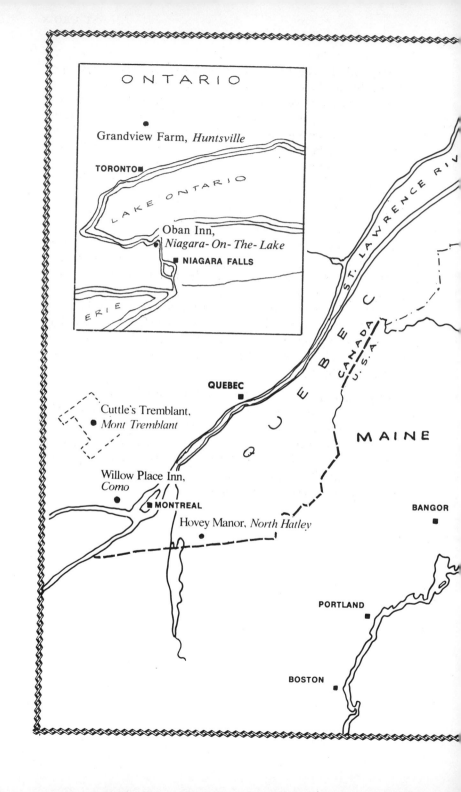

GULF OF ST. LAWRENCE

CAPE BRETON

Kilmuir Place, *Northeast Margaree*

Shaw's Hotel, *Brackley Beach*

SYDNEY

NEW

P. E. I.

Inverary Inn, *Baddeck*

BRUNSWICK

MONCTON

Marshlands, *Sackville*

NOVA SCOTIA

Elm Lodge, *t. Stephen*

HALIFAX

LAIS

Marathon Hotel, *Grand Manan Island*

ATLANTIC

ANNAPOLIS ROYAL

Milford House, *South Milford*

YARMOUTH

OCEAN

Eastern and Maritime Canada

Nova Scotia

INVERARY INN
Baddeck, Nova Scotia

Baddeck, Nova Scotia, is a small Scottish village on the shores of Loch Bras d'Or. By air, it's about 2½ hours away from Boston via Halifax and Sydney, Nova Scotia. In terms of more ethereal measurements, it might as well be the moon.

And yet I probably have received more mail about people visiting the Inverary Inn than any other country inn in this book! Here's an example from a recent letter.

"Dear Berkshire Traveller, I have read your book, stayed at several of your country inns, and found myself on some back roads you may not have discovered, but these few days at the Inverary Inn have been a delight with excellent food and comfortable beds. We've enjoyed thoughtfulness and reading lamps, freshly-squeezed orange juice, a fire in the fireplace, and new friends — all made possible by the imagination and concern of Isobel MacAulay.

"When we mentioned *Country Inns and Back Roads,* the conversation continued well into the night over tea and lemon pie in the kitchen. This inn is a fine example of the spirit of the country inns. I'll certainly be returning to the Inverary as soon as I can." That was from a lady in New Jersey.

Here's an excerpt from some guests from Calgary: "We're coming back for the food! The salmon was heavenly and so fresh! For breakfast, we've never tasted anything like that Scottish oatmeal porridge and bannoch (a Scottish scone made with buttermilk and sour cream). And the oatcakes — oh, the oatcakes."

Another letter spoke of the warmth, graciousness, and hospitality at the Inverary and took me to task for omitting some of the historic events of Nova Scotia history. They were particularly complimentary toward the staff of the inn who, they said, seemed to be enjoying themselves as they went about their work.

Literally dozens and dozens of people have found their way to the Inverary with copies of *Country Inns and Back Roads* in their hands and Isobel MacAulay has made them all feel as though their arrival was the most important day in her life. In 1975 I said that the Inverary might just be the most famous country inn in Nova Scotia and I think it is safe to say in 1978 that it *is* the most famous country inn in Nova Scotia. However, such well-deserved fame does not go unnoticed, and so it is most necessary in all seasons of the year to have advance reservations.

Thank you Isobel for being so warm and generous to our "Travellers."

INVERARY INN, Box 190, Baddeck, Cape Breton, N.S., Canada 902-295-2674. A 40-room village inn on the Cabot Trail, 52 mi. from Sydney, N.S. On the shores of Lake Bras d'Or. European plan. Some rooms with shared bath. Breakfast and dinner served to travelers daily. Open from May 15 to Nov. 1. Bicycles and children's playground on grounds. Boating and small golf course nearby. Isobel MacAulay, Innkeeper.

Directions: Follow Trans-Canada Hwy. to Canso Causeway to Baddeck.

KILMUIR PLACE
Northeast Margaree, Cape Breton, Nova Scotia

Here are some excerpts from a most recent letter from Isabel Taylor and her husband Ross who have a tiny country inn on the Cabot Trail on Cape Breton, in Nova Scotia.

"Good morning, 'Mr. Norman', you've been neglected recently. The number one reason — I was having the chaise reupholstered and couldn't write in any other corner. The number two reason — I had to stir myself and work a little more in the kitchen so there is not as much leisure. Number three — the garden grew so well it kept me busy picking vegetables and flowers.

"We have had a good summer, many calls from CIBR friends and a lot of young people and that is interesting. I like to see young folk coming this way, as you sort of feel they'll be back.

"Our friend, Isobel MacAulay from the Inverary Inn, gives

us a call on the phone every so often. She has been busy as a beaver herself.

"Ross is busy helping with breakfast at the moment. The blueberry muffins and chocolate cake are in demand and he keeps the supply moving. I see a lot of birds gathering outside my kitchen window. They are ready to depart south. All look plump and ready to stand the long journey to warmer climates. The hummingbirds are gone, but the warblers are still here, soon to be on their way also."

Kilmuir Place is where Ross and Isabel have their home, and they can accommodate six comfortably. The inn operates on the American plan serving breakfast and dinner to houseguests only. It's necessary to have firm reservations. The home is filled with treasures that belonged to their relatives, and other dear things they've collected over the years. In the dining room, the beautiful mahogany set is their pride.

On a visit in June, before the season really got underway, I had lobster caught fresh from the Gulf of St. Lawrence and we did something that I've never done—I understand it's an old Cape Breton thing—I sprinkled (at their suggestion) some vinegar on the lobster. It was delicious.

All of the rooms were taken at that time and the guests were doing some of the fabulous salmon fishing, playing cards or just sitting and rocking on the porch.

At Kilmuir Place they know how to live.

KILMUIR PLACE, Northeast Margaree, Cape Breton, N.S., Canada B0E 2H0; 902-248-2877. A 5-room country inn on Rte. 19, 28 mi. from Baddeck. Some rooms with shared baths. Modified American plan. Breakfast and dinner served to houseguests only. Open from June to mid-October. Salmon fishing in the Margaree River, touring the Cabot Trail and both fresh water and salt water swimming nearby. Mr. and Mrs. Ross Taylor, Innkeepers.

Directions: After crossing Canso Causeway to Cape Breton, follow either Rte. 19 (coast road to Inverness) and turn right on Cabot Trail at Margaree Forks, or follow Rte. 105 and turn left on Cabot Trail at Nyanza.

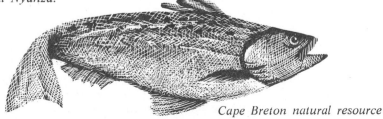

Cape Breton natural resource

MILFORD HOUSE
South Milford, Nova Scotia

For those of you who are reading about the Milford House for the first time, let me explain that it is a flashback to the early days of the twentieth century when people from Canada and the United States stayed at resort-inns like this for months at a time. It is an old-fashioned place with turn-of-the-century furniture and decor. The neat parlors and living rooms have a "country elegance."

Lodgings are in the main house and also in extremely well-furnished cabins that are spread out along a series of lakes within a short walk from the main house. Each has a dock, a fireplace, and all the conveniences, including electricity and maid service. Meals are taken at the inn dining room.

So much for the basic character. Now I would like to quote from a letter I received from Bud, Margaret and Wendy Miller telling me about some of the things that went on during the summer of 1977:

"It seems to me there was an unusually warm feeling of good fellowship last summer. Maybe it was the small fries who are always good for morale. This was the year for babies and we all had fun making a big fuss over them. Baby Victoria was a very good girl as befitted the daughter of two ministers! Baby Salinda's parents have been coming here for the past ten years; in fact, since their honeymoon. She played on the big mat in front of the fireplace with Victoria while the mothers compared notes.

"When Moms and Dads wanted to get away by themselves, we arranged for one of our local girls to babysit. Our own grandchildren, Simon and Jay, were also here. This is a good place to bring small children, and with Pampers, baby traveling beds, etc., it can be quite easy to travel. It is nice to have the children.

"Besides babies, we also had a good group of 17 to 21 year-olds. These children have been coming here since they were, themselves, babies and it hardly seems possible that they have grown up. One of them is now six feet tall and still growing. Last year he had a unique experience of living in Norway with a family on a farm; he had a very interesting slide presentation for us one evening. Another six-footer kept us supplied with striped bass from his many fishing expeditions in the Annapolis River. Incidentally, one of our young fellows caught a 35-pounder.

"July is one of the great times to come to this part of Nova Scotia. It is relatively free from rain and the weather is at its best. The days are longer, the nights are warmer and there are not so many people on the road."

We can all see that the Milford House is a great place for families with children of all ages (and even families without children). It is a place of enduring traditions, including that of guests standing on the front porch to wave good-bye to those who are departing. It's permitted to wave back until the car reaches the big tree at the edge of the property. Then the guest must look straight ahead, and not look back! It is really very hard to do; I know. I have done it.

MILFORD HOUSE, South Milford, R.R. #4, Annapolis Royal, N.S., Canada, B0S 1OA; 902-532-2617. A rustic resort-inn with 24 cabins on 600 acres of woodlands and lakes, 90 mi. from Yarmouth, N.S., near Kejimkujik National Park. Modified American plan. Breakfast and dinner served daily with picnic lunches available. Open from June 18 to Sept 15. Tennis, fishing, croquet, canoeing, bird-watching and swimming on grounds. Deep-sea fishing and golf nearby. Warren and Margaret Miller, Innkeepers.

Directions: From Yarmouth follow Rte. 1 to traffic lights in Annapolis Royal. Turn right and continue on to Rte. 8, 15 mi. to inn.

Prince Edward Island

Prince Edward Island is one of the great surprises of North America. For one thing, ocean water temperatures along the wide P.E.I. beaches average 68 to 70 degrees in summer and the sun is excellent for tanning. It has one of Canada's finest national parks stretching 25 miles along the Gulf of St. Lawrence. There are wild seascapes, breathtaking views and an atmosphere of hospitality because this has been a resort area for more than a century.

During the summer months there is an excellent theatre at the Confederation Centre of the Arts in Charlottetown offering a choice of musicals which play to capacity houses most every night. Cavendish Beach is the locale of Lucy Maude Montgomery's stories of "Ann of Green Gables." A small, gabled, green cottage has been built with some reminders of "Ann" stories.

Prince Edward Island is very popular in July and August so reserve well in advance and be sure to obtain ferry information.

SHAW'S HOTEL
Brackley Beach, Prince Edward Island

I first visited P.E.I. and Shaw's Hotel in 1974 and never thought that I could be this far north and find ocean water so wonderfully warm and enjoyable. Here on the Gulf of St. Lawrence it was comfortable and pleasant and reminded me of Palm Beach in February.

I had taken the ferry from Caribou, Nova Scotia that morning. There is another ferry from Cape Tormentine, New Brunswick. It is possible to stay at the Marshlands Inn in Sackville and take the ferry over the next morning. I had driven down from the Inverary Inn on Cape Breton in northern Nova Scotia, so the Caribou crossing was more convenient.

I found that Shaw's was part of an original pioneer farm started in 1793, had become a hotel in 1860, and today still has many of the characteristics of an operating farm.

Some of the accommodations are single and double rooms in the main building which is a Victorian house with a brilliant red mansard third story. There are also individual cottages which can accommodate from two to eight people. This is most convenient for families that return every summer. They are spaced far enough apart to insure privacy. Five of them have their own fireplaces.

Shaw's Hotel is surrounded by many trees and broad meadows. The view from the dining room might include a sailboat bobbing along on the bay. There is a good mix of both Canadian and American guests, and Mr. Shaw tells me that in 1977 there were quite a few people from California, Washington and New York.

One of the most attractive features about Shaw's Hotel is the fact that it is only a short distance through the woods to the beach. All of this summertime outdoor activity including swimming, sailing on the bay, deep sea tuna fishing, golf, tennis, bicycling, walking, and horseback riding contribute to very big appetites, so the main dishes include fresh salmon, lobster, mackerel, cod and halibut. Dinners are fun because everyone is eager for a hearty meal, and enthusiasm is high after the day of recreation.

Children are particularly happy in this atmosphere. Gordon Shaw said he has had as many as 20 to 30 children at one time in the height of the season. "There is always plenty of elbow room," he said. "We don't have any trouble keeping the parents of the children amused either. Besides the beach, there are riding horses nearby and it is fun to ride along the beach and on the bridle paths. I have been doing it all my life."

One of our readers summed up their experience at Shaw's Hotel like this:

"It is not easy to get from Hannibal, Missouri to Brackley Beach, Prince Edward Island. But my husband and I and our two children, 9 and 11, made an adventure out of it stopping at inns in your book all along the way. When that big sheep dog bounded out to greet us when we pulled up to the hotel I knew that we were in the right place."

SHAW'S HOTEL and Cottages, Brackley Point Road, Brackley Beach, Prince Edward Island, Canada COA 2HO; 902-672-2022. A 24-room country hotel within walking distance of Brackley Beach, 15 mi. from Charlottetown. American plan. Some rooms with shared baths. 10 guest cottages. Breakfast, lunch, dinner served to travelers daily. Open from June 15 to Sept. 15. Pets allowed in cottages only. Tennis, golf, bicycles, riding, sailing, beach and summer theatre nearby. Gordon Shaw, Innkeeper.

Directions: Prince Edward Island is reached either by ferry from Cape Tormentine, New Brunswick (near Moncton), or Caribou, Nova Scotia. In both cases, after arriving on P.E.I., follow Rte. 1 to Charlottetown, then Rte. 15 to Brackley Beach. P.E.I. is also reached by Eastern Provincial Airways, Canadian National Railways and Air Canada.

New Brunswick

ELM LODGE INN
St. Stephen, New Brunswick

In each of the guest bedrooms of this Canadian Victorian inn on the border between the United States and Canada, there is a copy of a poem which, I believe, was mutually written by the innkeepers Zena and Pat Garbutt. Perhaps this conveys more than anything I can say; the true spirit expressed by these lovely Christian people whose religion dominates their lives. Their inn is not only a place of business but an open house for all who may need help:

And so to Bed ...

To rise with gratitude,
   To find one's sphere,
To feel that work is good,
   And hold it dear,
To take life's winding road,
   With laughter and with song,
Nor grumble at the load,
   Though the way be long ...
To pluck a harmful weed
   And plant a blossom there,
To see another's need,
   His burdens share;
To laugh and joke a bit,
   To cherish one true friend,
Preserve a gentle wit
   Until the end ...
To find in little things
   One's greatest happiness,
The bird that sweetly sings,
   The wind's caress;
To reach the Inn of rest,
   And know the day has sped
To breathe "I've done my best"
   And so to bed.
A restful night to you.

Best wishes,

Zena and Pat Garbutt

345

Elm Lodge Inn is a beautifully restored building with three huge elm trees on the front lawn, handsome coach lamps flanking the entrance, and large green shutters which enhance the building considerably. There are flowerbeds on the lawn, including a number of rose bushes. On one of my visits, bluebells were in full array.

The interior of the inn tells a marvelous story. Pat and Zena Garbutt, who also own the Willow Place Inn in Como, Quebec, have worked very hard over the past few years restoring this truly elegant house. Floors, walls, and woodwork are all cleaned, polished, and refurbished until everything shines like a schoolboy's face. Victorian antiques and an improvisation of different types of furniture make each of the three little dining rooms a separate experience. Zena and Pat have been aided in their efforts by young people, some of whom have come from the Willow Place.

Upstairs are nine very handsome, comfortable rooms. Mine overlooked the lawn and the broad street, and had a canopied bed, which Clare MacMillan explained was very popular with honeymooners.

Clare and his wife are also an important part of Elm Lodge: he is the chef, and has the best interests of the inn very much at heart. The duckling with orange sauce, the steak and kidney pie, and clam chowder are very popular. Clare's wife does the baking for the inn, and I had a piece of her delicious, spicy walnut-raisin pie for dinner, as well as some homemade bread.

During my most recent visit in 1977, I was delighted to learn that St. Stephen's University, Canada's only four-year, degree-granting, interdominational Christian university, which was started at the Elm Lodge just a few years ago, is now making progress. More buildings have been acquired in St. Stephen, and students from both America and Canada are attending each year.

Let me elaborate a little on the directions for reaching the inn: coming east on Route 9 (the "airline route") from Bangor, be on the lookout in Milltown, Maine for the Texaco station on the left, which is next to the Milltown border-crossing into Canada. While I was talking to the Canadian customs man, I could see Elm Lodge just over the St. Croix River. If the traveler has been following the coastal route in Maine, proceed through Calais and ignore the first customs crossing and go two miles into Milltown, Maine and look for the border crossing on the right. Coming from New Brunswick, follow Water Street in St. Stephens, past the border point and on into Milltown. The road winds along the river and into the tree-lined and gracious main street, and on out to the border point. The inn with the sign "Auberge Elm Lodge Inn" is on the right.

The American or Canadian traveler on a first visit to New Brunswick does well to stop at the Auberge Elm Lodge Inn.

ELM LODGE INN, 477 Milltown Blvd., St. Stephen, New Brunswick, Canada; 506-466-3771. A 9-room village inn on a quiet street near the Canadian-American border crossing at Calais, Maine. European plan and Modified American plan which omits lunch. Breakfast, lunch and dinner served daily. Open every day from Jan. 12 through Dec. 14. Dining room closed on Sundays from Jan. to May. Children welcome and pets who act like English gentlemen. Bicycles, sailing, swimming, nature trails, horseback riding, golf, canoeing, jogging nearby. Patrick and Zena Garbutt, Innkeepers.

Directions: From Bangor, Maine, follow Rte. 9. Cross at Milltown-St. Stephen border crossing. Inn is kitty-cornered to and within sight of Canadian customs.

MARATHON INN
Grand Manan Island, New Brunswick

Grand Manan, Campobello, and Deer Islands are known as New Brunswick's Fundy Isles. Grand Manan was settled by United Empire Loyalists. It's even possible that the Vikings may have arrived hundreds of years earlier.

Grand Manan is a quiet, unspoiled island of great natural beauty 15 miles long and 4 miles wide, a paradise for naturalists, bird watchers, photographers, artists, divers, and rock hounds. The best way to experience the island is by walking.

There have been a few changes here on the island since my last

Ferry to Grand Manan

visit. For one thing, the Marathon Hotel is now the Marathon Inn and the new owners are Jim, Judy, and Fern Leslie. Jim and Judy are husband and wife, and Fern is Jim's mother. They have approached their new profession of country innkeeping with zeal and enthusiasm and have instituted some remarkably optimistic innovations.

"Well, for one thing," said Jim, "we are going to be open year round. We think that Grand Manan Island has its own charm twelve months of the year. Of course, it is not the same in the winter as in the summer, but for people who want to have a quiet, natural experience, I am certain we can provide something most unusual."

Jim and Judy are apparently go-getters. Almost as soon as they took up residence, they made many new friends and I believe that the new Marathon Inn is going to be humming with new ideas.

It is exactly the kind of country inn that I was hoping to find on this unusual island. The design is Victorian and there are spotlessly clean rooms with white walls and furniture painted in gay colors. The open staircase reminds me of a flying bridge aboard a boat. All of the rooms on the front have a spectacular view of the harbor.

Extensive restoration work has already been done including painting the exterior, adding a new roof, and improving the landscaping.

Grand Manan is reached by ferry from Black's Harbor, and in 1978 another ferry will be added to the schedule, which means that there will be twice as many sailings each day.

During the summer months the island is literally covered with wild flowers. Wild berries are found everywhere — Marathon guests bring them back by the pailsful to devour with cream. Audubon visited the island in 1833 and gave a glowing report: "It is the birds that really own Grand Manan. There are over 300 species that live at least a part of their lives here and that includes the Bald Eagle." Grand Manan Island may be one of the last accessible unspoiled environments on the Northeast coast.

MARATHON INN, North Head at Grand Manan, New Brunswick, Canada EOG 2MO; 506-662-8144. A 38-room resort-inn on Grand Manan Island in the Bay of Fundy, 40 mi. from St. John in New Brunswick. Modified American and European plans. Open all year. Breakfast and dinner served to travelers daily. Pets allowed on ground floor annex. Beach combing, bird watching, swimming, fishing, hiking, diving, bicycles, golf, and tennis nearby. Jim, Judy, and Fern Leslie, Innkeepers.

Directions: Grand Manan Island is reached by ferry from Black's Harbour which is just off Rte. 1, midway between Calais, Maine and St. John, New Brunswick.

MARSHLANDS INN
Sackville, New Brunswick

We were an interesting little group. There was a gentleman from Saskatchewan who was on his way to Cape Breton to do some fishing. A lady and gentleman from Toronto were on their way home from visiting some relatives in Halifax, Nova Scotia. There was also a young honeymooning couple from Detroit who had stayed in a different Berkshire Traveller Inn for the past four nights. They would be leaving in the morning for the Inverary at Baddeck, Nova Scotia.

We were all sitting together in front of the fireplace in the living room sipping the delicious hot chocolate offered every evening at the Marshlands. Innkeeper Herb Read says. "This is for guests who simply aren't able to wait until breakfast time."

The Marshlands Inn is literally at the crossroads. It is a perfect, single day's drive from the two inns in Cape Breton or the Milford House which is near Annapolis Royal. It is also a comfortable day's ride on the land route from Calais, Maine or St. Stephen, New Brunswick, if the traveler is using the land route to Nova Scotia and Prince Edward Island. Many of the guests stay on for an extra night or two to see the famous "tidal bore" which is visible in the nearby Bay of Fundy, or to play some golf and enjoy some hiking and swimming. There is also curling.

The only major change since my first visit in 1973 is that Herb and Alice Read have purchased the older home next to the inn, which means that there are now six additional rooms available. They also

own a modern 20-unit motel a short distance away.

Almost all of the letters I get from our readers who have visited here mention two things: first, the unusually extensive collection of 19th century antiques throughout the inn and guest rooms, which have obviously been here from the very beginning; and second, the food.

We were talking about the food while enjoying the hot chocolate that evening. The gentleman from Saskatchewan had had the Atlantic salmon and couldn't say enough about it. I had thoroughly enjoyed one of my favorite dishes, curried lamb served with the Marshlands' own chutney. The young honeymooning couple had tried the fresh Miramichi salmon. His was served grilled and hers was poached with an egg sauce. Everyone agreed that the fiddlehead greens were a delicacy.

While we were exchanging travel experiences, I somewhat shamefacedly admitted that before my first visit I thought that Sackville was about fifteen miles south of the polar icecap. The Canadian couple came to my rescue by admitting that they, too, had a total misconception of New Brunswick.

The hour was getting late. Someone remarked that breakfast was served starting at 7 a.m. so we could get an early start.

We all said "good night" and promised to meet for breakfast, unwilling to break the chain of friendship we had begun in the handsome inn in not-so-faraway New Brunswick.

MARSHLANDS INN, Box 1440, Sackville, N.B., Canada EOA 3CO; 506-536-0170. A 16-room village inn near Tantramar Marshes and Fundy Tides. European plan. Eight rooms with private baths. Breakfast, lunch and dinner served to travelers daily. Closed during the Christmas season. Golf, xc skiing, curling, hiking and swimming nearby. Herb and Alice Read, Innkeepers.

Directions: Follow Trans-Canada Highway to Sackville, then Rte. 6, 1 mi. to center of town.

Quebec

CUTTLE'S TREMBLANT CLUB
Mont Tremblant, Quebec

I cast off the trim Laser sailboat and immediately started the jib. Jim Cuttle kept us heading out into Lac Tremblant and trimmed the mainsheet. Things were all shipshape and we were set for a good sail. "These Lasers really respond very adroitly," I remarked. "Yes, they do," said Jim, "and we introduce many Americans to them for the first time. In fact, we have a sailing instructor who is particularly expert in handling them."

From the center of the lake we enjoyed a most unusual perspective of the Laurentians. Straight ahead was Mont Tremblant, one of the most famous ski areas in the world. Behind us was the grassy lakeside beach of Cuttle's Tremblant Club, where I counted several other sailboats and motorboats for waterskiing. Next to the beach house, the tennis courts were already busy on this early morning, and some young children were playing in the sandbox. The main house of the Club was farther up the side of the hill with a very commanding view of the lake and mountain.

All of my visits with Jim and Betty Cuttle have been in the summer, so it was quite natural for me to be curious about what it was like in the winter. "Just imagine six to eight feet of snow," said Jim. "I'm sure you know that heavy snow is a way of life up here and everybody welcomes it. We've had our own ski school here at the Club for many years. In fact, Betty and I were instructors in the early days. Today our guests board our bus right after breakfast and head for the mountain where all of the teaching is done. The Club has eight instructors who are busy all day long. They use video cameras, and in the evening after dinner, everybody sits around in front of the fire and the tapes are shown which enables the guests

to improve their technique. The evenings are really great fun; that's where everybody gets together and a lot of new friendships are made. We have lots of singing and dancing."

Winter is a magic time here at Cuttle's. In addition to the downhill skiing there is snowshoeing and excellent cross-country skiing. Many trails begin at the front door. Mont Tremblant Park offers fifty miles of marked and groomed trails for Nordic skiers of all abilities. Box lunches are available at the Club, and there is a waxing room and repair bench.

Jim painted an attractive word picture of Cuttle's in winter, but it has a great deal of appeal to me in summer and fall as well. Besides the active sports, I like to sit by the graceful pool in the sunshine and walk the green woods. Laurentian back roads are a joy, and the little French-speaking villages remind me of northern Provence.

With so many opportunities to spend days out of doors, the food at Cuttle's takes on an added importance. The emphasis is on French dishes, including onion soup, a cold seafood plate featuring fish from the Gaspé Peninsula, roast leg of veal, braised calves' sweetbreads, and boned chicken Bayonnaise. The menus are bilingual so everyone can practice his French.

Jim and I decided to head back to the pier where Charlie, the collie, and Meg, the Irish setter, were scampering up and down the shore awaiting our return. "They're lots of fun," he said. "Meg particularly likes to go for walks in the forest with our guests."

CUTTLE'S TREMBLANT CLUB, Mont Tremblant, Quebec, Canada JOT IZO, 819-425-2731. A 32-room resort inn on Lac Tremblant facing Mont Tremblant, the highest peak in the Laurentians. Modified American plan omits lunch. Breakfast, lunch and dinner served daily to travelers. Open year-round. No pets. Tennis, swimming, sailing, boating, fishing and xc skiing on grounds. Golf, riding, trap shooting, Alpine skiing nearby. Jim and Betty Cuttle, Innkeepers.

Directions: From Montreal, 85 mi. northwest via Laurentian Auto Rte. 15 to St. Jovite. Turn right at church on Rte. 327N, 7 mi. to Lac Tremblant. Cuttle's is on the west shore facing the mountain.

HOVEY MANOR
North Hatley, Quebec

Bob Brown and I were taking an early morning walk in mid-July. We started from the front veranda of Hovey Manor and picked our way along the dirt roads through the maples, birches, beeches, and evergreens. Bob, the perfect picture of the Canadian innkeeper, pointed with his pipe to the many varieties of birds. There was a light mist on Lake Massawippi which would burn off shortly after breakfast.

He was telling me about the many beautiful mansions which dot the lake's shore. "Quite a few Americans discovered North Hatley about the turn of the century, and Hovey Manor, along with many other houses on this side of the lake, was built by people from the southern United States. The inn was built by a man from Georgia."

Hovey Manor is a delightfully friendly resort-inn on the shores of this beautiful lake. The choice of accommodations includes comfortable large rooms in the main portion of the inn, plus a series of cottages scattered about the grounds, many with a view of the lake and tennis courts, and the vast expanse of fields, and forests. There are canoes, sailboats, rowboats, good swimming, golf, fishing, and in fact just about everything to make a summer or fall vacation totally enjoyable.

The Inn even has a haunted clock which has been featured in Ripley's "Believe it or not" column.

At this point we made a turn onto the hardtop road where we could see five miles down the lake. There were meadows on the uphill side of the road that stretched back to the birch forest, and a hint of honeysuckle and wild flowers in the air.

"I came up here in 1950 and have had a wonderful time ever since," Bob continued. "There has been a great deal of expansion, but

the important things have always been here: the beautiful, unspoiled lake, the marvelous fresh air, the fishing, the wildlife, and the really wonderful people who make North Hatley their home.

"We are open year-round," he said, "because there are five ski areas within an easy driving distance, and we have become a sort of family ski resort as well as a family summer resort. There are also five golf courses within twenty minutes of us."

By this time we had reached the rear door of the inn and walked through the living room with its considerable collection of antiques which Bob has acquired over the years. We passed through the great doors leading to the front terrace and decided to have breakfast out there in full view of the lake. Betty Brown was waiting and we all sat down to some scrambled eggs.

What a beautiful way to start the day!

HOVEY MANOR, Box 60, Rtes. 10 and 55, North Hatley, Quebec, Canada JOB 2CO; 819-842-2421. A 34-room resort-inn, 85 mi. from Montreal, 35 mi. from Newport, Vt. On Lake Massawippi and near major ski areas. European plan or Modified American plan which omits lunch. Breakfast, lunch, and dinner served to travelers daily. Open year-round. Tennis on grounds. Golf, Alpine, and xc ski nearby. Bob and Betty Brown, Innkeepers.

Directions: From U.S., take I-91 across border to Rte. 55. From Rte. 55, take North Hatley Exit 18 and follow Rte. 108 east. Turn right at blinker, approximately 5 mi.

WILLOW PLACE INN "AUBERGE"
Como, Quebec

"There certainly *is* a resemblance to Lake Como in Italy." Pat Garbutt, the innkeeper at the "Willow," and I were taking a short drive from the inn to the village of Hudson. I was feeling very much the world traveler because I had visited Lake Como just a few weeks earlier.

"And this area has long been a favorite of artists and antique hunters, as well as dog-sled racers, horsemen, sailors, and cross-country skiers," Pat added.

The "Willow" is about thirty-five miles from the heart of Montreal on the Lake of Two Mountains, surrounded by ancient rolling hills, historic villages, and century-old homes. It's a world of peaceful countryside and quiet roads. The inn was built about 1820 as a private house. It later became a store; then a boarding house, a residential hotel, and finally the local inn and pub run by Zena and Pat Garbutt, their family and loyal staff.

The inn has fourteen comfortably furnished guest rooms. This time I had room number six, up under the eaves—the bed had an attractive green headboard and there was a tiny little bathroom which was fun. I got a kick out of looking through the old *Life* magazines and seeing what life was like twenty years ago. There were pictures of Ingrid Bergman and advertisements of products that are no longer in existence today.

Pat and Zena also have an inn at the border-crossing at Calais, Maine in St. Stephen, New Brunswick—the Elm Lodge Inn. Pat has been commuting for the past few years between the two places, both of which are most comfortable and accommodating.

The inn is located on a lake where there is a great deal of sports both winter and summer, and we had great fun at breakfast watching

the sailboats and looking at the small town with its church spires on the other side of the lake. The inn has a grassy lawn leading down to the lakeshore and a small swimming pool.

Furnishings in the dining room are most unusual, with a collection of round and square tables, a mixture of Victorian chairs and several horse prints adorning the walls. There were dried flower arrangements on every table, a very handsome silver candelabra overhead, and a collection of polished silver dish covers. In the evening, dinner is served by candlelight.

Another attractive room is a side parlor where overnight guests can gather to get acquainted. I had a most enjoyable conversation with people from western Canada, as well as with guests from the southern United States. I was happy to be able to direct the Canadians to Cuttles Inn at Mont Tremblant, because this was their first time in eastern Canada. I suggested they take the direct road instead of the Laurentian Autoroute.

The dinner menu at the Willow Place Inn is a very balanced mix of both English and French dishes. As in France, I found an excellent house pate, and also some escargots de bourgogne, coq au vin, caneton roti avec sauce a l'orange, and Dover sole were on the menu, along with an excellent local cheese: fromage d'Oka and a sharp Canadian cheddar.

I had a little problem with my Audi on this trip, but Pat directed me to the AutoRode, a garage nearby. They had me fixed up in no time and at a very reasonable cost.

I've always found the Willow Place a happy experience, because it enables me to mingle freely with the Canadians who consider the inn their home pub. It is a meeting place for many kinds of people of varied interests.

WILLOW PLACE INN, Box 100, Como, Hudson, Quebec, Canada JOP 1AO, 514-458-4656. A 14-room Coach House, 25 mi. from Montreal on the shores of the "Lake of Two Mountains." European plan or Modified American plan which omits lunch. Coach House rooms only with shared bath. Breakfast, lunch, and dinner served to travelers daily. Closed Christmas Day, Boxing Day (St. Stephen's Day), New Year's Day, and Good Friday. Swimming and xc skiing on grounds. Tennis, golf, sailing, bicycles, and Alpine skiing nearby. Pat and Zena Garbutt, Innkeepers.

Directions: From Trans-Canada Hwy., take Exit 17 and follow Hwy. 342 north to Como Station Rd. and Bellevue Blvd. Turn left to inn. Near Oka Ferry.

Ontario

GRANDVIEW FARM
Huntsville, Ontario

One of the most gratifying letters that I received in recent years came from a reader in Montreal who said, "After examining the Canadian section of your book, I discovered that if there wasn't a Canada you would invent one."

I think Canada and the Canadians are marvelous, and I am happy to say that our group of inns from this great country is growing every year. Here are some notes I made on a visit to Grandview Farm Inn in Huntsville, Ontario about two and a half hours from Toronto:

"I wish you could see that tree during the Fall season. It turns the most gorgeous scarlet," said Bruce Craik. He and I were taking a leisurely walk around the grounds and buildings of Grandview Farm. "Yes, and during the summer, our dock has canoes, Lasers, and inboards for touring the lakes or waterskiing. That's Fairy Lake, part of a chain of five lakes in this section of Ontario."

It was a strikingly beautiful day in early January. I had driven up from Toronto and then turned east on route 60 for a few miles through snow-covered fields which were bathed in brilliant sunshine. The daisies and buttercups would carpet them in a few short months.

I turned off at the little sign and drove to the top of the knoll where there was a series of friendly-looking buildings. Two equally friendly dogs pranced out to greet me and the young man flooding the skating pond waved a cheery greeting. As I walked across the crunchy snow toward the front door of the main house, which was flanked by trees, Judy Craik stepped out and said, "Welcome to Grandview Farm. I saw you coming."

The first thing the Craik family did was to take me into a living room where a most welcome fire was crackling away on a raised hearth and a big picture window overlooked the lake. I was revived by some hot chocolate and we started visiting.

It is easy to visit with the Craiks because there are so many of them. In fact, a needlepoint design on one wall carried the message: The Craik Family: Bruce, Judy, Ian, Peter, Ginny, Sandy, Tim, and Heather—Grandview Farm 1975.

"Yes, everyone is involved here," said Bruce. "We are a resort-inn where most families have fun because we are a big family ourselves."

I found that in addition to being an inn with lots of different things to do during summer as well as winter, Grandview Farm Inn is also a restaurant serving three meals a day. "One of our specialties is roast beef with Yorkshire pudding which we serve on Wednesday and Saturday nights," explained Judy. "Other nights we offer three different entrees, such as chicken done in many different ways, and we serve fish every night and there is stuffed roast pork, and veal. We pass the vegetables and offer seconds on everything."

Lodgings are in the main house and in six other attractive cottages set among some fine old trees on or near the lake shore, each with its own name. All the rooms are very comfortable, from the corner room in the inn with the four-poster to the fireplace rooms in the "Tree Tops" and those in the little waterside cottage called "Puffin Hill."

While I was browsing in the Rafters, the small gift shop at the inn, I picked up the Grandview Farm brochure. It was extremely handsome with full color photographs of all of the activities, the lake views, and the lodging rooms. I found it very helpful when writing this account.

Bruce and I had returned to the main house and he pointed out the patio which is on the west side overlooking the lake. "We serve lunch and dinner out here in the summertime." The scene reminded me of another most attractive Canadian inn, Hovey Manor, south of Montreal in North Hatley, Quebec, overlooking Lake Massawippi.

*GRANDVIEW FARM, Huntsville, Ontario, Canada POA 1KO;
705-789-7462. A 25-room resort-inn on Fairy Lake, 142 mi. north of
Toronto in a beautiful lake and mountain resort area. American and
Mod. American plans. Breakfast, lunch, and dinner served to
travelers daily. Open from mid-May to mid-October; Dec. 26 to
Mar. 31. Closed Christmas Eve and Christmas Day. No pets. Tennis,
swimming, sailing, waterskiing, canoeing, xc skiing trails; Alpine
skiing nearby. The Craik Family, Innkeepers.*

*Directions: From Toronto follow Route 400 North above Barrie,
then Rte. 11 North, approx. 80 mi. near Huntsville. Turn right on
Rte. 60 for 4 mi. Inn is on right.*

OBAN INN
Niagara-on-the-Lake, Ontario

"The building," said Gary Burroughs, "has a great deal of very
interesting history. It was once the home of Captain Duncan Malloy,
a lake captain whose home was in Oban, Scotland, a beautiful
seaport town. It was built about 1824 and later turned into an inn. In
1914 there were additions made, and the Oban Inn became an
officers' mess. It's been in my family for some years now, and I'm very
pleased to make my home here in Niagara-on-the-Lake and make the
inn a part of my way of life."

In many ways the Oban Inn reminds me of the Willow Place Inn
in Como, Quebec, and its English innkeeper, Patrick Garbutt. The
Oban is essentially a Canadian inn. However, because of its evident
English heritage, I recalled other English inns I had visited such as
the Crown in Chiddingfold which has the same cozy village air, and
the Mermaid Tavern in Rye, where the atmosphere is also drenched
in history.

359

The menu indicated that the Oban really has a mix of the Old World and the new. For example, among the appetizers was a homemade pate which is a tradition in England and the Continent. The main menu items have the ring of the English countryside: roast prime ribs of beef with Yorkshire pudding, and calves sweetbreads with bacon on toast.

We were talking about the intermingling of cultures at the Oban when Gary said, "There is one thing that we have here that is undeniably British. Come with me and you will see what I mean." We walked from the main dining room down the corridor into a pub room that might well have been in Surrey or Sussex. It was decorated with many photographs of actors and actresses that have appeared at the Shaw Festival. At the center of a buffet bar was the star of the repast, a turkey pie with a big beautiful crust. There was also a large salad bowl, cold cauliflower, mixed peas and lima beans, cold sliced meats, sliced eggs and generous helpings of tomatoes, beets and pickles. It was quite British.

There was a mixture of patrons at that hour including business men from the town as well as a few Canadian and American visitors who were enjoying Niagara-on-the-Lake in the off-season. I noted a piano in one corner, and Gary said that in the evening there were informal, jolly sing-alongs as well as quiet entertainment. With the fire crackling away on a rather chilly day, it was all very heart-warming and hospitable.

The hospitality at the Oban Inn extends to some very homelike lodging rooms. Some of them have a view of Lake Ontario and all are neat and quite typical of country inns with individual color schemes and furniture.

Gary and I talked extensively about local history, and as we were leaving, he said warmly, "I am sure that your readers will enjoy Niagara-on-the-Lake." I'm equally sure that they will also enjoy a visit at the Oban Inn.

THE OBAN INN, 160 Front St., Box 94, Niagara-on-the-Lake, Ontario LOS IJO 416-468-2165. A 23-room village inn on a quiet street in one of Canada's historic villages approx. 12 mi. from Niagara Falls, N.Y., on the shores of Lake Ontario. Near Ft. George and Ft. Niagara, the Shaw Festival and Mime Theatre. All plans available. Breakfast, lunch, dinner served daily to travelers. Open every day of the year. Owner-controlled pets welcome. Golf, xc skiing, sailing, fishing, tennis nearby. Gary Burroughs, Innkeeper.

Directions: Exit Hwy. 55 at St. Catherines from the Queen Elizabeth Hwy. Follow signs to Niagara-on-the-Lake.

INDEX

ALEXANDER-WITHROW HOUSE
Lexington, Virginia, 238

ALGONQUIN HOTEL
New York, New York, 150

ALMSHOUSE INN
Ghent, New York, 152

ASA RANSOM HOUSE
Clarence, New York, 154

ASTICOU INN
Northeast Harbor, Maine, 74

BARROWS HOUSE
Dorset, Vermont, 123

BAY SHORE YACHT CLUB
Fort Lauderdale, Florida, 252

BEEKMAN ARMS
Rhinebeck, New York, 156

BENBOW INN
Garberville, California, 305

BIRD AND BOTTLE
Garrison, New York, 158

BLACK POINT INN
Prouts Neck, Maine, 76

BLUEBERRY HILL
Goshen, Vermont, 125

BOONE TAVERN HOTEL
Berea, Kentucky, 208

BOTSFORD INN
Farmington Hills, Michigan, 277

BOULDERS INN
New Preston, Connecticut, 20

BRADFORD GARDENS INN
Provincetown, Massachusetts, 33

BRAMBLE INN
Brewster, Massachusetts, 35

BRAZILIAN COURT
Palm Beach, Florida, 254

BULL'S HEAD INN
Cobleskill, New York, 160

BUXTON INN
Granville, Ohio, 293

CAPTAIN LORD MANSION
Kennebunkport, Maine, 78

CAPTAIN WHIDBEY INN
Coupeville, Washington, 322

CENTURY INN
Scenery Hill, Pennsylvania, 184

CHALET SUZANNE
Lake Wales, Florida, 256

CHESHIRE INN
St. Louis, Missouri, 286

CHESTER INN
Chester, Vermont, 126

THE CLAREMONT COTTAGES
Southwest Harbor, Maine, 80

CLARKSON HOUSE
Lewiston, New York, 162

COLBY HILL INN
Henniker, New Hampshire, 98

COUNTRY INN
Berkeley Springs,
West Virginia, 242

CURTIS HOUSE
Woodbury, Connecticut, 22

CUTTLE'S TREMBLANT CLUB
Mont Tremblant,
Quebec, Canada, 351

DANA PLACE INN
Jackson, New Hampshire, 100

DEXTER'S INN
Sunapee, New Hampshire, 102

DOCKSIDE GUEST QUARTERS
York, Maine, 82

DOE RUN INN
Brandenburg, Kentucky, 210

DURBIN HOTEL
Rushville, Indiana, 273

EDSON HILL MANOR
Stowe, Vermont, 128

ELM LODGE
St. Stephen,
New Brunswick, Canada, 345

ELMWOOD INN
Perryville, Kentucky, 212

FAIRFIELD INN
Fairfield, Pennsylvania, 187

FARMHOUSE
Port Townsend, Washington, 324

GENERAL LEWIS INN
Lewisburg, West Virginia, 244

GLEN IRIS INN
Castile, New York, 164

GOLDEN LAMB
Lebanon, Ohio, 295

GRAVES MOUNTAIN LODGE
Syria, Virginia, 236

GRANDVIEW FARM
Huntsville,
Ontario, Canada, 357

GREEN MOUNTAIN INN
Stowe, Vermont, 131

GREENVILLE ARMS
Greenville, New York, 165

GREY ROCK INN
Northeast Harbor, Maine, 84

GRISTMILL SQUARE
Warm Springs, Virginia, 240

GRISWOLD INN
Essex, Connecticut, 24

HARBOR HOUSE
Elk, California, 307

HEMLOCK INN
Bryson City, North Carolina, 221

HERITAGE HOUSE
Little River, California, 309

HICKORY BRIDGE FARM
Orrtanna, Pennsylvania, 189

HOLLOWAY HOUSE
East Bloomfield, New York, 168

HOLLYMEAD INN
Charlottesville, Virginia, 232

HOMEWOOD INN
Yarmouth, Maine, 85

HOUND EARS LODGE
Blowing Rock, North Carolina, 223

HOVEY MANOR
North Hatley,
Quebec, Canada, 353

INN AT CASTLE HILL
Newport, Rhode Island, 64

INN AT HUNTINGTON
Huntington, Massachusetts, 39

INN AT PLEASANT HILL
Shakertown, Kentucky, 214

INN AT PRINCETON
Princeton, Massachusetts, 42

INN AT SAWMILL FARM
West Dover, Vermont, 132

INN AT STARLIGHT LAKE
Starlight, Pennsylvania, 191

INN FOR ALL SEASONS
Scituate Harbor, Massachusetts, 37

INN ON THE COMMON
Craftsbury Common, Vermont, 134

INVERARY INN
Baddeck,
Nova Scotia, Canada, 338

ISLAND HOUSE
Ogunquit, Maine, 88

JAMES HOUSE
Port Townsend, Washington, 326

JARED COFFIN HOUSE
Nantucket Island,
Massachusetts, 44

JOHN HANCOCK INN
Hancock, New Hampshire, 104

KEDRON VALLEY INN
South Woodstock, Vermont, 136

KILMUIR PLACE
Northeast Margaree,
Nova Scotia, Canada, 339

KING CHRISTIAN HOTEL
Christiansted, St. Croix,
Virgin Islands, 334

LAKE QUINAULT LODGE
Quinault, Washington, 328

LAKESIDE INN
Mt. Dora, Florida, 257

LAMOTHE HOUSE
New Orleans, Louisiana, 260

LARCHWOOD INN
Wakefield, Rhode Island, 67

LINCKLAEN HOUSE
Cazenovia, New York, 170

LODGE ON THE DESERT
Tucson, Arizona, 300

LONGFELLOW'S WAYSIDE INN
South Sudbury, Massachusetts, 46

LOVETT'S
BY LAFAYETTE BROOK
Franconia, New Hampshire, 106

LOWELL INN
Stillwater, Minnesota, 284

LYME INN
Lyme, New Hampshire, 107

MAINSTAY INN
Cape May, New Jersey, 148

MARATHON HOTEL
Grand Manan Island,
New Brunswick, Canada, 347

MARSHLANDS INN
Sackville,
New Brunswick, Canada, 349

MARYLAND INN
Annapolis, Maryland, 216

MILFORD HOUSE
South Milford,
Nova Scotia, Canada, 341

MOSELEM SPRINGS INN
Moselem Springs,
Pennsylvania, 193

MOUNTAIN VIEW INN
Norfolk, Connecticut, 26

NATIONAL HOUSE INN
Marshall, Michigan, 280

NAUSET HOUSE
East Orleans, Massachusetts, 47

NEW HARMONY INN
New Harmony, Indiana, 269

NEW LONDON INN
New London, New Hampshire, 109

NORMANDY INN
Carmel, California, 311

NORTH HERO HOUSE
North Hero, Vermont, 138

NU-WRAY INN
Burnsville, North Carolina, 225

OBAN INN
Niagara-On-The-Lake,
Ontario, Canada, 359

OJAI VALLEY INN
Ojai, California, 313

OLD CLUB RESTAURANT
Alexandria, Virginia, 234

OLD DROVERS INN
Dover Plains, New York, 172

OLD FORT CLUB
Kennebunkport, Maine, 89

OLIVER HOUSE
Ancram, New York, 174

OVERLOOK INN
Canadensis, Pennsylvania, 195

PARTRIDGE INN
Underwood, Washington, 330

PATCHWORK QUILT
Middlebury, Indiana, 275

PHILBROOK FARM INN
Shelburne, New Hampshire, 112

PINE BARN INN
Danville, Pennsylvania, 197

PINE CREST INN
Tryon, North Carolina, 226

PUMP HOUSE
Canadensis, Pennsylvania, 198

RABBIT HILL INN
Lower Waterford, Vermont, 141

RALPH WALDO EMERSON
Rockport, Massachusetts, 49

RANCHO DE LOS CABALLEROS
Wickenburg, Arizona, 302

REDCOAT'S RETURN
Tannersville, New York, 176

RED GERANIUM and
SHADBLOW RESTAURANTS
New Harmony, Indiana, 271

RED INN
Provincetown, Massachusetts, 51

RED LION INN
Stockbridge, Massachusetts, 53

RIVERSIDE INN
Pence Springs, West Virginia, 246
ROBERT MORRIS INN
Oxford, Maryland, 219
ROCKHOUSE MOUNTAIN FARM
Eaton Center, New Hampshire, 114
ST. GEMME BEAUVAIS INN
Ste. Genevieve, Missouri, 288
1740 HOUSE
Lumberville, Pennsylvania, 200
1661 INN
Block Island, Rhode Island, 69
SHAW'S HOTEL
Brackley Beach,
Prince Edward Island, Canada, 343
SILVERMINE TAVERN
Norwalk, Connecticut, 28
SNOWBIRD MOUNTAIN LODGE
Robbinsville, North Carolina, 228
SPALDING INN CLUB
Whitefield, New Hampshire, 116
SPRINGSIDE INN
Auburn, New York, 178
SQUIRE TARBOX HOUSE
Westport Island, Maine, 91
STAFFORD'S BAY VIEW INN
Petoskey, Michigan, 282
STAFFORD'S-IN-THE-FIELD
Chocorua, New Hampshire, 118
STAGECOACH HILL INN
Sheffield, Massachusetts, 55
STERLING INN
South Sterling, Pennsylvania, 202
SUTTER CREEK INN
Sutter Creek, California, 314
SWISS HUTTE
Hillsdale, New York, 180
SWORDGATE INN
Charleston, South Carolina, 261
TANQUE VERDE
Tucson, Arizona, 303

THE TAVERN
New Wilmington,
Pennsylvania, 204
THE INN
Rancho Santa Fe, California, 316
THREE VILLAGE INN
Stony Brook, New York, 182
TOWN FARMS INN
Middletown, Connecticut, 30
VAGABOND HOUSE
Carmel, California, 318
VICTORIAN INN
Whitinsville, Massachusetts, 56
VILLAGE INN
Landgrove, Vermont, 143
VILLAGE INN
Lenox, Massachusetts, 59
WAYSIDE INN
Middletown, Virginia, 230
WELLS INN
Sistersville, West Virginia, 248
WELSHFIELD INN
Burton, Ohio, 297
WHISTLING OYSTER
Ogunquit, Maine, 94
WHITEHALL INN
Camden, Maine, 95
WHITE HART INN
Salisbury, Connecticut, 32
WILDERNESS LODGE
Lesterville, Missouri, 290
WILLOW PLACE INN
Como, Quebec, Canada, 355
WINE COUNTRY INN
St. Helena, California, 320
WOODBOUND INN
Jaffrey, New Hampshire, 121
YANKEE CLIPPER
Rockport, Massachusetts, 61
YANKEE PEDLAR INN
Holyoke, Massachusetts, 62

The Last Word ...

Remember, to avoid disappointment, telephone ahead to all inns for reservations.

Country Inns and Back Roads, North America is completely rewritten each year. The new edition is available every March. Your bookstore will be happy to reserve your copy in advance. For a complete catalog of other Berkshire Traveller Press books write: Berkshire Traveller Press, Pine Street, Stockbridge, Massachusetts 01262.